Praise for Now and Then

"*Now and Then* provides multiple views of contemporary American issues juxtaposed against the backdrop of their historical underpinnings. The author provides essays by prominent authors, articles from the media, cartoons, and visuals that allow students to develop awareness of the roots of today's social context and to explore their attitudes regarding topics within that context. . . . I found the material thought-provoking and likely to be engaging to students."—*Mary J. Faure, Ohio State University–Newark*

"The strength of this reader is its fresh take on longstanding controversies. Novel angles of approach such as class in affirmative action enliven an old yet very relevant debate."—*Karin Burns, La Pierce College*

"*Now and Then* is a well-conceived text that could serve as either the primary text or as a strong supplemental text in any research-oriented composition course. . . . Its strengths are legion, especially its visual literacy/rhetoric and its presentation of solid principles of research methodology. . . . The competition doesn't present anything close to Stanford's 'Chapter Two: The Processes and Aims of Writing.' "—*Lyle W. Morgan, Pittsburg State University*

"The historical context broadens the themes in ways that suggest that they are not passing fads but perennial questions."—*Scott A. Leonard, Youngstown State University*

"This text eliminates the fluff and gets to the nitty-gritty."—*Emmett Lombard, Gannon University*

"The most innovative part is its structure—the idea of having historically contextualized readings combined with very recent texts makes for an interesting approach that can help students see the issues discussed as not an artificially constructed theme/problem, but a recurring issue in our culture/society."—*Ditlev S. Larsen, Winona State University*

"This book provides stimulating and provocative readings that are short, accessible, and contemporary. The material reflects diversity and the issues require thought."—*David L. Cooper, Jefferson Community College*

"The 'now and then' framework is a productive way to demonstrate how cultural narratives change across time and space."—*Aimee Carrillo Rowe, University of Iowa*

"I find the focus of the book very appealing."—*Beth Reynolds, Ferris State University*

"This is a text that offers challenging, up-to-date readings that encourage students to take a broader historical perspective on current controversies and debates. It activates students' critical ability to see correlations between image and text."—*Sharon Jaffe, Santa Monica College*

"I would recommend *Now and Then* to any of my colleagues teaching Composition and Rhetoric classes."—*Sandra Griffin, Western New Mexico University*

Now and Then

Current Issues in Historical Context

Judith A. Stanford
Rivier College

Boston   Burr Ridge, IL   Dubuque, IA   Madison, WI   New York
San Francisco   St. Louis   Bangkok   Bogotá   Caracas   Kuala Lumpur
Lisbon   London   Madrid   Mexico City   Milan   Montreal   New Delhi
Santiago   Seoul   Singapore   Sydney   Taipei   Toronto

For Alexis Walker and Anne Stameshkin

The McGraw·Hill Companies

Mc Graw Hill Higher Education

Now and Then: Current Issues in Historical Context

Published by McGraw-Hill, a business unit of The McGraw-Hill Companies, Inc., 1221 Avenue of the Americas, New York, NY 10020.

Some ancillaries, including electronic and print components, may not be available to customers outside the United States.

1 2 3 4 5 6 7 8 9 0 DOC/DOC 0 9 8 7 6 5

This book is printed on acid-free paper.

Editor in chief: *Emily Barosse*; publisher: *Lisa Moore*; senior sponsoring editor: *Alexis Walker*; development editor: *Anne Stameshkin*; marketing manager: *Lori DeShazo*; senior project manager: *Christina Gimlin*; manuscript editor: *Patricia Ohlenroth*; senior design manager: *Cassandra Chu*; cover designer: *Cassandra Chu and Jeff Brick*; interior designer: *Linda Robertson*; associate art editor: *Ayelet Arbel*; senior photo research coordinator: *Nora Agbayani*; photo researcher: *Robin Sand*; associate production supervisor: *Jason Huls*; senior media producer: *Todd Vaccaro*

Composition: 10.5/12 Times New Roman by Thompson Type

Printing: 45# New Era Matte, RR Donnelley, Crawfordsville

ISBN: 0-07-298121-0

Cover photo: top, © Adam Crowley/Getty Images; bottom, © Fototeca Storica Nazionale/Getty

The credits section for this book begins on C-1 and is considered a continuation of the copyright page.

Library of Congress Cataloging-in-Publication Data
Now and then : current issues in historical context / [compiled by] Judith A. Stanford.
     p. cm.
   Includes index.
   ISBN 0-07-298121-0 (alk. paper)
    1. College readers. 2. English language—Rhetoric—Problems, exercises, etc. 3. Report writing—Problems, exercises, etc. 4. Current events—Problems, exercises, etc. 5. Readers—Current events. I. Stanford, Judith Dupras, 1941–
PE1417.N67 2005
808'.0427—dc22

                2004061013

www.mhhe.com

Contents in Brief

Contents

Alternate Table of Contents: Rhetorical Strategy

Illustration and Example

Definition

Classification and Division

Comparison and Contrast

Alternate Table of Contents: Disciplines/Areas of Academic Interest

Ethnic Studies

History

Preface to the Instructor

THE STORY BEHIND *NOW AND THEN*

Like previous textbooks I have written, *Now and Then: Current Issues in Historical Context* was inspired and influenced by the observations and questions of students, colleagues, and editors. However, this time the context of these conversations seemed— and was—radically different: they took place in a world utterly changed by the events of September 11, 2001. Our conversations and ideas were now framed by new and different concerns. How would the events of 9/11 affect the world in which students would live? How had these events, and their repercussions, affected what and how students learned, and how instructors taught? Did it make sense to look at the changes in our lives in terms of "lessons learned," or was it impossible to draw "lessons" at all from events of that magnitude? How does history affect our lives *now,* and how does 9/11, along with the changes in the way we view the world since that time, affect the way we evaluate—and even re-member—what was *then?*

Now and Then presents complex current issues, themes, and questions in a way that invites both critical analysis and the syn-thesis of ideas and resources. In each thematic chapter, an array of high-interest articles from recent periodicals offers varied per-spectives on current controversies, capturing the moment of change in which we are living. These fresh, new readings and their accompanying apparatus encourage students to ask why each question or controversy is relevant in today's world (***now***), while additional classic selections and contextual introductions further engage students in questions of how history (***then***) has created, shaped, and altered the conversation.

Twenty-First-Century Readings in Historical Context

The main body of *Now and Then* is an anthology made up of **seven thematically arranged chapters.** Each theme opens with an **intro-duction,** followed by two or sometimes three **"Then"** selections that establish historical context. Following the **"Then"** section is **"Now,"** which consists of one or two subthemes, each focused on a specific current issue within the larger theme—for example, "How Do Gender and Society Influence How We Dress?" and "For Better or for Worse: Defining 'Marriage.'"

Readings are taken from a variety of print and Web sources, including magazines, journals, newspapers, and student newspapers from colleges and universities across the nation. "Now" pieces are mostly very recent (nearly all published since 9/11) and brief (3–5 pages); select pieces are longer, providing opportunities for in-depth reading.

Stimulating Apparatus

A variety of apparatus encourage critical thinking and involved student writing. **Suggestions for Prereading or Journal Writing** introduce each "Then" section, as well as each of the specifically focused "Now" sections. Each reading opens with a brief **headnote,** providing information on the author (where possible) and the original source and date of publication, as well as contextual information. Accompanying each selection are **Topics for Writing and Discussion,** many of which call for an informative or persuasive aim.

Concluding each "Then" and "Now" subtheme, **Making Connections** questions invite students to draw comparisons among the selections and to use the processes of synthesis and analysis to evaluate the similarities and differences they observe. Finally, at the end of each chapter, **Extended Connections** topics provide opportunities for thinking and writing in the context of further **research.** In every chapter and its many subthemes, there is an emphasis on argument through grouped readings: Opposing Viewpoints and Multiple Perspectives.

KEY FEATURES

- *Seven exciting themes.* The themes in *Now and Then*—which range from "Freedom and Security after 9/11" to "Exploring Pop Culture: Media Messages" and "Redefining Gender and Marriage: Men, Women, and Couples"—are designed to spark controversy and discussion.

- *68 readings, classic and cutting-edge.* The majority of readings ("Now") are very short, very recent articles—most published within the past three years—taken from a wide range of in-print and on-line periodicals. Additionally, several historical ("Then") pieces set the context for each thematic chapter. Selections go beyond "pro and con" thinking to offer a variety of opposing viewpoints, prompting students to think about and consider various issues related to reading, evaluating, and writing argument. Many "Now" selections have never before been anthologized.
- *47 relevant, high-interest visual texts.* A carefully chosen array of visuals promote engaged discussion and writing; photographs, paintings, advertisements, cartoons, charts, and graphs accompany all themes, "Now" and "Then," addressed in the anthology of readings. In addition, a compelling photo essay on the American flag through history—a collection of 13 images—is featured in a full-color insert. A **section on reading and evaluating images in Chapter 1** encourages students to see the visuals in *Now and Then* as complex texts that require careful consideration and critical thinking.
- *Flexible apparatus.* Each reading or visual text is accompanied by prompts for writing and discussion; additional chapter apparatus provide opportunities for making connections between readings and visuals as well as among and across themes. For more details on apparatus, please see above: "Stimulating Apparatus."
- *A sustained emphasis on critical reading and writing.* Two chapters, one on **critical reading and thinking** and one on the **processes and aims of writing,** provide instruction, models, and practice exercises that help students understand and build the skills needed to discuss and write about the wide variety of topics introduced in the anthology section. In these chapters and throughout the book's apparatus, there is an emphasis on **informative and argumentative writing,** with particular attention to the skills of **synthesis and analysis.**
- *A detailed chapter on research and documentation.* The book's final chapter leads students through the steps of the **research process,** including up-to-the-minute suggestions for finding, evaluating, and using online resources effectively.

A **student-written research paper** demonstrates the skills required to use sources thoughtfully and correctly, including examples of **MLA documentation** (both in-text parenthetical citation and Works Cited).

Supplements and Media

In addition to what you see in the book in your hand, we offer the following supplements for instructors and students:

- **www.mhhe.com/nowandthen.** This companion Web site offers three types of links—cultural, biographical, and bibliographical—to additional information on selected authors and issues from the text.
- **Instructor's Manual to accompany *Now and Then.*** Co-written by Judith Stanford and Lorraine Lordi, this teacher's guide includes sample syllabi, teaching tips, and ideas for class discussions, group work, and paper assignments. It is available for download online at www.mhhe.com/nowandthen; please contact your local sales representative to obtain a username and password. You can find your school's representative with our "rep locator" feature at www.mhhe.com/catalog.

ACKNOWLEDGMENTS

The first acknowledgment must go to my colleague and collaborator, Lorraine Lordi, who researched selections for Chapters 5 and 8. In addition, she has written the accompanying apparatus and the materials related to these chapters that appear in the instructor's guide and on the Online Learning Center. As always, she brings to this work her profound understanding of pedagogy and her love of teaching and of students. Her wit, intellect, and support have been essential to the completion of this project.

At McGraw-Hill, I extend my deep gratitude and thanks to Alexis Walker, Sponsoring Editor, and to Anne Stameshkin, Development Editor. The creative vision that led me to propose and pursue this project came from these two wise, sensible, and energetic women. I appreciate the thoughtful way they worked with me to shape this project, suggesting new selections, thought-provoking images, and useful apparatus, to mention only a few of their invaluable contributions. Finally, I deeply appreciate their outstanding willingness and ability to communicate clearly and promptly. For all these reasons and so much more, I dedicate this book to them.

I also wish to thank Jesse Hassenger, whose able research led to the discovery of several essential selections. In addition, he has coordinated many aspects of this project, particularly in the crucial final weeks of production. Christina Gimlin, project manager, ably focused the production with grace, energy, and efficiency. Patricia Ohlenroth copyedited this book, making many astute and thoughtful suggestions, which have made the book stronger. Once again, I have been fortunate to have Marty Granahan attending to the challenging task of obtaining permissions. I also want to thank Lori DeShazo for her commitment to this project and for making sure that *Now and Then* launches successfully into the world of its intended audience.

As always, I thank my family—my husband, Don; my sons David and Aaron; and my mother, Arline Dupras. All these people offer encouragement and support. Best of all, they are all thoughtful readers, and the many challenging conversations we have had over the years—and continue to have—offer me inspiration and lead me to examine and re-examine my own ideas.

Last, but by no means least of all, I thank my colleagues who reviewed this project at various stages, offering many invaluable suggestions for shaping it:

Emmett Lombard, Gannon University
Lyle W. Morgan, Pittsburg State University
Beth Reynolds, Ferris State University
Scott A. Leonard, Youngstown State University
M. Todd Harper, Kennesaw State University
Mary J. Faure, Ohio State University–Newark
Karin Burns, La Pierce College
David L. Cooper, Jefferson Community College
Ditlev S. Larsen, Winona State University
Sandra Griffin, Western New Mexico University
Emmett Lombard, Gannon University
Jay Rubin, College of Alameda
Sharon Jaffe, Santa Monica College

About the Author

Judith Stanford has taught composition and literature at Rivier College, in Nashua, New Hampshire, for the past 20 years. She has edited a number of composition textbooks, including *Responding to Literature, Connections, Developing Connections, The Writing Connection* (with Rebecca Burnett), *The Art of Reading* (with Robert DiYanni, Eric Gould, and William Smith), and *Guidelines for Writers.* Professor Stanford received her Ph.D. from the University of California at Santa Barbara; her interests include canoeing, walking, traveling, reading, and—especially—spending time at the family "camp" in Maine. Judith is married to Don Stanford, who worked for 23 years as international marketing director for MIT press, and is the mother of David, 29, a Seattle resident with a strong interest in music composition, and Aaron, 27, who is currently (successfully) pursuing an acting career in New York City.

PART ONE

On Reading and Writing

CHAPTER 1

Critical Reading and Thinking

Reading thoughtfully and productively in today's rapidly changing world calls for an open mind and courage, as well as the skills necessary to understand and evaluate complex ideas and issues. Critical reading and thinking require readers to approach each writer's work with a mind that remains alert to multiple possibilities and points of view. This process demands a willingness to see and acknowledge differences, yet also to look for similarities and connections. Most of all, critical reading and thinking ask readers to avoid hasty judgments, to discard clichéd responses, and to tolerate ambiguity.

Reading to Respond

When you first read any work, fiction or nonfiction, one of the best critical reading and thinking strategies you can use is to begin by skimming through the work, noting your responses as you move quickly from point to point. Being aware of initial responses is particularly important when you encounter unfamiliar ideas, images, and values. Try not to censor your responses as you read, but also try expressing some of your reactions in the form of questions or open-ended statements that could lead to, rather than close off, discussion. By using this approach during your first reading, you'll be able to keep an honest record of your thoughts and feelings, and you'll help yourself remain alert to the many different ideas, possibilities, and points of view presented by the author.

Marginal Notes   As an example of initial responses, consider the notes one student, Cassandra Lineman, wrote in the margins

of her book as she read "Tattoos Today," an excerpt from an article by Andres Martin, M.D., a specialist in child psychiatry.

Tattoos Today
Andres Martin

Tattoos and piercing have become a part of our
everyday landscape. They are ubiquitous, having
entered the circles of glamour and the mainstream
of fashion, and they have even become an increasingly common feature of our urban youth. Legislation in most states restricts professional tattooing
to adults older than 18 years of age, so "high end"
tattooing is rare in children and adolescents, but
such tattoos are occasionally seen in older teenagers. Piercings, by comparison, as well as self-

*Why are self-
made tattoos
called
"jailhouse"
type?*

made or "jailhouse" type tattoos, are not at all rare
among adolescents or even among school-age children. Like hairdo, makeup, or baggy jeans, tattoos

*How are
"school-age
children"
different from
"adolescents"?*

and piercings can be subject to fad influence or peer
pressure in an effort toward group affiliation. As
with any other fashion statement, they can be con-
strued as bodily aids in the inner struggle toward
identity consolidation, serving as adjuncts to the
defining and sculpting of the self by means of external manipulations. But unlike most other body
decorations, tattoos and piercings are set apart by
their irreversible and permanent nature, a quality at
the core of their magnetic appeal to adolescents.

*He only talks
about parents
here. What
about other
adults who
object, like
teachers?*

Adolescents and their parents are often at odds
over the acquisition of bodily decorations. For the
adolescent, piercing or tattoos may be seen as personal and beautifying statements, while parents
may construe them as oppositional and enraging
affronts to their authority. Distinguishing bodily
adornment from self-mutilation may indeed prove
challenging, particularly when a family is in disagreement over a teenager's motivations [. . .]. At

such times it may be most important to realize jointly that the skin can all too readily become but another battleground for the tensions of the age, arguments having less to do with tattoos and piercings than with core issues such as separation from the family matrix.

[. . .]

Tattoos and piercing can offer a concrete and readily available solution for many of the identity crises and conflicts normative to adolescent development. In using such decorations, and by marking out their bodily territories, adolescents can support their efforts at autonomy, privacy, and insulation. Seeking individuation, tattooed adolescents can become unambiguously demarcated from others and singled out as unique. The intense and often disturbing reactions that are mobilized in viewers can help to effectively keep them at bay, becoming tantamount to the proverbial "Keep Out" sign hanging from a teenager's door.

Alternatively, feeling prey to a rapidly evolving body over which they have no say, self-made and openly visible decorations may restore adolescents' sense of normalcy and control, a way of turning a passive experience into an active identity. By indelibly marking their bodies, adolescents can strive to reclaim their bearings within an environment experienced as alien, estranged, or suffocating or to lay claim over their evolving and increasingly unrecognizable bodies. In either case, the net outcome can be a resolution to unwelcome impositions: external, familial, or societal in one case; internal and hormonal in the other. In the words of a 16-year-old girl with several facial piercings, and who could have been referring to her body just as well as to the position within her family: "If I don't fit in, it is because I say so."

[. . .]

Imagery of a religious, deathly, or skeletal nature, the likenesses of fierce animals or imagined

What does "family matrix" mean?

But don't tattoos also make adolescents like their peers—so how is this unique?

Great example—This is just how it feels to want your own freedom.

creatures, and the simple inscription of names are some of the time-tested favorite contents for tattoos. In all instances, marks become not only memorials or recipients for dearly held persons or concepts: they strive for incorporation, with images and abstract symbols gaining substance on becoming a permanent part of the individual's skin. Thickly embedded in personally meaningful representations and object relations, tattoos can become not only the ongoing memento of a relationship, but at times even the only evidence that there ever was such a bond. They can quite literally become the relationship itself. The turbulence and impulsivity of early attachments and infatuations may become grounded, effectively bridging oblivion through the visible reality to tattoos.

I don't understand what he means here—How do "abstract symbols" become part of someone's skin?

[. . .]

The popularity of the anchor as a tattoo motif may historically have had to do less with guild identification among sailors than with an intense longing for rootedness and stability. In a similar vein, the recent increase in the popularity and acceptance of tattoos may be understood as an antidote or counterpoint to our urban and nomadic lifestyles. Within an increasingly mobile society, in which relationships are so often transient—as attested by the frequencies of divorce, abandonment, foster placement, and repeated moves, for example—tattoos can be a readily available source of grounding. Tattoos, unlike many relationships, can promise permanence and stability. A sense of constancy can be derived from unchanging marks that can be carried along no matter what the physical, temporal, or geographical vicissitudes at hand. Tattoos stay, while all else may change.

So is he saying that tattoos are more popular with unstable people? I disagree!

[. . .]

Adolescents' bodily decorations, at times radical and dramatic in their presentation, can be seen in terms of figuration rather than disfigurement, of the natural body being through them transformed into a personalized body (Brain, 1979). They can

"Figuration"? Meaning?

often be understood as self-constructive and adorning efforts, rather than prematurely subsumed as mutilatory and destructive acts. If we bear all of this in mind, we may not only arrive at a position to pass more reasoned clinical judgment, but become sensitized through our patients' skins to another level of their internal reality.

REFERENCES
Brain, R. 1979. *The Decorated Body.* New York: Harper & Row.

As Cassandra read this article, she jotted in the margin any question or observation that came to mind. Look closely both at the *content* of Cassandra's notes and at the *types* of comments and questions she wrote. You'll notice that many of her observations fall loosely into the following categories:

1. Questions that ask about people (paragraphs 1, 2).
2. Questions that ask about actions (paragraph 1).
3. Questions that ask about policies, laws, or customs (paragraphs 1, 2).
4. Questions that address the writer's style, including such things as choice of examples, vocabulary, sentence structure, and even unusual punctuation (paragraphs 2, 4).
5. Questions or comments that challenge or call for closer examination of the writer's observations, judgments, evaluations, or inferences (paragraphs 2, 3, 6).
6. Comments that affirm or expand on the writer's observations, judgments, evaluations, or inferences (paragraph 4).

While there are many more ways of responding to a reading, this list suggests the wide range of reactions a reader might have when first encountering a text. As you form your first responses, never be afraid of these early reactions—don't worry that tentative, initial probings will be "wrong" or "silly" or "simplistic." You may later change your mind and decide to revise or even reject entirely one or more of your original reactions. But these changes, which you will base on rereading, on writing in response to reading, and perhaps on discussions with your fellow classmates and your instructor, represent progress and development. Rather than indicating that your first responses were unworthy or embarrassing, such changes demonstrate a willingness to apply new avenues of critical thinking to your work and a willingness to remain open to new possibilities.

Journal Entries   Another useful way of responding to what you read is to write about it in a journal. Such journals take many different forms. They may be kept strictly as personal exploratory writing or they may be a course requirement. If you write a journal as a class assignment, the instructor may ask you to write a certain number of entries each week and may specify approximately how long these entries should be. The instructor may also suggest topics or approaches to help you determine the focus of the entries.

Whether or not you are keeping a journal as a course requirement, writing entries in response to your initial readings can be a helpful way of engaging your mind with the ideas and feelings the writer expresses. Here are several examples of journal entries that students wrote following their first quick reading of Andres Martin's "Tattoos Today" (pages 4–7.)

1. I like the way the writer does not condemn tattoos as evil or stupid. I was surprised because this is what I expected. I did notice that he talked about "jailhouse" type tattoos, so it seemed like he might be saying that a lot of people with tattoos are criminals. I do not think this is true, in my experience. I have a tattoo and so do a lot of my friends. None of us are criminals. Plus, there are a lot of celebrities who have tattoos and they are not criminals. This is a topic that is not really followed up in the article.

   Frances Paglia

2. Martin just seems to describe why adolescents would want to get tattoos, but he does not talk about all the harm that can come from them. For instance, what about getting infections from dirty needles? What about later in life when maybe you want a job where the boss does not think tattoos are appropriate. Why doesn't he say more about the negative aspects? I have some friends with tattoos who now wish they did not have them.

   Anne Janocha

3. I thought it was interesting that Dr. Martin thinks people may be getting tattoos because they want stability. Yes,

tattoos are stable, I suppose, because they are very hard to get rid of. But I really don't see how anyone would think that a tattoo would be a way to feel more stable. It seems to me that tattoos are more a way of expressing your individuality than of trying to fit in and be stable. I would see tattoos as isolating people who have them from certain parts of society.

Steve O'Hare

As you can see from these journal entries, different readers can respond very differently to the same material. The following list briefly evaluates and comments on each of the entries:

1. Frances Paglia identifies one particular detail that she found interesting and then goes on to explain that she felt this reference was not fully developed. She also questions the inference she believes the writer is making about people who have tattoos.

2. In her entry, Anne Janocha asks many questions about the neutral, or even positive, position Martin takes toward the subject of tattoos. She wonders why he is not more critical, and she seems to imply there may be some bias in the article.

3. Steve O'Hare's initial response is to agree with a statement Martin makes. Yet he goes on to disagree with Martin's subsequent inference.

These three entries suggest ways of writing journal entries as initial responses to reading. Notice that the entries may question the writer, yet they keep open many possible interpretations rather than seeking one simple, easy answer. These entries also reflect the way early responses draw heavily on the reader's own experiences and knowledge. In addition, they take many different approaches to the article. The point here is that there is no one "correct" way to respond to any piece of writing, neither the first time you read nor upon subsequent readings. When these students returned to Martin's essay to read it for a second or third time, many of them changed or modified their initial responses. Points that may have seemed puzzling during the first reading became clear during the second; issues that seemed straightforward revealed previously unnoted complexities; opinions that seemed convincing appeared unsupported by sufficient evidence. The richness in reading often lies in the diversity and the possibilities a selection offers.

EXERCISE 1

Read the following essay written by Judith Illes. This piece first appeared in the online magazine *Tour Egypt Monthly* in December 2000. As you read, make notes in the margins to record your responses. Then write a journal entry expanding on at least one of those responses.

Tattoos in Ancient Egypt
Judith Illes

Not that long ago, in Western industrialized culture, tattooing was associated exclusively with those perceived as "primitive," "marginal" or even "criminal." Sailors and convicts were associated with tattoos as were women of a certain repute and perhaps the occasional nobleman gone slumming. This attitude has changed drastically in the last decade or so. Tattooing has become popular enough among the general population as to seem virtually commonplace. [. . .]

As far as we know, the history of tattooing starts in ancient Egypt. The phrase *"as far as we know"* is key because body ornamentation is an ephemeral art. Skin does not ordinarily survive in the archaeological context, with the exception of certain unique circumstances (the bog people of Northern Europe) or certain unique preservation techniques (the mummies of ancient Egypt). [. . .] However, the earliest documented evidence for the tattoo is in Egypt. [. . .]

The earliest intimations of tattoos come from clay figurines dating to roughly 4000 BCE These female figurines are decorated with dots, dashes and lozenges. This was inconclusive evidence until the discovery and examination of preserved, mummified bodies, whose body designs closely echo the patterns etched on the figurines.

Among the best-preserved mummies is that of a woman from Thebes from Dynasty XI (2160–1994 BCE), whose tomb identifies her as Amunet, Priestess of Hathor. Sometimes described as a concubine of Mentuhotep II, [she has] tattoo patterns that remain clearly visible on her flesh. No amulet designs for Amunet. Instead, she bore parallel lines on her arms and thighs and an elliptical pattern below the navel in the pelvic region.

5   Several other female mummies from this period also clearly show similar tattoos as well as ornamental scarring (cicatrization, still popular in parts of Africa) across the lower abdomen. The tattoos are all seemingly abstract: a series of dots, dashes and lozenges and for this reason they are often dismissed as random and meaningless. Yet in many ways the designs are similar to those sported by traditional, rural North African and Western Asian women. This strong non-representational geometric style is influenced by the precepts of Islam but also stretches its roots back farther into the past, back into the Paleolithic. Those dots and dashes, so abstract to the non-initiated, actually hold protective and fertility-promoting significance. The lozenges are anciently and traditionally connected to the primal female power of the universe, the Great Mother, so appropriate for a priestess of Hathor. [. . .]

The earliest known tattoo, which is not an abstraction, which is clearly a picture of *something,* is an image of the demi-god Bes. Bes' image appears as a tattoo on the thighs of dancers and musicians in many Egyptian paintings. Female Nubian mummies from around 400 B.C.E. have been discovered with Bes placed similarly on their flesh.

Bes' appearance leads to an interesting point. Up until very recently in the West, tattoos have been considered very macho, exclusively male. If the evidence of the mummies can be given credence, it appears in ancient Egypt, quite the opposite scenario was true. Tattooing seems to be virtually an exclusively female province. Perhaps there isn't enough conclusive evidence to report that only women wore tattoos. There are images of male figures bearing what may be tattoo marks. However, Bes as a god throws the art back into the women's camp.

Bes is a very interesting little spirit. Not a grand creator, not a giver of profound societal gifts, he is a very basic protector of the home, a little male figure devoted to women's concerns. Half dwarf, half lion, he is the only Egyptian god traditionally shown full-face rather than in profile. Bes dances and bangs his noisy percussion instruments to drive off evil spirits. Ugly little Bes was believed to have a special love for women and children, to expend his energy protecting them. [. . .]

What kind of protection did the women who wore his image expect from Bes? As an amulet, Bes was expected to provide easy childbirth, conception itself and to protect the subsequent children. Perhaps he was a special patron of dancers and musicians, a patron saint of sorts. Because the pictorial images of tattooed women often include dancers, acrobats and musicians, some consider that his tattoo might have been expected to protect against venereal disease or dangerous male clientele, the assumption being that the tattooed women were also prostitutes.

It is very hard at this stage to determine how much of this is   10 true and how much Western bias. Because tattoos in the West were considered disreputable, there was an automatic association among some early anthropologists that these ancient tattooed women had to be "*that*" kind of woman. Perhaps they were and perhaps they weren't. Because of the placement of the tattoos—on the upper thigh, over the pelvic and pubic region—there certainly seems to be a reproductive and/or erotic component to these tattoos. From our vantage point, at this time at least, it is very difficult to pinpoint exactly the nature of that component. Perhaps these tattoos did mark and protect women in certain professions or perhaps [tattooing] was just considered visually erotic and seductive and nothing more than that.

Reading to Understand

After exploring initial responses to something you have read, the next step is to return to the selection and reread carefully to be certain you have an accurate understanding of what the writer is saying and how he or she is saying it. It is easy during the first reading to skip over essential points, to miss important evidence, or to be overwhelmed by the emotions the piece arouses.

Writing down and talking about initial responses and then returning to the text before making firm evaluations are essential parts of critical thinking. Especially when you read something written from a viewpoint that is different from your own, it is easy to jump quickly to unwarranted conclusions or to fail to see clearly the point the author is making.

One way to delay the rush to judgment as you read and reread is to look for the author's main idea as well as for the points that support that idea. Until you fully understand what the writer is saying, it is impossible to move from an initial response to a logical and carefully thought-out evaluation of those ideas.

Summarizing to Identify the Main Idea and Supporting Ideas A useful strategy for gaining a clear sense of what the author is saying is to try writing a summary of the selection. When you summarize, you move from your own initial responses to an objective view of the writer's ideas. In a summary, you briefly restate in your own words the author's main idea or ideas and, often, the most important supporting points. Useful summaries usually share the following qualities:

1. They clearly identify the author's main point or points.
2. They identify the most important supporting points.
3. They make clear the relationship between the main point and the supporting points.
4. They condense these points without omitting essential ideas.
5. They are stated primarily in your own words. If you use any of the author's words, they should be enclosed in quotation marks and properly documented.
6. They focus on the author's ideas and feelings and do not include your own observations or evaluations.

Here are sample paragraphs written by three different students who read "Tattoos Today" and had been asked to write a summary of what they had read. As you read these paragraphs, consider which one best demonstrates the qualities just listed for summaries and note your reasons for making this judgment.

A. Andres Martin talks about how tattoos have become popular in today's society. They are like makeup or hairstyles to teenagers. Parents are often at odds with their teenagers over the acquisition of bodily decorations. Tattoos can be like a "keep out" sign on the bedroom door. A sixteen-year-old girl says that if she doesn't fit in, it is because she says so. Some tattoos have a religious meaning. At one time anchors were popular as tattoos. Some adolescents' tattoos are radical.

B. The central idea of this essay is that the author talks about adolescents and tattoos. But even though he points out that the tattoos often cause problems between teenagers and their parents, he does not talk about many other problems with this kind of self-mutilation. Since he is a doctor, why doesn't he talk about the dangers? For instance, he talks about piercing, which can cause infection. Why doesn't he say this? I am against tattooing because it is a permanent action that may be regretted later in life. Martin should be thinking more about the problems that can be caused by tattooing. The end of the article says that tattoos can be seen as "adorning" efforts rather than "disfigurement," but I think he is just plain wrong.

C. In his essay "Tattoos Today," Andres Martin discusses the reasons that tattoos are popular with adolescents, even though they often cause conflicts between teenagers and their parents. As Martin points out, a tattoo is relatively permanent and so can be a way for a teenager to strongly establish a separate identity from his or her parents. Also, getting a tattoo may give teenagers a sense of control over their bodies at a time when most physical changes that are happening to them cannot be controlled. Another reason Martin believes tattoos appeal to adolescents is that they provide a way to mark important events or relationships in ways that will permanently become part of the teen's body. The desire for this kind of permanence may come from the increasing lack of stability in our society, caused by such things as divorce or repeated family moves. Martin concludes by urging that tattoos may be looked at as "self-constructive and adorning efforts" and not simply as rebellious or "destructive acts" (7).

Example A does not fit the definition of a summary, First, this sample does not clearly identify the central point, and it does not differentiate between main ideas and supporting ideas. Instead, it simply plows chronologically through the essay, picking up details here and there, especially from the first sentences of paragraphs. Some of the details are main points—for example, the idea of parents being in conflict with teenagers over tattoos. Yet the next sentence talks about tattoos being like a "keep out" sign—a minor point. In addition, the example of the sixteen-year-old girl's comment is only marginally related to the main points the author makes.

Another problem with Example A shows up in this sentence: "Some tattoos have a religious meaning." While Martin does make this point, Example A does not show how the point relates to the central idea of the meanings tattoos can have for teenagers.

Finally, several sentences take words directly from the essay without enclosing them in quotation marks or providing correct documentation. For a clear example of this problem, note this sentence: "Parents are often at odds with their teenagers over the acquisition of bodily decorations." The words "are often at odds" and "over the acquisition of bodily decorations" are taken directly from the essay and must be enclosed in quotation marks and documented in the summary. In addition to using the words without quotations, the writer often fails to provide a proper context. For instance, the final sentence uses words directly from the article, does not document those words, and then gives no context for the idea of the sentence to show how it fits with other points in the summary.

The summary provided in Example A demonstrates problems that can arise from failing to read carefully to establish a clear overview of the author's ideas and to understand how the author uses details, reasons, and examples to support those ideas.

Example B is not really a summary at all. Instead, it is a response. While responding freely to a text is essential, a different process is required for summarizing. Without summarizing—or a similar clarifying strategy—the reader never moves beyond initial responses to carefully considered judgments.

The writer of Example B starts off with a sentence that might well start a summary since it does suggest Martin's main idea. The rest of Example B, however, expresses opinions and asks questions. While it's important to react and respond to what you read throughout the reading process, it's also essential to be able to set aside those responses at some point and to look objectively at what the author is saying. You cannot move on to evaluate the author's ideas—or to evaluate your own responses to those ideas—until you understand the main and supporting points clearly.

Example C provides a useful summary of "Tattoos Today." In the opening sentence, the writer provides a context by mentioning both the author's name and the title of the essay being summarized as well as by suggesting the author's central idea. In the second sentence, the student writer moves from the main idea to one of the central purposes of the essay. This sentence show that the student understands that the conflict between parents and teens is a primary motive for Martin to write about the central idea. The next three sentences skillfully abstract the main reasons Martin has identified for adolescents choosing to have tattoos, while the next-to-last sentence extends the point summarized in the previous sentence. The final sentence deftly sums up Martin's concluding thoughts. In addition, this student correctly uses quotation marks and documentation to identify words taken directly from Martin's essay and refrains from making evaluations.

The act of writing the summary accomplishes a number of goals. Perhaps the two most important goals are to help the student writer understand what an author is saying and to provide the student an opportunity to think about the essay and thus avoid a rush to unconsidered judgments of the author's ideas.

EXERCISE 2

Reread the excerpt from Judith Illes's online essay, "Tattoos in Ancient Egypt," then read the following summaries of that essay. Applying the criteria given on page 13 and following the process used in the evaluations on pages 14–15, state which summary you believe demonstrates the clearest understanding of Illes's observations and explain the reasons for your choice.

A. In "Tattoos in Ancient Egypt," Judith Illes talks about how tattooing first began in ancient Egypt. She describes a mummy of an Egyptian woman who had tattoos. Also, she talks about a god names Bes and says he proves that it was mainly Egyptian women who got tattooed and not men. But since he was a male god, this does not make sense. Also, why would only Egyptian women get tattooed? It would seem to me that men would, too, since I think women in ancient Egypt did not have the same rights as men, so why would they be getting tattoos when men did not?

B. In this excerpt from "Tattoos in Ancient Egypt," Judith Illes's main point is that the art of tattooing, which has become quite popular in Western society, actually began in ancient Egypt. She explains that tattooing may have appeared in other cultures, but the record is clear in Egypt because the skin of mummies is so well-preserved. Illes describes various tattoo patterns, all found on the mummies of Egyptian women, and all made up of a series of dots and dashes. She makes an argument that these patterns hold fertility-related significance, which may account for the fact that tattoos have been found only on female mummies, not on males. Another common tattoo is that of Bes, an Egyptian god known as a protector of women. He was believed to aid in conception and childbirth, yet he was also the protector of performers, such as dancers. Because the tattoos were often in the pelvic area, there is speculation that they may have been thought to protect women, yet they may also have been "visually erotic and seductive" (12).

C. In "Tattoos in Ancient Egypt," Judith Illes starts with the main idea that in Western culture tattooing has been associated with sailors, convicts, and women of a certain repute. Noblemen also sometimes got tattoos. The skin does not survive except in special cases like mummies, which is how we know that Egyptian women wore tattoos. There were clay figurines that dated to about 4000 BCE and they had decorations on them that were dots and dashes. There was a mummy of a woman called Amunet, Priestess of Hamor, and she did not have amulet designs. She had parallel lines on her arms and thighs and an elliptical pattern below her navel. There were also other mummies from Egypt. Women in North Africa and Western Asia also have tattoos that are something like the ones on Egyptian mummies. In Egypt, there was a god called Bes. He is a very interesting little spirit. Bes was supposed to provide easy childbirth. He was also the patron saint of dancers and musicians, so tattoos may have also been erotic.

EXERCISE 3

Choose a reading from the anthology section of this book, read it carefully, and then write a summary. As you write, keep in mind the examples you have just read as well as the qualities of a strong summary that are listed on page 13.

Reading to Understand Inferences

When you make inferences, you use the hints or suggestions that are embedded in the language you read or hear to understand more completely what a writer or speaker is saying. For example, if you show your uncle the hiking boots you have decided to buy, he might note that the high tops of the boots will be uncomfortable on summer hikes. Though your uncle has not stated that you should reconsider your decision, you can infer that meaning from his comment. To understand his advice, you have to go beyond understanding the words he has used and recognize the implications of his words.

In a similar manner, to understand fully what you are reading you need to go beyond recognizing an author's main points and supporting points. You need to think more deeply so that you can see ideas, feelings, and values that are not directly stated but are instead implied. For instance, in the excerpt from "Tattoos Today" Andres Martin provides several reasons why teenagers may decide to get tattoos. In addition, he closes his article by suggesting that tattoos may not be completely negative but instead might be considered an attempt by teenagers to build, rather than to negate, a "self." While he does not actually state that he would urge parents and other authorities to accept tattoos as positive, he implies that position.

When you read to make inferences, you "read between the lines" to see what the writer suggests as well as what he or she actually states. As you develop your ability to make inferences, keep in mind the following points:

1. Notice the writer's choice of words and be sensitive to both the *connotations* (the emotional associations) and the *denotations* (the dictionary definitions) of the words.
2. Notice the examples the writer chooses to describe an individual or a place or to explain a point. Consider the responses these examples evoke from readers.
3. Notice any value judgments the writer makes and consider whether these stated judgments help you understand the writer's attitude toward other topics he or she discusses.
4. Notice any biases the writer states and consider how these views might relate to what he or she discusses.

Reading to Evaluate

While the process of reading is highly complex and varies widely from individual to individual, most effective critical reading moves through the two stages just described—responding and understanding—to a third stage: evaluating.

To evaluate what you read (and your responses to what you read), you need to think carefully both about what the author states and implies and about the way you initially react to those statements and inferences. You have to work diligently to establish intelligent, fair criteria (standards) by which to make sensible, balanced judgments about what you have read. Finally you must be able to substantiate your evaluation in written or oral form.

Establishing Criteria When you make judgments about anything, you begin by establishing your criteria. For example, when you decide to buy a new pair of shoes, before you even begin looking, you have a list of criteria forming in your head. These criteria are, of course, affected by many circumstances and they do not remain exactly the same for every pair of shoes you buy. If you are buying shoes to wear to work at a job that requires standing on your feet for eight hours a day, your criteria might include comfortable fit, sturdy material, cushioned innersoles, and low cost. If you are buying shoes to wear as part of a wedding party, your criteria might change to include a formal style, a certain color, comfortable fit, and low cost. Notice that while some of the criteria changed to suit the specific circumstances, other criteria (comfortable fit and low cost) remained the same.

As you evaluate what you read, you'll find the process similar. Some criteria will remain important to you no matter what you are reading. Other criteria may be relevant only to a particular text. For instance, if you are reading an essay written by someone from a culture very different from your own, you may find that to make a fair judgment of the work, you have to revise or even discard some of your old standards. You may need to look at such writing in a new way.

As you develop criteria for evaluating what you read, keep the following considerations in mind:

1. *Consider the author.* What do you know about the author? Do the author's credentials give you confidence in his or her knowledge of the selection's topic? Do you have any reason to expect bias in the selection?
2. *Consider the audience.* For whom was the author originally writing? (In this book, the headnote often provides this information by telling you where the selection was first published.) To what extent do you believe the author would have been successful in communicating with this

audience? For instance, how well does he or she seem to
consider both *who the readers are* (their age, sex, ethnic
background, political philosophy, religious beliefs, occu-
pation, economic status) and *what they might already
know* (level of education, experience with the topic, pre-
conceptions about the topic).

To what extent do you believe this author is successful
in communicating with you and your fellow students as an
audience? (Consider the same questions related to audience analysis that are listed in the previous paragraph).

3. *Consider the author's aim.* It's usually not possible to
neatly ascribe one specific reason for an author's writing
any given selection, but in general there are three broad
aims that writers have:

a. *Writing to express emotions, ideas, incidents, observations.* When authors write expressively, they are usually
describing something, often by telling a true story about
something they have experienced or observed. Their
purpose is to create a picture made of words that will
show the reader a new way of looking at some aspect
of life.

b. *Writing to explain.* When authors write to explain, they
convey information and often prove a point about the
subjects they explore. To accomplish their purpose,
they may analyze, evaluate, synthesize, describe a
process, make a comparison, define an unfamiliar concept, or explain the causes and effects of an action or
decision—or they may use a combination of two or
more of these strategies.

c. *Writing to persuade.* When authors write to persuade,
they offer evidence or make emotional appeals designed
to convince the reader to acknowledge and accept as true
the idea they are promoting. Often, in addition to urging
the reader to accept a certain idea, the author hopes to
move the audience to certain actions.

Identifying the author's aim helps you establish criteria for
judging how well he or she has accomplished that aim.

4. *Consider the author's use of details, reasons, and examples.* After you have identified the author's intended audience and purpose, you need to look carefully at the way he
or she works to communicate to the audience and thus ac-

complish his or her aim. Depending on the audience and
the aim you have identified, you may want to consider the
following:

a. *Use of evidence:* Does the author provide evidence that
convincingly supports the points he or she is making?
For instance, if statistics are used, are they clearly explained and do they come from sources you believe to
be reliable? If the author quotes experts, are these individuals' qualifications mentioned so that you can determine their reliability?

b. *Use of emotional appeals:* Does the author use examples, anecdotes, or specific words that appeal strongly
to the readers' emotions? If so, do these emotional appeals help the writer communicate effectively, or are
these appeals a hindrance? Many readers find that emotional appeals enhance a writer's efforts when these appeals seem honest. When emotional appeals seem
manipulative, many readers resent them. There are no
easy tests to separate "honest" use of emotion from
"manipulative" use of emotion. You'll need to establish
your own reading sensibilities to make such judgments.

5. *Consider the values represented.* Finally, as you evaluate
how effectively the author communicates, you may also
want to think about the values that the author presents in
his or her writing. When you make judgments about an author's values, you also think about and explore your own
values, which serve as criteria for judging the writer. As
you read selections by writers who may share some, but
not all, of your own values, you'll often need to rethink
both the views of the author and the views that you hold.
This rethinking is the most challenging, and often disturbing, part of reading critically. It is challenging because it
requires you to examine what you believe to be true about
the way people should interact with one another, with their
institutions, and with their environment. It is often disturbing because as you read the thoughts and feelings of writers
who hold views different from your own, you may sometimes find yourself questioning some of your own beliefs
and ideals. The process may be less distressing if you consider that changing an opinion or belief—or, conversely,
affirming in a new way an old belief or opinion—is an

essential part of becoming an educated woman or man. If you were to pass through college entirely untouched by what you read or heard, you would be wasting a great deal of time and money.

Reading Images Critically

As we become more and more inundated with images from television, newspapers, Web sites, and many other sources, it becomes increasingly important to develop strategies for thinking critically about these visual texts. Throughout this book, you will find photographs, cartoons, graphs, advertisements, and other images that relate to the chapter's theme. As you engage with these selections, consider the following strategies for understanding, analyzing, and evaluating them.

1. Look at the whole image. What is your first impression? What message do you think this image is intended to convey?
2. Notice as many details as possible. What is in the foreground? To what elements is your eye immediately drawn? What elements are in the background? How do the background and foreground elements relate?
3. What purpose does this image serve? Can you tell why its creator might have produced it?
4. Are there any details in the image that you find shocking, confusing, or contradictory? In what way do those images, and the responses they evoke, contribute to the message of the image?
5. How are elements such as shadow, light, color, or shape used to contribute to the message of the image?
6. What is the tone of the image? Somber? Angry? Humorous? What elements create the tone? How does the tone contribute to the message of the image?
7. Does the image use familiar symbols or words in traditional or nontraditional ways? What do these familiar symbols or words, and their use in this image, contribute to its message?
8. Are there any words, phrases, or sentences incorporated into the image? If so, how do they relate to the visual details? In what ways do the words emphasize, contradict, or provide an ironic contrast to the visual details?

EXERCISE 4

Using the suggestions on page 22 for evaluating images, carefully examine and think critically about the following images of people with tattoos.

This married couple has formed a band called "Human Marvel." "Katzen" has whisker implants; "Enigma" has horn implants. Photographed at the 2003 Woodstock Tattoo Festival.

A young woman shows off a new tattoo to her friends, c. 2000

A man displays his tattoos at the Cornerstone Festival (a Christian music festival), in Bushnell, Illinois, July 3, 2004

A young girl shows her dolphin-shaped henna tattoo (a temporary tattoo made from a paste of henna plant leaves), April 2002

A U.S. marine from the 1st Battalion, 5th Marines Regiment, shows his tattoo, which reads "Death Before Dishonor," at the marine base in Fallujah, Iraq, April 20, 2004

EXERCISE 5

Suggestions for Writing and Discussion

1. Choose one of these images and describe the details in it that you find most compelling. What do you see as the central message of this image? Explain.

2. Choose two images that you believe have significant differences. Describe their differences and explain the significance you see in these contrasts.

3. What do you see as the relationship between the tattoos (as images) and the people who have chosen to make these tattoos a part of themselves? Explain.

SUMMARY: Critical Reading Process

- Initial Response
- Second Response (reacting to initial response)
- Clarifying Meaning (summarizing, making inferences)
- Evaluating (establishing criteria, forming judgments)

CHAPTER **2**
. . . .

The Processes and Aims of Writing

Chapter 1 discusses processes for reading effectively to explore, understand, synthesize, analyze, and evaluate an author's work. Writing is a natural companion to reading, and it can be a valuable tool for helping you understand your own responses to a text. Writing can also help you investigate more fully an author's ideas and observations and can help you argue for or against an author's proposals. This chapter explores a number of processes that can lead to thoughtful and coherent writing. It also provides descriptions of possible aims for writing and offers examples of students' papers that demonstrate ways you can write to inform a reader or to argue a position. As you write your own papers, you will not necessarily follow each step described here. But after reading this chapter you should understand more about your own writing process and about the possible ways you can approach various writing assignments.

CONSIDERING YOUR OWN WRITING PROCESS

To begin thinking about your writing process, try this exercise:

> Draw an image that represents the way you approach a writing assignment. Then write a brief description of the image and explain how it suggests your approach to writing.

Here are some examples of students' responses to this exercise:

> My image is a long, flat line and then at the very end a lot of up and down lines. This is like a monitor that shows a brain that is

turned off, but at the last minute comes to life with a lot of frantic movement. I just can't get myself started until the last minute, but then I work very fast and usually everything turns out all right.

Brenda Toohey

I see a path that curves through a garden and as I go along this path sometimes I find a beautiful flower to pick but also many weeds. Sometimes there are side paths and I take them. Often there is nothing on the side path, but sometimes I find another flower that fits with those I have gathered. At the end, I must arrange all the flowers carefully together. In writing, I am very slow, and I don't find good ideas very easily. Finding the ideas is hard, but arranging them right is even harder.

Dana Warschek

I think of beginning a writing project as if it's a big set of high stairs. The only way I can do it is to think of just getting up the next step. Because if I think of having to write maybe ten pages I just can't do it. But if I think that first I have to get a list of ideas, which is like step one, I can do that. Then I have to think of step two, three, etc. I usually do a little bit every day.

Albert Lowell

Each of these students describes a very different approach to writing. Brenda takes a long time to get started but then works in an intensive—and apparently productive—burst of energy. Albert sees writing as a fairly straightforward task that he approaches systematically and gradually. Dana, on the other hand, does not see writing as going primarily in one direction. Instead of proceeding in lines or steps, Dana's writing process follows a curving path that leads in many different directions, revealing useful ideas and images (flowers) but also material that will not work (weeds).

From reading the descriptions of their approaches to a writing assignment, which of these students would you judge to be the best writer? Which would you say follows the best process? It's tempting to say that Albert's is best because he makes a plan and works at it step by step, or to praise Brenda, whose last-minute surge of inspiration apparently leads to outstanding insights, or to admire Dana's ability to search in many directions and choose only the worthiest images and ideas for the final paper. Yet none of these students has discovered the process that is right for every-body. They have only discovered approaches that seem to work for them. Perhaps by considering the experiences of other writers, they might develop new strategies. In addition, they might iden-tify and address any weaknesses in their current processes. For in-stance, Brenda says that "usually everything turns out all right," but perhaps she can develop ways of initiating her burst of in-sights sooner so that she has time to revise and edit her papers. Dana, who finds it difficult to arrange ideas, might focus on de-veloping ways to organize information effectively. Albert might discover that a writing project cannot always be broken down into clear steps. Sometimes there may be a series of false starts and side trips that eventually leads to a fuller, more insightful paper than would a series of neat stages.

As you develop your own writing process, it is important to remain open to other possible ways of working. Staying with a process that has usually worked may be safe, but trying new ways and taking risks with your writing will allow you to grow. To grow with your writing, you need to understand the three basic elements of any writing project: (1) the writing task, (2) the process of writ-ing, and (3) the aim of your writing.

UNDERSTANDING THE WRITING TASK

Sometimes writing tasks are generated entirely by our own needs. We may decide to keep a journal, to write a letter to a friend, or to compose a reply to an editorial in the local newspaper. More often, however, a writing task is assigned by an instructor at school or by a supervisor at work. Before beginning to write, it is essential to understand what the writing task will require. To do this, you need to know the subject you will address, the purpose of the as-signment, the audience for whom it is intended, and any special requirements.

The Subject

Sometimes a subject will be extremely broad. For example, "Choose an issue related to a multicultural society and write about it." Sometimes it will be relatively narrow. For instance, "Write a paper on interracial adoption." Whether a subject is extremely broad or somewhat narrow, you usually have to refine it even more so that you have a clear, specific topic to pursue. Here, for example, are possible ways of refining the assignment "Write a paper on interracial adoption":

1. Legal issues related to interracial adoption.
2. Cultural problems with interracial adoption.
3. Advantages of interracial adoption.
4. Interracial adoption in the United States compared to interracial adoption in Great Britain.

As you work at refining your topic, it is usually helpful to check with the person who has given you the assignment to ask for confirmation or advice about the direction you have decided to take.

The Purpose of the Assignment

Next, consider the purpose of the assignment. To write effectively, you must understand what you hope to accomplish. For example, consider a scenario in which your supervisor asks you to write about safety hazards. Is your supervisor asking you to explain safety hazards you have observed in the workplace or does she want you to argue that those safety hazards must be corrected in a certain way and within a certain time frame? Of course, sometimes you have more than one motive for writing and sometimes you must pursue one purpose in order to accomplish a second. For example, you would have to explain why a certain waste disposal process creates an environmental hazard before you could effectively argue that it should be discontinued.

The Audience

As you plan your writing, you should also consider your readers.

1. *Keep in mind how much your audience knows about your subject.* What information, explanations, or definitions do you need to provide? On the one hand, you do not want to insult readers by telling them things that they already know, but on the other hand, you do not want them to be puzzled because your subject matter or approach is entirely unfamiliar.
2. *Keep in mind your readers' values.* You determine readers' values in many different ways. Sometimes you have talked

with your readers, and they have told you that (for instance) they consider getting an education absolutely essential or, conversely, that they believe practical experience to be more important than the theories learned in formal schooling. Sometimes you can guess at readers' values if you know such things as their political affiliations or their religious beliefs (or rebellion against certain religious beliefs). While it is dangerous to make generalizations without recognizing exceptions, you can guess that a group whose motto is "Save the whales" will hold considerably different values than a group who sums up their philosophy with the phrase "Save jobs not owls." If you were writing a paper on environmental issues, knowing that most of your readers belonged to one or the other of these groups would most certainly affect the way you would approach your topic. If the values you are explaining are significantly different from those of your readers, consider how you will approach your discussion so that your audience will not immediately become alienated or dismiss your ideas without considering the possible connections your ideas may have with their own values.

3. *Keep in mind that your audience will probably not be made up entirely of a single, easily definable group.* Occasionally, you may write for readers who all have very nearly the same level of knowledge about your subject and who hold similar values relating to your subject. More often, however, you'll be writing for people who, although they may be alike in some ways, are dramatically different in others. For instance, within an introductory writing class, there will often be students whose ages, ethnic background, work experience, and previous education vary widely. When you are writing to such a mixed audience, you have to decide how to meet the needs of as many readers as possible without making your paper a mishmash that fails to communicate clearly because it is trying to be all things to all people.

Special Requirements

In addition to understanding and narrowing the topic on which you will write, identifying your purpose for writing, and analyzing your audience, you need to recognize any special requirements that your assignment might have. For example, consider the following questions:

1. *Does the assignment specify a length?* If you are asked to write a two-page paper, you'll need to plan it differently than you would if you were asked to address the same subject in a ten-page paper. For example, the shorter paper might be stronger if you narrowed your topic as much as possible. On the other hand, the longer paper might require a complex and detailed exploration of several aspects of the topic.

2. *Does the assignment require (or forbid) using secondary sources?* If you are asked to use sources other than your own knowledge, you need to know what kinds of sources are required (journals, books, newspapers, interviews, Web resources) and whether a specific number of sources is expected. Be aware that library searches, including electronic searches, can often be frustrating; start early so that you can locate the materials you need. If you are having difficulty, ask the reference librarian for help. When you cite from sources (either direct quotations or paraphrases), be sure to document them correctly. For further information on documenting sources, see pages 379–410.

   If you are supposed to use only your own ideas, do not consult outside sources. Whether or not you use direct quotations, using the ideas of others as if they were your own (without proper documentation) is considered plagiarism.

3. *Does the assignment specify a particular organization?* For example, an assignment might ask you to compare two or more concepts or ideas or require you to explain the details of an event in chronological order.

4. *Was the assignment given in written form?* If so, be sure to read the instructions carefully and to follow any guidelines that have been provided.

5. *Was the assignment given orally?* If so, be sure to take careful notes and to follow the instructions and guidelines given.

6. *Are you confused about any aspect of the assignment?* Ask for clarification from your instructor.

UNDERSTANDING THE PROCESSES OF WRITING

As the exercise at the beginning of this chapter suggests, there is no single, correct process for any writer or for any writing assignment. Instead, an individual writer may work in many different ways to address varied assignments, and several writers may successfully address the same assignment in different ways. Nevertheless, it is helpful to be aware of four stages that are usually part of any writer's approach to a writing task: prewriting, drafting, revising, and editing.

Prewriting

Prewriting includes the thinking, discovery, and planning that take place in your mind, in conversations with others, on paper, or on a computer screen before you begin actually drafting your response to a writing task. As you begin prewriting, consider these possible approaches:

1. Making lists: Listing ideas, observations, reactions, and details related to your topic can help you discover what you want to say about that topic.
2. Freewriting: Writing continuously about your topic and jotting down whatever comes to mind can help you find possibilities for planning and writing your paper.
3. Mapping: Mapping, which is similar to listing and freewriting, encourages a visual rather than a linear exploration of ideas. While there are no precise rules, you generally begin mapping by writing your topic in the middle of a page, circling it, and then coming up with possible subdivisions of that topic. These new possibilities are circled and attached by lines to the original topic. Note the example of mapping that Kimberly Waibel used when she wrote the sample paper "In the Best Interest of the Child" (pages 56–59).
4. Incubation: Incubating takes place in your head, rather than on paper. When you are first given a topic, you consciously implant it in your mind and tell yourself to think about it whenever you can. For example, you can incubate ideas while you are exercising, while you are waiting in

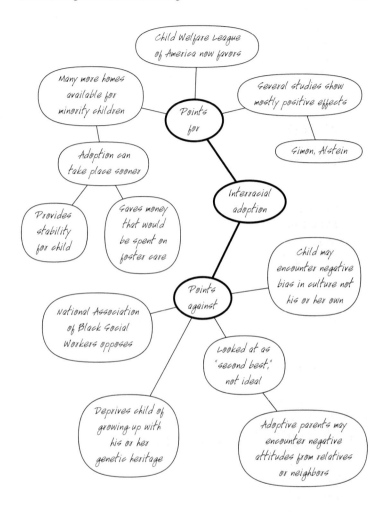

line, while you are doing chores such as lawn mowing or washing dishes, or while you are walking to class. Focusing on a topic through incubation often leads to insights when you least expect them.

5. Conversations or interviews: Talking with a friend or interviewing someone who is knowledgeable about your topic can help you find new ways of thinking about it.

6. Journalist's questions: Using the traditional journalist's questions can prompt different approaches to thinking or

writing about your topic. See how these questions might apply to your topic: Who? What? When? Where? Why? How?

7. Outlining: Outlines provide a way of organizing the thoughts, images, and ideas that are discovered through listing, brainstorming, or mapping.

Drafting

After you have narrowed your topic and explored possibilities through various prewriting strategies, you are ready to begin drafting. The draft is the first version of your final paper.

Thesis Statement   While drafting can be done in various ways, one useful process begins with writing a *thesis statement:* a sentence or two that not only state your topic but also tell what you intend to say about the topic. For example, if your topic was "illegal immigration," your thesis statement might look like this:

> Illegal immigration into the United States may pose practical problems, but it also raises complicated moral issues that must be considered.

During the drafting stage, the thesis is tentative; you use it as a guide, but you may change it as you develop and revise your paper.

Planning   To write the draft, you should have a plan for organizing your ideas. You might, for instance, arrange the points you are making in chronological order, or perhaps move from describing an event to explaining the effects of that event. To help sort the information you have gathered, you can make an informal outline, or you might sort notecards into piles (which can easily be rearranged) to see how you want to organize your paper.

Getting Started   To begin drafting, you do not need to have the perfect introduction. Some writers start with their tentative thesis; others just plunge right in and work on the main body of the paper. Introductions and conclusions are often the most difficult to write, so many writers set aside those parts until they have worked with the draft for a while. The important thing is to get started and not to procrastinate because you do not have a polished opening sentence.

Revising

Revising can be the most important step in the writing process because it is at this stage that you are refining and polishing your ideas, developing your examples, evaluating the evidence you have used to support your points, and working to develop effective introductions and conclusions. As you revise, consider the following checklist:

1. Have you focused on a subject that is specific enough to allow for full treatment in a paper of the length you've been asked to write?
2. Do you have a clear understanding of the purpose of your paper? Do you communicate the purpose of your paper to your readers through a thesis statement?
3. Have you organized the ideas, information, and descriptions you are presenting so that they make sense to your audience?
4. Does each paragraph deal with one main idea and does each paragraph logically follow from the paragraph before it?
5. Does every paragraph offer sufficient information (details, examples, reasons) to support the idea it expresses?
6. Do all paragraphs relate clearly to the purpose of your paper?
7. Have you analyzed and evaluated your audience, considering their abilities, beliefs, values, opinions, knowledge, and interest? And have you written with your audience analysis in mind?
8. Have you provided an opening paragraph that catches the interest of your audience and makes them want to read further?
9. Have you written a concluding paragraph that provides an original analysis, evaluation, solution, option, insight? (A strong conclusion usually does more than simply summarize what you've already said.)
10. Does every paragraph in the paper lead logically to the conclusion?

Editing

After you have revised your paper, the final step is editing. Editing can be divided into two categories: issues of style and issues of grammar and mechanics. As you edit your paper, consider the following checklist:

Issues of Style

1. Have you used a variety of sentence structures to avoid sounding dull and monotonous?
2. Have you chosen words carefully, considering both denotation (the dictionary meaning) and connotation (the emotional overtones readers attach to words)?
3. Have you avoided *repetition* (unless, of course, the repetition is used for emphasis)?
4. Have you avoided overuse of *passive voice*?

> *Example: Passive voice*   The map was read by the visitor.
> *Active voice*   The visitor read the map.

5. Have you avoided using long, ornate words when a shorter, more concise word would convey your meaning just as accurately?
6. Have you avoided using unnecessary words (for example, saying "due to the fact that" when you could just say "because")?

Issues of Grammar and Mechanics

1. Does each sentence express a complete thought?
2. Have you avoided fusing two complete thoughts together with no mark of punctuation or with only a comma?
3. Do descriptive words or phrases (*modifiers*) relate clearly to the word or words they are intended to describe?
4. Do all subjects and verbs agree?
5. Does every pronoun have a clear *antecedent* (a noun to which it refers)?
6. Do all pronouns agree with their antecedents?
7. Is the *tense* (time reference) of verbs consistent throughout the paper (except when you intend to indicate change in time)?

8. Are commas, semicolons, and other punctuation marks used correctly?
9. Are possessives formed correctly, using apostrophes with nouns (the girl's book; two girls' books) but not with personal pronouns (the book is hers; its cover is torn)?
10. Are all words spelled correctly?

Peer Editors

All writers should develop strategies for revising and editing their own writing, but it's also extremely helpful to have the benefit of additional readers during the process of revising and editing. In many classrooms, as well as in many workplace situations, peers may be called on to help a writer see his or her work with new eyes.

The concept of peer editors suggests that there are mutual responsibilities. The writer and editor may not be experts in either the writing process or the subject that is being addressed. However, through preparation, concentration, and goodwill on the part of both writer and editor, the peer editing process can be extremely useful. Here are some suggestions that have come from more than 200 students who, during the past ten years, have participated in the peer editing process, both as editors and as readers. Their suggestions were made as part of evaluations they wrote at the end of the semester.

Advice for Writers

1. Read the assignment carefully and do what it asks. It's a waste of time for the peer editor to read a paper that does not address the assignment.
2. Complete the paper before the date for the peer editing. Do not count on peer editors to finish the paper for you.
3. Do as much revising and editing as you can *before* you bring the paper to the peer editing session. Doing this will give you the full benefit of the peer editors' work. The peer editors will not be pointing out things you already know or could easily see yourself.
4. Come to the peer editing session with a list of questions that you would like your editors to consider. (*Note:* To formulate these questions, look at the revision checklist on

page 37.) As you write your list, begin with larger issues of revising before thinking about questions related to style and editing.

5. Pay attention to what your editors say. Maybe you don't agree with everything, but you'll probably find some points that offer very good advice.

6. Take notes during the editing discussion so that you will be able to remember what was said when you begin to work on revising your paper later.

7. If you do get to the point of discussing issues of style (see page 38) or issues of grammar and mechanics (pages 38–39) and you disagree with your peer editors, you might want to consult another source, such as a handbook, your instructor, or a tutor at your campus writing center.

8. Remember that the writer makes the final decision about what gets changed and what does not. You don't have to do everything your editors suggest, and your readers (including the instructor) will hold you responsible for the content, organization, and correctness of your paper.

Advice for Peer Editors

1. Come to the peer editing session prepared. If you were supposed to read the paper ahead of time, make sure that you have done so.

2. Start by reading the essay through without a pencil or pen in your hand. Just read for an initial overall impression. As you read, keep in mind large issues such as these:
   a. Does the paper do what the assignment asks?
   b. What is the main idea of this paper?
   c. How well is the main idea supported?
   d. Is the paper well organized?

3. When you have completed your first reading, stop and write three or four comments. Include the following:
   a. What one aspect do you like best about the paper?
   b. What one aspect do you think most needs attention for revision?

4. If the writer has prepared questions for you, read them before you do your second reading.

5. Then read the essay a second time, this time with a pen or pencil in your hand. Make notes in the margins about

points you really admire or aspects you think need to be changed. Remember to keep in mind the writer's questions (if she or he has provided them). *Note:* To help with this process, you should also consider the points raised in the revision checklist, pages 37–39.

6. As you talk with the writer, it sometimes helps to ask questions rather than just give advice. For example, "Is the main idea of your paper that divorce is too easy or that divorce should be made illegal?" A question like this will often be more helpful than a statement like "I don't get your main idea."

7. Even if the paper seems nearly perfect to you, try to find some worthwhile suggestions for revision. Going over the revision checklist, pages 37–39, may give you ideas.

8. Even if the paper seems to need changes in nearly every paragraph and sentence, try to find some positive points to give the writer encouragement.

9. If you have addressed all the issues on the revision checklist, then (and only then) you should go on to address issues of style (page 38).

10. If you have addressed all the issues of revision and the issues of style, then (and only then) you should go on to address issues of grammar and mechanics (pages 38–39).

UNDERSTANDING THE AIMS OF WRITING

Like reading, writing is a complex activity. Both critical reading and thoughtful writing require many strategies and stages rather than a single rigid approach. This section explains and demonstrates the three primary aims of writing: to express, to inform, and to persuade. Understanding these aims can help you develop a process for successfully completing any writing project, whether personal, academic, or professional. Expressive writing often uses stories (narratives) to describe people, places, and events and to communicate the author's external and internal experiences to readers. While most of the selections in this text demonstrate primarily informative and persuasive writing, these examples are not exclusive. For example, within an essay written by an author whose purpose is primarily informative, there may also be short stories (anecdotes) to illustrate a point. In nearly all persuasive writing, there are paragraphs or sections that are informative. So, as you read about the informative and persuasive aims of writing, keep in mind that they are not mutually exclusive.

Informative Writing

While informative writing often incorporates description and narrative, it aims primarily to explain ideas, processes, and concepts, as in this textbook's selections "The Lost Boys" (pages 164–67), "'Pantelets' and 'Turkish Trousers,'" (pages 201–4), and "Tips for Teens" (pages 293–96).

Writing that explains takes many different forms, but all forms share the broad purpose of seeking to convey new information to readers. Writers explain by using a variety of approaches; so as you begin to read an essay, article, or book that explains, you may find it helpful to identify the writer's approach. The following are some of the ways writers choose to convey new ideas or to offer new ways of looking at familiar ideas.

1. *Informing.* When writers seek to inform, they usually are concerned mainly with providing facts: giving readers access to details, statistics, anecdotes, and so on, with which they were previously unacquainted. An essay that is strictly informative almost always takes an objective stance. In other words, the writer does not offer an opinion about the information provided. Rather, the author provides the data, usually ends with a brief summary, and leaves the reader to draw conclusions or to discover the implications of the new information. Articles in scientific journals are often written primarily to inform. On a more mundane level, a set of directions telling someone how to get somewhere is also an example of informative writing.

   More common than the strictly informative essay, however, is writing that offers information but, in addition, uses that information for another purpose—for example, *defining, analyzing, synthesizing,* or *evaluating.*

2. *Defining.* If a complex concept is involved, a writer may explain the concept by developing a detailed, extended definition. Obviously, such an essay goes far beyond the brief notations given in dictionaries. Rather than providing

the short—and often simplistic—definitions found in reference books, selections that explain through defining explore complexities and ambiguities, offering examples and details that help the reader see the richness of the subject being discussed.

In this book, a number of selections provide extended definitions. They include "'Blaxicans' and Other Reinvented Americans" (pages 87–93) and "Bakke and Beyond: A History and Timeline of Affirmative Action" (pages 344–48).

3. *Analyzing.* Analysis means looking at the parts to see how they work together to create the whole. To write an analysis, a writer looks closely at the aspects and qualities that constitute a place, a person, an idea, an emotion, or, perhaps, a work of literature or an object of art. Then, focusing on those aspects or qualities that seem most significant, the writer explains what he or she has discovered. Note particularly that the purpose of analysis is not simply to see the components of a whole but, rather, to see the significance of those components in relationship with one another.

A practical example of analysis is the process most of us go through when we are trying to fix something that isn't working as it should. Consider, for example, a photocopier that does not make clean, clear copies. To solve the problem, we would probably consult the owner's guide. After identifying the components of the copier, we would recognize that the paper tray, the power plug, and the front cover could not be sources of the problem, but we'd certainly want to check the glass, the chargers, and the toner box. We'd consider how these parts should be working together to produce a readable copy. And if our analysis was successful, we'd learn what needs to be done to get the machine to function smoothly once again.

A writer who makes an analysis may look at a complicated principle, a common assumption, a geographic phenomenon, or a distinguished and unusual person's life. By looking at the parts that make up any of these (or many other) subjects, the writer discovers new and significant ideas and possibilities, which she or he then explains to the reader. Examples of selections that analyze include "Wheel of Misfortune" (pages 78–84) and "The New Gender Gap" (pages 170–79).

4. *Synthesizing.* The ability to synthesize information, ideas, and observations is essential for anyone truly interested in learning and growing. This process is particularly important for thinking, reading, and writing across cultures because when you synthesize, you look for connections, disjunctions, differences, and similarities. More important, you look for the significance of the comparisons and contrasts you have observed. Writers who explain through synthesis work to see relationships among apparently different people, places, ideas, concepts, or emotions.

We all use the process of synthesis when we meet a new person who will be significant in our lives (coworker, roommate, supervisor, in-law). We observe the differences between ourselves and these people as we strive to discover how we'll address those differences. However, we also look for similarities and for ways to make connections with those who are important to us.

Several selections provide examples of writers who explain their ideas through making syntheses, for example, "The Great Enigma of Our Times" (pages 285–89) and "Pondering Condoleezza Rice's Affirmative Action Problem—and Mine" (pages 349–52).

5. *Evaluating.* When writers evaluate, they provide readers with information about a particular person, place, idea, action, or theory. Then they go on to define or imply criteria for judging this subject and to apply those criteria. Evaluating requires the writer to form an opinion about the subject and to provide evidence to convince the reader that this opinion deserves attention. An evaluation may be as straightforward as formulating a judgment of a book or film. For example, when we recommend a particular movie to a friend and then offer reasons why we think this movie is worthwhile, we are making and expressing an evaluation.

A more complex yet equally common way of evaluating is for a writer to define a problem and then explain what he or she sees as the significant causes or effects of that problem. An evaluation of a problem may also include suggestions for solving the problem, as in the selections "Indian Gaming: Why Is the Backlash Growing?" (pages 84–86) and "With Fewer Distractions Students Will Do Better" (pages 168–69).

As you read selections written to inform or explain, you'll almost certainly notice that many of your own writing tasks require explanation of one kind or another. For example, professors may ask you to write a review or critique of an article, essay, book, or chapter in a book. Such an assignment calls for evaluation. Also, many essay exams require you to compare or contrast various aspects of the course's subject. The essay question may not directly instruct you to explain the significance of these similarities and differences, but you are usually expected to synthesize the information you have gathered, providing a useful conclusion rather than merely a list of things that are alike and things that are not alike. As another example, a history instructor may assign a paper on the causes and effects of the French Revolution or the Great Depression, a writing task that can be accomplished through analysis. Or a philosophy course may focus on a semester-long exploration of a concept such as truth or love that leads to a paper defining the complexities of one of these terms.

Writing to explain requires developing a process that allows you to explore ideas, gather data effectively, and formulate a clear thesis that will serve as your focus. Whatever approach you take to explaining—informing, defining, analyzing, synthesizing, or evaluating—you need to keep in mind that your primary purpose is to convey new information or a new way of thinking to your reader. To convince readers that this new information or new way of thinking is worthy of their attention and consideration, you need to provide details, reasons, and examples that will show— not just tell—them what you want them to think about. Remember, also, that when you write to explain, you rarely use one approach exclusively. For instance, a paper that analyzes may also include an extended definition of an important term. An essay that synthesizes two apparently different ideas may also evaluate the significance the writer sees in newly discovered similarities between these two ideas.

Here is an example of an informative paper, written by student writer Kimberly Waibel.

Changing Views toward Interracial Adoption

While not all positions for social workers require dealing directly with issues related to adoption, many social service agencies encounter concerns related to today's changing family structure. Because adoption is an important part of that changing structure, it is essential that future social workers understand the complexities of interracial adoption. (The terms "interracial" and "transracial" adoption, which are interchangeable, refer to adoptions in which the child belongs to one race and the prospective parents, or one of the prospective parents, to another.) Transracial adoption has historically followed a dramatically changing pattern. For example, during the thirty years from 1958 to 1988, the Child Welfare League of America (CWLA) issued four different policy statements reflecting the League's view of interracial adoption (Simon, Alstein, *A.R.I.*). Considering the four different policy views of the CWLA and examining possible reasons for the changes will provide essential background information on this controversial topic.

The Child Welfare League of America is an agency that lobbies for and develops policy statements related to the well-being of children and adolescents in the United States. One of their concerns is adoption, and they would certainly have been aware of the fact that following World War II, there was a great increase in international adoption, with many of the children having fathers who had been in the American military (Bagley, Young, Scully). The placement of these children, some of whom were of mixed race, led adoption agencies within the United States to try interracial adoption as a way to find homes for the minority children they served. These adoptions, however, often faced condemnation by the families and communities of the adopting parents, as well as challenges from the legal system. In 1955, a case known as *In re Adoption of a Minor* was decided in Washington, D.C. The case involved a child born to an unmarried white couple. The birth mother then married a black man. With the mother's permission, the black man filed a petition to adopt the child. The court refused, citing that the child would lose the social status of a white man because his "official father" would be black (Simon, Alstein, *A.R.I.* 40). Although the court of appeals reversed the district court's ruling, the first ruling is an example of the strong prejudices of this time period.

In 1958, the CWLA published its guide *Standards for Adoption Service,* which reflects the racist attitudes of the era. This publication gave guidelines that specifically promote inracial (same-race) adoption as the only acceptable form of adoption. Under the subtitle "Matching," the CWLA held that "Physical resemblances should not be a determining factor in the selection of a home, with the exception of such racial characteristics as color" (Simon, Alstein, *A.R.I.* 4). During the same year that this policy was issued, 1958, the rate of interracial adoption, which had risen every year since 1945, began to drop. Several experts agree that the position stated by the CWLA, as well as the public attitudes leading to that position, influenced many adoption agencies to stop encouraging or even permitting interracial adoption (Austin; Bagley, Young, Scully).

As the country moved into the 1960s, however, changes occurred to bring pressure on agencies such as the CWLA to change their views. For example, Martin Luther King, Jr., was leading the nation's civil rights movement, which promoted racial harmony and the full integration of black people into society. According to Janet Marent, Ph.D., professor of sociology, this movement led some social workers to argue strongly that transracial adoption should be looked at as acceptable. In addition, Dr. Marent stated, some proponents of the civil rights movement believed that interracial adoption would further the cause of racial integration. Furthermore, both the National Association for the Advancement of Colored People (NAACP) and the National Urban League made statements endorsing transracial adoption as a reasonable alternative to traditional adoption (McRoy). Subsequently, in the late 1960s, the CWLA reversed its earlier position, now stating that "families who have the capacity to adopt a child whose racial background is different from their own . . . should be encouraged to consider such a child" (McRoy 149). In response to the changing times, as reflected by the reversal of the CWLA policy, approximately 5,000 to 10,000 transracial adoptions occurred between 1967 and 1972 (Simon, Alstein, *Transracial Adoption* 156).

5   In 1972, however, a new influence, which was to influence yet another change in CWLA policy, made its voice heard. At its annual conference, the National Association of Black Social Workers (NABSW) developed an official statement strongly opposed to interracial adoption. The 5,000 members of the association passed a resolution stating that "black children in white homes are cut off

from the healthy development of themselves as black people"
(McRoy 150). Furthermore, the NABSW went so far as to call transracial adoption "a form of genocide" (Simon, Alstein, *A.R.I.* 15). Support for the NABSW came from the African American separatists
who surfaced in response to the civil rights movement. These separatists believed that integration would destroy the sense of black
identity and pride. Several of these separatist groups reinforced the
NABSW's position by stating that the adoption of black children by
white families would be detrimental to the African American community as a whole (Hayes 30). As a result, the CWLA again reversed
its position, restating the importance of inracial placements in order
to facilitate a child's integration into its adoptive family (McRoy 150).
Following the statements made by the NABSW and the CWLA, the
rate of transracial adoptions decreased dramatically. In 1975, the last
year the federal government collected information on adoption statistics, the number of transracial adoptions was 831, as reported by
the Department of Health, Education, and Welfare. This number is
much lower than the record high in 1971 when 2,574 transracial
adoptions were recorded (Simon, Alstein, *A.R.I.* 5).

The most recent statement from the CWLA, its 1988 *Standards
for Adoption Services,* shows yet another change. While the organization still maintains inracial adoption to be the best alternative, the
new policy states, "If aggressive, ongoing recruitment efforts are
unsuccessful in finding families of the same ethnicity or culture,
other families should be considered" (Simon, Alstein, *A.R.I.* 32). This
statement indicates that the objections of such organizations as the
NABSW are being taken seriously, yet interracial adoption is now
looked at as a reasonable alternative to having the children remain
in the custody of the state where, according to social worker Eric
Blogden, they are often simply moved from one crowded foster home
to the next. The latest change in the CWLA's statement is supported
by the results of a twenty-year study, carried out from 1971 until
1991 by sociologists at the University of Illinois. This study included
133 families who adopted children interracially. The families and
children were contacted regularly and were found by researchers to
have done very well. In fact, in publishing some of the results of the
survey, sociology professor Rita Simon notes the following:

> In conclusion, I want to emphasize that the findings in our
> study are neither unique nor unusual. All of the studies, even
> those carried out by researchers who were initially skeptical,
> reported that transracial adoptees grow up emotionally and

socially adjusted, and aware of and comfortable with their racial identity. (76)

For future social workers, continuing to watch the policy statements of organizations such as the CWLA and the NABSW will provide a way to follow the developing views on interracial adoption. This topic continues to be highly controversial, and because it may well touch the lives of people who seek help from various social service agencies, future social workers should make themselves aware of the complex history and the continuing changes related to this important issue.

WORKS CITED

Austin, Judy, ed. Adoption: The Inside Story. Washington, D.C.: American University Press, 1991.

Bagley, Christopher, Loretta Young, and Anne Scully. International and Transracial Adoptions. Montpelier, Vermont: Ashgate, 1993.

Blogden, Eric. Personal interview. 10 November 1998.

Hayes, Peter. "Transracial Adoption: Politics and Ideology." Child Welfare 72 (1993): 301–10.

Marent, Janet, Ph.D. Personal interview. 13 November 1998.

McRoy, Ruth G. "An Organizational Dilemma: The Case of Transracial Adoptions." Journal of Applied Behavioral Science 25.2 (1989): 145–60.

Simon, Rita James. "Transracial Adoptions: Experiences of a Twenty-Year Study." American Sociologist 27.3 (1996): 79–90.

Simon, Rita James, and Howard Alstein. Transracial Adoption. New York: Wiley, 1977.

———. Adoption, Race, and Identity. New York: Praeger, 1992.

Suggestions for Informative Writing

1. As you are prewriting, keep in mind the many approaches that help a writer to explain: informing, defining, analyzing, synthesizing, and evaluating.
2. As you think about your subject and plan your draft, consider your audience. Consider such things as their knowledge, interests, concerns, and values.
3. As you write the opening of an essay that informs, remember that your audience needs to understand your purpose.

Readers need to know the subject of your essay as well as what you are going to say about that subject. A standard way to convey this information is in a thesis statement.

4. As you develop your ideas, remember that your purpose is to inform readers of a new idea or a new way of looking at the world. To accomplish this purpose, you'll need to provide specific details, reasons, and examples. You want to show your readers what you are talking about rather than overwhelming, and perhaps confusing, them with unsupported generalizations.

5. As you write your conclusion, remember that it should follow logically from the information you have given your reader in the rest of the essay. Remember, too, that the conclusion should do more than summarize. It should provide an original analysis, evaluation, solution, option, or insight.

Persuasive Writing

Although persuasive writing may include descriptions, stories, and explanations, its main goal is to persuade readers to see a particular point of view as important and valid. In this textbook, examples of such persuasive writing include "Don't Turn on the Flag" (pages 124–25), "If You're a Woman in Saudi Arabia, Just Cover Up. (For Now)" (pages 212–16), and "Why the Record Companies Have to Play Hardball" (pages 263–65).

Whenever you read, you pay attention to the writer's main ideas and to the way he or she supports and develops those ideas. However, as mentioned in chapter 1, when you are reading thoughtfully and critically, once you are aware of these literally stated points, you also need to consider what is being implied. It is particularly important to be aware of the power of implication when you read essays or articles that aim to persuade.

To make inferences—that is, to "read between the lines"— you need to pay special attention to the distinction between fact and the author's opinion. In addition, note carefully the author's *tone* (the author's attitude toward the subject and toward the audience), which often reflects biases, beliefs, and values.

Rational Appeals   As you read persuasive writing, notice the way the writer seeks to convince you that a particular point of view is worthy of your consideration—and, ultimately, of your adoption. Most writers use a combination of facts and opinions. There's certainly nothing wrong with giving your attention to another's opinion—but do not be lulled into thinking that because an idea is stated in print, it has to be the truth. *Facts* are statements or statistics that can be verified through a source (or sources) that most knowledgeable people believe to be reliable. For instance, a writer may state that American journalist Harriet Quimby was the second woman to be a licensed pilot and, in 1912, the first woman to fly across the English Channel, citing the *1996 Information Please Almanac* as the source. You could easily check to verify these details, so accepting them as facts is certainly reasonable. On the other hand, if the writer then stated that Quimby contributed more to the advancement of women in aviation than did Amelia Earhart, that would be an opinion. For you, as a reader, to be convinced that this opinion was worthy of consideration would require much more evidence than a simple statement.

In judging the evidence you expect the writer to provide, you should ask yourself the following questions:

1. *Has the writer provided sufficient evidence?* In the example just given, for instance, providing just one or two comparisons between Quimby and Earhart would not be enough. Instead, the writer might list significant contributions made by Quimby and significant contributions made by Earhart, pointing out the reasons that Quimby's list shows her influence to have been greater than Earhart's. In addition, the writer might cite the views of scholars who are well respected in such fields as women's studies and aviation history and whose evaluations corroborated the writer's contention.

2. *Has the writer used only relevant evidence?* For example, it may be interesting to know the high school or college backgrounds of these two aviators. But their grade point averages or extracurricular activities could hardly be used to persuade an intelligent reader that one or the other had made more significant contributions to the field of women in aviation.

3. *Has the writer qualified the evidence, where needed?* Very seldom can words such as *all, every,* and *never* be used accurately. To be believable, statements often require such qualifying words as *some, most,* or *in many cases.* For

example, "Everyone agrees that Quimby's flight across the English Channel marked the beginning of women's history in aviation" is subject to challenge if even one dissenting example can be found. A more careful writer would, instead, say something like this: "Many aviation enthusiasts agree that Quimby's flight across the English Channel marked the beginning of women's history in aviation."

4. *Has the writer successfully avoided* logical fallacies *(flaws in reasoning)?* Logical fallacies often sound reasonable, but critical reading shows that the writer's thinking has gone astray. Sometimes fallacies result from a writer's carelessness; other times, a writer may purposely use fallacious reasoning, hoping to manipulate the unwary reader. Logical fallacies include—but are not limited to—the following types:

 a. *Begging the question*—using circular statements to claim that something is true. For instance, "Amelia Earhart is well known as a woman pilot only because she has gained much publicity as a female aviator" begs the question. This statement says that Earhart is well known only because she is well known and does not make a sensible point.

 b. *Hasty generalization*—making a generalization from only one or two examples. *Stereotyping*—making broad claims about all members of a particular group on the basis of the actions or beliefs of some of that group—is a type of hasty generalization that is particularly relevant to reading and writing about cross-cultural issues. For example, if someone were to say that because Earhart and Quimby were both United States citizens, American women must have a natural talent for flying, that would be a hasty generalization that stereotypes American women. Note that stereotyping can identify either a positive trait or a negative trait. It's just as illogical—and potentially damaging—to assume that all members of one race, religion, or social group share a particular talent as it is to suggest that they all share a specific weakness or deficiency.

 c. *Ad hominem (Latin for "to the man") appeals*—claiming that irrelevant personal qualities should be considered reason to qualify or disqualify an individual for a particular office, position, honor, or role. For example, noting that a candidate for mayor fails to keep her house neatly painted has nothing to do with how she might lead the city.

d. *Post hoc, ergo propter hoc (Latin for "after this, therefore because of this")*—assuming that because one action or event preceded another, the first event or action caused the second to happen. For instance, noting that Harriet Quimby received her pilot's license shortly before ratification of the Nineteenth Amendment, which gave women in the United States the right to vote, is accurate. However, to suggest that Quimby's licensing somehow caused the Nineteenth Amendment to be passed would be illogical.

e. *Red herring*—introducing an irrelevant issue that sidetracks the audience from the main argument. For instance, in the Quimby versus Earhart issue, a red herring might be a question like "Why worry about Quimby's and Earhart's contributions when so many men have made more significant contributions?" Whether men have made more significant contributions is an entirely different issue and not relevant to the Quimby-Earhart topic.

f. *False dilemma (either-or fallacy)*—offering only two possibilities when other alternatives clearly exist. For instance, suppose someone said that women who want to have careers in aviation should either devote themselves to full-time flying or work at desk jobs. This statement ignores the many other options that are available (part-time work, work in maintenance, work related to building aircraft, for example).

g. *Bandwagon*—stating or implying that because many people are doing something, it is justified. For example, someone might say that since many people still prefer to fly with a male pilot than to fly with a female pilot, male pilots must be better at their work than female pilots. This statement suggests that simply because a biased action is supported by a large number of people, that action should be respected and emulated.

Emotional Appeals   In addition to differentiating fact and opinion and evaluating the various rational appeals a writer uses, you should pay close attention to the way the writer of a persuasive essay appeals to your emotions.

Criteria for evaluating emotional appeals cannot be defined as easily as criteria for judging rational appeals. Traditional discussions of argument and persuasion often suggest that any appeal to the emotions is somehow dishonest and suspect. Yet as humans, we make most of the decisions in our lives—including choosing the values we live by—not only from what our minds know to be true but also from what our emotions lead us to see as valid. Most of us agree that a balance between intellect and emotion is desirable; few of us would want to live in a world controlled solely by thought or solely by feelings.

The problem, then, is to recognize how a writer appeals to our feelings and to reject false manipulation while not ignoring the claims of emotions we see as genuine and worthy of our response. An example of an argument based primarily on emotional appeals is Martin Luther King's "I Have a Dream" (pages 104–8).

Appeals to the emotions are made in many ways. Consider these points as you evaluate such appeals:

1. *Word choice.* Remember that words have both literal (*denotative*) and emotional (*connotative*) meanings. For instance, although *clever* and *cunning* both describe a person as skillful and talented, most people would prefer to be called clever, because *cunning* also implies a crafty slyness. As you read persuasive writing, watch carefully for the connotations of words. Decide whether the other evidence offered convinces you that the word chosen truly describes the person or situation or whether, instead, it has been used primarily to divert your attention from making a fair assessment.
2. *Figurative language.* An extension of word choice is the use of figurative language. A writer or speaker may use startling or unusual metaphors or similes to gain the attention and sympathy of the audience. You'll find examples of figurative language in Sojourner Truth's "Ain't I a Woman?" (page 200).
3. *Sentence patterns.* Certain sentence patterns—for example, repetition of a key word or phrase—can fire the emotions in either a positive or a negative way. Repetition can

lead, and has led, to terrifying mob violence; yet in other instances, it has inspired selfless and idealistic actions. Once again, as a responsible listener and reader, you need to be aware of the way these devices are used and decide for yourself whether you consider the argument worthy of your emotional response.

4. *Imitative language patterns.* A writer or speaker may use language patterns familiar from other respected sources, thus tacitly asking the audience to give to this argument the same emotional responses that would have been given to the original source. For example, in "My People" Seattle refers to the documents that established the United States government, often directly echoing key phrases from those documents (pages 65–68).

Topics Worth Arguing About If you understand both rational and emotional appeals, you are prepared to write persuasively. But you should understand that persuasion is not always an appropriate approach; some topics are not worthy of argument. Keep these guidelines in mind:

1. *Matters of fact* are not worthy of argument. If you know that Ingrid Bergman and Yul Brynner won the Oscars for best actress and best actor in 1956 but your friend insists these awards went, instead, to Joanne Woodward and Alec Guinness, you can easily prove that you are right by consulting an almanac or entertainment encyclopedia. There's no sense wasting time and energy trying to convince someone to believe a fact that can be verified through a source you both consider accurate and reliable.

2. *Matters of taste* are not worthy of argument. While you might reasonably argue that your coworker should at least try the salad you have made of fiddlehead ferns and dandelion greens, you can't reasonably expect to persuade her that she likes the concoction. Our tastes (in food, pleasure reading, style of dressing, and so on) do change, of course, but not because someone else has given us a list of reasons to make the change.

A reasonable subject for a persuasive argument, then, is a subject that raises questions that are controversial. Usually, such a subject has many aspects. For instance, if the subject concerns the solution to a problem, ordinarily no one answer shows itself as the only correct answer. In addition, most controversial issues are extremely broad and complex. When you choose to write about them, you need to narrow your topic to suit the time and space you have to devote to writing the argument. For instance, to try to write a three- to five-page paper arguing for or against legalized abortion or capital punishment would be extremely difficult. Instead, you would narrow the topic so that you were arguing, say, about the use of tax money to pay for abortions for welfare patients or about the rights of those convicted of a capital crime to appeal their sentences.

Here is an example of a persuasive argument, written by student writer Kimberly Waibel.

In the Best Interest of the Child

In the 1995 film *Losing Isaiah,* a white social worker adopts a black baby who has been abandoned. Later, Isaiah's birth mother, now recovered from drug addiction, seeks to regain custody. The birth mother's lawyer makes this statement: "You might raise a black child with the best intentions in the world—colorblind. But in the end the world is still out there. He needs to know who he is" (Brant 29). In this way, the film raises the highly controversial topic of interracial adoption. In the film, the Hollywood solution is that both the adoptive mother and the birth mother work out a way to care for him together. However, in real life such solutions are extremely rare, and instead minority children are being denied the opportunity to become part of a family that wants them just because that family is of a different race. It is important to examine the issues related to interracial adoption and to find a solution that will really be in the best interest of the children involved.

To fully understand the controversy, it is important to examine its history and development. Interracial (or transracial) adoption has been an issue of great concern since the 1950s. (The terms "interracial" and "transracial" adoption, which are interchangeable, refer to adoptions in which the child belongs to one race and the prospective parents, or one of the prospective parents, to another.) In the 1950s, prejudice against minority groups led to legal rulings making transracial adoption extremely difficult. Then in the 1960s, the civil rights movements promoted the value of integration, and as a result, social service agencies were urged by such organizations as the Child Welfare League of America to view interracial adoption as a reasonable possibility for homeless minority children. In 1972, however, the National Association of Black Social Workers developed a statement strongly opposing the interracial adoption of minority children, and following this statement interracial adoption was barred, officially or unofficially, in forty-three states (Brant). In spite of recent legal efforts, such as the passage of the Multiethnic Placement Act of 1994, to abolish race as the key factor in an adoption, transracial adoption is still not a completely accepted practice (Brooks et al. 169).

There are many reasons why agencies are still reluctant to place minority children with white families. In an article published by the *National Black Law Journal,* Valerie Phillips Hermann describes some of these reasons. First of all, there is the view that minority children who are adopted by families from races different from their own will grow up without an understanding of their own culture and so will have identity problems. Second, there is a concern that transracially adopted children will experience more racial prejudice because of the way some white people might respond to families who adopt minority children. Third, there is a belief that minority children who grow up in white families will have difficulty being accepted into either the white culture or the black culture because of their mixed identities (Hermann).

All of these concerns lead many social service agencies to the view that transracial adoption cannot be the ideal placement and because of this it should not be seen as an equal alternative to inracial adoption. When children are placed transracially, it is often seen as a "last chance" case and, therefore, as "second best" (Simon, Alstein, *A.R.I.* 32). Such an attitude creates a situation in which adoption agencies go to extreme measures to find same-race homes for a child, causing the child to spend additional time in foster or institutional care. Ironically, the older the child gets, the more developed his or her identity is and the more difficult it can be for him or her to integrate into an adoptive family, whether from the same or a different ethnic background as the child.

5   All three of the major concerns expressed by opponents of interracial adoption are addressed in the twenty-year study done by sociology professors Rita James Simon and Howard Alstein. Simon and Alstein began their study in 1971, considering 143 families from Chicago, St. Louis, Minneapolis, and Ann Arbor, Michigan. A point that is highly significant comes from the early years of the study

during the first contact with the adopting families. Simon and Alstein gave the adopted nonwhite children (as well as white birth children in families that had them) the Kenneth Clark "doll" test. In this test, children are shown dolls of various ethnic backgrounds and are asked to pick out which one is smarter, prettier, nicer and so on. Simon and Alstein report:

> Unlike all other previous "doll studies," our respondents did not favor the white doll. It was not considered smarter, prettier, nicer, etc. than the black doll by either the white or black children. . . . Yet the black and white children in our study accurately identified themselves as white or black on those same tests. (*A.R.I.* 155)

As Simon and Alstein continued to follow the experiences of these families, in 1983–84, they asked the children in the study to complete a "self-esteem scale," which was designed to show how much respect the child has for him- or herself. In giving this test, Simon and Alstein looked at scores of the following groups: black transracially adopted children, other transracially adopted children, white birth children, and white adopted children. The scores for all four groups of children were nearly the same. Simon and Alstein state, "No one group of respondents manifested higher or lower self-esteem than the others" (*A.R.I.* 234).

Finally, in 1991, during the final phase of the study, Simon and Alstein polled black transracially adopted young adults from the 93 families still participating. Of these individuals, 80 percent disagreed with the view of the National Association of Black Social Workers, which strongly opposes transracial adoption. In addition, these young adults made comments such as these:

> I feel lucky to have been adopted when I was very young [24 days]. I was brought up to be self-confident—to be the best I can. I was raised in an honest environment.

> Multicultural attitudes develop better children. I was brought up without prejudice. The experience is fulfilling and enriching for parents and children. (Simon 81)

In addition to the extensive studies of Simon and Alstein, several other studies support the idea that interracial adoption is not harmful to children. One of the studies most often cited was carried out by William Feigelman and Arnold R. Silverman of Nassau Community College. They found that "[transracially adopted] children's adjustments were generally similar to those of inracially adopted children" (602).

In response to the claim that the general public would be prejudiced against transracial adoption, we can look at a survey carried out by the television program "CBS This Morning," which polled 975 adults. They asked the question "Should race be a factor in adoption?" Seventy percent of white Americans said "no," and 71 percent of black Americans said "no."

Considering the results of the Simon and Alstein study as well as the results of the CBS poll should certainly lead us to think carefully about the benefits of transracial adoption. Social workers need to stop looking at transracial adoption as a second-rate alternative and start treating it as an equally valuable alternative to inracial adoption. With the passage of the Multiethnic Placement Act in 1994, a step was taken in the right direction. This bill, which was supported by both Republicans and Democrats, now makes it illegal to use race to delay or deny adoption placements. However, this bill does not make clear the extent to which race may still be considered before being in violation of the provisions of the bill. Therefore, the government and the media, as well as the general public, need to continue to promote finding the best home possible for children, without using racial concerns as a barrier.

WORKS CITED

Brant, Martha. "Storming the Color Barrier." Newsweek 20 March 1995: 29.

Brooks, Devon, et al. "Adoption and Race: Implementing the Multiethnic Placement Act and the Interethnic Adoption Provisions." Social Work 44.2 (1999): 167–79.

Feigelman, William, and Arnold R. Silverman. "The Long-Term Effects of Transracial Adoption." Social Service Review 68 (1994): 588–609.

Hermann, Valerie Phillips. "Transracial Adoption: 'Child-Saving' or 'Child-Snatching'?" National Black Law Journal 13 (1993): 147–64.

Simon, Rita James. "Transracial Adoptions: Experiences of a Twenty-Year Study." American Sociologist 27.3 (1996): 79–90.

Simon, Rita James, and Howard Alstein. Adoption, Race, and Identity. New York: Praeger, 1992.

———. Transracial Adoption. New York: Wiley, 1997.

Suggestions for Persuasive Writing

1. Determine the main idea you will argue for or against. For example, you might try to persuade readers to question a previously accepted point of view. You might try to convince your audience to accept a proposal for solving a problem. Or you might challenge a law or rule you see as unjust.

2. Gather data related to your main idea. Make certain that you have enough evidence to support your idea before you begin to write. Remember that as you gather evidence you may change your mind and see that you cannot, in fact, support the idea you began with. Then you will have to begin again with a revised thesis idea.

3. Evaluate your audience carefully, and then consider the voice and tone you will use.

4. Consider points that might be made against your argument, and plan ways to address these points.

5. Plan and write your draft(s) so that the evidence you offer moves smoothly and logically from one point to the next.

6. Revise your draft(s), paying particular attention to the evidence you have offered and your use of rational and emotional appeals.

7. Consider your word choice, making certain you have established a convincing, reasonable, and reliable voice.

8. Evaluate your conclusion to make sure that it does more than summarize what you have already said. For example, you might provide a solution for a problem or suggest related issues worthy of further exploration.

PART TWO

....

Readings

CHAPTER 3

Coming to America:
The Immigrant Experience

INTRODUCTION

A common image of the United States is the rather convivial melting pot of immigrants. If this country were a melting pot it would be the case that all who arrived and remained here mixed together easily into a diverse new whole. However, a thoughtful examination of the many waves of immigrants, their relationships with one another, and the impact of immigrants on the native population of America shows that the mixing has been anything but easy. As Richard Rodriguez, one of this chapter's authors, ironically notes in his article about immigrants, "Just when Americans think we know who we are—we are Protestants, culled from Western Europe, are we not?—then new immigrants appear from Southern Europe or from Eastern Europe. We—we who are already here—we don't know exactly what the latest comers will mean to our community." The selections in this chapter examine both historical and contemporary views of America's diverse population.

Chief Seattle's speech addressed to the governor of Washington in 1854 suggests some of the issues raised by the early immigrants' desire to occupy and own land formerly inhabited by native people. His words offer a chilling prediction of the massacres and relocations that decimated Native American tribes beginning in 1869.

Moving ahead to the twenty-first century, Pulitzer Prize–winning investigative journalists Donald L. Barlett and James B. Steele focus on what they see as the abuses coming from the growth of casinos on reservation land, arguing that revenues do not raise the standard of living for most Native Americans. An editorial from the *Native American Times* responds sharply to Barlett and Steele, challenging their findings and claiming that casinos provide a way for American Indian people to regain some of the resources that were taken from them by arriving immigrants.

On the other hand, Irving Howe, the son of immigrants, describes the ordeals faced by those arriving in New York and finding themselves challenged by the bewildering and often heartbreaking processes of Ellis Island. Writing about life on the opposite coast of the United States, Maxine Hong Kingston explains the fears and anxieties she experienced growing up in California in a community of Chinese immigrants, some of whom had arrived in the country illegally.

Kingston's controversial theme of illegal immigrants and the challenges they and their children face continues in the twenty-first century. A *Chicago Tribune* editorial and a newspaper column by University of Arizona student Cara O'Connor examine the complex issues related to immigrant students seeking in-state tuition rates.

The questions raised in this chapter suggest only a tiny fraction of the hard-won strengths, as well as the frightening injustices, that contribute to the character of this nation of immigrants and native peoples.

· *THEN* ·

SETTING THE CONTEXT: COMING TO AMERICA THEN

Suggestions for Prereading or Journal Writing

1. What do you know about your ancestry? Write a few paragraphs retelling some of the stories you've heard about your grandparents or great-grandparents. Do any of these stories deal with injustice, personal triumphs, or family tragedies? Pick one story from your family's past to write about more extensively.

2. Think back to a time you left familiar surroundings and people to visit a new or strange place (your first day at school or at summer camp; your first plane ride alone; moving to a new city, state, or country). Write about the actual trip you took—from your departure to your arrival. As you describe the details of the trip, include both the external physical details and your inner thoughts and feelings.

My People
Chief Seattle (1786–1866)

Chief of the Suquamish and leader of other tribes in what is now Washington State, Chief Seattle was born around 1786. In 1854, the governor of Washington Territories, Isaac Stevens, proposed buying two million acres of land from the tribes Seattle led. This speech is Seattle's reply to the offer.

Yonder sky that has wept tears upon my people for centuries untold, and which to us appears changeless and eternal, may change. Today is fair. Tomorrow may be overcast with clouds. My words are like the stars that never change. Whatever Seattle says the great chief at Washington can rely upon with as much certainty as he can upon the return of the sun or the seasons. The White Chief says that Big Chief at Washington sends us greetings of friendship and goodwill. That is kind of him for we know he has little need of our friendship in return. His people are many. They are like the grass that covers vast prairies. My people are few. They resemble the scattering trees of a storm-swept plain. The great, and—I presume—good, White Chief sends us word that he wishes to buy our lands but is willing to allow us enough to live comfortably. This indeed appears just, even generous, for the Red Man no longer has rights that he need respect, and the offer may be wise also, as we are no longer in need of an extensive country. . . . I will not dwell on, nor mourn over, our untimely decay, nor reproach our paleface brothers with hastening it, as we too may have been somewhat to blame.

Youth is impulsive. When our young men grow angry at some real or imaginary wrong, and disfigure their faces with black paint, it denotes that their hearts are black, and then they are often cruel and relentless, and our old men and old women are unable to restrain them. Thus it has ever been. Thus it was when the white men first began to push our forefathers further westward. But let us hope that the hostilities between us may never return. We would have everything to lose and nothing to gain. Revenge by young men is considered gain, even at the cost of their own lives, but old men who stay at home in times of war, and mothers who have sons to lose, know better.

Our good father at Washington—for I presume he is now our father as well as yours, since King George has moved his boundaries further north—our great good father, I say, sends us word that if we do as he desires he will protect us. His brave warriors will be to us a bristling wall of strength, and his wonderful ships of war will fill our harbors so that our ancient enemies far to the northward—the Hydas and Tsimpsians—will cease to frighten our women, children, and old men. Then in reality will he be our father and we his children. But can that ever be? Your God is not our God! Your God loves your people and hates mine. He folds his strong and protecting arms lovingly about the paleface and leads him by the hand as a father leads his infant son—but He has forsaken His red children—if they really are his. Our God, the Great Spirit, seems also to have forsaken us. Your God makes your people wax strong every day. Soon they will fill the land. Our people are ebbing away like a rapidly receding tide that will never return. The white man's God cannot love our people or He would protect them. They seem to be orphans who can look nowhere for help. How then can we be brothers? How can your God become our God and renew our prosperity and awaken in us dreams of returning greatness? If we have a common heavenly father He must be partial—for He came to his paleface children. We never saw Him. He gave you laws but He had no word for His red children whose teeming multitudes once filled this vast continent as stars fill the firmament. No; we are two distinct races with separate origins and separate destinies. There is little in common between us.

To us the ashes of our ancestors are sacred and their resting place is hallowed ground. You wander far from the graves of your ancestors and seemingly without regret. Your religion was written upon tables of stone by the iron finger of your God so that you could not forget. The Red Man could never comprehend nor remember it. Our religion is the traditions of our ancestors—the dreams of our old men, given them in solemn hours of night by the Great Spirit; and the visions of our sachems; and it is written in the hearts of our people.

5 Your dead cease to love you and the land of their nativity as soon as they pass the portals of the tomb and wander way beyond the stars. They are soon forgotten and never return. Our dead never forget the beautiful world that gave them being.

Day and night cannot dwell together. The Red Man has ever fled the approach of the White Man, as the morning mist flees before the morning sun. However, your proposition seems fair and I think that my people will accept it and will retire to the reservation you offer them. Then we will dwell apart in peace, for the words of the Great White Chief seem to be the words of nature speaking to my people out of dense darkness.

It matters little where we pass the remnant of our days. They will not be many. A few more moons; a few more winters—and not one of the descendants of the mighty hosts that once moved over this broad land or lived in happy homes, protected by the Great Spirit, will remain to mourn over the graves of a people once more powerful and hopeful than yours. But why should I mourn at the untimely fate of my people? Tribe follows tribe, and nation follows nation, like the waves of the sea. It is the order of nature, and regret is useless. Your time of decay may be distant, but it will surely come, for even the White Man whose God walked and talked with him as friend with friend, cannot be exempt from the common destiny. We may be brothers after all. We will see.

We will ponder your proposition, and when we decide we will let you know. But should we accept it, I here and now make this condition that we will not be denied the privilege without molestation of visiting at any time the tombs of our ancestors, friends and children. Every part of this soil is sacred in the estimation of my people. Every hillside, every valley, every plain and grove, has been hallowed by some sad or happy event in days long vanished. . . . The very dust upon which you now stand responds more lovingly to their footsteps than to yours, because it is rich with the blood of our ancestors and our bare feet are conscious of the sympathetic touch. . . . Even the little children who lived here and rejoiced here for a brief season will love these somber solitudes and at eventide they greet shadowy returning spirits. And when the last Red Man shall have perished, and the memory of my tribe shall have become a myth among the White Men, these shores will swarm with the invisible dead of my tribe, and when your children's children think themselves alone in the field, the store, the shop, upon the highway, or in the silence of the pathless woods, they will not be alone. . . . At night when the streets of your cities and villages are silent and you think them deserted, they will throng with the returning hosts that once filled and still love this beautiful land. The White Man will never be alone.

Let him be just and deal kindly with my people, for the dead are not powerless. Dead, did I say? There is not death, only a change of worlds.

Suggestions for Writing and Discussion

1. What is the main point of Chief Seattle's speech? What details and examples does he provide to support his message?
2. Notice the images and comparisons Seattle chooses to explain his ideas. What does his language suggest about his view of the world?
3. In paragraph 2, Seattle describes the young men of his tribe in this way: "Youth is impulsive. When our young men grow angry at some real or imaginary wrong . . . then they are often cruel and relentless." What is his attitude toward this cruelty and relentlessness? Comment on the application of Seattle's observations to your own observations of present-day circumstances in the United States and in other countries.

Ellis Island
Irving Howe

The son of immigrant Jewish parents, Irving Howe was born in New York in 1920. In addition to teaching as a professor of English at Brandeis, Stanford, and the City University of New York, Howe published several articles and books related to the immigrant experience, including *World of Our Fathers,* from which this excerpt was taken.

Ellis Island, now a restored landmark and museum in New York Harbor, functioned from 1892 until 1965 as the point of entry for European immigrants.

"The day of the emigrants' arrival in New York was the nearest earthly likeness to the final Day of Judgment, when we have to prove our fitness to enter Heaven." So remarked one of those admirable journalists who in the early 1900's exposed themselves to the experience of the immigrants and came to share many of their feelings. No previous difficulties roused such overflowing anxiety, sometimes self-destructive panic, as the anticipated test of Ellis Island. Nervous chatter, foolish rumors spread through each cluster of immigrants:

> "There is Ellis Island!" shouted an immigrant who had already been in the United States and knew of its alien laws. The name acted like magic. Faces grew taut, eyes narrowed. There, in those red buildings, fate awaited them. Were they ready to enter? Or were they to be sent back?
>
> "Only God knows," shouted an elderly man, his withered hand gripping the railing.

Numbered and lettered before debarking, in groups corresponding to entries on the ship's manifest, the immigrants are herded onto the Customs Wharf. "Quick! Run! Hurry!" shout officials in half a dozen languages.

On Ellis Island they pile into the massive hall that occupies the entire width of the building. They break into dozens of lines, divided by metal railings, where they file past the first doctor. Men whose breathing is heavy, women trying to hide a limp or deformity behind a large bundle—these are marked with chalk, for later inspection. Children over the age of two must walk by themselves, since it turns out that not all can. (A veteran inspector recalls: "Whenever a case aroused suspicion, the alien was set aside in a cage apart from the rest [. . .] and his coat lapel or shirt marked with colored chalk, the color indicating why he had been isolated.") One out of five or six needs further medical checking—H chalked for heart, K for hernia, Sc for scalp, X for mental defects.

An interpreter asks each immigrant a question or two: can he respond with reasonable alertness? Is he dull-witted? A question also to each child: make sure he's not deaf or dumb. A check for TB, regarded as "the Jewish disease."

5   Then a sharp turn to the right, where the second doctor waits, a specialist in "contagious and loathsome diseases." Leprosy? Venereal disease? Fauvus, "a contagious disease of the skin, especially of the scalp, due to a parasitic fungus, marked by the formation of yellow flattened scabs and baldness"?

Then to the third doctor, often feared the most. He

> stands directly in the path of the immigrant, holding a little stick in
> his hand. By a quick movement and the force of his own compelling
> gaze, he catches the eyes of his subject and holds them. You will
> see the immigrant stop short, lift his head with a quick jerk, and
> open his eyes very wide. The inspector reaches with a swift move-
> ment, catches the eyelash with his thumb and finger, turns it back,
> and peers under it. If all is well, the immigrant is passed on . . .
> Most of those detained by the physician are Jews.

The eye examination hurts a little. It terrifies the children.
Nurses wait with towels and basins filled with disinfectant. They
watch for trachoma, cause of more than half the medical deten-
tions. It is a torment hard to understand, this first taste of America, with its poking of flesh and prying into private parts and
mysterious chalking of clothes.

Again into lines, this time according to nationality. They are
led to stalls at which multilingual inspectors ask about character,
anarchism, polygamy, insanity, crime, money, relatives, work. You
have a job waiting? Who paid your passage? Anyone meeting you?
Can you read and write? Ever in prison? Where's your money?

For Jewish immigrants, especially during the years before
agencies like the Hebrew Immigrant Aid Society (HIAS) could
give them advice, these questions pose a dilemma: to be honest or
to lie? Is it good to have money or not? Can you bribe these fellows, as back home, or is it a mistake to try? Some are so accustomed to bend and evade and slip a ruble into a waiting hand that
they get themselves into trouble with needless lies. "Our Jews,"
writes a Yiddish paper,

> love to get tangled up with dishonest answers, so that the officials
> have no choice but to send them to the detention area. A Jew who
> had money in his pocket decided to lie and said he didn't have a
> penny. . . . A woman with four children and pregnant with a fifth,
> said her husband had been in America fourteen years. . . . The
> HIAS man learned that her husband had recently arrived, but she
> thought fourteen years would make a better impression. The
> officials are sympathetic. They know the Jewish immigrants get
> "confused" and tell them to sit down and "remember." Then they let
> them in.

Especially bewildering is the idea that if you say you have a job
waiting for you in the United States, you are liable to deporta-

tion—because an 1885 law prohibits the importation of contract labor. But doesn't it "look better" to say a job is waiting for you? No, the HIAS man patiently explains, it doesn't. Still, how can you be sure *he* knows what he's talking about? Just because he wears a little cap with those four letters embroidered on it?

10 Except when the flow of immigrants was simply beyond the staff's capacity to handle it, the average person passed through Ellis Island in about a day. Ferries ran twenty-four hours a day between the island and both the Battery and points in New Jersey. As for the unfortunates detained for medical or other reasons, they usually had to stay at Ellis Island for one or two weeks. Boards of special inquiry, as many as four at a time, would sit in permanent session, taking up cases where questions had been raised as to the admissibility of an immigrant, and it was here, in the legal infighting and appeals to sentiment, that HIAS proved especially valuable.

The number of those detained at the island or sent back to Europe during a given period of time varied according to the immigration laws then in effect . . . and, more important, according to the strictness with which they were enforced. It is a sad irony, though familiar to students of democratic politics, that under relatively lax administrations at Ellis Island, which sometimes allowed rough handling of immigrants and even closed an eye to corruption, immigrants had a better chance of getting past the inspectors than when the commissioner was a public-spirited Yankee intent upon literal adherence to the law.

Two strands of opinion concerning Ellis Island have come down to us, among both historians and the immigrant masses themselves: first, that the newcomers were needlessly subjected to bad treatment, and second, that most of the men who worked there were scrupulous and fair, though often overwhelmed by the magnitude of their task.

The standard defense of Ellis Island is offered by an influential historian of immigration, Henry Pratt Fairchild:

> During the year 1907 five thousand was fixed as the maximum number of immigrants who could be examined at Ellis Island in one day; yet during the spring of that year more than fifteen thousand immigrants arrived at the port of New York in a single day.
>
> As to the physical handling of the immigrants, this is [caused] by the need for haste. . . . The conditions of the voyage are not calculated to land the immigrant in an alert and clear-headed state. The bustle, confusion, rush and size of Ellis Island complete the

work, and leave the average alien in a state of stupor. . . . He is in no condition to understand a carefully-worded explanation of what he must do, or why he must do it, even if the inspector had the time to give it. The one suggestion which is immediately comprehensible to him is a pull or a push; if this is not administered with actual violence, there is no unkindness in it.

Reasonable as it may seem, this analysis meshed Yankee elitism with a defense of the bureaucratic mind. Immigrants *were* disoriented by the time they reached Ellis Island, but they remained human beings with all the sensibilities of human beings; the problem of numbers *was* a real one, yet it was always better when interpreters offered a word of explanation than when they resorted to "a pull or a push." Against the view expressed by Fairchild, we must weigh the massive testimony of the immigrants themselves, the equally large body of material gathered by congressional investigators, and such admissions, all the more telling because casual in intent, as that of Commissioner Corsi: "Our immigration officials have not always been as humane as they might have been." The Ellis Island staff was often badly overworked, and day after day it had to put up with an atmosphere of fearful anxiety which required a certain deadening of response, if only by way of self-defense. But it is also true that many of the people who worked there were rather simple fellows who lacked the imagination to respect cultural styles radically different from their own.

One interpreter who possessed that imagination richly was a 15 young Italo-American named Fiorello La Guardia, later to become an insurgent mayor of New York. "I never managed during the years I worked there to become callous to the mental anguish, the disappointment and the despair I witnessed almost daily. . . . At best the work was an ordeal." For those who cared to see, and those able to feel, there could finally be no other verdict.

Suggestions for Writing and Discussion

1. Create a chart to show the various stages an immigrant followed when entering the United States through Ellis Island. Then discuss the effect these stages had on the chances that an immigrant would be admitted. Why were some immigrants allowed in and others excluded?

2. What tone does Howe take toward his topic? Is he angry, sad, neutral, or something else as he describes the entry of immigrants through Ellis Island?
3. At the beginning of paragraph 12, Howe says that "two strands of opinion concerning Ellis Island have come down to us." What are those two strands? What is your own response to each of these strands?

Secrets

Maxine Hong Kingston

Best known for her collection of essays, *The Woman Warrior* (1976), and *China Men* (1980), Maxine Hong Kingston was born in Stockton, California, in 1940. She grew up listening to the stories of friends and relatives who gathered in the laundry her parents operated. The following memoir reflects the fears and hopes of her sources.

We have so many secrets to hold in. Our sixth-grade teacher, who liked to explain things to children, let us read our files. My record shows that I flunked kindergarten and in first grade had no IQ—a zero IQ. I did remember the first-grade teacher calling out during a test, while students marked X's on a girl or a boy or a dog, which I covered with black. First grade was when I discovered eye control; with my seeing I could shrink the teacher down to a height of one inch, gesticulating and mouthing on the horizon. I lost this power in sixth grade for lack of practice, the teacher a generous man. "Look at your family's old addresses and think about how you've moved," he said. I looked at my parents' aliases and their birthdays, which variants I knew. But when I saw Father's occupations I exclaimed, "Hey, he wasn't a farmer, he was a . . ." He had been a gambler. My throat cut off the word—silence in front of the most understanding teacher. There were secrets never to be said in front of the ghosts,[1] immigration secrets whose telling could get us sent back to China.

Sometimes I hated the ghosts for not letting us talk; sometimes I hated the secrecy of the Chinese. "Don't tell," said my parents,

---

1. A term used to describe Caucasians.

though we couldn't tell if we wanted to because we didn't know. Are there really secret trials with our own judges and penalties? Are there really flags in Chinatown signaling what stowaways have arrived in San Francisco Bay, their names, and which ships they came on? "Mother, I heard some kids say there are flags like that. Are there? What colors are they? Which buildings do they fly from?"

"No. No, there aren't any flags like that. They're just talking-story. You're always believing talk-story."

"I won't tell anybody, Mother. I promise. Which building are the flags on? Who flies them? The benevolent associations?"

"I don't know. Maybe the San Francisco villagers do that; our 5
villagers don't do that."

"What do our villagers do?"

They would not tell us children because we had been born among ghosts, were taught by ghosts, and were ourselves ghost-like. They called us a kind of ghost. Ghosts are noisy and full of air; they talk during meals. They talk about anything.

"Do we send up signal kites? That would be a good idea, huh? We could fly them from the school balcony." Instead of cheaply stringing dragonflies by the tail, we could fly expensive kites, the sky splendid in Chinese colors, distracting ghost eyes while the new people sneak in. Don't tell. "Never tell."

Occasionally the rumor went about that the United States immigration authorities had set up headquarters in the San Francisco or Sacramento Chinatown to urge wetbacks and stowaways, anybody here on fake papers, to come to the city and get their files straightened out. The immigrants discussed whether or not to turn themselves in. "We might as well," somebody would say. "Then we'd have our citizenship for real."

"Don't be a fool," somebody else would say. "It's a trap. You 10
go in there saying you want to straighten out your papers, they'll deport you."

"No, they won't. They're promising that nobody is going to go to jail or get deported. They'll give you citizenship as a reward for turning yourself in, for your honesty."

"Don't you believe it. So-and-so trusted them, and he was deported. They deported his children too."

"Where can they send us now? Hong Kong? Taiwan? I've never been to Hong Kong or Taiwan. The Big Six? Where?" We don't belong anywhere since the Revolution. The old China has disappeared while we've been away.

"Don't tell," advised my parents. "Don't go to San Francisco until they leave."

15   Lie to Americans. Tell them you were born during the San Francisco earthquake. Tell them your birth certificate and your parents were burned up in the fire. Don't report crimes; tell them we have no crimes and no poverty. Give a new name every time you get arrested; the ghosts won't recognize you. Pay the new immigrants twenty-five cents an hour and say we have no unemployment. And, of course, tell them we're against Communism. Ghosts have no memory anyway and poor eyesight. And the Han people won't be pinned down.

Suggestions for Writing and Discussion

1. After reading this memoir, what do you think Kingston means by the opening sentence, "We have so many secrets to hold in"? Do most children have to hold in secrets, or were Kingston and the children she knew especially burdened with secrets to keep?

2. Why do you think the parents described in this essay tell their children to lie? How justified do you think they are?

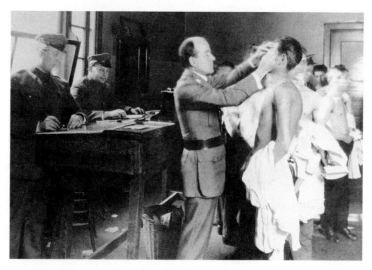

Newly arrived immigrant health inspection at Ellis Island, New York, c. 1900

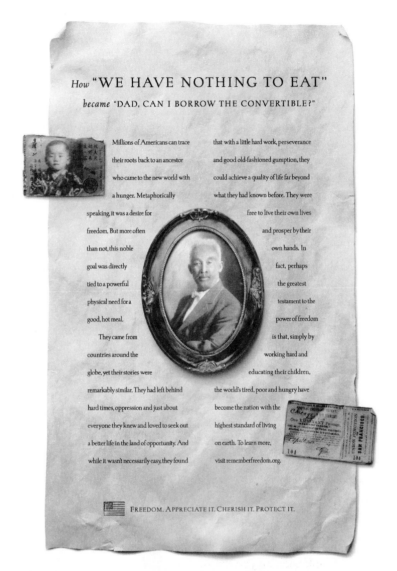

How **"WE HAVE NOTHING TO EAT"** *became* "DAD, CAN I BORROW THE CONVERTIBLE?"

Millions of Americans can trace their roots back to an ancestor who came to the new world with a hunger. Metaphorically speaking, it was a desire for freedom. But more often than not, this noble goal was directly tied to a powerful physical need for a good, hot meal.

They came from countries around the globe, yet their stories were remarkably similar. They had left behind hard times, oppression and just about everyone they knew and loved to seek out a better life in the land of opportunity. And while it wasn't necessarily easy, they found that with a little hard work, perseverance and good old-fashioned gumption, they could achieve a quality of life far beyond what they had known before. They were free to live their own lives and prosper by their own hands. In fact, perhaps the greatest testament to the power of freedom is that, simply by working hard and educating their children, the world's tired, poor and hungry have become the nation with the highest standard of living on earth. To learn more, visit rememberfreedom.org.

FREEDOM. APPRECIATE IT. CHERISH IT. PROTECT IT.

A public service announcement from the AdCouncil as part of their ongoing "Explore Freedom" campaign, 2002

Topics for Writing and Discussion

1. What do the photo of Ellis Island and the public service announcement suggest about the circumstances for immigrants who came to the United States in the late nineteenth and early twentieth centuries? What similarities do you see in these visuals? What contrasts do you see?

2. Compare the messages sent by the photo of Ellis Island and the public service announcement with the ideas expressed by Irving Howe in "Ellis Island" and Maxine Hong Kingston in "Secrets." What significance do you see in the comparisons and contrasts you have identified?

Making Connections: Synthesis and Analysis

1. Briefly identify the differences in the situations described by Chief Seattle, Howe, and Kingston. Then discuss the similarities among the experiences of the people the three writers are describing.

2. Citing specific details and examples from each of the selections in this section, what qualities do you see reflected in the people described that you consider to be a positive part of the character of America today?

· NOW ·

WHAT HAPPENS TO THE NATIVE POPULATION WHEN IMMIGRANTS ARRIVE?

Suggestions for Prereading or Journal Writing

1. Think back on your earliest impressions of Native Americans. Where did you get this impression—from family and friends, a book, a television show, a film, something else? Try to remember the specific source that shaped your views on Native Americans. Did this source present you with what you would now consider a fair picture? Explain.

2. Think of the images of gambling casinos as shown in the media. From your own impressions, or from interviews with others, compare those images with the actual scenes one might encounter when visiting a casino. For instance, how do the people in casino advertising on television compare with the people you (or the person you interviewed) observed in the casinos?

EVALUATING AN ARGUMENT: TWO POINTS OF VIEW

Wheel of Misfortune

Donald L. Barlett and James B. Steele

Investigative reporters Donald L. Barlett and James B. Steele won the Pulitzer Prize in 1989 for reporting that led to the 1992 publication of their book *America: What Went Wrong.* Continuing their collaboration, they have researched and explored the question of gaming on Indian reservations and what they see to be the abuse of the Indian Gaming Regulatory Act. The following article first appeared in *Time* magazine, December 16, 2002.

Imagine, if you will, Congress passing a bill to make Indian tribes more self-sufficient that gives billions of dollars to the white backers of Indian businesses—and nothing to hundreds of thousands of Native Americans living in poverty. Or a bill that gives hundreds of millions of dollars to one Indian tribe with a few dozen members—and not a penny to a tribe with hundreds of thousands of members. Or a bill that allows select Indian tribes to create businesses that reap millions of dollars in profits and pay no federal income tax—at the same time that the tribes collect millions in aid from American taxpayers. Can't imagine Congress passing such a bill? It did. Here's how it happened—and what it means.

Maryann Martin presides over America's smallest tribe. Raised in Los Angeles in an African-American family, she knew little of her Indian ancestry until 1986, when at age 22 she learned that her mother had been the last surviving member of the Augustine Band of Cahuilla Mission Indians. In 1991, the Bureau of Indian Affairs (BIA) certified Martin and her two younger brothers as members of the tribe. Federal recognition of tribal status opened the door for Martin and her siblings to qualify for certain types of government aid. And with it, a far more lucrative lure beckoned: the right to operate casinos on an Indian reservation.

As Indian casinos popped up like new housing developments across Southern California, Martin moved a trailer onto the long-abandoned Augustine reservation in Coachella, a 500-acre desert tract then littered with garbage, discarded household appliances and junk cars, about 25 miles southeast of Palm Springs. There she lived with her three children and African-American husband William Ray Vance. In 1994, membership in the tiny tribe dwindled from three adults to one when Martin's two brothers were killed during separate street shootings in Banning, Calif. Police said both men were involved in drug deals and were members of a violent Los Angeles street gang.

Subsequently, Martin negotiated a deal with Paragon Gaming, a Las Vegas company, to develop and manage a casino. Paragon is headed by Diana Bennett, a gaming executive and daughter of Vegas veteran and co-founder of the Circus Circus Casino William Bennett. Martin's Augustine Casino opened last July. With 349 slot machines and 10 gaming tables, it's the fifth and by far the most modest casino in the Palm Springs area. But it stands to make a lot of non-Indian investors—and one Indian adult—rich.

5   And get this: Martin still qualifies for federal aid, in amounts far greater than what many needy Native Americans could even dream of getting. In 1999 and 2000 alone, government audit reports show, she pulled in more than $1 million from Washington—$476,000 for housing, $400,000 for tribal government and $146,000 for environmental programs.

It wasn't supposed to be this way. At the end of the 1980s, in a frenzy of cost cutting and privatization, Washington perceived gaming on reservations as a cheap way to wean tribes from government handouts, encourage economic development and promote tribal self-sufficiency. After policy initiatives by the Reagan Administration and two U.S. Supreme Court rulings that approved gambling on Indian reservations, Congress enacted the Indian Gaming Regulatory Act in 1988. It was so riddled with loopholes, so poorly written, so discriminatory and subject to such conflicting interpretations that 14 years later, armies of high-priced lawyers are still debating the definition of a slot machine.

Instead of regulating Indian gambling, the act has created chaos and a system tailor-made for abuse. It set up a powerless and underfunded watchdog and dispersed oversight responsibilities among a hopelessly conflicting hierarchy of local, state and federal agencies. It created a system so skewed—only a few small tribes and their backers are getting rich—that it has changed the face of Indian country. Some long-dispersed tribes, aided by new, non-Indian financial godfathers, are regrouping to benefit from the gaming windfall. Others are seeking new reservations—some in areas where they never lived, occasionally even in other states—solely to build a casino. And leaders of small, newly wealthy tribes now have so much unregulated cash and political clout that they can ride roughshod over neighboring communities, poorer tribes and even their own members.

The amount of money involved is staggering. Last year 290 Indian casinos in 28 states pulled in at least $12.7 billion in revenue. Of that sum, *Time* estimates, the casinos kept more than $5 billion as profit. That would place overall Indian gaming among *Fortune* magazine's 20 most profitable U.S. corporations, with earnings exceeding those of J.P. Morgan Chase & Co., Merrill Lynch, American Express and Lehman Bros. holdings combined.

But who, exactly, is benefiting? Certainly Indians in a few tribes have prospered. In California, Christmas came early this year for the 100 members of the Table Mountain Rancheria, who over Thanksgiving picked up bonus checks of $200,000 each as their share of the Table Mountain Casino's profits. That was in addition to the monthly stipend of $15,000 each member receives. But even those amounts pale beside the fortunes made by the behind-the-scenes investors who bankroll the gaming palaces. They walk away with up to hundreds of millions of dollars.

Meanwhile, the overwhelming majority of Indians get noth- 10
ing. Only half of all tribes—which have a total of 1.8 million members—have casinos. Some large tribes like the Navajo oppose gambling for religious reasons. Dozens of casinos do little better than break even because they are too small or located too far from population centers. The upshot is that a small number of gaming operations are making most of the money. Last year just 39 casinos generated $8.4 billion. In short, 13% of the casinos accounted for 66% of the take. All of which helps explain why Indian gaming has failed to raise most Native Americans out of poverty. What has happened instead is this:

A LOSING HAND

Revenue from gaming is so lopsided that Indian casinos in five states with almost half the Native American population—Montana, Nevada, North Dakota, Oklahoma and South Dakota—account for less than 3% of all casino proceeds. On average, they produce the equivalent of about $400 in revenue per Indian. Meanwhile, casinos in California, Connecticut and Florida—states with only 3% of the Indian population—haul in 44% of all revenue, an average of $100,000 per Indian. In California, the casino run by the San Manuel Band of Mission Indians pulls in well over $100 million a year. That's about $900,000 per member.

THE RICH GET RICHER

While federal recognition entitles tribes to a broad range of government benefits, there is no means testing. In 2001, aid to Indians amounted to $9.4 billion, but in many cases more money went to wealthy members of tribes with lucrative casinos than to destitute Indians. From 1995 to 2001, the Indian Health Service, the agency responsible for looking after the medical needs of Native Americans, spent an average of $2,100 a year on each of the 2,800 members of the Seminole tribe in Florida. The Seminoles' multiple casinos generated $216 million in profits last year, and each tribe member collected $35,000 in casino dividends. During the same six years, the health service spent an annual average of just $470 on each of the 52,000 members of the Muscogee (Creek) Nation in Oklahoma, whose tiny casinos do little more than break even.

BUYING POLITICIANS

Wealthy Indian gaming tribes suddenly are pouring millions of dollars into political campaigns at both state and federal levels. They are also influencing gaming and other policies affecting Native Americans by handing out large sums to influential lobbying firms. In 2000 alone, tribes spent $9.5 million on Washington lobbying. Altogether they spend more to influence legislation than such longtime heavyweights as General Motors, Boeing, AT&T— or even Enron in its heyday.

GAMING TRIBES AS EXCLUSIVE CLUBS

Tribal leaders are free to set their own whimsical rules for admission, without regard to Indian heritage. They may exclude rivals, potential whistle-blowers and other legitimate claimants. The fewer tribe members, the larger the cut for the rest. Some tribes are booting out members, while others are limiting membership. Among them: the Pechanga Band of Mission Indians in Riverside County, Calif., whose new Las Vegas–style gaming palace, the Pechanga Resort & Casino, is expected to produce well over $100 million in revenue.

GOLD RUSH

Since only a federally recognized tribe can open a casino, scores [15] of groups—including long-defunct tribes and extended families—have flocked to the BIA or Congress seeking certification. Since 1979, as gambling has boomed, the number of recognized tribes on the U.S. mainland has spiked 23%, to a total of 337. About 200 additional groups have petitioned the bureau for recognition. Perhaps the most notorious example of tribal resurrection: the Mashantucket Pequots of Connecticut, proud owners of the world's largest casino, Foxwoods. The now billion-dollar tribe had ceased to exist until Congress re-created it in 1983. The current tribe members had never lived together on a reservation. Many of them would not even qualify for government assistance as Indians.

THE IMPOTENT ENFORCER

Congress created the National Indian Gaming Commission (NIGC) to be the Federal Government's principal oversight-and-enforcement agency for Indian gaming—and then guaranteed that it could do neither. With a budget capped at $8 million, the agency has 63 employees to monitor the $12.7 billion all-cash business in more than 300 casinos and small gaming establishments nationwide. The New Jersey Casino Control Commission, by contrast, has a $59 million budget and a staff of 720 to monitor 12 casinos in Atlantic City that produce one-third the revenue. The NIGC has yet to discover a single major case of corruption—despite numerous complaints from tribe members.

THE WHITE MAN WINS AGAIN

While most Indians continue to live in poverty, many non-Indian investors are extracting hundreds of millions of dollars—sometimes in violation of legal limits—from casinos they helped establish, either by taking advantage of regulatory loopholes or cutting backroom deals. More than 90% of the contracts between tribes and outside gaming-management companies operate with no oversight. That means investors' identities are often secret, as are their financial arrangements and their share of the revenue. Whatever else Congress had in mind when it passed the regulatory act, presumably the idea was not to line the pockets of a Malaysian gambling magnate, a South African millionaire or a Minnesota leather-apparel king.

FRAUD, CORRUPTION, INTIMIDATION

The tribes' secrecy about financial affairs—and the complicity of government oversight agencies—has guaranteed that abuses in Indian country growing out of the surge in gaming riches go undetected, unreported and unprosecuted. Tribal leaders sometimes rule with an iron fist. Dissent is crushed. Cronyism flourishes. Those who question how much the casinos really make, where the money goes or even tribal operations in general may be banished. Indians who challenge the system are often intimidated, harassed and threatened with reprisals or physical harm. They risk the loss of their jobs, homes and income. Margarite Faras, a member of the San Carlos Apache tribe, which owns the Apache Gold Casino in San Carlos, Ariz., was ousted from the tribal council after exposing corruption that led to the imprisonment of a former tribal leader. For three years, Faras says, those in control mounted nighttime demonstrations at her home, complete with loudspeakers. They initiated a boycott of her taco business, telling everyone she used cat meat. They telephoned her with death threats. Says Faras: "I don't know what else to say, other than it's been a nightmare."

Indian Gaming: Why Is the Backlash Growing?

Editorial, *Native American Times*

In a strongly worded editorial, the *Native American Times* responds to Donald L. Barlett's and James B. Steele's contention that allowing gambling casinos on Native American reservations has been a disaster, both for Native Peoples and for the entire United States. This essay appeared on December 17, 2002.

The December 16, 2002 edition of *Time Magazine* in its story "Look who's cashing in at Indian Casinos" a special (sic) investigation by Donald L. Barlett, and James B. Steele, the once proud publication at best distorts and shamefully lies at its worst in presenting its story.

Recently, the *Wall Street Journal* and the *Tulsa World* have both decided to take their integrity for a spin and write editorials and articles, which fan the flames of racism with lies.

But, let's start with the first sentence in the story: "Imagine, if you will, Congress passing a bill to make Indian tribes more self-sufficient that gives billions of dollars to the white backers of Indian businesses—and nothing to hundreds of thousands of Native Americans living in poverty." It asks the reader to "imagine" which is exactly what the article did in making its premise. If someone imagines some thought or concept then the idea comes from the reader not the writer. Congress never passed a bill, which gives billions of dollars to one Indian to fund gaming or enrich an investor. Never, never and no matter how many times *Time Magazine* says it, doesn't make it true. Unfortunately, *Time* has a good reputation and most people will read that first sentence and believe the rest of the article.

They make much of the fact that Oklahoma doesn't share in the wealth even though there are more Native Americans here than any other state. But they fail to mention the fact that the state of Oklahoma and the Governor have resisted allowing Class III gaming in Oklahoma. Indians in Oklahoma would like nothing better than to escape the reality of abject poverty, but they will have to fight to get their foot in the door. That will take lobbying; something *Time Magazine* has a problem with according to their reporting. Tribes are fighting for their collective lives and have to fight with every resource available to them to hold off those who would send them back to the metaphoric reservation.

5   Most people know that tribal success with gaming is as varied as the rainbow. One tribe is doing well and another doesn't make a penny. The reasons are just as varied. But to read these articles is to believe that Indian gaming is just a ruse to enrich certain tribes.

The examples of bad gaming are certainly compelling, but are certainly not representative of what Indian gaming has done for many of the poorest tribes in America.

While they may look at some rich tribes with contempt, it is closer to justice. The writers who once won a Pulitzer Prize for reporting take issue with the Shakopee tribe and their lucrative casino Mystic Lake in Minnesota. If any tribe deserves a break it is that tribe. Mass hangings and one of the most harrowing trips ever taken under arms by an Indian tribe is part of their history. There are so few members because they were almost wiped out. They point accusingly at the per capita payments the tribe shares with its members, we hope the tribe doubles the amount. It belongs to them and what and how they spend it is not the business of two racially insensitive reporters.

They have declared war on Indians who are among the richest people in this country and we believe that is the crux of the article. The thought of rich Indians is against nature we can only assume. *Time* doesn't care about those poor Indians who are not sharing in the profits of more fortunate tribes. The history of this country and wealth is shameful and has never changed. When the Osages struck oil in the 1920's it set off a grisly series of murders to separate the tribe and their money. There remain over 50 unsolved murders during the Osage reign of terror. Back in New York City, one of the first streets name[d] was Wall Street. It was so named to keep Indians away from the collective wealth of foreign immigrants.

Despite the wealth of some tribes, Indian people are still the poorest race of people in the country. They still have the highest instances of infant mortality. They still have the lowest life expectancy. They are still the victims of more acts of racist violence among any racial group.

Time would have Indian people put in a position to never be able to correct these numbers. Indian people are no longer going to give away their resources for pennies on the ton or stop making profits just because a multi-million dollar media giant is envious of tribal wealth. 10

Suggestions for Writing and Discussion

1. Identify two or three central points made by Barlett and Steele and refuted by the *Native American Times*. Regardless of your own beliefs, analyze the points you have identified and explain which writer(s) you find more convincing on each particular point.

2. Compare your own views on gambling and on the ways various segments of our society, including state governments, benefit from gambling with the views expressed by one of these articles.

Seminole Indian Herbert Jim and his wife, April Jim, walk through the Seminole Hard Rock Hotel and Casino in Hollywood, Florida, May 11, 2004

Topics for Writing and Discussion

1. Describe the details of the photo of the Native Americans in a gambling casino. Then compare this image with the image of Native Americans conveyed in Chief Seattle's letter. What significance do you see in the comparisons and contrasts you have identified?
2. In what ways do the details of this photo support or challenge the arguments made by Donald L. Barlett and James B. Steele or the refutation by the editorial in the *Native American Times*?

HOW DOES AMERICA WELCOME IMMIGRANTS?

Suggestions for Prereading or Journal Writing

1. Under what circumstances would you leave your home and your country for a foreign land?
2. Describe your ideal country or your idea of utopia. How would you compare your description of utopia with your description of the United States today?

"Blaxicans" and Other Reinvented Americans

Richard Rodriguez

Born to Mexican immigrant parents in 1944, Richard Rodriguez struggled during his childhood with the conflicting pressures of loyalty to his home community and the desire to become part of the larger culture of his country. Best known for his autobiography, *Hunger of Memory* (1982), Rodriguez has written extensively about issues related to the culture of immigrants and their children. He is also the author of a trilogy, including the final volume, *Brown: The Last Discovery of America* (2002). This selection, which is an excerpt from a speech given at the University of Pennsylvania, appeared in the *Chronicle of Higher Education,* September 12, 2003.

There is something unsettling about *immigrants* because . . . well, because they chatter incomprehensibly, and they get in everyone's way. *Immigrants* seem to be bent on undoing America. Just when Americans think we know who we are—we are Protestants, culled from Western Europe, are we not?—then new *immigrants* appear from Southern Europe or from Eastern Europe. We—we who are already here—we don't know exactly what the latest comers will mean to our community. How will they fit in with us? Thus we—we who were here first—we begin to question our own identity.

After a generation or two, the grandchildren or the great-grandchildren of *immigrants* to the United States and the grand-children of those who tried to keep *immigrants* out of the United States will romanticize the immigrant, will begin to see the immi-grant as the figure who teaches us most about what it means to be an American. The immigrant, in mythic terms, travels from the outermost rind of America to the very center of American mythol-ogy. None of this, of course, can we admit to the Vietnamese im-migrant who served us our breakfast at the hotel this morning. In another 40 years, we will be prepared to say to the Vietnamese immigrant that he, with his breakfast tray, with his intuition for travel, with his memory of tragedy, with his recognition of peer-less freedoms, he fulfills the meaning of America.

In 1997, Gallup conducted a survey on race relations in America, but the poll was concerned only with white and black Americans. No question was put to the aforementioned Viet-namese man. There was certainly no question for the Chinese gro-cer, none for the Guatemalan barber, none for the tribe of Mexican Indians who reroofed your neighbor's house.

The American conversation about race has always been a black-and-white conversation, but the conversation has become as bloodless as badminton.

I have listened to the black-and-white conversation for most   5
of my life. I was supposed to attach myself to one side or the other, without asking the obvious questions: What is this perpetual di-alectic between Europe and Africa? Why does it admit so little reference to anyone else?

I am speaking to you in American English that was taught me by Irish nuns—immigrant women. I wear an Indian face; I answer to a Spanish surname as well as this California first name, Richard. You might wonder about the complexity of historical fac-tors, the collision of centuries, that creates Richard Rodriguez. My brownness is the illustration of that collision, or the bland memorial of it. I stand before you as an Impure-American, an Ambiguous-American.

In the 19th century, Texans used to say that the reason Mexicans were so easily defeated in battle was because we were so dilute, being neither pure Indian nor pure Spaniard. Yet, at the same time, Mexicans used to say that Mexico, the country of my ancestry, joined two worlds, two competing armies. José Vasconcelos, the Mexican educator and philosopher, famously described Mexicans as la raza cosmica, the cosmic race. In Mexico what one finds as early as the 18th century is a predominant population of mixed-race people. Also, once the slave had been freed in Mexico, the incidence of marriage between Indian and African people there was greater than in any other country in the Americas and has not been equaled since.

Race mixture has not been a point of pride in America. Americans speak more easily about "diversity" than we do about the fact that I might marry your daughter; you might become we; we might become us. America has so readily adopted the Canadian notion of multiculturalism because it preserves our preference for thinking ourselves separate—our elbows need not touch, thank you. I would prefer that table. I can remain Mexican, whatever that means, in the United States of America.

I would propose that instead of adopting the Canadian model of multiculturalism, America might begin to imagine the Mexican alternative—that of a mestizaje society.

10   Because of colonial Mexico, I am mestizo. But I was reinvented by President Richard Nixon. In the early 1970s, Nixon instructed the Office of Management and Budget to identify the major racial and ethnic groups in the United States. OMB came up with five major ethnic or racial groups. The groups are white, black, Asian/Pacific Islander, American Indian/Eskimo, and Hispanic.

It's what I learned to do when I was in college: to call myself a Hispanic. At my university we even had separate cafeteria tables and "theme houses," where the children of Nixon could gather— of a feather. Native Americans united. African-Americans. Casa Hispanic.

The interesting thing about Hispanics is that you will never meet us in Latin America. You may meet Chileans and Peruvians and Mexicans. You will not meet Hispanics. If you inquire in Lima or Bogotá about Hispanics, you will be referred to Dallas. For "Hispanic" is a gringo contrivance, a definition of the world according to European patterns of colonization. Such a definition suggests I have more in common with Argentine-Italians than with American Indians; that there is an ineffable union between the white Cuban and the mulatto Puerto Rican because of Spain. Nixon's conclusion has become the basis for the way we now organize and understand American society.

The Census Bureau foretold that by the year 2003, Hispanics would outnumber blacks to become the largest minority in the United States. And, indeed, the year 2003 has arrived and the proclamation of Hispanic ascendancy has been published far and wide. While I admit a competition has existed—does exist—in America between Hispanic and black people, I insist that the comparison of Hispanics with blacks will lead, ultimately, to complete nonsense. For there is no such thing as a Hispanic race. In Latin America, one sees every race of the world. One sees white Hispanics, one sees black Hispanics, one sees brown Hispanics who are Indians, many of whom do not speak Spanish because they resist Spain. One sees Asian-Hispanics. To compare blacks and Hispanics, therefore, is to construct a fallacious equation.

Some Hispanics have accepted the fiction. Some Hispanics have too easily accustomed themselves to impersonating a third race, a great new third race in America. But Hispanic is an ethnic term. It is a term denoting culture. So when the Census Bureau says by the year 2060 one-third of all Americans will identify themselves as Hispanic, the Census Bureau is not speculating in pigment or quantifying according to actual historical narratives, but rather is predicting how by the year 2060 one-third of all Americans will identify themselves culturally. For a country that traditionally has taken its understandings of community from blood and color, the new circumstance of so large a group of Americans identifying themselves by virtue of language or fashion or cuisine or literature is an extraordinary change, and a revolutionary one.

People ask me all the time if I envision another Quebec forming in the United States because of the large immigrant movement from the south. Do I see a Quebec forming in the Southwest, for example? No, I don't see that at all. But I do notice the Latin American immigrant population is as much as 10 years younger   15 than the U.S. national population. I notice the Latin American immigrant population is more fertile than the U.S. national population. I see the movement of the *immigrants* from south to north as a movement of youth—like approaching spring!—into a country that is growing middle-aged. I notice *immigrants* are the archetypal Americans at a time when we—U.S. citizens—have become post-Americans, most concerned with subsidized medications.

I was at a small Apostolic Assembly in East Palo Alto a few years ago—a mainly Spanish-speaking congregation in an area along the freeway, near the heart of the Silicon Valley. This area used to be black East Palo Alto, but it is quickly becoming an Asian and Hispanic Palo Alto neighborhood. There was a moment in the service when newcomers to the congregation were introduced. Newcomers brought letters of introduction from sister evangelical churches in Latin America. The minister read out the various letters and pronounced the names and places of origin to the community. The congregation applauded. And I thought to myself: It's over. The border is over. These people were not being asked whether they had green cards. They were not being asked whether they arrived here legally or illegally. They were being welcomed within a new community for reasons of culture. There is now a north-south line that is theological, a line that cannot be circumvented by the U.S. Border Patrol.

I was on a British Broadcasting Corporation interview show, and a woman introduced me as being "in favor" of assimilation. I am not in favor of assimilation any more than I am in favor of the Pacific Ocean or clement weather. If I had a bumper sticker on the subject, it might read something like ASSIMILATION HAPPENS. One doesn't get up in the morning, as an immigrant child in America, and think to oneself, "How much of an American shall I become today?" One doesn't walk down the street and decide to be 40 percent Mexican and 60 percent American. Culture is fluid. Culture is smoke. You breathe it. You eat it. You can't help hearing it—Elvis Presley goes in your ear, and you cannot get Elvis Presley out of your mind.

I am in favor of assimilation. I am not in favor of assimilation. I recognize assimilation. A few years ago, I was in Merced, Calif.—a town of about 75,000 people in the Central Valley where the two largest immigrant groups at that time (California is so fluid, I believe this is no longer the case) were Laotian Hmong and Mexicans. Laotians have never in the history of the world, as far as I know, lived next to Mexicans. But there they were in Merced, and living next to Mexicans. They don't like each other. I was talking to the Laotian kids about why they don't like the Mexican kids. They were telling me that the Mexicans do this and the Mexicans don't do that, when I suddenly realized that they were speaking English with a Spanish accent.

On his interview show, Bill Moyers once asked me how I thought of myself. As an American? Or Hispanic? I answered that I am Chinese, and that is because I live in a Chinese city and because I want to be Chinese. Well, why not? Some Chinese-American people in the Richmond and Sunset districts of San Francisco sometimes paint their houses (so many qualifiers!) in colors I would once have described as garish: lime greens, rose reds, pumpkin. But I have lived in a Chinese city for so long that my eye has taken on that palette, has come to prefer lime greens and rose reds and all the inventions of this Chinese Mediterranean. I see photographs in magazines or documentary footage of China, especially rural China, and I see what I recognize as home. Isn't that odd?

I do think distinctions exist. I'm not talking about an America **20** tomorrow in which we're going to find that black and white are no longer the distinguishing marks of separateness. But many young people I meet tell me they feel like Victorians when they identify themselves as black or white. They don't think of themselves in those terms. And they're already moving into a world in which tattoo or ornament or movement or commune or sexuality or drug or rave or electronic bombast are the organizing principles of their identity. The notion that they are white or black simply doesn't occur.

And increasingly, of course, one meets children who really don't know how to say what they are. They simply are too many things. I met a young girl in San Diego at a convention of mixed-race children, among whom the common habit is to define one parent over the other—black over white, for example. But this girl said that her mother was Mexican and her father was African. The girl said "Blaxican." By reinventing language, she is reinventing America.

America does not have a vocabulary like the vocabulary the Spanish empire evolved to describe the multiplicity of racial possibilities in the New World. The conversation, the interior monologue of America cannot rely on the old vocabulary—black, white. We are no longer a black-white nation.

So, what myth do we tell ourselves? The person who got closest to it was Karl Marx. Marx predicted that the discovery of gold in California would be a more central event to the Americas than the discovery of the Americas by Columbus—which was only the meeting of two tribes, essentially, the European and the Indian. But when gold was discovered in California in the 1840s, the entire world met. For the first time in human history, all of the known world gathered. The Malaysian stood in the gold fields alongside the African, alongside the Chinese, alongside the Australian, alongside the Yankee.

That was an event without parallel in world history and the beginning of modern California—why California today provides the mythological structure for understanding how we might talk about the American experience: not as biracial, but as the re-creation of the known world in the New World.

25   Sometimes truly revolutionary things happen without regard. I mean, we may wake up one morning and there is no black race. There is no white race either. There are mythologies, and—as I am in the business, insofar as I am in any business at all, of de-mythologizing such identities as black and white—I come to you as a man of many cultures. I come to you as Chinese. Unless you understand that I am Chinese, then you have not understood anything I have said.

Suggestions for Writing and Discussion

1. What does Rodriguez think about the mixture of cultures in the United States? How does the term "Blaxicans" reflect the way he views individual groups who wish to maintain their own cultures within the larger culture of the United States?

2. What is meant by the term "assimilation"? Why does Rodriguez say he is not in favor of assimilation but still believes that it is inevitable for any immigrant (or minority) population? Do you agree with him? Explain.

3. Why does Rodriguez tell interviewer Bill Moyers that he thinks of himself as Chinese? What point is he trying to make? What is your response to his claim?

EVALUATING AN ARGUMENT: TWO POINTS OF VIEW

In these two related articles from 2003, the *Chicago Tribune* and Cara O'Connor, a reporter for the *Arizona Daily Wildcat,* the student newspaper at the University of Arizona, present viewpoints on legislation that would allow illegal immigrants to pay in-state tuition in the states where they reside.

An Education in Citizenship

Editorial, *The Chicago Tribune*

By a vote of 112–4 (with 2 voting present), the Illinois House recently passed a bill that would allow young people who are in the U.S. illegally to pay in-state tuition rates at Illinois colleges and universities. The lopsided margin suggests this was an easy vote for most of the lawmakers. It shouldn't have been.

One hopes the state Senate will give the measure a more thorough examination and airing than it got in the House, because the issue at stake is nothing less than the meaning and significance of American citizenship.

Sponsored by Rep. Edward Acevedo (D-Chicago), the tuition measure would treat as an in-state student any undocumented immigrant who has lived in Illinois for three years and graduated from an Illinois high school.

In dollars and cents, the implications of such a policy are substantial. For the average entering freshman at the University of Illinois in Urbana-Champaign, for example, it would be the difference between $5,302, the current in-state rate, and $13,906, the out-of-state rate. At Illinois State University in Normal, the corresponding figures would be $5,037 and $9,227.

No one wants to see any able student deprived of a good 5 higher education. But neither should we wish to see the concept of citizenship bent, folded, spindled or mutilated. This legislation, unfortunately, would do that. It is of a piece with laws like New York's of several years ago that forbade city employees to inquire as to the citizenship status of people who seek city services.

It is one thing for cities and states to dispense emergency services—health care, fire and rescue, police—without regard to citizenship. When life and immediate health are at stake, whether your citizenship papers are in order ought to be the last of society's concerns.

But it is another thing entirely to begin routinely setting aside citizenship as a consideration in dispensing public services. The practice is troubling on two accounts.

First, it makes cities and states usurpers of the prerogative granted by the Constitution to Congress "To establish an [sic] uniform Rule of Naturalization. . . ." In other words, it's Congress that decides who becomes a citizen and how, and it is not for any other unit of government—federal, state or local—to modify it or set it aside.

Second, it deprives citizens—of the nation and the states—of what they have a reasonable right to expect: that all the activities of their various governments will be conducted within a framework of law, the most basic element of which is a definition of citizenship and its rights and responsibilities.

10   This nation sorely needs to reform its complex, often-unenforced immigration laws. But until that day comes, it cannot blithely ignore those laws. The notion that someone can have no legal right to be present in the country but be entitled to a very expensive and valuable benefit of citizenship is absurd on its face.

Advocates for immigrants estimate there are 3,000 young people in Illinois in this awkward position. It might be argued—and is—that their parents pay taxes here, so the main practical criterion for access to in-state tuition status is satisfied. Why insist on citizenship?

But students from any of the 49 other states could make the same argument, since their parents' federal tax dollars help support the Pell Grants and federal loans and research grants that are part of an Illinois university's budget. So on what basis do we justify charging them more for tuition?

Almost any distinction can be challenged on some basis. But to be in the country legally—whether as a citizen, a permanent resident or on some other basis—seems the most reasonable distinction of all. Illinois' senators ought to consider that before they chip away at that distinction with this ill-advised piece of legislation.

Immigrant Students Seek Lower Tuition
Cara O'Connor

LAW WOULD ALLOW IMMIGRANTS TO PAY IN-STATE COLLEGE TUITION

This week, groups in Tucson and across the nation held vigils, marches, rallies and press conferences to support federal legislation that would allow long-time resident immigrants to receive green card status to go to college at an in-state price.

The legislation, known as the DREAM Act in the Senate and the Student Adjustment Act in the House of Representatives, would repeal a provision of a 1996 law that requires students to have lawful immigration status in order to qualify for state residency when entering college.

According to the Illegal Immigration Reform and Immigrant Responsibility Act of 1996, foreign nationals who are not lawfully residing in the United States cannot get reduced in-state tuition rates unless the college offers that rate to any U.S. citizen, state resident or not.

If the legislation passes, states would be allowed to decide whether to offer in-state tuition rates to the 50,000 to 65,000 immigrant students who graduate nationally from high school every year.

Current UA policy set by the Arizona Board of Regents states: 5 "A non-citizen with a visa that prohibits establishing a domicile in Arizona during any portion of the durational period may not be granted resident status."

Other non-citizens may qualify for resident status by meeting all general residency requirements or "having been granted refugee status and meeting all other requirements for domicile," the policy states.

"To deny them the chance to receive higher education . . . is nothing but hatred," said Richard Ortiz, a high school teacher in the Flowing Wells School District. "They exemplify good citizenship."

Many of the students who would be affected by this legislation were brought to the United States by their parents at a very young age and attended primary and secondary school in the country.

Federal law prohibits public school from inquiring about a student's immigration status, said Estella Zavala, communication specialist for Tucson Unified School District.

10 TUSD requires families to provide proof of residence in the form of a lease, utility bill, or driver's license, but does not ask for proof of legal residency status, Zavala said.

However, when students without legal residency apply for college they must provide a social security number.

"There is always that little spot where I have to put my social security number, and I just look at it and want to rip it apart," said Jose, an immigrant student who spoke at Wednesday's press conference at the Chicanos por la Causa building. He asked that his last name not be revealed because he is still waiting to receive his green card.

"Next year I might be doing some landscaping job," said the high school senior who came to the United States before he was 10 years old. "I have been educated here. I speak the language. I have friends here."

"He is an American. He just doesn't have the papers to tell him he is," said Lorraine Lee, vice president of Chicanos por la Causa.

15 The legislation would also expand students' eligibility for relief to adjust their status to that of a legal permanent resident.

To be eligible under the DREAM Act, one must be at least 12 years old at the time the law is enacted, but under 21 when he or she applies for legal status. If applying for college, the student must also have a high school diploma or GED certificate, have resided in the United States for at least five years and cannot have a criminal record.

The DREAM Act, short for the Development, Relief and Education for Alien Minors Act, was introduced by Senators Orrin Hatch (R-Utah) and Richard Durbin (D-Ill.).

The act was approved by the Senate Judiciary Committee in June 2002 during the 107th Congress and is waiting now for reintroduction in the 108th session of Congress.

The Student Adjustment Act was introduced by Representatives Chris Cannon (R-Utah) and Howard Berman (D-Calif.) and had 61 cosponsors at the end of the 107th Congress. The act, which was reintroduced April 9, has a bipartisan list of 62 cosponsors including Ed Pastor of Arizona.

The legislation has drawn the support of many leaders and or- 20
ganizations in the Tucson community, including Congressman Raul
Grijalva and Pima County Supervisor Richard Elias. Both lent their
support to the legislation at Wednesday's press conference.

The conference also included Chicanos por la Causa, Youth
on Their Own, the League of United Latin American Citizens
and the Human Rights Coalition along with local teachers and
students.

Many supporters believe the legislation would be a good deal
for taxpayers. If these people achieve legal residency status and
higher education they will make more money, pay more taxes and
require fewer social services, according to the Human Rights
Coalition.

The press conference was part of a larger National Week of
Action for Immigrant Students, according to the Human Rights
Coalition.

The week began Saturday with a march of about 400 people
to the state capitol in Phoenix in support of the legislation.

Suggestions for Writing and Discussion

1. Identify the key issues related to the in-state tuition controversy. List the reasons the writers of the two articles
   identify for opposing in-state tuition, and then list the reasons the writers see for supporting in-state tuition. Which
   argument do you find is stronger? Explain your reasons.
2. Discuss how you think Richard Rodriguez would address
   this issue. What points that he makes in his article might
   be relevant to the circumstances and situations of students
   seeking in-state tuition? What points might be relevant to
   those who oppose the legislation?

Topics for Writing and Discussion

1. Rall's cartoon says, "Close the borders!" Is this what he is
   supporting? Explain your response.
2. What are the problems Rall's cartoon suggests would be
   the results of closing the borders?
3. Who, according to Rall's cartoon, would benefit from a
   ban on illegal immigrants?

Political cartoon by Ted Rall, Close the Borders, from the New York Times, *October 16, 2003. Copyright © 2003 Ted Rall. Reprinted with permission of Universal Press Syndicate. All rights reserved.*

4. What message is sent by the warning sign from the U.S. and Mexican border? How does this sign relate to the question "How does America welcome immigrants?" and to the selections related to that question (pages 86–98)?

EXTENDED CONNECTIONS: FOR CRITICAL THINKING, WRITING, AND RESEARCH

1. Through careful analysis of one selection from this chapter, find a research question related to a controversy about immigration. After exploring this question through various sources (books, online databases, interviews), formulate a thesis that explains the viewpoint you now hold. Write an argument supporting that viewpoint.

2. Compare the challenges faced by the people described in the selections by Chief Seattle, Irving Howe, and Maxine Hong Kingston. In addition, do research using various

A road sign by the side of a California freeway warns of illegal immigrants crossing near the U.S.–Mexico border

sources (books, online databases, interviews), and then determine what single most important challenge each group of people faced. Write an argument proposing that the challenges these people faced make them alike (or make them distinctively different).

3. Read "Wheel of Misfortune" and "Indian Gaming: Why Is the Backlash Growing?" as well as additional sources (books, online databases, interviews) about gaming on reservations. Then write an argument proposing that casinos on reservations have primarily hurt (or primarily helped) Native Americans.

4. Read "The Great Unmentionable in American Society: Class" (pages 364–67), "An Education in Citizenship," and "Immigrant Students Seek Lower Tuition." Then consult additional sources related to the benefits and costs of educating students who are illegal immigrants (books, online databases, interviews) and write an argument proposing that states should (or should not) offer in-state tuition to these students.

CHAPTER 4

Finding Our Way: The American Dream after 9/11

INTRODUCTION

Looking back, everyone who was over the age of about five on September 11, 2001, remembers the perfect, bright blue sky pierced by the unspeakable smoke, fire, and destruction of human life in New York City and Washington, D.C. After the disbelief, horror, anger, and mourning of that day have come the retrospectives. We examine our own thoughts and the thoughts of others on those few hours that have changed forever the lives of those who live in the United States, and those whose lives are affected by the United States. For many Americans, the response of former poet laureate Stanley Kunitz captures the deep sense of questioning, disillusion, and loss engendered by the terrorist attack on the country we call home. "There is the thought that there must be something wrong with the world itself, with what we have done in the organization of states and society at large, that there is so much hatred and distrust in the world" (Interview, *Articles,* 2002).

To examine how the American dream has changed since 9/11, this chapter looks first at two speeches that define the dream before that date. Martin Luther King Jr.'s familiar "I Have a Dream" speech sets before us the possibility of a country that will fulfill the promise made in the Declaration of Independence: the assurance that all people will be "guaranteed the inalienable rights of life, liberty and the pursuit of happiness." Speaking in 1963, King looks back at the foundations of the American republic as well as the principles of the Emancipation Proclamation, the decree that formally ended slavery in the United States. Still, he notes, the dream of equality and freedom for all has not been fully realized.

In the second speech, William Jefferson Clinton's second inaugural address (1997), echoes of King's longing for the dream sound throughout. Although Clinton notes that much has been accomplished, he also points out that much is left to be done, stating that King's "dream was the American dream" and that "his quest is our quest: the ceaseless striving to live out our true creed." Although Clinton notes the work that lies ahead, his speech is filled with optimism and hope. In retrospect, perhaps most poignant is his assertion that "The world is no longer divided into two hostile camps. Instead, now we are building bonds with nations that were once our adversaries."

Following the two speeches that offer possible definitions of the American dream before September 11, 2001, is a photo essay filled with images that suggest many ways of looking at our flag. The complex ideas and feelings expressed in the essay that follows, "Seeing Stars and Stripes," indicate how one writer, artist Jessica De Poyen, changed in the way she viewed the flag after the terrorist attack.

Her thoughtful affirmation of the flag is followed by a series of writings that look at the relationships between people's various loyalties to the flag, to the country, and to the right to peaceful protest. Sparked by college basketball player Toni Smith's decision to turn her back on the flag during the playing of the national anthem, these writings look at the reasons behind Smith's decision and at the very strong reactions to her action.

Moving from questions of Toni Smith's rights, responsibilities, and patriotism to larger questions of civil rights, three selections examine the Patriot Act, analyzing and evaluating just how the legal rights of Americans have been changed by this act, which was passed in response to the threat of terrorism.

How each individual's view of the American dream prior to 9/11 has been affected by the changes we have all experienced, including legislation such as the Patriot Act, must be given careful consideration as we move into the uncharted space of our future.

· THEN ·

SETTING THE CONTEXT: THE DREAM THEN

Suggestions for Prereading or Journal Writing

1. Make a list of the phrases and words that come to mind when you hear the phrase "American dream." Then choose two or three items from your list and write about how these items might be viewed by some people as positive and by others as negative.
2. To what extent and in what ways do you believe that you (or your family) have achieved what you consider to be the American dream.
3. Has your view of the American dream changed at all following the events of 9/11? Explain.

I Have a Dream

Martin Luther King Jr.

Born in 1929, Martin Luther King Jr. gained great acclaim and admiration for his tireless advocacy of civil rights during the years from 1958 until he was assassinated in 1968. In 1963, standing at the base of the Lincoln Memorial in Washington, D.C., he delivered to a crowd of 250,000 civil rights protestors his powerful "I Have a Dream" speech.

I am happy to join with you today in what will go down in history as the greatest demonstration for freedom in the history of our nation.

Five score years ago, a great American, in whose symbolic shadow we stand today, signed the Emancipation Proclamation. This momentous decree came as a great beacon light of hope to millions of Negro slaves who had been seared in the flames of withering injustice. It came as a joyous daybreak to end the long night of their captivity. But one hundred years later, the Negro still is not free. One hundred years later, the life of the Negro is still sadly crippled by the manacles of segregation and the chains of discrimination. One hundred years later, the Negro lives on a lonely island of poverty in the midst of a vast ocean of material prosperity. One hundred years later, the Negro is still anguished in the corners of American society and finds himself in exile in his own land. And so we have come here today to dramatize a shameful condition.

In a sense we have come to our nation's capital to cash a check. When the architects of our republic wrote the magnificent words of the Constitution and the Declaration of Independence, they were signing a promissory note to which every American was to fall heir. This note was the promise that all men—yes, black men as well as white men—would be guaranteed the inalienable rights of life, liberty, and the pursuit of happiness.

It is obvious today that America has defaulted on this promissory note insofar as her citizens of color are concerned. Instead of honoring this sacred obligation, America has given the Negro people a bad check, a check which has come back marked "insufficient funds." But we refuse to believe that the bank of justice is bankrupt. We refuse to believe that there are insufficient funds in the great vaults of opportunity of this nation; and so we have come to cash this check, a check that will give us upon demand the riches of freedom and the security of justice.

5   We have also come to this hallowed spot to remind America of the fierce urgency of *now*. This is no time to engage in the luxury of cooling off or to take the tranquilizing drug of gradualism. *Now* is the time to make real the promises of democracy. *Now* is the time to rise from the dark and desolate valley of segregation to the sunlit path of racial justice. *Now* is the time to lift our nation from the quicksands of racial injustice to the solid rock of brotherhood. *Now* is the time to make justice a reality for all of God's children.

It would be fatal for the nation to overlook the urgency of the moment. This sweltering summer of the Negro's legitimate discontent will not pass until there is an invigorating autumn of freedom and equality. Nineteen sixty-three is not an end, but a beginning. And those who hope that the Negro needed to blow off steam and will now be content will have a rude awakening if the nation returns to business as usual. There will be neither rest nor tranquility in America until the Negro is granted his citizenship rights. The whirlwinds of revolt will continue to shake the foundations of our nation until the bright day of justice emerges.

But there is something that I must say to my people who stand on the warm threshold which leads into the palace of justice. In the process of gaining our rightful place, we must not be guilty of wrongful deeds. Let us not seek to satisfy our thirst for freedom by drinking from the cup of bitterness and hatred. We must forever conduct our struggle on the high plane of dignity and discipline. We must not allow our creative protest to degenerate into physical violence. Again and again we must rise to the majestic heights of meeting physical force with soul force. And the marvelous new militancy which has engulfed the Negro community must not lead us to a distrust of all white people; for many of our white brothers, as evidenced by their presence here today, have come to realize that their destiny is tied up with our destiny, and they have come to realize that their freedom is inextricably bound to our freedom.

We cannot walk alone. And as we walk we must make the pledge that we shall always march ahead. We cannot turn back. There are those who are asking the devotees of civil rights, "When will you be satisfied?" We can never be satisfied as long as the Negro is the victim of the unspeakable horrors of police brutality. We can never be satisfied as long as our bodies, heavy with the fatigue of travel, cannot gain lodging in the motels of the highways and the hotels of the cities. We cannot be satisfied as long as the Negro's basic mobility is from a smaller ghetto to a larger one. We can never be satisfied as long as our children are stripped of their selfhood and robbed of their dignity by signs stating "For Whites Only." We cannot be satisfied as long as the Negro in Mississippi cannot vote and a Negro in New York believes he has nothing for which to vote. No, no, we are not satisfied, and we will not be satisfied until justice rolls down like waters and righteousness like a mighty stream.

I am not unmindful that some of you have come here out of great trials and tribulations. Some of you have come fresh from narrow jail cells. Some of you have come from areas where your quest for freedom left you battered by the storms of persecution and staggered by the winds of police brutality. You have been the veterans of creative suffering. Continue to work with the faith that unearned suffering is redemptive.

Go back to Mississippi, and go back to Alabama. Go back to **10** South Carolina. Go back to Georgia. Go back to Louisiana. Go back to the slums and ghettos of our Northern cities, knowing that somehow this situation can and will be changed. Let us not wallow in the valley of despair.

I say to you today, my friends, even though we face the difficulties of today and tomorrow, I still have a dream. It is a dream deeply rooted in the American dream. I have a dream that one day this nation will rise up and live out the true meaning of its creed: "We hold these truths to be self-evident, that all men are created equal." I have a dream that one day, on the red hills of Georgia, sons of former slaves and the sons of former slave owners will be able to sit down together at the table of brotherhood. I have a dream that one day even the state of Mississippi, a state sweltering with the heat of injustice, sweltering with the heat of oppression, will be transformed into an oasis of freedom and justice. I have a dream that my four little children will one day live in a nation where they will not be judged by the color of their skin, but by the content of their character.

I have a dream today. I have a dream that one day down in Alabama—with its vicious racists, with its governor's lips dripping with the words of interposition and nullification—one day right there in Alabama, little black boys and black girls will be able to join hands with little white boys and white girls as sisters and brothers.

I have a dream today. I have a dream that one day every valley shall be exalted and every hill and mountain shall be made low, the rough places will be made plain and the crooked places will be made straight, and the glory of the Lord shall be revealed, and all flesh shall see it together.

This is our hope. This is the faith that I go back to the South with. And with this faith we will be able to hew out of the mountain of despair a stone of hope. With this faith we will be able to transform the jangling discords of our nation into a beautiful symphony of brotherhood. With this faith we will be able to work together, to play together, to struggle together, to go to jail together, to stand up for freedom together, knowing that we will be free one day.

15   And this will be the day—this will be the day when all of God's children will be able to sing with new meaning.

> My country, 'tis of thee,
> Sweet land of liberty,
>   Of thee I sing;
> Land where my fathers died,
> Land of the Pilgrims' pride,
> From every mountainside
>   Let freedom ring.

And if America is to be a great nation, this must become true.

And so let freedom ring from the prodigious hilltops of New Hampshire. Let freedom ring from the mighty mountains of New York. Let freedom ring from the heightening Alleghenies of Pennsylvania. Let freedom ring from the snow-capped Rockies of Colorado. Let freedom ring from the curvaceous slopes of California.

But not only that. Let freedom ring from Stone Mountain of Georgia. Let freedom ring from Lookout Mountain of Tennessee. Let freedom ring from every hill and molehill of Mississippi. "From every mountainside let freedom ring."

And when this happens—when we allow freedom to ring, when we let it ring from every village and every hamlet, from every state and every city—we will be able to speed up that day when all of God's children, black men and white men, Jews and Gentiles, Protestants and Catholics, will be able to join hands and sing in the words of the old Negro spiritual: "Free at last! Free at last! Thank God Almighty. We are free at last!"

Suggestions for Writing and Discussion

1. As you read this speech, put yourself in the place of King as he thought about who his audience for this speech would be. How do you think he would have defined that audience to himself? Cite specific details of his speech that suggest to you how he hoped to communicate effectively to various segments of his audience.

2. As you read King's speech, what parts of his argument do you see as using what might be called objective facts? What parts use ethical or emotional appeals? How effective do you find these different ways of building an argument?

A New Sense of Responsibility

William Jefferson Clinton

Born in Arkansas in 1946, William Clinton was elected governor of his native state at age 32, only five years after graduating from Yale Law School. In 1992 and again in 1996, he was elected president of the United States. The following speech is the full text of his second inaugural address, delivered, as he notes, on Martin Luther King Jr.'s birthday in January of 1997.

My fellow citizens:

At this last presidential inauguration of the 20th century, let us lift our eyes toward the challenges that await us in the next century. It is our great good fortune that time and chance have put us not only on the edge of a new century, in a new millennium, but on the edge of a bright new prospect in human affairs. A moment that will define our course and our character for decades to come. We must keep our old democracy forever young. Guided by the ancient vision of a promised land, let us set our sights upon a land of new promise.

The promise of America was born in the 18th century out of the bold conviction that we are all created equal. It was extended and preserved in the 19th century, when our nation spread across the continent, saved the union and abolished the scourge of slavery.

Then, in turmoil and triumph, that promise exploded onto the world stage to make this the American Century.

5   What a century it has been. America became the world's mightiest industrial power; saved the world from tyranny in two world wars and a long Cold War; and time and again, reached across the globe to millions who longed for the blessings of liberty.

Along the way, Americans produced the great middle class and security in old age; built unrivaled centers of learning and opened public schools to all; split the atom and explored the heavens; invented the computer and the microchip; and deepened the wellspring of justice by making a revolution in civil rights for African Americans and all minorities, and extending the circle of citizenship, opportunity and dignity to women.

A NEW CENTURY IS UPON US

Now, for the third time, a new century is upon us, and another time to choose. We began the 19th century with a choice to spread our nation from coast to coast. We began the 20th century with a choice to harness the Industrial Revolution to our values of free enterprise, conservation and human decency. Those choices made all the difference.

At the dawn of the 21st century, a free people must choose to shape the forces of the Information Age and the global society, to unleash the limitless potential of all our people and form a more perfect union.

When last we gathered, our march to this new future seemed less certain than it does today. We vowed then to set a clear course, to renew our nation.

In these four years, we have been touched by tragedy, exhilarated by challenge, strengthened by achievement. America stands alone as the world's indispensable nation. Once again, our economy is the strongest on Earth.

Once again, we are building stronger families, thriving communities, better educational opportunities, a cleaner environment.

Problems that once seemed destined to deepen now bend to our efforts: Our streets are safer, and record numbers of our fellow citizens have moved from welfare to work.

And once again, we have resolved for our time a great debate over the role of government. Today, we can declare: Government is not the problem, and government is not the solution. We, the American people, we are the solution. Our founders understood that well and gave us a democracy strong enough to endure for centuries, flexible enough to face our common challenges and advance our common dreams.

As times change, so government must change. We need a new government for a new century, a government humble enough not to try to solve all our problems for us but strong enough to give us the tools to solve our problems for ourselves. A government that is smaller, lives within its means and does more with less. Yet where it can stand up for our values and interests around the world, and where it can give Americans the power to make a real difference in their everyday lives, government should do more, not less. The preeminent mission of our new government is to give all Americans an opportunity, not a guarantee, but a real opportunity to build better lives.

THE FUTURE IS UP TO US

Beyond that, my fellow citizens, the future is up to us. Our founders taught us that the preservation of our liberty and our union depends upon responsible citizenship.

And we need a new sense of responsibility for a new century. There is work to do, work that government alone cannot do: Teaching children to read. Hiring people off welfare rolls. Coming out from behind locked doors and shuttered windows to help reclaim our streets from drugs and gangs and crime. Taking time out from our own lives to serve others.

Each and every one of us, in our own way, must assume personal responsibility—not only for ourselves and our families but for our neighbors and our nation.

Our greatest responsibility is to embrace a new spirit of community for a new century. For any one of us to succeed, we must succeed as one America.

The challenge of our past remains the challenge of our future: Will we be one nation, one people, with one common destiny—or not? Will we all come together or come apart?

THE DIVIDE OF RACE

20 The divide of race has been America's constant curse. Each new wave of immigrants gives new targets to old prejudices. Prejudice and contempt, cloaked in the pretense of religious or political conviction, are no different. They have nearly destroyed us in the past. They plague us still. They fuel the fanaticism of terror. They torment the lives of millions in fractured nations around the world.

These obsessions cripple both those who are hated and, of course, those who hate. Robbing both of what they might become.

We cannot—we will not—succumb to the dark impulses that lurk in the far regions of the soul, everywhere. We shall overcome them, and we shall replace them with the generous spirit of a people who feel at home with one another.

Our rich texture of racial, religious and political diversity will be a godsend in the 21st century. Great rewards will come to those who can live together, learn together, work together, forge new ties that bind together.

As this new era approaches, we can already see its broad outlines. Ten years ago, the Internet was the mystical province of physicists. Today, it is a commonplace encyclopedia for millions of schoolchildren. Scientists now are decoding the blueprint of human life. Cures for our most feared illnesses seem close at hand.

The world is no longer divided into two hostile camps. In- 25 stead, now we are building bonds with nations that once were our adversaries. Growing connections of commerce and culture give us a chance to lift the fortunes and spirits of people the world over. And for the very first time in all of history, more people on this planet live under democracy than dictatorship.

WE WILL SUSTAIN AMERICA'S JOURNEY

My fellow Americans, as we look back at this remarkable century, we may ask, "Can we hope not just to follow, but even to surpass the achievements of the 20th century in America and to avoid the awful bloodshed that stained its legacy?" To that question, every American here and every American in our land today must answer a resounding, "Yes."

This is the heart of our task. With a new vision of government, a new sense of responsibility, a new spirit of community, we will sustain America's journey. The promise we sought in a new land we will find again in a land of new promise.

In this new land, education will be every citizen's most prized possession. Our schools will have the highest standards in the world, igniting the spark of possibility in the eyes of every girl and every boy. And the doors of higher education will be open to all.

The knowledge and power of the Information Age will be within reach not just to the few, but of every classroom, every library, every child. Parents and children will have time not only to work but to read and play together. And the plans they make at their kitchen table will be those of a better home, a better job, the certain chance to go to college.

Our streets will echo again with the laughter of our children 30 because no one will try to shoot them or sell them drugs anymore. Everyone who can work will work, with today's permanent underclass part of tomorrow's growing middle class.

New miracles of medicine at last will reach not only those who can claim care now but the children and hard-working families too long denied. We will stand mighty for peace and freedom, and maintain a strong defense against terror and destruction. Our children will sleep free from the threat of nuclear, chemical or biological weapons. Ports and airports, farms and factories will thrive with trade and innovation and ideas. And the world's greatest democracy will lead a whole world of democracies.

THIS LAND OF NEW PROMISE

Our land of new promise will be a nation that meets its obligations, a nation that balances its budget but never loses the balance of its values; a nation where our grandparents have secure retirement and health care, and their grandchildren know we have made the reforms necessary to sustain those benefits for their time; a nation that fortifies the world's most productive economy even as it protects the great natural bounty of our water, air and majestic land.

And in this land of new promise, we will have reformed our politics so that the voice of the people will always speak louder than the din of narrow interest, regaining the participation and deserving the trust of all Americans.

Fellow citizens, let us build that America, a nation ever moving forward toward realizing the full potential of all its citizens. Prosperity and power: Yes, they are important, and we must maintain them, but let us never forget the greatest progress we have made and the greatest progress we have yet to make is in the human heart.

35   In the end, all the world's wealth and a thousand armies are no match for the strength and decency of the human spirit.

KING'S DREAM WAS AMERICAN DREAM

Thirty-four years ago, the man whose life we celebrate today spoke to us down there at the other end of this mall in words that moved the conscience of a nation. Like a prophet of old, he told of his dream that one day America would rise up and treat all its citizens as equals before the law and in the heart.

Martin Luther King's dream was the American dream. His quest is our quest: the ceaseless striving to live out our true creed.

Our history has been built on such dreams and labors, and by our dreams and labors we will redeem the promise of America in the 21st century. To that effort, I pledge all my strength and every power of my office.

I ask the members of Congress here to join in that pledge. The American people returned to office a president of one party and a Congress of another.

Surely they did not do this to advance the politics of petty bickering and extreme partisanship they plainly deplore. No, they call all of us instead to be repairers of the breach and to move on with America's mission. America demands and deserves big things from us, and nothing big ever came from being small.

Let us remember the timeless wisdom of Cardinal Bernardin when facing the end of his own life: He said, "It is wrong to waste the precious gift of time on acrimony and division."

Fellow citizens, we must not waste the precious gift of this time, for all of us are on that same journey of our lives. And our journey too will come to an end, but the journey of our America must go on.

LET US BUILD OUR BRIDGE

And so, my fellow Americans, we must be strong, for there is much to dare.

The demands of our time are great, and they are different. Let us meet them with faith and courage, with patience and a grateful happy heart. Let us shape the hope of this day into the noblest chapter in our history. Yes, let us build our bridge, a bridge wide enough and strong enough for every American to cross over to a blessed land of new promise.

May those generations whose faces we cannot yet see, whose names we may never know, say of us here that we led our beloved land into a new century with the American dream alive for all her children, with the American promise of a more perfect union a reality for all her people, with America's bright flame of freedom spreading throughout all the world.

From the height of this place and the summit of this century, let us go forth. May God strengthen our hands for the good work ahead, and always, always bless our America.

Suggestions for Writing and Discussion

1. What prospects does Clinton envision for the United States as the country approaches the new century? To what extent do you think these dreams have been realized?

*Painting by E. Percy Moran,
George Washington looking
on as Betsy Ross sews the
first American flag, c. 1908*

*U.S Armed Forces recruitment
poster showing figure of
Liberty with the flag, 1917*

See questions on pp. 115–16.

Comedian Richard Pryor,
June 1968

Astronaut Buzz Aldrin during
an Apollo 11 Extravehicular
Activity (EVA) on the moon's
surface, July 20, 1969

See questions on pp. 115–16. **2**

Young woman wearing flag-patterned bikini

An original pastel painting by S. Thomas Sierak, an exponent of contemporary American realism, "United We Stand"

See questions on pp. 115–16.

*Photojournalist Joe Rosenthal captures U. S. Marines
raising the American flag on Iwo Jima, February 3, 1945*

See questions on pp. 115–16. **4**

Photojournalist Thomas E. Franklin's photo of New York firefighters raising a flag at Ground Zero is featured on U.S. postage stamp, 2002

5

See questions on pp. 115–16.

Over 5,000 Australians on Gold Coast beach form human flag in an anniversary tribute to the victims of September 11, September 11, 2002

Young Filipina girl burning an American flag as President George W. Bush's motorcade passes through Manila, October 18, 2003

See questions on pp. 115–16.

6

Silhouette of raised hands behind an American flag

*Protestors against the war
on Iraq near the Washington
Monument in Washington,
D.C., March 15, 2003*

7
See questions on pp. 115–16.

Front page of the Seattle Times, *April 18, 2004. The image was used amid debate over the U.S. administration's ban on photos of soldiers' coffins at U.S. military bases. Photographer Tami Silicio, who took the photo while working for the U.S. military at Kuwait International Airport, was dismissed from her job on April 21, 2004.*

See questions on pp. 115–16.

2. Clinton says that "Our greatest responsibility is to embrace a new spirit of community for a new century. For any one of us to succeed, we must succeed as one America." Explain why you do or do not agree with this part of his vision for the country. Be sure to give specific reasons to support the points you make.

3. In what ways do you think Clinton's speech might have changed if he were making it in January 2005 instead of January 1997?

Making Connections: Synthesis and Analysis

1. What do you see as the basic similarities and differences between the American dream as envisioned in King's speech and the American dream as envisioned in Clinton's?

2. Imagine that King had lived to hear Clinton's second inaugural address and that the two had met in private shortly after Clinton delivered his speech. Write the dialogue that might have occurred.

· NOW ·

WHAT DOES THE FLAG MEAN?

Suggestions for Prereading or Journal Writing

1. Do you think that residents of the United States should be compelled to respect the flag by law? Or should they be convinced in others ways to show respect for the flag?

2. Describe any images you have of the American flag being used as a means of protest. What has your response been to such protests?

Topics for Writing and Discussion

1. Choose any of these images that you find relates to the American dream as suggested by either Martin Luther King Jr.'s or William Jefferson Clinton's speech. What comparisons do you see? What contrasts can you identify? What significance do you see in these comparisons and contrasts?

2. Do you see any of these images as projecting disrespect for the flag? Explain your response. Do you see any images that others might find disrespectful, but you do not? How would you defend your point of view?

3. What relationship do you see between any of these images and the series of essays that respond to the question "What Does the Flag Mean?" (pages 116–28)? If you had to choose three or four of these images to accompany that set of selections, which would you choose? Explain your reasons.

4. In what way do any of these images relate to the question "How do we balance security and freedom?"? Does the flag, and the response of individuals to the flag, relate in any way to the way you define patriotism? To your definition of loyalty to the United States? Explain.

Seeing Stars and Stripes

Jennifer de Poyen

Born and raised in Canada by a Canadian mother and an American father, Jennifer de Poyen considers herself "bi-national." She is an artist and scriptwriter and also works as dance and theater critic and columnist for the *San Diego Union-Tribune.* This selection, which appeared in the 2002 edition of the publication *ARTicles,* shows her complicated responses toward the American flag and details the changes in her response following the events of 9/11.

Last spring [. . .] I wanted to sort through my feelings about a symbol that had suddenly taken on a new meaning for so many Americans. [. . .] I wanted to see if I could really *see* the flag for what it is meant to represent: freedom, liberty, possibility. As long as I'd been alive, the flag had been the property of right-wing so-called "patriots," who had appropriated it to promote certain ideas of what it means to be American. It had been scorned by pro-flag-burning, free-speech liberals who saw flag-waving as a cover for ill-considered and sometimes illegal practices of the United States government. And it had been largely shrugged at— invoked at school events, sporting matches and national holidays— by the great, moderate expanse in between. I wanted to explore the possibility that the post-9/11 flag-waving was not proof of a terror-induced political and cultural shift to the right, but a broadening of the definition of what it means to love America. I wanted to believe what the choreographer Paul Taylor, who has used patriotic images (however ambiguously) in his work, told a *New York Times* writer about the flags flying all over New York in the wake of Sept. 11: "When you used to see a flag on a car, it usually meant a redneck. Now everybody's doing it. It's kind of nice!"

[. . .]

After the devastation of Sept. 11, there was a renewed interest in art objects that incorporate the flag, presumably for the same reason that there was renewed interest in the flag itself: as a locus for grief about the missing, the dead and the devastated; as a gesture of solidarity with those who labored to find bodies in the horrifying rubble; as an attempt to make sense of a desperately senseless act of violence; as an expression of defiance in the face of fear and loathing for those who had attacked us, and would attack again. [. . .] In the post-9/11 context, it was an easy image from which to begin to construct a visual response to a horrific, but undeniably visual, event. For all the horror of the actual attack, and for all the suffering of family, friends and residents of Lower Manhattan, there was the added terror of images emblazoned in our minds through repeated viewings in the media: the towers struck with planes, stuck with planes, billowing smoke, collapsing into rubble. With such harrowing pictures in our mind's eye, is it any wonder that the flag, to which children are conditioned to pledge allegiance, became the symbol of our collective sorrow, our shared resolve?

Not surprisingly, the patriotic art that arose from the ashes of Sept. 11 did not come from academically, institutionally and critically approved artists, and still less from New York artists, who were daily confronted with the grim reality of the attacks. The responses came, instead, from folk artists, who have historically deployed flag imagery, from ordinary people, and from pop-culture sources—from culture-makers, who are happy to swim in the mainstream and are traditionally less troubled by the notion that their work is unsophisticated, or simple.

Will we ever forget the tragedy's first *memento mori*—that spontaneous gesture, captured and in some sense created by the photojournalist Thomas E. Franklin, of three firemen raising the flag in the ashes of the World Trade Center? Hauntingly, it echoed the famous Iwo Jima scene and, like that World War II–era photograph, it asserted a triumph of the spirit that no one, in the moment, actually felt. And who—especially heartbroken New Yorkers—failed to be moved by the spontaneous art of flower-strewn, flag-laden, candlelit memorials, full of prayers, poetry and pictures of the lost, that sprouted everywhere?

After those first, wrenching memorials to the dead came a 5 slew of artistic responses to the terrorist attacks on New York and Washington. A week later, on Sept. 18, a group of schoolchildren in Atlanta put together a 16-by-18-foot rock-garden-cum-flag made of stones they had painted red, white and blue. Mort Kunstler, an artist in Cove Neck, N.Y., turned his art into a fundraising project by selling prints of his flag-themed painting "Old Glory"; for every $25 donation to the Red Cross, he would ship a print to the donor at his own expense. The Yale-trained Baltimore artist Tony Shore, best known for his large-scale works on black velvet, persuaded organizers of his "Oktavec Fish," a public art project that needed refurbishing, to allow him to repaint his sculpture red, white and blue (he too renamed it "Old Glory").

[. . .]

But people also seemed hungry for responses from cultural institutions, from the realm of high art; perhaps we were eager for prominent picture-makers to substitute soothing, or at least sense-making, images for the hideous ones we kept seeing in the media. As Americans in their confusion and helplessness turned to other institutions—all branches of government, various state agencies, the Big Three network news organizations—to package and explain the unimaginable horror of the terrorist attacks, so too were arts organizations under pressure to provide cultural ballast. How many orchestras and operas opened their seasons with the playing and singing of the American national anthem, often with the Stars and Stripes flying overhead? After Mayor Rudy Giuliani urged New Yorkers to "see a show" and asked Broadway to reopen its doors on Sept. 13, dispirited casts joined sorrowful audiences in moments of silence before finding their way back into plays that suddenly seemed irrelevant.

[. . .]

And Lord, did we need those patriotic images. In the first hours after the attacks, walking around Greenwich Village in a daze of despair, I was amazed to see that people were already showing their colors—fatigue pants for the guys, flag head-scarves for the girls. Those who weren't sitting in bars waiting for the end of the world—remember how it felt like the end of the world?—were raiding stores for flags; soon the merchants were out in the streets, hawking everything from flag pins to patriotic T-shirts to NYFD baseball caps. It's hard not to believe that the months after Sept. 11 formed the most patriotic period in American history. (Possible exception: the months after Pearl Harbor. In July 1942, every major magazine across the land agreed to feature the flag on the cover in celebration of Independence Day.)

After 9/11, aside from commentary from the left, there was little internal debate over the pervasive use of flag imagery as a palliative for grief, a substitute for dialogue, a muzzle for debate. Even some devout liberals embraced the Stars-and-Stripes symbolism after Sept. 11. Todd Gitlin, a Columbia University professor and former leader of the radical '60s group Students for a Democratic Society, hung a flag across the balcony of his Greenwich Village apartment. Gitlin's gesture caused a stir on the left, but he echoed a common sentiment of the swelling post-9/11 mainstream when he told a *San Francisco Chronicle* writer, "I want to affirm solidarity with my people, who have suffered and are showing in a variety of ways a solidarity with each other and thereby expressing the best of American values. And I don't want to leave the flag to those who affirm the most bombastic and aggressive or punitive of national values."

[. . .]

And what was the fate of those who dared resist the magnetic pull of flag imagery? In Colorado, a controversy erupted when Marcelee Gralapp, the library director at the Boulder Public Library's main branch, refused to display a 10-by-15-foot flag, either because (as she initially said) she thought that the library should welcome people of all beliefs and that the flag might alienate some visitors, or because (as she later said) she thought the flag so large that "people would have had to walk through it to get into the building." The library eventually installed a smaller flag in the lobby, but that did not satisfy disgruntled observers, who flew into a particular rage when it came to light that, over the same period, the library had been displaying a phallus-themed art project. Calling the exhibit of Susanne Walker's colorful ceramic penises, intended to call attention to domestic violence, "a kick in the groin for our boys overseas," Bob Rowan, the self-styled 49-year-old "Dildo Bandito" filched the penises from the library in full view of silent onlookers, and took them home; he later called a local radio station to confess to the crime. (In a Nov. 11 interview, El Dildo Bandito offered a perfect précis of the post-9/11 culture war he was waging over flags and phalluses: "I detest the fact that they're hanging there, number one, but the timing; it's the wrong time to do something like this. And it should never belong in something I pay taxes for.") And there was an uproar in Berkeley when city administrators removed American flags from all fire trucks before a Sept. 20 anti-war rally at the University of California/Berkeley, a liberal stronghold since the '60s. A war of words broke out between the city manager, who made the call to remove the flags, and mayor Shirley Dean, who was bombarded with angry phone calls from around the country. He said he feared the kind of violent clashes between protesters and firemen—bottle- and rock-throwing—that had broken out during the Persian Gulf War in 1991; she said his decision was "flat-out wrong." At a time when even such a tireless defender of the Constitution as Floyd Abrams became an apologist for limiting civil rights for security reasons, such haggling over Stars-and-Stripes symbolism became hard for some to swallow.

[. . .]

Walking around Manhattan in the months after the attacks, you 10 could see all kinds of violations of the Flag Code: people wearing flag T-shirts, of course, but also tattered flags, flags flying at the rear of a car or draped over a back seat, flags hung with the canton on the wrong side, and flags flying unilluminated through the night. Such violations—mostly faults of devotion—don't seem to raise anybody's hackles. But artists who employ patriotic imagery without patriotic zeal—and whose devotion may be to raising questions or exploring form—those Americans risk both censure and censor. What if this year's Whitney Biennial had included Mexican sculptor Marcos Ramirez's tribute to Johns' flags, which didn't so much as raise a stir at the museum's 2000 showcase of contemporary art? How would viewers have reacted to that piece, which re-imagines the Stars and Stripes as a corrugated metal fence on the U.S.-Mexican border, in this cultural moment? Would the Whitney have dared even show it?

[. . .]

. . . With all the fetishistic behavior surrounding the flag, the argument went, you could forget about your constitutional right to burn the flag and, by extension, your freedom of expression. The most radical provision of the Constitution—the one most pertinent to an artist's practice—was no longer safe. It was an extension of a visceral reaction I had had on Sept. 12, when I saw all those flags flying all over New York: I'm not safe anywhere anymore. Not because of the terrorists; I knew that on Sept. 11. No—now I realized I wasn't safe from my own government, my fellow Americans, my fellow New Yorkers. I wasn't safe from the evil that the Founding Fathers fought hardest to banish from the fledgling United States: tyranny. The tyranny of the majority, the iron-clad might of the masses, the totalitarian urge that has surged up in every time and in every place since humans started running in herds.

I thought, why not burn the flag? Not in a tasteful indoor crematorium, not in a private ceremony of patriotic decorum, but out in the open, in Central Park, where children play in the petting zoo, and lovers pet on the Great Lawn, and John Lennon fans imagine peace in Strawberry Fields, and muggers lurk in the Rambles, and joggers circle the reservoir, and tourists ride in stinky horse-drawn carriages, and . . .

In the end, I didn't have the heart for it. After 9/11, I was aggrieved by the command from on high to be "patriotic" and to defend "the American way of life"—dangerous abstractions, to my mind—but I was also moved by the solace so many people seemed to get from the flag. When push came to shove, I didn't want to add to anyone's pain.

Have my feelings about the flag changed since 9/11? Did the day that seemed to change everything really alter my sense of what the flag represents? Yes and no. I still see it as an object of fetish, a sacred cow that gets hoisted on the petard of patriotism every time *they* want to shut someone up. I still think, good liberal that I am, that it sometimes provides cover—like the sheep's clothing in which the wolf is wrapped—for dubious, sometimes immoral actions on the part of both individuals and the nation. On the other hand, I no longer bristle when I see it waving in the wind on a car going down the road. I no longer see it hanging in someone's window and think, I'm not welcome in *there*. [. . .] As visual nutrition, the flag is comfort food, and the hunger for it, post-9/11, was voracious. Created more than 250 years ago by a seamstress working in a folk tradition, the flag became a blanket with which we tucked ourselves to bed at night, a charm against nightmares about incinerated buildings, Osama bin Laden and his unfathomable followers, our unburied dead.

[. . .]

Suggestions for Writing and Discussion

1. Read the first paragraph and then write a brief explanation of the way de Poyen regarded the flag before 9/11 and her reasons for those opinions.
2. Why does de Poyen regard art as an important response to the events of 9/11? How, in particular, does she see images of the flag as significant?
3. Describe the responses of those who, according to de Poyen, resisted "the magnetic pull of flag imagery"? Why might those people have turned away from the flag during those traumatic days immediately following 9/11?
4. Why does de Poyen think that artistic freedom was particularly challenged by the strong surge of patriotism after the terrorist attacks?
5. In the end, to what conclusion does de Poyen come regarding her own feelings about the flag? How do her views compare with your own?

EVALUATING AN ARGUMENT: MULTIPLE POINTS OF VIEW

The Fight about the Flag
Tara Tripaldi

Writing for the Manhattanville College student newspaper, Tara Tripaldi describes the controversy sparked by basketball cocaptain Toni Smith's decision to turn her back on the flag during the opening ceremonies of games. This article appeared in the February 27, 2003, edition of *The Touchstone.*

Toni Smith, a senior co-captain, chooses to turn her back on the flag during the National Anthem. This has sparked controversy that has been covered in the "Journal News," "Newsday" and ESPN, which has caused Smith to get taunted by opposing fans during games.

Smith has been criticized by many for her actions, but many people do not know her reasons. When asked about the issue Smith said, "Before I do something I love, I have to salute this flag and say thank you when I feel like this flag has never done anything for me and my family."

Originally, Smith used to look away from the flag or put her head down, but after a conversation with her boyfriend, Smith wondered why should she salute the flag when she disagrees with what it stands for. "The way the American system is set up is that the rich get richer and the poor get poorer," said Smith.

Due to the media coverage, it no longer has become a Manhattanville issue. Smith has received numerous emails and letters of support since, including a letter from a firefighter who was at Ground Zero. However, there has also been a ton of negative feedback, but Smith is pleased with the support that she has received from her family and friends.

5   With the playoffs approaching the focus has been put on this issue rather than the team. When asked if it became an issue with the team, Smith declined to comment but did say, she appreciated the support her team gave her during the Kings Point game and although everyone has their own personal beliefs, they are still a team and she hopes to be able to continue through the season without it affecting the game.

Suggestions for Writing and Discussion

1. According to Tripaldi's article, why does Toni Smith choose to turn her back on the flag during the national anthem?
2. If you could have a conversation with Toni Smith, how would you address her statement that she feels "like this flag has never done anything for me and my family"?

Don't Turn on the Flag

Editorial, *San Francisco Chronicle*

Commenting on Toni Smith's turning her back on the flag at Manhattanville College basketball games, the *San Francisco Chronicle* argues that both Smith and her critics "have it all wrong." The writer proposes a third way of looking at the American flag. This editorial appeared on February 27, 2003.

Toni Smith's protest is misdirected. Smith, a 21-year-old senior guard for the Manhattanville College basketball team in suburban Purchase, N.Y., has been attracting national attention by turning her back to the American flag during the national anthem. "It is clear that the government's priorities are not on bettering the quality of life for all of its people, but rather on expanding its own power," she has said. "I cannot, in good conscience, salute the flag."

The resulting outrage has been regrettable but predictable. Hecklers have urged her to "leave the country." One Vietnam War veteran ran onto the court and shook an American flag in her face. In a recent game against the U.S. Merchant Marine Academy, a group of midshipmen waved flags and chanted "U-S-A, U-S-A."

Both Smith and her critics have it wrong.

Neither side in the national debates about Iraq, civil liberties and national priorities should be allowed to claim exclusive rights to expressions of patriotism or the symbolism of the flag. The flag has not been copyrighted by the Bush-Cheney re-election committee. The national anthem is not the official theme song for Operation Regime Change or the dividend tax cut.

If, as she suggests, Smith is angry at an administration that is 5 turning away from American ideals, then she should be turning toward the flag to express her concern with the direction of this government.

And she has a good case to make.

After all, to challenge the Bush administration's proposed pre-emptive war on Iraq—a revolutionary turn from our historic definition of defense—is not an unpatriotic act. To question the administration's plans to unravel more than two centuries of basic constitutional protections—with secret searches, expanded surveillance, vast dossiers on ordinary citizens, even secret arrests—

would surely draw approval from many, perhaps most, of our founding fathers.

The notion that "flag waving" or "patriotism" equates with a particular position on the use of military force should have vanished long ago. The anti-war movement of the 1960s fell into the trap of allowing hawks to appropriate the flag and other symbols of U.S. values. The critics of the rush to war in Iraq, or of Attorney General John Ashcroft's efforts to peel back the U.S. Constitution in the name of security, must not let it happen again.

Toni Smith, there is nothing inconsistent about your ideals and the symbolism of the American flag. The same applies to the anti-war demonstrators who have been encountering packs of counter-protesters waving the Stars and Stripes.

10 Don't turn on the flag. Display it and wave it proudly as you stand tall for the history and many noble principles it represents.

Suggestions for Writing and Discussion

1. What are two primary arguments that this editorial states against Toni Smith's turning her back on the flag? Do you agree or disagree with these arguments? Explain.
2. The editorial states that Smith's challenge to the "preemptive war on Iraq" is not unpatriotic. What does the phrase "pre-emptive war" mean?

A Silent Protest on the Basketball Court
Janet Paskin

During her undergraduate years at Oberlin College, Janet Paskin wrote for the campus newspaper. Currently, she works as a sportswriter for *Newsday* and also as a freelance journalist. This article explains further details of Toni Smith's protest, quoting Smith on her reasons for turning her back on the flag. In addition, Paskin describes the responses of Smith's critics. This article originally appeared on February 21, 2003, in the White Plains, New York, *Journal News.*

NEWBURGH—Fans packed the stands before the women's basketball game at Mount St. Mary College last night. They held flags. And they waited.

They got what they came for. As Mount St. Mary student Sara Klemeshefsky sang "The Star-Spangled Banner," Manhattanville's Toni Smith turned to the side, away from the American flag, and faced the floor.

She held tight the hand of freshman teammate Dionne Walker. When the anthem was done, Walker gave Smith a hug.

Smith has made the same quiet quarter-turn all season, usually without incident. But on Feb. 11, the team traveled to the U.S. Merchant Marine Academy, where more than 300 flag-waving midshipmen greeted Smith with chants of "U-S-A" and "Leave our country." Since then, word has spread.

The Mount St. Mary student government spent more than $100 on small flags and handed them out before the game. More than 500 filled the small gym and jeered Smith at every opportunity. Smith picked up two fouls in the first 2:16 and sat the rest of the half, prompting a dissatisfied crowd to chant, "We want Toni." The crowd dwindled by halftime and quieted, more interested in the two-point game that Mount St. Mary won, 67–65. The remaining fans stood and sang "God Bless America" as the clock ran out.

"It's disgraceful," said Mount St. Mary junior Jess Varvatsas, who wore a Stars and Stripes halter top and brought a flag to the gym. "I'm against the war, but the flag stands for more than war."

They, like everyone else, assumed that Smith turns away to protest America's march toward the war with Iraq. That's part of it, Smith said in a written statement.

"For some time now, the inequalities that are embedded into the American system have bothered me," Smith wrote. "As they are becoming progressively worse and it is clear that the government's priorities are not on bettering the quality of life for all of its people, but rather on expanding its own power, I cannot, in good conscience, salute the flag."

Until last night, Smith had kept her rationale to herself. She refused to discuss her views with the media and Manhattanville President Richard Berman, who offered Smith a hug and words of support early in the season.

"I told her I think what she's doing is courageous and difficult," said Berman, who protested the Vietnam War while a student at Michigan in the 1960s. "But that in this community we respect one another's views, and whether I agree or disagree is irrelevant. I asked her if she wanted to talk about the issues, and she said no."

In Smith's online profile, which is linked to the team's roster, Smith posted two quotes: "If you don't stand for something, you will fall for anything" and "It will be a great day when our schools get all the money they need and the military has to hold a bake sale to buy a bomber."

Smith's refusal to face the flag, however, went unnoticed until some players and their parents mentioned it to first-year coach Shawn Lincoln. He spoke with Smith, then held a team meeting.

"The team is like any other collection of people," Lincoln said. "Everybody has their own beliefs and opinions, and we're no different."

Lincoln refused to discuss the team's reaction.

15   That was the end of the issue internally for the team, which, at 15-9, has proceeded to have one of the best seasons in the history of Manhattanville women's basketball.

But Smith's protest did not fade into the background for opponents. By a fluke of scheduling, Manhattanville played Skyline conference rival St. Joseph's twice in a week. Three of St. Joseph's players have friends or family in active military service, and after the second game, St. Joseph's Christine Argentina yelled at Smith.

"After the game, we were walking down the line, and my point guard called her a jerk and (said) 'You've got a lot of nerve' and got in her face," said St. Joseph's coach Dennis Case, whose son, Dwayne, is with the Merchant Marine in the Mediterranean Sea.

"I supported her," Case said of Argentina, whose brother is in the Middle East. "If Toni Smith has First Amendment rights to not face the flag, then my point guard has First Amendment rights to tell her what she thinks of that. Under no circumstances would I ever reprimand her for that."

Argentina's comments were mild compared to what Smith faced at USMMA six days later. More than 300 midshipmen packed the stands, a record turnout for the winless Mariners. The fans hung flags from the rafters, waved them in the stands and wrapped them around their shoulders. During "The Star-Spangled Banner," Smith looked at the floor—the only place in the gym that wasn't red, white and blue. At halftime, 50 plebes (freshmen), each carrying a flag, marched into the gym and stood across from the Valiants' bench. They stayed there until the game was over.

20   "Every time she got a ball, (the fans) were yelling and waving their flags," USMMA sports information director Kim McNulty said. "We were proud of the professionalism with which

the midshipmen displayed their feelings. They did nothing to offend or make the game an unsafe atmosphere. They were expressing their opinion."

Smith has stood firm in the face of her detractors. In her statement, she wrote, "It is my right as an American to stand for my beliefs the way others have done against me. . . . Patriotism can be shown in many ways, but those who choose to do so by saluting the flag should recognize that the American flag stands for individuality and freedom. Therefore, any true patriot must acknowledge and respect my right to be different."

Suggestions for Writing and Discussion

1. In what ways do you think the guarantee of free speech under the First Amendment to the Constitution applies to Toni Smith's actions and to the actions of those who oppose her? Cite examples and references to the First Amendment from Paskin's article.

2. In the final paragraph, Smith is quoted as saying that "any true patriot must acknowledge and respect [her] right to be different." Do you agree with this definition of a "true patriot"? Explain.

Making Connections: Synthesis and Analysis

1. After reading all three articles about Toni Smith and the American flag, briefly summarize the controversy. Remember that in a summary you simply state the facts, not your own opinion.

2. Gathering information, including direct quotations of Smith's statements, make a list of the reasons that Smith decided to turn her back on the flag. In addition, make note of what those who support her actions say. Do they all agree with Smith? If not, why do they support her actions?

3. Gathering information from all three articles, explain the reasons Smith's critics oppose her actions. Explain how convincing you find each of these reasons.

4. The editorial from the *San Francisco Chronicle* suggests an approach to the flag that is different from either Smith's

point of view or that of her critics. How do you think Smith and her critics would respond to the *Chronicle* writer?

HOW DO WE BALANCE FREEDOM AND SECURITY?

Suggestions for Prereading or Journal Writing

1. How would you define the words "security" and "freedom"? What do you see as the relationship between these two words?
2. Think of ways in which your own freedom may have been curtailed, at home, at work, or at school. What freedom was taken away? Why was it removed? To what extent did this action contribute to your own security or to the security of others? Explain.

EVALUATING AN ARGUMENT: MULTIPLE POINTS OF VIEW

Terrorist Attacks Prompt Changes in Americans' Legal Rights
David Kravets

In this article, which appeared in the *Chicago Sun-Times* on September 8, 2002, David Kravets explains the basic changes to Americans' legal rights as a result of the passage of the Patriot Act. Kravets, the legal affairs correspondent for the Associated Press, has been covering state and federal courts and their rulings for more than a decade.

The government has imposed many new limits on Americans' legal rights as it fights a war on terror, fundamentally altering the nation's delicate balance between liberty and security.

The changes—including the authority in terror cases to imprison Americans indefinitely, without charges or defense lawyers—substantially expand the government's ability to investigate, arrest, try and detain.

They grant law enforcement easier access to Americans' personal lives while keeping many government operations secret. And the idea that law-abiding citizens can freely associate with other law-abiding citizens without the threat of government surveillance no longer holds.

The Bush administration will not abuse these far-reaching powers, said Viet Dinh, an assistant U.S. attorney general: "I think security exists for liberty to flourish and liberty cannot exist without order and security," Dinh said.

Still, even supporters are wary.   5

"One has to pray that those powers are used responsibly," said Charlie Intriago, a former federal prosecutor and money laundering expert in Miami who said the new provisions could help intercept terrorists' finances.

The USA Patriot Act, hurriedly adopted by Congress and signed by Bush six weeks after the terror attacks, tipped laws in the government's favor in 350 subject areas involving 40 federal agencies.

The Bush administration has since imposed other legal changes without congressional consent, such as allowing federal agents to monitor attorney-client conversations in federal prisons, and encouraging bureaucrats to deny public access to many documents requested under the Freedom of Information Act.

The FBI can monitor political and religious meetings inside the United States now, even when there's no suspicion a crime has been committed—a policy abandoned in the 1970s amid outrage over J. Edgar Hoover's surveillance of the Rev. Martin Luther King Jr. and other activists.

The American Civil Liberties Union, media companies and   10
other organizations are challenging many of the changes.

"Are we any safer as a nation? I don't know," said Anthony Romero, the ACLU's executive director. "Are we less free? You bet."

In a poll conducted for The Associated Press by ICR/International Communications Research of Media, Pa., 63 percent said they were concerned that the new measures could end up restricting Americans' individual freedoms. Of those, 30 percent of the 1,001 responding adults were "very concerned" and 33 percent "somewhat concerned."

The telephone poll taken Aug. 2–6 has an error margin of 3 percentage points.

"I don't think government should interfere too much in our lives," said Kelly Beaver, 19, a student in North Carolina.

15   But Arizona caregiver Daniel Martell, 42, said he wasn't concerned at all—"To me, it's not restricting my freedom. There's all kinds of things going on every day to protect freedom."

Americans may never know how valid their concerns are, since everything about terror-related investigations is secret. The administration isn't required to disclose how it is implementing the fundamental changes, making oversight—let alone court challenges—exceedingly difficult.

The Patriot Act allows "black bag" searches for medical and financial records, computer and telephone communications, even for the books Americans borrow from the library.

Judges approve these top-secret warrants in the secret Foreign Intelligence Surveillance Act court. Established to target "foreign powers," FISA now also applies to U.S. citizens, who are no longer protected by the bread-and-butter legal standard of probable cause—prosecutors need only say the search will assist a terror probe.

Dinh credited these changes with reducing the risk of terror, but he wouldn't reveal specifics. "Many of our successes will have to be celebrated in secret," he said.

20   What is known is that thousands of Middle Eastern men who entered the United States since 2000 have been questioned and detained. Many were quietly deported after immigration hearings that are no longer public.

The administration is appealing a judge's order to reveal their names, saying the president's prosecution of the terror war can't be challenged, and that civilian courts have no authority over their detention.

Some of the new surveillance measures expire by 2006, but Congress can extend them if the open-ended war on terror continues.

"At what time is this war over?" Dinh said. "That I cannot answer."

CHANGES TO LEGAL RIGHTS

Some of the fundamental changes to Americans' legal rights by the Bush administration and the USA Patriot Act following the terror attacks:

- **Freedom of association:**
  Government may monitor religious and political institutions without suspecting criminal activity to assist terror investigation.
- **Freedom of information:**
  Government has closed once-public immigration hearings, has secretly detained hundreds of people without charges, and has encouraged bureaucrats to resist public records requests.
- **Freedom of speech:**
  Government may prosecute librarians or keepers of any other records if they tell anyone that the government subpoenaed information related to a terror investigation.
- **Right to legal representation:**
  Government may monitor federal prison jailhouse conversations between attorneys and clients, and deny lawyers to Americans accused of crimes.
- **Freedom from unreasonable searches:**
  Government may search and seize Americans' papers and effects without probable cause to assist terror investigation.
- **Right to a speedy and public trial:**
  Government may jail Americans indefinitely without a trial.
- **Right to liberty:**
  Americans may be jailed without being charged or being able to confront witnesses against them.

Suggestions for Writing and Discussion

1. According to David Kravets, what are some of the significant changes in the legal rights of Americans since the events of September 11, 2001?
2. Kelly Beaver, a student from North Carolina, is quoted in the article as saying, "I don't think government should interfere too much in our lives." Do you agree or disagree with her? Explain.

Conservative Backlash
Editorial, *Baltimore Sun*

This editorial, which appeared in the *Baltimore Sun* on Friday, August 22, 2003, traces the growing concern about the powers of the Patriot Act not only among liberals but also among some of the country's best-known conservative organizations.

John Ashcroft must be sweating bullets.

A grass-roots drive to resist the attorney general's broad expansion of police powers in the name of fighting terrorism has picked up so much support in the American heartland it threatens not only repeal of the legislation but political damage to President Bush as well.

Try as he might, Mr. Ashcroft can no longer dismiss opponents of the USA Patriot Act as a small but whiny band of liberals. Some of the nation's top conservative groups as well as a huge majority of the Republican-led House of Representatives—in other words, the Bush base—are now leading the drive to eliminate portions of the law that allow secret spying on anyone.

So the attorney general is out stumping in the presidential battleground states of Pennsylvania, Ohio and Michigan, as well as the first caucus state of Iowa, trying to sell the Patriot Act as vital to the war on terrorism while a Justice Department Web site seeks to dispel "myths" put out by critics.

5   This spin control performance is offensive both in its message and its tactics. Mr. Ashcroft, who bullied Congress into granting law enforcement agencies sweeping new powers while the nation was still traumatized by the Sept. 11 attacks, is once again using fear to get his way.

Most outrageously, he asserts that the nation is "safer" now because of the broader police powers and that "if we knew then what we know now, we would have passed the Patriot Act six months before Sept. 11."

Well, perhaps—if the FBI, so hidebound, so risk-averse and so technologically outmoded that it ignored many clues within its grasp, would somehow have been transformed. But the new police powers in the Patriot Act don't fix any of that.

In his stump speech, Mr. Ashcroft doesn't address the concerns that have inspired three states and 154 local governments, including Baltimore, to pass resolutions in protest of the Patriot Act. Among these is the power granted to police to secretly obtain records of phone calls, Internet use, library visits and other personal information without probable cause of criminal activity.

Lawmakers also worry about "sneak and peek" searches of homes and property, about which targets learn much later.

The Justice Department's Patriot Act Web site (www   10 .lifeandliberty.gov) maintains that "terrorism investigators have no interest in the library habits of ordinary Americans" and that searches must be secret so terrorists don't get tipped off. But Patriot Act powers are not limited to terrorism investigations.

Mr. Ashcroft speaks only to selected audiences not open to the public. He wants U.S. attorneys in each state to take questions in town meetings, trying to use prosecutors as lobbyists. Thomas M. DiBiagio, the U.S. attorney for Maryland who considers himself politically independent, has no such plans.

The Ashcroft road show seems likely to backfire, and actually fuel the drive for a thorough review by Congress of the Patriot Act to weed out its onerous parts. Mr. Ashcroft should be weeded out as well.

Suggestions for Writing and Discussion

1. This editorial discusses the responses of both liberals and conservatives to the Patriot Act. What is the definition of the term "liberal" when it is used to describe a political philosophy? What is the definition of the term "conservative" when it is used to describe a political philosophy?

2. What concerns might be raised by the provision of the Patriot Act that allows government agencies to secretly examine records of phone calls as well as an individual's use of the Internet or of library resources?

Scientists Raise Concerns about Impact of Patriot Act

Sandra Guy

Sandra Guy, a freelance writer and business reporter, explains why leading scientists are finding fault with the Patriot Act. Guy's article, which appeared in the *Chicago Sun-Times* on July 30, 2003, argues that the controversial act angers not only journalists and civil libertarians but also those who work within the scientific and technological communities.

It is little surprise that President Bush's controversial USA Patriot Act has enraged journalists and civil libertarians, but scientists are now voicing their dismay about its consequences.

Critics cited in an article titled "Biotech's Big Chill," in *Technology Review*'s July-August editions, blast the Patriot Act and ensuing federal regulations. They argue that the new laws unfairly restrict scientific research and impose enormous paperwork burdens on colleges, which must now monitor foreign students.

As an example, many microbiologists are reported to be worried that the federal government's requirement that anthrax samples be inventoried and locked up, along with other new security rules, will hinder basic research, biotechnology and even efforts to stop bioterrorism.

Linked with these concerns are obstacles that foreign students encounter in obtaining visas to study here, and, in some cases, to be involved in scientific research.

5 The Illinois Institute of Technology has run smack into the problem, since 17 percent of the undergraduate population at the Chicago university is foreign-born, and 43 percent of graduate students are from overseas.

Because the federal government now prohibits citizens of blacklisted "enemy" countries from working in high-security sites, two IIT students have been locked out of working at Argonne National Laboratory, said Ali Cinar, Ph.D., vice provost for research and dean of the graduate college.

As a result, the students have had to revamp their research, since they no longer can conduct necessary experiments and have no access to equipment critical to their work.

Cinar believes the government should more carefully balance security risks with the benefits the United States receives by educating the world's most talented science students, many of whom become naturalized citizens or who return to take leadership roles in their home countries.

A State Department spokeswoman said 80 percent of the foreign students who undergo security review complete the process within two weeks.

10 A spokesman for the Department of Homeland Security reiterated the government's stance that it must know who is entering the country and whether they pose a danger to national security.

Yet Cinar is concerned that students will decide to avoid certain fields of study because they will run into security hassles.

Cinar said he believes that politicians must understand the long-term consequences of the rules they impose, especially those that are applied ham-handedly.

"There are a lot of inefficiencies in the system," Cinar said. "Hopefully, they will disappear."

Students also are running into a security bureaucracy before they start their studies.

The Patriot Act requires colleges and universities to track all   15 foreign students, including prospective students, and visiting faculty and researchers who enter the country, by logging details about them into a federal database, called the Student Exchange Visitor Information System.

The details include where a student lives, if the student moves, the student's intended major, whether he or she drops below a full course-load, and whether the student brings a spouse or child to the U.S., among other details.

Celia Bergman, director of IIT's International Center, said her office is inundated with data entry duties, which take time away from cultural aspects of the job such as student exchanges.

"From some countries, the background checks are taking months," said Cinar, who worries that students will decide to pursue higher education in Canada, Australia, U.K. or another country because of the restrictions here.

Suggestions for Writing and Discussion

1. What are two reasons that some scientists are arguing against the Patriot Act?
2. What effects might the Patriot Act have on students from other countries who are studying in the United States?

Topics for Writing and Discussion

1. What details of the Statue of Liberty in this advertisement differ from the actual statue? What do these differences suggest about the intention and message of the ad?
2. Each of the sentences that appear under the image of the altered Statue of Liberty begins with "we." To whom does the "we" refer?

We will roll up our sleeves.

We will move forward together.

We will overcome.

We will never forget.

A message from

A full-page ad by the General Electric company, run by the New York Times *and the* Washington Post *on September 21, 2001*

Making Connections: Synthesis and Analysis

1. After reading David Kravets's article and the accompanying list of "Changes to Legal Rights," write a summary explaining some of the changes in the rights of Americans following the passage of the Patriot Act.

2. After reading the three articles on the Patriot Act, what do you think are the main reasons that support having such an act? How do these reasons relate to the events of 9/11? To what extent do you think these changes in Americans' rights are a justifiable response to terrorist attacks?

3. After reading these articles, explain the main arguments against the Patriot Act. How convincing do you find these arguments? Focus on one or two points of argument and explain your response—either pro or con—in detail.

EXTENDED CONNECTIONS: FOR CRITICAL THINKING, WRITING, AND RESEARCH

1. Through careful analysis of one selection from this chapter (pre-9/11 or post-9/11), find a research question related to the idea of the American dream. For instance, how have the events of 9/11 affected the dream of equality in the United States, or how have the events of 9/11 affected the way Americans view the rights granted to them by the Constitution and the Bill of Rights? After exploring your question through various sources (books, online databases, interviews), formulate a thesis that explains the viewpoint you now hold. Write an argument supporting that viewpoint.

2. Compare the views of the American flag that are suggested in the photo essay, as well as in the essays in the section titled "What Does the Flag Mean?" Then do research on the various ways the flag has been used to register protest (for instance, during the Vietnam War era or during Civil Rights actions). Consult various sources (books, online databases, interviews) and formulate a thesis leading to an argument for or against using the flag in such protests.

3. Both the controversy regarding the flag and the controversy regarding the Patriot Act relate to First Amendment rights. Find a copy of the entire text of the First Amendment in the

Bill of Rights (the first ten amendments to the Constitution of the United States). Then formulate a research question related to another recent First Amendment controversy, such as a controversy related to rock music or videos or to highly violent or sexually explicit films. After exploring this controversy through various sources (books, online databases, interviews, DVDs, or films), formulate a thesis that explains the viewpoint you now hold. Write an argument supporting that viewpoint.

CHAPTER **5**

··

Passing and Failing: Education, Formal and Informal

INTRODUCTION

Why is it that we learn? Is it because we are born naturally bright and curious? Is it because our parents expect us to learn? Is it because one teacher—or an assortment of them—looked at our learning as the single most important factor in our development as human beings? Whatever answers we find to these questions are important. However, the answers to the other side of this question are equally as important and, in the balance of things, much more troubling: Why is it that we do NOT learn?

In this chapter, we see how learning depends on a combination of factors. In the essays that reflect three past educational experiences, we see how a young person's curiosity played a key role. Eudora Welty is "clamorous to learn," while Frederick Douglass's appetite for learning began with a quest to gain knowledge not only for his own sake but for the sake of his whole race. Malcolm X sees that unless he can decipher the words in a book, he is left out of the white man's American system. In addition to a thirst for knowledge, though, other factors contributed to the education of these writers, both in and out of the classroom. They all were motivated by personal issues or by historical factors, and they all had teachers whom they found in books, on the streets, or in a schoolroom.

Thus, the stage is set for probing the ways in which children today learn best—and what factors impede their road to learning. While men had the educational advantage over women in the early years of our country, we're seeing a shift in this balance of power today. As Elaine McArdle shows in her piece, "The Lost Boys," female students outnumber their male counterparts by nearly one-third. In "The New Gender Gap," Michelle Conlin shows how females outscore males in the elementary and high school levels as well—a trend that a Harvard Medical School psychologist calls "a national crisis." What's the cause of this crisis, and how can all students, regardless of gender, succeed in school? Some people argue for single-sex schools ("With Fewer Distractions, Students Will Do Better"), but is that really the best answer?

Not only is gender a factor in a student's education, but as recent studies have shown, children of poverty in America do not receive the same educational benefits as children of middle-class status. In fact, many educators report an inequality based on race and ethnicity that mirrors the days prior to the 1960s, when federal laws mandated integration and justice in our nation's schools. Sonia Nieto, a college professor, raises poignant questions about the reality of social justice in our educational system, while Richard Williams, a member of the Lakota Indian tribe, questions the practicality of the "No Child Left Behind" initiative for children on reservations. Finally, Suzanne Fields recommends charter schools as an equitable solution for inner-city children who live in poverty. Her recommendation raises the question of whether such a solution encourages "separate but equal" education. In the end, we must all ask an even more probing question, the answer to which is anything but simple: When it comes to educating our children, how well are we really doing?

· *THEN* ·

SETTING THE CONTEXT: EDUCATION THEN

Suggestions for Prereading or Journal Writing

1. Think back to your own early school days, and write a reflection as to how you felt about school and learning and how these impressions may have changed as you advanced in years. Looking back on it now, who or what would you

say contributed most to your success as a student? Who or what kept you from learning as much as you could have?

2. What's your initial reaction to the photograph of the one-room schoolhouse in this chapter? Imagine that you are a student in this school. Who are your classmates? What, specifically, are you learning? What might you have had then that you do not have in your education today? What might you have been missing then that you have today? What conclusions can you draw between education "then" and your own education now?

A nineteenth-century schoolroom

Topics for Writing and Discussion

1. Think about this room in terms of symbolic value. What do the following specifics symbolize about America's past education: American flag, wood-burning stove, table and bench, large open windows, sunlight, open space, bare walls?

2. How does this room compare/contrast with a typical classroom today? Through this comparison, what conclusions can you draw about what we've gained in education and what we've lost?

Learning to Read and Write
Frederick Douglass (1818–1895)

Although Frederick Douglass was born a slave and was, by law, forbidden to read or write, as this excerpt from his autobiography, *Narrative of the Life of Frederick Douglass,* reveals, once the seed for learning was planted in the soil of his soul, he did everything in his power to continue educating himself so that one day he might be freed from the white man's laws which imprisoned him. Eventually, he escaped from his owners in Maryland and became a freedman and a Northern advocate for blacks who were still enslaved in the South. That Douglass, through his own ingenuity and persistence, achieved such a high level of reading, writing, and thinking is amazing. And it was through this sophisticated and rhetorical understanding of the English language that Douglass was able to help free his people and alter for the better the course of America's future.

I lived in Master Hugh's family about seven years. During this time, I succeeded in learning to read and write. In accomplishing this, I was compelled to resort to various stratagems. I had no regular teacher. My mistress, who had kindly commenced to instruct me, had, in compliance with the advice and direction of her husband, not only ceased to instruct, but had set her face against my being instructed by any one else. It is due, however, to my mistress to say of her, that she did not adopt this course of treatment immediately. She at first lacked the depravity indispensable to shutting me up in mental darkness. It was at least necessary for her to have some training in the exercise of irresponsible power, to make her equal to the task of treating me as though I were a brute.

My mistress was, as I have said, a kind and tender-hearted woman; and in the simplicity of her soul she commenced, when I first went to live with her, to treat me as she supposed one human being ought to treat another. In entering upon the duties of a slaveholder, she did not seem to perceive that I sustained to her the relation of a mere chattel, and that for her to treat me as a human being was not only wrong, but dangerously so. Slavery proved as injurious to her as it did to me. When I went there, she was a pious, warm, and tender-hearted woman. There was no sorrow or suffering for which she had not a tear. She had bread for the hungry, clothes for the naked, and comfort for every mourner that came within her reach. Slavery soon proved its ability to divest her of these heavenly qualities. Under its influence, the tender heart became stone, and the lamblike disposition gave way to one of tigerlike fierceness. The first step in her downward course was in her ceasing to instruct me. She now commenced to practise her husband's precepts. She finally became even more violent in her opposition than her husband himself. She was not satisfied with simply doing as well as he had commanded; she seemed anxious to do better. Nothing seemed to make her more angry than to see me with a newspaper. She seemed to think that here lay the danger. I have had her rush at me with a face made all up of fury, and snatch from me a newspaper, in a manner that fully revealed her apprehension. She was an apt woman; and a little experience soon demonstrated, to her satisfaction, that education and slavery were incompatible with each other.

From this time I was most narrowly watched. If I was in a separate room any considerable length of time, I was sure to be suspected of having a book, and was at once called to give an account of myself. All this, however, was too late. The first step had been taken. Mistress, in teaching me the alphabet, had given me the *inch,* and no precaution could prevent me from taking the *ell.*

The plan which I adopted, and the one by which I was most successful, was that of making friends of all the little white boys whom I met in the street. As many of these as I could, I converted into teachers. With their kindly aid, obtained at different times and in different places, I finally succeeded in learning to read. When I was sent on errands, I always took my book with me, and by doing one part of my errand quickly, I found time to get a lesson before my return. I used also to carry bread with me, enough of which was always in the house, and to which I was always welcome; for I was much better off in this regard than many of the poor white children in our neighborhood. This bread I used to bestow upon the hungry little urchins, who, in return, would give me that more valuable bread of knowledge. I am strongly tempted to give the names of two or three of those little boys, as a testimonial of the gratitude and affection I bear them; but prudence forbids:—not that it would injure me, but it might embarrass them; for it is almost an unpardonable offence to teach slaves to read in this Christian country. It is enough to say of the dear little fellows, that they lived on Philpot Street, very near Durgin and Bailey's ship-yard. I used to talk this matter of slavery over with them. I would sometimes say to them, I wished I could be as free as they would be when they got to be men. "You will be free as soon as you are twenty-one, *but I am a slave for life!* Have not I as good a right to be free as you have?" These words used to trouble them; they would express for me the liveliest sympathy, and console me with the hope that something would occur by which I might be free.

5   I was now about twelve years old, and the thought of being *a slave for life* began to bear heavily upon my heart. Just about this time, I got hold of a book entitled "The Columbian Orator." Every opportunity I got, I used to read this book. Among much of other interesting matter, I found in it a dialogue between a master and his slave. The slave was represented as having run away from his master three times. The dialogue represented the conversation which took place between them, when the slave was retaken the third time. In this dialogue, the whole argument in behalf of slavery was brought forward by the master, all of which was disposed of by the slave. The slave was made to say some very smart as well as impressive things in reply to his master—things which had the desired though unexpected effect; for the conversation resulted in the voluntary emancipation of the slave on the part of the master.

In the same book, I met with one of Sheridan's mighty speeches on and in behalf of Catholic emancipation. These were choice documents to me. I read them over and over again with unabated interest. They gave tongue to interesting thoughts of my own soul, which had frequently flashed through my mind, and died away for want of utterance. The moral which I gained from the dialogue was the power of truth over the conscience of even a slaveholder. What I got from Sheridan was a bold denunciation of slavery, and a powerful vindication of human rights. The reading of these documents enabled me to utter my thoughts, and to meet the arguments brought forward to sustain slavery; but while they relieved me of one difficulty, they brought on another even more painful than the one of which I was relieved. The more I read, the more I was led to abhor and detest my enslavers. I could regard them in no other light than a band of successful robbers, who had left their homes, and gone to Africa, and stolen us from our homes, and in a strange land reduced us to slavery. I loathed them as being the meanest as well as the most wicked of men. As I read and contemplated the subject, behold! that very discontentment which Master Hugh had predicted would follow my learning to read had already come, to torment and sting my soul to unutterable anguish. As I writhed under it, I would at times feel that learning to read had been a curse rather than a blessing. It had given me a view of my wretched condition, without the remedy. It opened my eyes to the horrible pit, but to no ladder upon which to get out. In moments of agony, I envied my fellow-slaves for their stupidity. I have often wished myself a beast. I preferred the condition of the meanest reptile to my own. Any thing, no matter what, to get rid of thinking! It was this everlasting thinking of my condition that tormented me. There was no getting rid of it. It was pressed upon me by every object within sight or hearing, animate or inanimate. The silver trump of freedom had roused my soul to eternal wakefulness. Freedom now appeared, to disappear no more forever. It was heard in every sound, and seen in every thing. It was ever present to torment me with a sense of my wretched condition. I saw nothing without seeing it, I heard nothing without hearing it, and felt nothing without feeling it. It looked from every star, it smiled in every calm, breathed in every wind, and moved in every storm.

I often found myself regretting my own existence, and wishing myself dead; and but for the hope of being free, I have no doubt but that I should have killed myself, or done something for which I should have been killed. While in this state of mind, I was eager to hear any one speak of slavery. I was a ready listener. Every little while, I could hear something about the abolitionists. It was some time before I found what the word meant. It was always used in such connections as to make it an interesting word to me. If a slave ran away and succeeded in getting clear, or if a slave killed his master, set fire to a barn, or did any thing very wrong in the mind of a slaveholder, it was spoken of as the fruit of *abolition.* Hearing the word in this connection very often, I set about learning what it meant. The dictionary afforded me little or no help. I found it was "the act of abolishing;" but then I did not know what was to be abolished. Here I was perplexed. I did not dare to ask any one about its meaning, for I was satisfied that it was something they wanted me to know very little about. After a patient waiting, I got one of our city papers, containing an account of the number of petitions from the north, praying for the abolition of slavery in the District of Columbia, and of the slave trade between the States. From this time I understood the words *abolition* and *abolitionist,* and always drew near when that word was spoken, expecting to hear something of importance to myself and fellow-slaves. The light broke in upon me by degrees. I went one day down on the wharf of Mr. Waters; and seeing two Irishmen unloading a scow of stone, I went, unasked, and helped them. When we had finished, one of them came to me and asked me if I were a slave. I told him I was. He asked, "Are ye a slave for life?" I told him that I was. The good Irishman seemed to be deeply affected by the statement. He said to the other that it was a pity so fine a little fellow as myself should be a slave for life. He said it was a shame to hold me. They both advised me to run away to the north; that I should find friends there, and that I should be free. I pretended not to be interested in what they said, and treated them as if I did not understand them; for I feared they might be treacherous. White men have been known to encourage slaves to escape, and then, to get the reward, catch them and return them to their masters. I was afraid that these seemingly good men might use me so; but I nevertheless remembered their advice, and from that time I resolved to run away. I looked forward to a time at which it would be safe for me to escape. I was too young to think of doing so immediately; besides, I wished to learn how to write, as I might have occasion to write my own pass. I consoled myself with the hope that I should one day find a good chance. Meanwhile, I would learn to write.

The idea as to how I might learn to write was suggested to me by being in Durgin and Bailey's ship-yard, and frequently seeing the ship carpenters, after hewing, and getting a piece of timber ready for use, write on the timber the name of that part of the ship for which it was intended. When a piece of timber was intended for the larboard side, it would be marked thus—"L." When a piece was for the starboard side, it would be marked thus—"S." A piece for the larboard side forward, would be marked thus— "L. F." When a piece was for starboard side forward, it would be marked thus—"S. F." For larboard aft, it would be marked thus— "L. A." For starboard aft, it would be marked thus—"S. A." I soon learned the names of these letters, and for what they were intended when placed upon a piece of timber in the shipyard. I immediately commenced copying them, and in a short time was able to make the four letters named. After that, when I met with any boy who I knew could write, I would tell him I could write as well as he. The next word would be, "I don't believe you. Let me see you try it." I would then make the letters which I had been so fortunate as to learn, and ask him to beat that. In this way I got a good many lessons in writing, which it is quite possible I should never have gotten in any other way. During this time, my copy-book was the board fence, brick wall, and pavement; my pen and ink was a lump of chalk. With these, I learned mainly how to write. I then commenced and continued copying the Italics in Webster's Spelling Book, until I could make them all without looking on the book. By this time, my little Master Thomas had gone to school, and learned how to write, and had written over a number of copybooks. These had been brought home, and shown to some of our near neighbors, and then laid aside. My mistress used to go to class meeting at the Wilk Street meetinghouse every Monday afternoon, and leave me to take care of the house. When left thus, I used to spend the time in writing in the spaces left in Master Thomas's copy-book, copying what he had written. I continued to do this until I could write a hand very similar to that of Master Thomas. Thus, after a long, tedious effort for years, I finally succeeded in learning how to write.

Suggestions for Writing and Discussion

1. What point does Douglass make about the change in his mistress's attitude toward teaching him to read? In what way might this point, made more than 150 years ago, still be applicable to Americans today?

2. What does Douglass mean when he writes, "The light broke in upon me by degrees"? What does the "light" refer to, and why is it important that this happened in "degrees"?

3. Based on the anecdotes that Douglass provides here, how would you characterize the white southern male of Douglass's time?

4. Examine all of the factors that Douglass needed in order to succeed in his pursuit of reading and writing. Which of these factors are present in your own educational journey today and which ones are lacking? What do you make of these differences?

Clamorous to Learn

Eudora Welty (1909–2001)

Born and raised in Jackson, Mississippi, Eudora Welty is one of America's most honored and prolific southern writers. The following essay, which is from her autobiography, *One Writer's Beginnings* (1984), reveals how one's early influences, including books, parents, and teachers, come to shape one's attitude and aptitude toward learning. In fact, books were so valued in Welty's family that when the house caught on fire, Welty's mother made sure that the books were safely out of the house before she left herself. Clearly, this same passion for learning burned in her daughter's heart as well.

From the first I was clamorous to learn—I wanted to know and begged to be told not so much what, or how, or why, or where, as when. How soon?

> Pear tree by the garden gate,
> How much longer must I wait?

This rhyme from one of my nursery books was the one that spoke for me. But I lived not at all unhappily in this craving, for my wild curiosity was in large part suspense, which carries its own secret pleasure. And so one of the godmothers of fiction was already bending over me.

When I was five years old, I knew the alphabet, I'd been vaccinated (for smallpox), and I could read. So my mother walked across the street to Jefferson Davis Grammar School and asked the principal if she would allow me to enter the first grade after Christmas.

"Oh, all right," said Miss Duling. "Probably the best thing you could do with her."

Miss Duling, a lifelong subscriber to perfection, was a figure of authority, the most whole-souled I have ever come to know. She was a dedicated schoolteacher who denied herself all she might have done or whatever other way she might have lived (this possibility was the last that could have occurred to us, her subjects in school). I believe she came of well-off people, well-educated, in Kentucky, and certainly old photographs show she was a beautiful, high-spirited-looking young lady—and came down to Jackson to its new grammar school that was going begging for a principal. She must have earned next to nothing; Mississippi then as now was the nation's lowest-ranking state economically, and our legislature has always shown a painfully loud reluctance to give money to public education. That challenge *brought* her.

5   In the long run she came into touch, as teacher or principal, with three generations of Jacksonians. My parents had not, but everybody else's parents had gone to school to her. She'd taught

most of our leaders somewhere along the line. When she wanted something done—some civic oversight corrected, some injustice made right overnight, or even a tree spared that the fool telephone people were about to cut down—she telephoned the mayor, or the chief of police, or the president of the power company, or the head doctor at the hospital, or the judge in charge of a case, or whoever, and calling them by their first names, *told* them. It is impossible to imagine her meeting with anything less than compliance. The ringing of her brass bell from their days at Davis School would still be in their ears. She also proposed a spelling match between the fourth grade at Davis School and the Mississippi Legislature, who went through with it; and that told the Legislature.

Her standards were very high and of course inflexible, her authority was total; why *wouldn't* this carry with it a brass bell that could be heard ringing for a block in all directions? That bell belonged to the figure of Miss Duling as though it grew directly out of her right arm, as wings grew out of an angel or a tail out of the devil. When we entered, marching, into her school, by strictest teaching, surveillance, and order we learned grammar, arithmetic, spelling, reading, writing, and geography; and she, not the teachers, I believe, wrote out the examinations: need I tell you, they were "hard."

She's not the only teacher who has influenced me, but Miss Duling, in some fictional shape or form, has stridden into a larger part of my work than I'd realized until now. She emerges in my perhaps inordinate number of schoolteacher characters. I loved those characters in the writing. But I did not, in life, love Miss Duling. I was afraid of her high-arched bony nose, her eyebrows lifted in half-circles above her hooded, brilliant eyes, and of the Kentucky R's in her speech, and the long steps she took in her hightop shoes. I did nothing but fear her bearing-down authority, and did not connect this (as of course we were meant to) with our own need or desire to learn, perhaps because I already had this wish, and did not need to be driven.

She was impervious to lies or foolish excuses or the insufferable plea of not knowing any better. She wasn't going to have any frills, either, at Davis School. When a new governor moved into the mansion, he sent his daughter to Davis School; her name was Lady Rachel Conner. Miss Duling at once called the governor to the telephone and told him, "She'll be plain Rachel here."

Miss Duling dressed as plainly as a Pilgrim on a Thanksgiving poster we made in the schoolroom, in a longish black-and-white checked gingham dress, a bright thick wool sweater the red of a railroad lantern—she'd knitted it herself—black stockings and her narrow elegant feet in black hightop shoes with heels you could hear coming, rhythmical as a parade drum down the hall. Her silky black curly hair was drawn back out of curl, fastened by high combs, and knotted behind. She carried her spectacles on a gold chain hung around her neck. Her gaze was in general sweeping, then suddenly at the point of concentration upon you. With a swing of her bell that took her whole right arm and shoulder, she rang it, militant and impartial, from the head of the front steps of Davis School when it was time for us all to line up, girls on one side, boys on the other. We were to march past her into the school building, while the fourth-grader she nabbed played time on the piano, mostly to a tune we could have skipped to, but we didn't skip into Davis School.

10   Little recess (open-air exercises) and big recess (lunch-boxes from home opened and eaten on the grass, on the girls' side and the boys' side of the yard) and dismissal were also regulated by Miss Duling's bell. The bell was also used to catch us off guard with fire drill.

It was examinations that drove my wits away, as all emergencies do. Being expected to measure up was paralyzing. I failed to make 100 on my spelling exam because I missed one word and that word was "uncle." Mother, as I knew she would, took it personally. "You couldn't spell *uncle*? When you've got those five perfectly splendid uncles in West Virginia? What would *they* say to that?"

It was never that Mother wanted me to beat my classmates in grades; what she wanted was for me to have my answers right. It was unclouded perfection I was up against.

My father was much more tolerant of possible error. He only said, as he steeply and impeccably sharpened my pencils on examination morning, "Now just keep remembering: the examinations were made out for the *average* student to pass. That's the majority. And if the majority can pass, think how much better *you* can do."

I looked to my mother, who had her own opinions about the majority. My father wished to treat it with respect, she didn't. I'd been born left-handed, but the habit was broken when I entered the first grade in Davis School. My father had insisted. He pointed out that everything in life had been made for the convenience of right-handed people, because they were the majority, and he often used "what the majority wants" as a criterion for what was for the best. My mother said she could not promise him, could not promise him at all, that I wouldn't stutter as a consequence. Mother had been born left-handed too; her family consisted of five left-handed brothers, a left-handed mother, and a father who could write with both hands at the same time, also backwards and forwards and upside down, different words with each hand. She had been broken of it when she was young, and she said she used to stutter.

"But you still stutter," I'd remind her, only to hear her say 15 loftily, "You should have heard me when I was your age."

In my childhood days, a great deal of stock was put, in general, in the value of doing well in school. Both daily newspapers in Jackson saw the honor roll as news and published the lists, and the grades, of all the honor students. The city fathers gave the children who made the honor roll free season tickets to the baseball games down at the grandstand. We all attended and all worshiped some player on the Jackson Senators: I offered up my 100's in arithmetic and spelling, reading and writing, attendance and, yes, deportment—I must have been a prig!—to Red McDermott, the third baseman. And our happiness matched that of knowing Miss Duling was on her summer vacation, far, far away in Kentucky.

Every school week, visiting teachers came on their days for special lessons. On Mondays, the singing teacher blew into the room fresh from the early outdoors, singing in her high soprano "How do you do?" to do-mi-sol-do, and we responded in chorus from our desks, "I'm ve-ry well" to do-sol-mi-do. Miss Johnson taught us rounds—"Row row row your boat gently down the stream"—and "Little Sir Echo," with half the room singing the words and the other half being the echo, a competition. She was from the North, and she was the one who wanted us all to stop the Christmas carols and see snow. The snow falling that morning outside the window was the first most of us had ever seen, and Miss Johnson threw up the window and held out wide her own black cape and caught flakes on it and ran, as fast as she could go, up and down the aisles to show us the real thing before it melted.

Thursday was Miss Eyrich and Miss Eyrich was Thursday. She came to give us physical training. She wasted no time on nonsense. Without greeting, we were marched straight outside and summarily divided into teams (no choosing sides), put on the mark, and ordered to get set for a relay race. Miss Eyrich cracked out "Go!" Dread rose in my throat. My head swam. Here was my turn, nearly upon me. (Wait, have I been touched—was that slap the touch? Go on! Do I go on without our passing a word? What word? Now am I racing too fast to turn around? Now I'm nearly home, but where is the hand waiting for mine to touch? Am I too late? Have I lost the whole race for our side?) I lost the relay race for our side before I started, through living ahead of myself, dreading to make my start, feeling too late prematurely, and standing transfixed by emergency, trying to think of a password. Thursdays still can make me hear Miss Eyrich's voice. "On your mark—get set—GO!"

Very composedly and very slowly, the art teacher, who visited each room on Fridays, paced the aisle and looked down over your shoulder at what you were drawing for her. This was Miss Ascher. Coming from behind you, her deep, resonant voice reached you without being a word at all, but a sort of purr. It was much the sound given out by our family doctor when he read the thermometer and found you were running a slight fever: "Um-hm. Um-hm." Both alike, they let you go right ahead with it.

20   The school toilets were in the boys' and girls' respective basements. After Miss Duling had rung to dismiss school, a friend and I were making our plans for Saturday from adjoining cubicles. "Can you come spend the day with me?" I called out, and she called back, "I might could."

"Who—said—MIGHT—COULD?" It sounded like "Fe Fi Fo Fum!"

We both were petrified, for we knew whose deep measured words those were that came from just outside our doors. That was the voice of Mrs. McWillie, who taught the other fourth grade across the hall from ours. She was not even our teacher, but a very heavy, stern lady who dressed entirely in widow's weeds with a pleated black shirtwaist with a high net collar and velvet ribbon, and a black skirt to her ankles, with black circles under her eyes and a mournful, Presbyterian expression. We children took her to be a hundred years old. We held still.

"You might as well tell me," continued Mrs. McWillie. "I'm going to plant myself right here and wait till you come out. Then I'll see who it was I heard saying 'MIGHT-COULD.'"

If Elizabeth wouldn't go out, of course I wouldn't either. We knew her to be a teacher who would not flinch from standing there in the basement all afternoon, perhaps even all day Saturday. So we surrendered and came out. I priggishly hoped Elizabeth would clear it up which child it was—it wasn't me.

"So it's you." She regarded us as a brace, made no distinction: 25 whoever didn't say it was guilty by association. "If I ever catch you down here one more time saying 'MIGHT-COULD,' I'm going to carry it to Miss Duling. You'll be kept in every day for a week! I hope you're both sufficiently ashamed of yourselves?" Saying "might-could" was bad, but saying it in the basement made bad grammar a sin. I knew Presbyterians believed that you could go to Hell.

Mrs. McWillie never scared us into grammar, of course. It was my first-year Latin teacher in high school who made me discover I'd fallen in love with it. It took Latin to thrust me into bona fide alliance with words in their true meaning. Learning Latin (once I was free of Caesar) fed my love for words upon words, words in continuation and modification, and the beautiful, sober, accretion of a sentence. I could see the achieved sentence finally standing there, as real, intact, and built to stay as the Mississippi State Capitol at the top of my street, where I could walk through it on my way to school and hear underfoot the echo of its marble floor, and over me the bell of its rotunda.

On winter's rainy days, the schoolrooms would grow so dark that sometimes you couldn't see the figures on the blackboard. At that point, Mrs. McWillie, that stern fourth-grade teacher, would let her children close their books, and she would move, broad in widow's weeds like darkness itself, to the window and by what light there was she would stand and read aloud "The King of the Golden River." But I was excluded—in the other fourth grade, across the hall. Miss Louella Varnado, my teacher, didn't copy Mrs. McWillie; we had a spelling match: you could spell in the dark. I did not then suspect that there was any other way I could learn the story of "The King of the Golden River" than to have been assigned in the beginning to Mrs. McWillie's cowering fourth grade, then wait for her to treat you to it on the rainy day of her choice. I only now realize how much the treat depended, too, on there not having been money enough to put electric lights in Davis School. John Ruskin had to come in through courtesy of darkness. When in time I found the story in a book and read it to myself, it didn't seem to live up to my longings for a story with that name; as indeed, how could it?

Suggestions for Writing and Discussion

1. Overall, what three words do you think Welty would use to describe her reactions to her early school days?
2. If you were a student in Miss Duling's class, how would you react? Based on the specific details, words, and examples Welty uses to describe Miss Duling, what do you think she feels about Miss Duling? How does that compare/contrast with your reaction? To what do you attribute the differences if, indeed, there are any?
3. What role do Welty's parents play in her education? Who is the greater influence: Welty's parents, her teachers, or do both exert equal influence? Explain.
4. What is Welty's final point about John Ruskin's story, "The King of the Golden River," being read by Mrs. McWillie, the stern, fourth-grade teacher? What might Welty be saying about reading, modernization, and the way students learn?

Can Prison Be a School?[1]
Malcolm X (1925–1965)

In the early 1960s, Malcolm X, a passionate organizer of the Nation of Islam, encouraged black separatism as well as violence in order to rise up against "white aggressors." His awareness of slavery and injustice began in the 1940s when he discovered the power of books and words during the several years he spent in jail for committing a burglary. However, while he may have started out as a passionate, angry preacher, a journey to Mecca in 1964 transformed him into a man who believed that the sins of a few could not be attributed to a whole race. Indeed, as he matured and grew in his own education, he upheld the belief that people could—and should—be united as a whole, and that this unity could be achieved through peaceful means. This shift in philosophy was apparently

---

1. Editor's title

the reason he was murdered in 1965. Today, he is regarded as a scholar, a leader, and a hero by many Americans. In this selection taken from *The Autobiography of Malcolm X,* he explores ways that being in prison can lead to a hunger for learning.

Many who today hear me somewhere in person, or on television, or those who read something I've said, will think I went to school far beyond the eighth grade. This impression is due entirely to my prison studies.

It had really begun back in the Charlestown Prison, when Bimbi first made me feel envy of his stock of knowledge. Bimbi had always taken charge of any conversation he was in, and I had tried to emulate him. But every book I picked up had few sentences which didn't contain anywhere from one to nearly all of the words that might as well have been in Chinese. When I just skipped those words, of course, I really ended up with little idea of what the book said. So I had come to the Norfolk Prison Colony still going through only book-reading motions. Pretty soon, I would have quit even these motions, unless I had received the motivation that I did.

I saw that the best thing I could do was get hold of a dictionary—to study, to learn some words. I was lucky enough to reason also that I should try to improve my penmanship. It was sad. I couldn't even write in a straight line. It was both ideas together that moved me to request a dictionary along with some tablets and pencils from the Norfolk Prison Colony school.

I spent two days just riffling uncertainly through the dictionary's pages. I'd never realized so many words existed! I didn't know *which* words I needed to learn. Finally, just to start some kind of action, I began copying.

In my slow, painstaking, ragged handwriting, I copied into 5 my tablet everything printed on that first page, down to the punctuation marks.

I believe it took me a day. Then, aloud, I read back, to myself, everything I'd written on the tablet. Over and over, aloud, to myself, I read my own handwriting.

I woke up the next morning, thinking about those words—immensely proud to realize that not only had I written so much at one time, but I'd written words that I never knew were in the world. Moreover, with a little effort, I also could remember what many of these words meant. I reviewed the words whose meanings I didn't remember. Funny thing, from the dictionary first page right now, that "aardvark" springs my mind. The dictionary had a picture of it, a long-tailed, long-eared, burrowing African mammal, which lives off termites caught by sticking out its tongue as an anteater does for ants.

I was so fascinated that I went on—I copied the dictionary's next page. And the same experience came when I studied that. With every succeeding page, I also learned of people and places and events from history. Actually the dictionary is like a miniature encyclopedia. Finally the dictionary's A section had filled a whole tablet—and I went on into the B's. That was the way I started copying what eventually became the entire dictionary. It went a lot faster after so much practice helped me to pick up handwriting speed. Between what I wrote in my tablet, and writing letters, during the rest of my time in prison I would guess I wrote a million words.

I suppose it was inevitable that as my word-base broadened, I could for the first time pick up a book and read and now begin to understand what the book was saying. Anyone who has read a great deal can imagine the new world that opened. Let me tell you something: from then until I left that prison, in every free moment I had, if I was not reading in the library, I was reading on my bunk. You couldn't have gotten me out of books with a wedge. Between Mr. Muhammad's teachings, my correspondence, my visitors—usually Ella and Reginald—and my reading of books, months passed without my even thinking about being imprisoned. In fact, up to then, I never had been so truly free in my life.

10   The Norfolk Prison Colony's library was in the school building. A variety of classes was taught there by instructors who came from such places as Harvard and Boston universities. The weekly debates between inmate teams were also held in the school building. You would be astonished to know how worked up convict debaters and audiences would get over subjects like "Should Babies Be Fed Milk?"

Available on the prison library's shelves were books on just about every general subject. Much of the big private collection that Parkhurst had willed to the prison was still in crates and boxes in the back of the library—thousands of old books. Some of them looked ancient: covers faded, old-time parchment-looking binding. Parkhurst, I've mentioned, seemed to have been principally interested in history and religion. He had the money and the special interest to have a lot of books that you wouldn't have in general circulation. Any college library would have been lucky to get that collection.

As you can imagine, especially in a prison where there was heavy emphasis on rehabilitation, an inmate was smiled upon if he demonstrated an unusually intense interest in books. There was a sizable number of well-read inmates, especially the popular debaters. Some were said by many to be practically walking encyclopedias. They were almost celebrities. No university would ask any student to devour literature as I did when this new world opened to me, of being able to read and *understand*.

I read more in my room than in the library itself. An inmate who was known to read a lot could check out more than the permitted maximum number of books. I preferred reading in the total isolation of my own room.

When I had progressed to really serious reading, every night at about ten P.M. I would be outraged with the "lights out." It always seemed to catch me right in the middle of something engrossing.

Fortunately, right outside my door was a corridor light that 15 cast a glow into my room. The glow was enough to read by, once my eyes adjusted to it. So when "lights out" came, I would sit on the floor where I could continue reading in that glow.

At one-hour intervals the night guards paced past every room. Each time I heard the approaching footsteps, I jumped into bed and feigned sleep. And as soon as the guard passed, I got back out of bed onto the floor area of that light-glow, where I would read for another fifty-eight minutes—until the guard approached again. That went on until three or four every morning. Three or four hours of sleep a night was enough for me. Often in the years in the streets I had slept less than that.

The teachings of Mr. Muhammad stressed how history had been "whitened"—when white men had written history books, the black man simply had been left out. Mr. Muhammad couldn't have said anything that would have struck me much harder. I had never forgotten how when my class, me and all of those whites, had studied seventh-grade United States history back in Mason, the history of the Negro had been covered in one paragraph, and the teacher had gotten a big laugh with his joke, "Negroes' feet are so big that when they walk, they leave a hole in the ground."

This is one reason why Mr. Muhammad's teachings spread so swiftly all over the United States, among *all* Negroes, whether or not they became followers of Mr. Muhammad. The teachings ring true—to every Negro. You can hardly show me a black adult in America—or a white one, for that matter—who knows from the history books anything like the truth about the black man's role. In my own case, once I heard of the "glorious history of the black man," I took special pains to hunt in the library for books that would inform me on details about black history.

I can remember accurately the very first set of books that really impressed me. I have since bought that set of books and have it at home for my children to read as they grow up. It's called *Wonders of the World.* It's full of pictures of archeological finds, statues that depict, usually, non-European people.

20   I found books like Will Durant's *Story of Civilization.* I read H. G. Wells' *Outline of History. Souls Of Black Folk* by W. E. B. Du Bois gave me a glimpse into the black people's history before they came to this country. Carter G. Woodson's *Negro History* opened my eyes about black empires before the black slave was brought to the United States, and the early Negro struggles for freedom.

J. A. Rogers' three volumes of *Sex and Race* told about race-mixing before Christ's time; about Aesop being a black man who told fables; about Egypt's Pharaohs; about the great Coptic Christian Empires; about Ethiopia, the earth's oldest continuous black civilization, as China is the oldest continuous civilization.

Mr. Muhammad's teaching about how the white man had been created led me to *Findings In Genetics* by Gregor Mendel. (The dictionary's G section was where I had learned what "genetics" meant.) I really studied this book by the Austrian monk. Reading it over and over, especially certain sections, helped me to understand that if you started with a black man, a white man could be produced; but starting with a white man, you never could produce a black man—because the white gene is recessive. And since no one disputes that there was but one Original Man, the conclusion is clear.

During the last year or so, in the *New York Times,* Arnold Toynbee used the word "bleached" in describing the white man. (His words were: "White (i.e. bleached) human beings of North European origin. . . .") Toynbee also referred to the European geographic area as only a peninsula of Asia. He said there is no such thing as Europe. And if you look at the globe, you will see for yourself that America is only an extension of Asia. (But at the same time Toynbee is among those who have helped to bleach history. He has written that Africa was the only continent that produced no history. He won't write that again. Every day now, the truth is coming to light.)

I never will forget how shocked I was when I began reading about slavery's total horror. It made such an impact upon me that it later became one of my favorite subjects when I became a minister of Mr. Muhammad's. The world's most monstrous crime, the sin and the blood on the white man's hands, are almost impossible to believe. Books like the one by Frederick Olmstead opened my eyes to the horrors suffered when the slave was landed in the United States. The European woman, Fannie Kimball, who had married a Southern white slaveowner, described how human beings were degraded. Of course I read *Uncle Tom's Cabin*. In fact, I believe that's the only novel I have ever read since I started serious reading.

Parkhurst's collection also contained some bound pamphlets 25 of the Abolitionist Anti-Slavery Society of New England. I read descriptions of atrocities, saw those illustrations of black slave women tied up and flogged with whips; of black mothers watching their babies being dragged off, never to be seen by their mothers again; of dogs after slaves, and of the fugitive slave catchers, evil white men with whips and clubs and chains and guns. I read about the slave preacher Nat Turner, who put the fear of God into the white slavemaster. Nat Turner wasn't going around preaching pie-in-the-sky and "non-violent" freedom for the black man. There in Virginia one night in 1831, Nat and seven other slaves started out at his master's home and through the night they went from one plantation "big house" to the next, killing, until by the next morning 57 white people were dead and Nat had about 70 slaves following him. White people, terrified for their lives, fled from their homes, locked themselves up in public buildings, hid in the woods, and some even left the state. A small army of soldiers took two months to catch and hang Nat Turner. Somewhere I have read where Nat Turner's example is said to have inspired John Brown to invade Virginia and attack Harper's Ferry nearly thirty years later, with thirteen white men and five Negroes.

I read Herodotus, "the father of History," or, rather, I read about him. And I read the histories of various nations, which opened my eyes gradually, then wider and wider, to how the whole world's white men had indeed acted like devils, pillaging and raping and bleeding and draining the whole world's non-white people. I remember, for instance, books such as Will Durant's story of Oriental civilization, and Mahatma Gandhi's accounts of the struggle to drive the British out of India.

Book after book showed me how the white man had brought upon the world's black, brown, red, and yellow peoples every variety of the sufferings of exploitation.

Suggestions for Writing and Discussion

1. Discuss what initially motivated Malcolm X to seek the meaning of words. What were the factors that aided him once he was determined to use words to his fullest advantage?

2. Malcolm X claims that black Americans are virtually invisible in books on American history in school. In order to test whether his allegations are still true today, write down a list of all the specific people, places, and events that you studied in school that focused on black Americans and their conflicts and contributions to U.S. history.

3. Malcolm X says about slavery, "the world's most monstrous crime, the sin and the blood on the white man's hands, are almost impossible to believe." Given that, what is your response to his story of Nat Turner in 1831?

4. In referring to Mendel's *Findings in Genetics,* what does Malcolm X mean when he says, "The conclusion is clear"? What conclusion is he drawing? What now is clear?

Making Connections: Synthesis and Analysis

1. Briefly discuss the major similarities and differences among Welty's, Douglass's, and Malcolm X's experiences. Given that all three ended up being successful in their educational endeavors, what conclusions can you draw about what a person might need most in order to learn?

2. Which American characteristics and ideals does each of these writers reflect? Give specific examples. What would be the most important messages from these three readings that students should pay attention to today?

· *NOW* ·

DOES GENDER AFFECT THE WAY WE LEARN?

Suggestions for Prereading or Journal Writing

1. Reflect on several generalizations that people make about schoolchildren, such as girls are usually quiet and well-behaved, while boys are usually noisy and unable to sit still in their seats. Also, some people say that girls are better with languages, while boys excel in math and science. Based on your own experiences and observations thus far, how "true" do you find these generalizations to be?

2. To what do you attribute the noticeable differences between males and females today: the environment, genetics, cultural influences, the media? Which one factor is most influential? Explain.

Two young students at work in the classroom.

Topics for Writing and Disussion

1. Describe the emotions and thoughts that may be going on within the boy and within the girl. Discuss these differences in relation to ways of learning.
2. What are some other noted differences between them that might reflect a difference in education as well?

The Lost Boys

Elaine McArdle

Elaine McArdle is a correspondent for the *Boston Globe.* The following article first appeared in the September 2003 *Boston Globe Magazine.*

Ann DuLong isn't someone you'd expect to have dating troubles.

A student and former cheerleader at Boston University, DuLong is in killer shape, with a pretty face and broad smile framed by long chestnut hair. She's outgoing, knows volumes about sports, and is really open to meeting the right guy.

But the odds are against her. These days, college life in Boston is a lot more like *The Bachelor* than *Animal House.*

"There just aren't that many guys around here to date," DuLong says. "The one or two handsome guys who've got their act together, there's a lot of competition for them. It's one cute guy and 50 girls looking at him. It leaves girls scrambling." The coeds in the aerobics classes she teaches are "really cute girls who take care of themselves." Yet they can't find men. "That's the biggest complaint I hear from girls. All of them are like, 'Are you kidding me? We go to BU—there's no one to date!' "

She sighs. "It's a little depressing."   5

DuLong and her friends aren't imagining things. BU is about 60 percent female at the undergraduate level, a gender gap that worries some students and continues to irk chancellor John Silber, who was ridiculed last year when he raised the issue (he asserted that the growing surplus of women was distracting to the men) and publicly raised questions about its implications.

Turns out Silber was onto something.

In a complete reversal that has taken only 30 years, today's universities and colleges are increasingly dominated by women, a trend that's only beginning to attract widespread attention. There are nearly 2 million more women than men in college now; by 2010, there will be 138 women for every 100 men. While it's highest among blacks, the gender gap holds true across all racial and ethnic groups, ages, and states. (Maine is at the very top with 154 women per 100 men in college.)

That makes achieving balance between men and women one of the hottest topics in university admissions. A school's survival depends on it. Campuses skewed too far toward one or the other gender can turn off students of both sexes.

10   "Obviously, students prefer gender balance," says Jack Dunn, spokesman for Boston College, which, after reaching a high of 55 percent female eight years ago, has wrestled the figure back down to 52 percent in this fall's incoming class. "Students will complain if the numbers are tilted that it's harder to meet people of the opposite sex and date."

"We'd all like to have parity and a 50/50 split," says Richard Nesbitt, who has achieved close to that goal (51 percent female this year) as admissions director at Williams College. If a gender gap grows too wide—say, beyond 60/40—top applicants from both genders may hesitate to enroll "for all kinds of reasons," Nesbitt says.

Schools like BC have comparatively little trouble attracting men, thanks in part to robust athletics programs. Other universities and colleges find it so tough that they're taking drastic measures. Brandeis, for example, whose entering class is 58 percent female, is experimenting this year with sending baseball caps bearing the university's logo to the first 500 men who return cards indicating interest in applying. "We don't know if it will work," says Deena Whitfield, director of enrollment. "But it's important to get men to respond to your first inquiry so you can at least get them in your database." (Like Brandeis, Emerson is nearly 60 percent female. Women comprise 54 percent of first-year students at Bates, 53 percent at Colby and Northeastern, and 52 percent at Tufts, Holy Cross, and Wesleyan. Only at MIT, with its focus on the traditionally male field of engineering, do there remain notably more men than women.)

Of Boston-area schools, BU, with the biggest imbalance, is taking the most aggressive approach. Silber has demanded more photographs of men and men's sports in recruitment brochures and catalogs. "For ROTC, there was only one picture and it was a female," he complains. "I said, 'Let's get it straight: ROTC is predominantly male, so put in pictures of men.'"

And while schools adamantly deny anything smacking of affirmative action based on gender (the University of Georgia dropped admissions preferences for male students after being socked with a lawsuit), there are ways to enroll more men without breaking the law. "Boys score higher on SATs, girls on grade point averages," Silber notes. "I said, 'Stop giving so much favoritism to GPAs.'" Since he started focusing on it three years ago, Silber says he's increased male enrollment by three percentage points. However, he adds, "We still have a long way to go."

Of course, fighting over the pool of male applicants misses the   15
bigger question: Why aren't more men going to college?

"It's been framed as a guild issue—how does one college compete against another—rather than what's happening in society with men and women," says William Pollack, director of the Centers for Men and Young Men at McLean Hospital in Belmont and author of the bestseller *Real Boys*. "Putting more men in catalogs is advertising. I don't think advertising will change national trends."

In Massachusetts, 83 percent of female high school graduates enroll in college. But only 70 percent of male grads do, according to a study by Northeastern University and the Boston Private Industry Council. Boys also drop out of high school at rates 30 percent higher than girls. One hundred thirty-three women will get bachelor's degrees in Boston for every 100 men.

"You'd call it a national crisis," says Pollack, a psychologist who teaches at Harvard Medical School—"*if* you were looking at it."

So what if men comprise 51 percent of the general public, but only 43 percent of the university and college population? So what if women have to date men with less education? In fact, the stakes are far more serious than the Saturday-night social woes of college coeds. There are economic and social implications, too.

College-educated men earn $1.25 million more over their life-   20
times than men who have only high school diplomas. They're more likely to have jobs and be productive at work, and they pay more in taxes while avoiding such government subsidies as welfare and Medicaid. They are less likely to father children out of wedlock or be convicted of crimes, and more likely to vote, volunteer for civic activities, and describe themselves as happy, according to a report by Northeastern University's Center for Labor Market Studies.

In New England's old mill towns, the number of births out of wedlock has soared, notes Andrew Sum, an economist and lead author of the study. In Pittsfield, for example, nearly half of children today are illegitimate, double the percentage of two decades ago, while in Lawrence, 63 percent of births are to unwed moms. "Today you have social disasters in a lot of these places," says Sum. "And part of it is that you can no longer do well, on average, without a college degree."

Because high-paying blue-collar jobs have all but disappeared in today's economy, a man without higher education is dooming himself. "They don't have jobs, and they're not looking," Sum says. "They're hanging out, they're chilling out, and we're going to support them for the next 30 years."

Yet this growing group of lost boys has garnered little national attention or interest. Tom Mortenson, a senior scholar at the Pell Institute for the Study of Opportunity in Higher Education, was the first to sound a warning when he noticed boys weren't keeping up with the gains that girls were making in higher education. But until recently, no one listened. "We have to find much better answers for boys," he says. "We have to. You can't write off half the population."

What's to blame? Popular culture, in part, which suggests it's not cool for boys to be smart or educated. High school boys spend more time partying, playing video games, and exercising, while girls are studying, doing volunteer work, and caring for their families, according to a UCLA study. There are biological factors at work, too. Girls learn to read and write earlier than boys, and because they're better at sitting still in class, they're less likely to be disciplined. Boys, who already find school difficult, fall behind, become discouraged, and give up.

25   "We should start teaching them according to how they learn, not according to some idea that boys and girls have to learn the same way," says Pollack, who's working on a pilot program for boys' education, "so boys can do equally well in the classroom without girls going down."

If we don't? "We're already seeing it," says Pollack. "Boys will be more likely to drop out of high school, less likely to go to college, more likely to drift into crime and drugs, less likely to get married or sustain a marriage, less likely to sustain relationships with their children."

Adds Mortenson, "If we can raise organized, purposeful young women, we have to figure out how to do the same thing for boys. And we're not doing it. We are *not* doing it."

Suggestions for Writing and Discussion

1. Reread the opening four lines in this piece. From these lines alone, what would a reader think the author's slant on this topic might be? Further, if the title of this piece is "The

Lost Boys," why do you think McArdle begins her article talking about a female student?

2. According to the author, John Silber, president of Boston University, contends that the "growing surplus of women" is "distracting" to the men. Analyze the phrase "growing surplus" as well as Silber's belief that women are a "distraction" to the men. Who (and what) is responsible for this distraction?

3. What future problems, according to this article, might arise if more men do not start going to college in the same numbers as females?

4. Analyze the arguments that popular culture and biology are to blame for boys falling behind in school. What other factors might contribute to this trend? What factors might be propelling women to pursue higher educational goals?

With Fewer Distractions, Students Will Do Better

Meg Milne Moulton and Whitney Ransome

Authors Meg Moulton and Whitney Ransome are co–executive directors of the National Coalition of Girls' Schools. Their article first appeared in the *Atlanta Journal-Constitution* on August 26, 2003.

"We're in favor of educational excellence."

Hardly a bold position, is it? Somewhat like declaring oneself a proponent of apple pie and Mother's Day. Yet in the ongoing debate over education reform, the statement has a subtle power about it: Even the most polarized of opponents share this simple goal.

Our organizational focus is on single-sex learning environments for girls, and we have watched with interest as the past decade's resurgence of all-girl private schools inspired a renewed interest in single-sex classrooms in public schools as well. We see clearly that there are some universal advantages of single-sex education for girls and boys alike, whether in private or public school.

For example, in a 2000 survey of 4,200 girls' school graduates, more than 80 percent reported they were better prepared to succeed in the coed world precisely because they went to a single-sex school, where students learn to measure their worth based on their own accomplishments rather than on the shifting whims of teen culture.

5   Single-sex classrooms offer the same benefit, particularly in the hormone-charged middle school years. With the distraction of the opposite sex removed for a time, girls and boys find their attitudes about learning are transformed. Notions of "fitting in" or "being cool" fade into the background, while academic achievement, intellectual inquiry and a child's natural desire to learn regain the prominence they deserve.

Atlanta Girls' School, a private school for girls in grades 6 through 12, takes as its motto, "Today a community of girls, tomorrow our community's leaders."

In doing so, it resumes a deep historical tradition in which generations of Atlantan leaders were drawn from the city's once-vibrant single-sex schools. Indeed, AGS was founded on the belief that this tradition must be renewed if the city of Atlanta is to continue to grow and prosper under the auspices of its native talent.

Today, however, critics of public single-sex education claim that it harkens back to the shameful days of racial segregation. That's exactly the charge leveled at King Middle School, where sixth-graders now take all-boy and all-girl classes. But it's a false—and deeply cynical—comparison.

Racial segregation was a way to deny opportunity, while single-sex education does just the opposite. Putting our young people on center stage at this crucial time in their lives empowers them by creating greater opportunities for achievement, leadership and success.

10   Sincere people can disagree on what school setting is best for their children, but we must not imagine that "one size fits all" when it comes to educational excellence. Every parent knows that children display a variety of learning styles, and new research on the human brain confirms that gender differences do show up in the classroom.

We need to offer learning environments that take these differences into account in a positive way, to maximize the school experience for all students. Single-sex classrooms—as one option among many available to Atlanta's families—are a way to do that.

Suggestions for Writing and Discussion

1. What is the authors' strongest reason for advocating single-sex schools, especially for girls? How effective is this reasoning?

2. As in "The Lost Boys" article, this piece also mentions the "distraction" of the opposite sex as being a problem in one's learning environment. What proof does this piece offer as support for this argument?

3. The authors suggest that students will be less apt to succumb to superficial peer pressure in single-sex classrooms. What's your thinking on this point?

4. In general, what is the authors' main purpose in this piece, and how effectively do they achieve this purpose?

The New Gender Gap
Michelle Conlin

Michelle Conlin is a writer for *Business Week*. This article initially appeared in the May 26, 2003, issue of that magazine.

FROM KINDERGARTEN TO GRAD SCHOOL, BOYS ARE BECOMING THE SECOND SEX

Lawrence High is the usual fortress of manila-brick blandness and boxy 1960s architecture. At lunch, the metalheads saunter out to the smokers' park, while the AP types get pizzas at Marinara's, where they talk about—what else?—other people. The hallways are filled with lip-glossed divas in designer clothes and packs of girls in midriff-baring track tops. The guys run the gamut, too: skate punks, rich boys in Armani, and saggy-panted crews with their Eminem swaggers. In other words, they look pretty much as you'd expect.

But when the leaders of the Class of 2003 assemble in the Long Island high school's fluorescent-lit meeting rooms, most of these boys are nowhere to be seen. The senior class president? A girl. The vice-president? Girl. Head of student government? Girl. Captain of the math team, chief of the yearbook, and editor of the newspaper? Girls.

It's not that the girls of the Class of 2003 aren't willing to give the guys a chance. Last year, the juniors elected a boy as class president. But after taking office, he swiftly instructed his all-female slate that they were his cabinet and that he was going to be calling all the shots. The girls looked around and realized they had the votes, says Tufts University–bound Casey Vaughn, an Intel finalist and one of the alpha femmes of the graduating class. "So they impeached him and took over."

The female lock on power at Lawrence is emblematic of a stunning gender reversal in American education. From kindergarten to graduate school, boys are fast becoming the second sex. "Girls are on a tear through the educational system," says Thomas G. Mortenson, a senior scholar at the Pell Institute for the Study of Opportunity in Higher Education in Washington. "In the past 30 years, nearly every inch of educational progress has gone to them."

5   Just a century ago, the president of Harvard University, Charles W. Eliot, refused to admit women because he feared they would waste the precious resources of his school. Today, across the country, it seems as if girls have built a kind of scholastic Roman Empire alongside boys' languishing Greece. Although Lawrence High has its share of boy superstars—like this year's valedictorian—the gender takeover at some schools is nearly complete. "Every time I turn around, if something good is happening, there's a female in charge," says Terrill O. Stammler, principal of Rising Sun High School in Rising Sun, Md. Boys are missing from nearly every leadership position, academic honors slot, and student-activity post at the school. Even Rising Sun's girls' sports teams do better than the boys'.

At one exclusive private day school in the Midwest, administrators have even gone so far as to mandate that all awards and student-government positions be divvied equally between the sexes. "It's not just that boys are falling behind girls," says William S. Pollock, author of *Real Boys: Rescuing Our Sons from the Myths of Boyhood* and a professor of psychiatry at Harvard Medical School. "It's that boys themselves are falling behind their own functioning and doing worse than they did before."

It may still be a man's world. But it is no longer, in any way, a boy's. From his first days in school, an average boy is already developmentally two years behind the girls in reading and writing. Yet he's often expected to learn the same things in the same way in the same amount of time. While every nerve in his body tells him to run, he has to sit still and listen for almost eight hours a day. Biologically, he needs about four recesses a day, but he's lucky if he gets one, since some lawsuit-leery schools have banned them altogether. Hug a girl, and he could be labeled a "toucher" and swiftly suspended—a result of what some say is an increasingly anti-boy culture that pathologizes their behavior.

If he falls behind, he's apt to be shipped off to special ed, where he'll find that more than 70% of his classmates are also boys. Squirm, clown, or interrupt, and he is four times as likely to be diagnosed with attention deficit hyperactivity disorder. That often leads to being forced to take Ritalin or risk being expelled, sent to special ed, or having parents accused of negligence. One study of public schools in Fairfax County, Va., found that more than 20% of upper-middle-class white boys were taking Ritalin-like drugs by fifth grade.

Once a boy makes it to freshman year of high school, he's at greater risk of falling even further behind in grades, extracurricular activities, and advanced placement. Not even science and math remain his bastions. And while the girls are busy working on sweeping the honor roll at graduation, a boy is more likely to be bulking up in the weight room to enhance his steroid-fed Adonis complex, playing Grand Theft Auto: Vice City on his PlayStation2, or downloading rapper 50 Cent on his iPod. All the while, he's 30% more likely to drop out, 85% more likely to commit murder, and four to six times more likely to kill himself, with boy suicides tripling since 1970. "We get a bad rap," says Steven Covington, a sophomore at Ottumwa High School in Ottumwa, Iowa. "Society says we can't be trusted."

As for college—well, let's just say this: At least it's easier for   10 the guys who get there to find a date. For 350 years, men outnumbered women on college campuses. Now, in every state, every income bracket, every racial and ethnic group, and most industrialized Western nations, women reign, earning an average 57% of all BAs and 58% of all master's degrees in the U.S. alone. There are 133 girls getting BAs for every 100 guys—a number that's projected to grow to 142 women per 100 men by 2010, according to the U.S. Education Dept. If current trends continue, demographers say, there will be 156 women per 100 men earning degrees by 2020.

Overall, more boys and girls are in college than a generation ago. But when adjusted for population growth, the percentage of boys entering college, master's programs, and most doctoral programs—except for PhDs in fields like engineering and computer science—has mostly stalled out, whereas for women it has continued to rise across the board. The trend is most pronounced among Hispanics, African Americans, and those from low-income families.

The female-to-male ratio is already 60–40 at the University of North Carolina, Boston University, and New York University. To keep their gender ratios 50–50, many Ivy League and other elite schools are secretly employing a kind of stealth affirmative action for boys. "Girls present better qualifications in the application process—better grades, tougher classes, and more thought in their essays," says Michael S. McPherson, president of Macalester College in St. Paul, Minn., where 57% of enrollees are women. "Boys get off to a slower start."

[. . .]

On the one hand, the education grab by girls is amazing news, which could make the 21st the first female century. Already, women are rapidly closing the M.D. and PhD gap and are on the verge of making up the majority of law students, according to the American Bar Assn. MBA programs, with just 29% females, remain among the few old-boy domains.

Still, it's hardly as if the world has been equalized: Ninety percent of the world's billionaires are men. Among the super rich, only one woman, Gap Inc. co-founder Doris F. Fisher, made, rather than inherited, her wealth. Men continue to dominate in the highest-paying jobs in such leading-edge industries as engineering, investment banking, and high tech—the sectors that still power the economy and build the biggest fortunes. And women still face sizable obstacles in the pay gap, the glass ceiling, and the still-Sisyphean struggle to juggle work and child-rearing.

15   But attaining a decisive educational edge may finally enable females to narrow the earnings gap, punch through more of the glass ceiling, and gain an equal hand in rewriting the rules of corporations, government, and society. "Girls are better able to deliver in terms of what modern society requires of people—paying attention, abiding by rules, being verbally competent, and dealing with interpersonal relationships in offices," says James Garbarino, a professor of human development at Cornell University and author of *Lost Boys: Why Our Sons Turn Violent and How We Can Save Them.*

Righting boys' problems needn't end up leading to reversals for girls. But some feminists say the danger in exploring what's happening to boys would be to mistakenly see any expansion of opportunities for women as inherently disadvantageous to boys. "It isn't a zero-sum game," says Susan M. Bailey, executive director of the Wellesley Centers for Women. Adds Macalester's McPherson: "It would be dangerous to even out the gender ratio by treating women worse. I don't think we've reached a point in this country where we are fully providing equal opportunities to women."

Still, if the creeping pattern of male disengagement and economic dependency continues, more men could end up becoming losers in a global economy that values mental powers over might—not to mention the loss of their talent and potential. The growing educational and economic imbalances could also create societal upheavals, altering family finances, social policies, and work-family practices. Men are already dropping out of the labor force, walking out on fatherhood, and disconnecting from civil life in greater numbers. Since 1964, for example, the voting rate in Presidential elections among men has fallen from 72% to 53%—twice the rate of decline among women, according to Pell's Mortenson. In a turnaround from the 1960s, more women now vote than men.

Boys' slide also threatens to erode male earnings, spark labor shortages for skilled workers, and create the same kind of marriage squeeze among white women that already exists for blacks. Among African Americans, 30% of 40- to 44-year-old women have never married, owing in part to the lack of men with the same academic credentials and earning potential. Currently, the never-married rate is 9% for white women of the same age. "Women are going to pull further and further ahead of men, and at some point, when they want to form families, they are going to look around and say, 'Where are the guys?'" says Mortenson.

Corporations should worry, too. During the boom, the most acute labor shortages occurred among educated workers—a problem companies often solved by hiring immigrants. When the economy reenergizes, a skills shortage in the U.S. could undermine employers' productivity and growth.

Better-educated men are also, on average, a much happier lot. **20** They are more likely to marry, stick by their children, and pay more in taxes. From the ages of 18 to 65, the average male college grad earns $2.5 million over his lifetime, 90% more than his high school counterpart. That's up from 40% more in 1979, the peak year for U.S. manufacturing. The average college diploma holder also contributes four times more in net taxes over his career than a high school grad, according to Northeastern's Sum. Meanwhile, the typical high school dropout will usually get $40,000 more from the government than he pays in, a net drain on society.

Certainly, many boys continue to conquer scholastic summits, especially boys from high-income families with educated parents. Overall, boys continue to do better on standardized tests such as the scholastic aptitude test, though more low-income girls than low-income boys take it, thus depressing girls' scores. Many educators also believe that standardized testing's multiple-choice format favors boys because girls tend to think in broader, more complex terms. But that advantage is eroding as many colleges now weigh grades—where girls excel—more heavily than test scores.

Still, it's not as if girls don't face a slew of vexing issues, which are often harder to detect because girls are likelier to internalize low self-esteem through depression or the desire to starve themselves into perfection. And while boys may act out with their fists, girls, given their superior verbal skills, often do so with their mouths in the form of vicious gossip and female bullying. "They yell and cuss," says 15-year-old Keith Gates, an Ottumwa student. "But we always get in trouble. They never do."

Before educators, corporations, and policymakers can narrow the new gender gap, they will have to understand its myriad causes. Everything from absentee parenting to the lack of male teachers to corporate takeovers of lunch rooms with sugar-and-fat-filled food, which can make kids hyperactive and distractable, plays a role. So can TV violence, which hundreds of studies—including recent ones by Stanford University and the University of Michigan—have linked to aggressive behavior in kids. Some believe boys are responding to cultural signals—downsized dads cast adrift in the New Economy, a dumb-and-dumber dude culture that demeans academic achievement, and the glamorization of all things gangster that makes school seem so uncool. What can compare with the allure of a gun-wielding, model-dating hip hopper? Boys, who mature more slowly than girls, are also often less able to delay gratification or take a long-range view.

Schools have inadvertently played a big role, too, losing sight of boys—taking for granted that they were doing well, even though data began to show the opposite. Some educators believed it was a blip that would change or feared takebacks on girls' gains. Others were just in denial. Indeed, many administrators saw boys, rather than the way schools were treating them, as the problem.

Thirty years ago, educational experts launched what's known 25 as the "Girl Project." The movement's noble objective was to help girls wipe out their weaknesses in math and science, build self-esteem, and give them the undisputed message: The opportunities are yours; take them. Schools focused on making the classroom more girl-friendly by including teaching styles that catered to them. Girls were also powerfully influenced by the women's movement, as well as by Title IX and the Gender & Equity Act, all of which created a legal environment in which discrimination against girls—from classrooms to the sports field—carried heavy penalties. Once the chains were off, girls soared.

Yet even as boys' educational development was flat-lining in the 1990s—with boys dropping out in greater numbers and failing to bridge the gap in reading and writing—the spotlight remained firmly fixed on girls. Part of the reason was that the issue had become politically charged and girls had powerful advocates. The American Association of University Women, for example, published research cementing into pedagogy the idea that girls had deep problems with self-esteem in school as a result of teachers' patterns, which included calling on girls less and lavishing attention on boys. Newspapers and TV newsmagazines lapped up the news, decrying a new confidence crisis among American girls. Universities and research centers sponsored scores of teacher symposiums centered on girls. "All the focus was on girls, all the grant monies, all the university programs—to get girls interested in science and math," says Steve Hanson, principal of Ottumwa High School in Iowa. "There wasn't a similar thing for reading and writing for boys."

Some boy champions go so far as to contend that schools have become boy-bashing laboratories. Christina Hoff Sommers, author of *The War Against Boys,* says the AAUW report, coupled with zero-tolerance sexual harassment laws, have hijacked schools by overly feminizing classrooms and attempting to engineer androgyny.

The "earliness" push, in which schools are pressured to show kids achieving the same standards by the same age or risk losing funding, is also far more damaging to boys, according to Lilian G. Katz, co-director of ERIC Clearinghouse on Elementary and

Early Childhood Education. Even the nerves on boys' fingers develop later than girls', making it difficult to hold a pencil and push out perfect cursive. These developmental differences often unfairly sideline boys as slow or dumb, planting a distaste for school as early as the first grade.

Instead of catering to boys' learning styles, Pollock and others argue, many schools are force-fitting them into an unnatural mold. The reigning sit-still-and-listen paradigm isn't ideal for either sex. But it's one girls often tolerate better than boys. Girls have more intricate sensory capacities and biosocial aptitudes to decipher exactly what the teacher wants, whereas boys tend to be more anti-authoritarian, competitive, and risk-taking. They often don't bother with such details as writing their names in the exact place instructed by the teacher.

30   Experts say educators also haven't done nearly enough to keep up with the recent findings in brain research about developmental differences. "Ninety-nine-point-nine percent of teachers are not trained in this," says Michael Gurian, author of *Boys and Girls Learn Differently.* "They were taught 20 years ago that gender is just a social function."

In fact, brain research over the past decade has revealed how differently boys' and girls' brains can function. Early on, boys are usually superior spatial thinkers and possess the ability to see things in three dimensions. They are often drawn to play that involves intense movement and an element of make-believe violence. Instead of straitjacketing boys by attempting to restructure this behavior out of them, it would be better to teach them how to harness this energy effectively and healthily, Pollock says.

As it stands, the result is that too many boys are diagnosed with attention-deficit disorder or its companion, attention-deficit hyperactivity disorder. The U.S.—mostly its boys—now consumes 80% of the world's supply of methylphenidate (the generic name for Ritalin). That use has increased 500% over the past decade, leading some to call it the new K-12 management tool. There are school districts where 20% to 25% of the boys are on the drug, says Paul R. Wolpe, a psychiatry professor at the University of Pennsylvania and the senior fellow at the school's Center for Bioethics: "Ritalin is a response to an artificial social context that we've created for children."

Instead of recommending medication—something four states have recently banned school administrators from doing—experts say educators should focus on helping boys feel less like misfits. Experts are designing new developmentally appropriate, child-initiated learning that concentrates on problem-solving, not just test-taking. This approach benefits both sexes but especially boys, given that they tend to learn best through action, not just talk. Activities are geared toward the child's interest level and temperament. Boys, for example, can learn math through counting pinecones, biology through mucking around in a pond. They can read *Harry Potter* instead of *Little House on the Prairie,* and write about aliens attacking a hospital rather than about how to care for people in the hospital. If they get antsy, they can leave a teacher's lecture and go to an activity center replete with computers and manipulable objects that support the lesson plan.

Paying attention to boys' emotional lives also delivers dividends. Over the course of her longitudinal research project in Washington (D.C.) schools, University of Northern Florida researcher Rebecca Marcon found that boys who attend kindergartens that focus on social and emotional skills—as opposed to only academic learning—perform better, across the board, by the time they reach junior high.

Indeed, brain research shows that boys are actually more empathic, expressive, and emotive at birth than girls. But Pollock says the boy code, which bathes them in a culture of stoicism and reticence, often socializes those aptitudes out of them by the second grade. "We now have executives paying $10,000 a week to learn emotional intelligence," says Pollock. "These are actually the skills boys are born with." 35

The gender gap also has roots in the expectation gap. In the 1970s, boys were far more likely to anticipate getting a college degree—with girls firmly entrenched in the cheerleader role. Today, girls' expectations are ballooning, while boys' are plummeting. There's even a sense, including among the most privileged families, that today's boys are a sort of payback generation—the one that has to compensate for the advantages given to males in the past. In fact, the new equality is often perceived as a loss by many boys who expected to be on top. "My friends in high school, they just didn't see the value of college, they just didn't care enough," says New York University sophomore Joe Clabby. Only half his friends from his high school group in New Jersey went on to college.

They will face a far different world than their dads did. Without college diplomas, it will be harder for them to find good-paying jobs. And more and more, the positions available to them will be in industries long thought of as female. The services sector, where women make up 60% of employees, has ballooned by 260% since the 1970s. During the same period, manufacturing, where men hold 70% of jobs, has shrunk by 14%.

These men will also be more likely to marry women who out-earn them. Even in this jobless recovery, women's wages have continued to grow, with the pay gap the smallest on record, while men's earnings haven't managed to keep up with the low rate of inflation. Given that the recession hit male-centric industries such as technology and manufacturing the hardest, native-born men experienced more than twice as much job loss as native-born women between 2000 and 2002.

Some feminists who fought hard for girl equality in schools in the early 1980s and '90s say this: So what if girls have gotten 10, 20 years of attention—does that make up for centuries of subjugation? Moreover, what's wrong with women gliding into first place, especially if they deserve it? "Just because girls aren't shooting 7-Eleven clerks doesn't mean they should be ignored," says Cornell's Garbarino. "Once you stop oppressing girls, it stands to reason they will thrive up to their potential."

40 Moreover, girls say much of their drive stems from parents and teachers pushing them to get a college degree because they have to be better to be equal—to make the same money and get the same respect as a guy. "Girls are more willing to take the initiative . . . they're not afraid to do the work," says Tara Prout, the Georgetown-bound senior class president at Lawrence High. "A lot of boys in my school are looking for credit to get into college to look good, but they don't really want to do the grunt work."

A new world has opened up for girls, but unless a symmetrical effort is made to help boys find their footing, it may turn out that it's a lonely place to be. After all, it takes more than one gender to have a gender revolution.

Suggestions for Writing and Discussion

1. Education expert Thomas Mortenson says that "the female lock on power" is a "stunning gender reversal in American

education." What facts and anecdotes support his statement? Does his statement ring true compared to your own
experiences and observations? Explain.

2. What evidence does the author provide to bolster the claim
that boys are, indeed, falling behind, and how serious do
you think this problem really is?

3. Although there are more female college graduates, the
males in America still make the most money, and as the
author states, "ninety percent of the world's billionaires
are men." To what might you attribute this dichotomy?

4. Examine all the possible causes, both stated in this article
and those not included, to the current trend that shows boys
doing poorly in school. What in your opinion has been the
biggest change in the past thirty years to initiate such a trend?

Making Connections: Synthesis and Analysis

1. Analyze the different arguments among these three pieces
that simultaneously point to gender being a detriment or
an asset, depending on the learning environment. Out of
these three pieces, which one sculpts the most convincing
argument? Explain why.

2. Compare/contrast your own educational experiences and
observations with the arguments put forth in the three
readings in this section, and write an essay that synthesizes your experiences with those arguments in order to
answer the question: To what extent does gender affect the
way you learn?

HOW EQUAL ARE THE EDUCATIONAL OPPORTUNITIES IN AMERICA TODAY?

Suggestions for Prereading or Journal Writing

1. Write about your past teachers. In general, how would you
"grade" them: as excellent, fair, or poor? How do your
grades reflect the community in which you were a student?

2. Write about a time when you felt you were treated unfairly
in school. What was the heart of the conflict, and how was
it resolved?

Merri Cyr, photo of a young schoolgirl

Topics for Writing and Discussion

1. What is your first impression of this photograph? What part of America, specifically, do you think it represents?
2. What inferences can you draw when you compare the size of the girl to that of the school buses? What conclusions can you draw from where the girl is situated between the buses and a chain-link fence? Finally, what conclusions can you draw from the fact that we only see the little girl from behind and that she is walking alone?

Profoundly Multicultural Questions
Sonia M. Nieto

Sonia M. Nieto is a professor of language, literacy, and culture in the Department of Teacher Education and Curriculum Studies at the University of Massachusetts. The following article appeared in the December 2002/January 2003 issue of *Educational Leadership.*

We must address the deeply ingrained inequities of today's schools by asking difficult questions related to equity and access.

I still recall the question that my friend Maddie, also an educator, asked me a number of years ago when I was describing an initiative to bring a multicultural program to a particular urban school district. A supporter of multicultural education, she was nonetheless becoming frustrated by the ways in which many districts were implementing it. She was especially concerned that many students from that particular district were doing poorly in school, and she asked impatiently, "But can they do math?"

[. . .]

Besides focusing on matters of culture and identity, educators also need to ask profoundly multicultural questions—that is, troubling questions that often go unanswered or even unasked. The answers tell us a great deal about what we value because the questions are about equity, access, and social justice in education. Here are a few of the questions that we must address if we are serious about giving all students of all backgrounds an equal chance to learn.

WHO'S TAKING CALCULUS?

I use "calculus" as a place marker for any number of other high-status and academically challenging courses that may open doors for students to attend college and receive advanced training. For instance, we find that although slightly more than 12 percent of white students are enrolled in calculus, only 6.6 percent of African Americans and 6.2 percent of Latinos and Native Americans are enrolled. In the case of physics, the numbers are 30.7 percent for whites, 21.4 percent for African Americans, 18.9 percent for Hispanics, and 16.2 percent for Native Americans (National Center for Education Statistics [NCES], 2002). This situation has serious implications for reforming such policies as rigid tracking, scheduling, and counseling services. Access to high-level and demanding academic courses has a long-term and dramatic effect in terms of college attendance and subsequent quality of life. For instance, the 2000 U.S. Census reported that annual average earnings for those with a bachelor's degree were nearly double the amount for those with just a high school diploma: $45,678 compared with $24,572 (U.S. Census Bureau, 2000b).

WHICH CLASSES MEET IN THE BASEMENT?

5 Language-minority students and students with special needs are too often hidden away in the basement—or in the hall closet, or the room with the leaky ceiling on the fourth floor, or the modular unit separated from the rest of the school. Administrators offer seemingly logical reasons for placing these students in these areas: There's no other available space in the building; these students were the last to arrive and therefore need to be placed where there's room; now they're closer to the English as a Second Language teacher. But placing programs for marginalized students in less desirable places is a powerful metaphor for the low status and little attention that they receive. It also serves in many cases to segregate these students from the so-called "regular" (English-speaking) or so-called "normal" (non–special needs) students, in this way creating an even greater gulf between them and the rest of the school.

The continuing segregation of students on the basis of race and ethnicity is a trend that has been escalating for the past 20 years. According to Gary Orfield (2001), most of the progress made toward desegregating schools in the two decades prior to 1988 has been lost in the past 15 years. For African Americans, the 1990s witnessed the largest backward movement toward segregation since the *Brown v. Board of Education* decision. Latinos are now the most segregated of all ethnic groups—not just in race and ethnicity, but also poverty. U.S. schools are becoming more separate and unequal than ever.

WHO'S TEACHING THE CHILDREN?

The question of who is teaching the children is inextricably linked to matters of social justice in education. Teachers working in poor urban schools tend to have less experience and less preparation than do those in schools that serve primarily white and middle-class students (Editorial Projects in Education, 1998). In addition, poor urban districts are more likely to hire teachers out of field than are suburban and middle-class school districts (David & Shields, 2001). These situations would be deemed unacceptable in more affluent districts.

Related to teachers' experience and training is the issue of teachers' race and ethnicity. Although all educators—teachers, administrators, curriculum coordinators, and others—need to develop the attitudes and skills to be effective with our increasingly diverse student population, we need a concerted effort to recruit a more diverse faculty. At present, the number of students of color in U.S. classrooms is growing dramatically at the same time that the number of teachers of color is declining. In 1972, just 22 percent of students in public schools were considered "minority"; by 1998, it was 37 percent (NCES, 2000a). The teaching force, on the other hand, is about 87 percent white. These trends show little sign of changing (U.S. Census Bureau, 2001).

The growing gap is problematic because mounting evidence indicates that a higher number of teachers of color in a school—particularly African American and Hispanic—can promote the achievement of African American and Hispanic students (Clewell, Puma, & McKay, 2001; Dee, 2000). In fact, one study found that a higher number of teachers of color can have an even greater impact on the achievement of white students (Meier, Wrinkle, & Polinard, 1999). Another study found that having same race and gender role models was "significantly and consistently predictive of a greater investment in achievement concerns" on the part of young people (Zirkel, 2002, p. 371).

Associated with teacher quality is the question of teachers' influence on their students. The proof is growing that all teachers—regardless of race, ethnicity, or gender—who care about, mentor, and guide their students can have a dramatic impact on their futures, even when these students face tremendous barriers related to poverty, racism, and other social ills (Flores-González, 2002; Noddings, 1992; Valenzuela, 1999). Stanton-Salazar, for instance, suggests that mentoring and support from teachers can provide students with the social capital they need to succeed, thus creating networks that "function as pathways of privilege and power"—pathways not generally available to poor students of color (1997, p. 4). 10

HOW MUCH ARE CHILDREN WORTH?

What do we pay for education, and how does the answer differ according to students' race, ethnicity, social class, and above all, home address? The well-known facts are that school financing is vastly unequal and that students with wealthier parents are fortunate to live in towns that spend more on their education, whereas young people who live in financially strapped urban or rural areas are much less fortunate (Kozol, 1991). Regrettably, the children who need the most get the fewest funds and resources (NCES, 2000b).

We also need to ask what our most vulnerable students are worth in terms of attention and care. A recent court case is a good example of the low value placed on students who attend poor urban schools. In June 2002, an appeals court in New York State ruled that youngsters who drop out of the New York City schools by 8th grade nevertheless receive "a sound basic education" (cited in González, 2002). The result of this astonishing ruling was to overturn a 2001 landmark decision that had found the state's formula for funding public schools unfair because it favored schools in suburban areas. The majority opinion in the appeals ruling, written by Judge Alfred Lerner, said in part,

> the skills required to enable a person to obtain employment, vote, and serve on a jury are imparted between grades 8 and 9. (cited in González, 2002)

Although Judge Lerner conceded that such a meager education might qualify young people for only the lowest-paying jobs, he added, "Society needs workers at all levels of jobs, the majority of which may very well be low-level" (cited in González, 2002). I am left wondering whether Judge Lerner would want this level of education for his own children or would think it fair and equitable.

These, then, are some of the profoundly multicultural questions that I suggest we ask ourselves. Certainly they are not the only questions that we can ask, but they give us an inkling of the vast inequities that continue to exist in U.S. public schools. My questions are not meant to diminish the noble efforts of educators who struggle daily to reach students through culturally responsive education or through an accurate representation in the curriculum of students' histories and cultures. But as we focus on these approaches—approaches that I wholeheartedly support—we also need to ask troubling questions about equity, access, and fair play. Until we do something about these broader issues, we will be only partially successful in educating all our young people for the challenges of the future.

REFERENCES

Clewell, B. C., Puma, M., & McKay, S. A. (2001). *Does it matter if my teacher looks like me? The impact of teacher race and ethnicity on student academic achievement.* New York: Ford Foundation.

D'Amico, J. J. (2001). A closer look at the minority achievement gap. *ERS Spectrum, 19*(2), 4–10.

David, J. L., & Shields, P. M. (2001). *When theory hits reality: Standards-based reform in urban districts, final narrative report.* Menlo Park, CA: SRI International.

Dee, T. S. (2000). *Teachers, race, and student achievement in a randomized experiment.* Cambridge, MA: National Bureau of Economic Research.

Editorial Projects in Education. (1998). *Education Week: Quality counts 1998.* Bethesda, MD: Author.

Flores-González, N. (2002). *School kids, street kids: Identity and high school completion among Latinos.* New York: Teachers College Press.

Gay, G. (2000). *Culturally responsive teaching: Theory, research, and practice.* New York: Teachers College Press.

González, J. (2002, June 27). Schools ruling defies logic. *New York Daily News,* p. 24.

Kahlenberg, R. D. (2000). *Economic school integration* (Idea Brief no. 2). Washington, DC: The Century Foundation.

Kozol, J. (1991). *Savage inequalities: Children in America's schools.* New York: Crown.

Ladson-Billings, G. (1994). *The dreamkeepers: Successful teachers of African American children.* San Francisco: Jossey-Bass.

Meier, K. J., Wrinkle, R. D., & Polinard, J. L. (1999). Representative bureaucracy and distributional equity: Addressing the hard question. *Journal of Politics, 61,* 1025–1039.

National Center for Education Statistics. (2000a). *Editorial projects in education, 1998.* Washington, DC: U.S. Department of Education, Office of Educational Research and Improvement.

National Center for Education Statistics. (2000b). *Trends in disparities in school district level expenditures per pupil.* Washington, DC: U.S. Department of Education, Office of Educational Research and Improvement.

National Center for Education Statistics. (2002). *Digest of education statistics, 2001.* Washington, DC: U.S. Department of Education, Office of Educational Research and Improvement.

Nieto, S. (1994). Affirmation, solidarity, and critique: Moving beyond tolerance in multicultural education. *Multicultural Education, 1*(4), 9–12, 35–38.

Nieto, S. (1999). *The light in their eyes: Creating multicultural learning communities.* New York: Teachers College Press.

Noddings, N. (1992). *The challenge to care in schools: An alternative approach to education.* New York: Teachers College Press.

Orfield, G. (2001). *Schools more separate: Consequences of a decade of resegregation.* Cambridge, MA: The Civil Rights Project, Harvard University.

Stanton-Salazar, R. D. (1997). A social capital framework for understanding the socialization of racial minority children and youth. *Harvard Educational Review, 67*(1), 1–40.

U.S. Census Bureau. (2000a). *Educational attainment in the United States: March 1999* (P20-528). Washington, DC: U.S. Department of Commerce.

U.S. Census Bureau. (2000b). *Educational attainment in the United States (Update): March 2000.* Washington, DC: U.S. Department of Commerce.

U.S. Census Bureau. (2001). *Statistical abstract of the United States: Education* [Online]. Available: www.census.gov/prod/2001pubs/statab/sec04.pdf.

Valenzuela, A. (1999). *Subtractive schooling: U.S.-Mexican youth and the politics of caring.* Albany, NY: SUNY Press.

Zirkel, S. (2002). "Is there a place for me?": Role models and academic identity among white students and students of color. *Teachers College Record, 104*(2), 357–376.

Suggestions for Writing and Discussion

1. What is Nieto's main point about multicultural education today?

2. What facts does Nieto use to support her point that schools are becoming more unequal today than they were 20 years ago? How does this claim link to the idea of social justice?

3. What might be the underlying causes behind children of poverty receiving teachers who would not be qualified to teach in suburban neighborhoods? How fair do you think it is that children with ethnic backgrounds are often taught in the worst rooms?

4. Nieto writes that "the children who need the most get the fewest funds." What solutions can you offer to remedy this injustice?

5. Nieto addresses the problems with school buildings, with teachers, and with funding. However, she does not address problems with the family or local community. Why does she omit these problems from her discussion?

No Child (Even Native American) Left Behind

Richard B. Williams

Richard B. Williams is an Oglala Lakota tribe member who wrote this opinion column in January 2003 in response to President Bush's "No Child Left Behind" Act.

In April 2001, No Child Left Behind was launched as the Bush administration's sweeping new educational initiative that was hailed as "revolutionary" in bringing our nation's public school systems into the 21st century. It was promoted as "the great equalizer" in transforming underperforming schools into models of educational efficiency and academic excellence. "Accountability" was the clarion call across the country in raising test scores in math and reading.

For Indian children and their parents on reservations across the country, however, this unfunded federal mandate has the potential for disaster. In a population that already has a 56 percent high-school dropout rate and more than a century of educational failure, the "corrective actions" imposed by NCLB are unrealistic and prohibitive in helping reservation schools achieve educational parity with their non-Native peers.

Indian children are not only being left further behind than before, but legislation without Indian consultation further illustrates the systemic failure of the federal government to uphold its responsibility to provide education to Indian tribes.

Consider the sanctions. Under NCLB, parents now have the right to transfer their children to a "successful" school within the same district. But the reality for Indian parents in remote areas like Pine Ridge, S.D., and Rock Point, Ariz., where there is likely only one school, busing and transfers are simply not viable alternatives.

Removing underperforming teachers also presents a problem. 5
On the reservations, the annual turnover rate is as high as 70 per-

cent. How will these school districts replace underperforming teachers when turnover is already a chronic issue?

Additionally, changing administrations or shutting down the schools in communities with very limited resources and trained personnel is simply not an option for a population with the least access to education of any racial or socio-economic group in the country.

"If you're a parent with a child in an underperforming school on a reservation, where are you going to go?" said John Cheek, executive director of the National Indian Education Association. "This act doesn't address the government's treaty obligations to the tribes at all."

Another mandate by NCLB is the training and educational requirements of teachers' aides, now known as "paraprofessionals." Under current law, paraprofessionals have until the 2005–06 school year to obtain at least an associate's degree. But many aides working for just above minimum wage on the reservation do not have the resources, the access to a local college or even the technology for long-distance learning to obtain their certificates.

Funding for tuition and training went out to states as block grants, but tribal schools are not eligible for these grants. Consequently, many Indian paraprofessionals in the ineligible schools may lose their jobs, although entities such as Lumina Foundation for Education are stepping forward to help them meet the higher education requirements.

10   "The law doesn't take into account the practical application of these requirements," said Verne Duus, legislative consultant for NIEA. "But the biggest problem is that the government has not even made a pretense of fully funding this initiative, and we simply cannot achieve these results without resources. This is going to be devastating for the schools, especially those on reservations."

But the main concern of those in Indian education is the long-term impact of inadequate education on Native communities. According to the 2000 Census, American Indians are the fastest-growing racial group in the country. As the population continues to grow, producing a skilled local workforce will become nearly impossible. Jobs will become even more critical in the areas of tribal law, accounting, medicine, education, technology and business in the decades to come.

NCLB has the promise of hope and recognizes the need for reform. The missing piece, however, is real change. The building blocks of success for Indian students include replacing competitive classrooms with cooperative ones; teaching to students' learning styles; modifying curricula so that children see themselves in stories and in the math assignments; and connecting culture and language as core components of the student's experience.

Most importantly, reform means caring about the children in the classroom. Let's stop the systemic failure and meet the needs of the students in a positive learning environment. Let's make changes that will reform our schools so that we can be proud of the good that is happening. We know what is possible based on the success of the tribal college movement. Let's make No Child Left Behind a reality for all of America's children.

Suggestions for Writing and Discussion

1. What is Williams's main point concerning the government's obligation to Indians now living on reservations in this country?
2. How would you characterize the tone and language in this piece? How does Williams present himself?
3. According to Williams, what flaws in the system will prevent "No Child Left Behind" from being effective for reservation schools, and, as he sees it, further damage educational opportunities for these children?
4. Why might reservations have a 70 percent turnover of teachers? Who is responsible for providing children on reservations with an equal and just education?

Charter Schools Blaze Trail to Real Racial Equality

Suzanne Fields

Suzanne Fields is a columnist for the *Washington Times*. This piece first appeared in the *Arizona Daily Star* on November 20, 2003.

The most troubling example of racial inequality in America today is the inner-city school. Civil-rights iniquities begin here.

You don't hear the two loudest ecclesiastical divines, the Revs. Jesse Jackson and Al Sharpton, complaining about self-indulgent, self-aggrandizing teachers whose unions support the cozy status quo.

You don't hear the educationist bureaucrats in the big cities, who pull down salaries wildly disproportionate to their talents and responsibilities, crying for the pain of what the schools are doing to black children.

White liberals usually don't want to clean up the wreckage, because if they did they wouldn't have convenient objects to pity to prove how compassionate they are.

5　But we're beginning to hear from educators who have looked closely at the data and see a consistent pattern in the awful gap that separates achieving whites and Asians and failing blacks and Hispanics. Abigail Thernstrom and Stephan Thernstrom, for example.

Their argument is not original. How they arrive at it is. Unequal skills and knowledge put blacks and Hispanics behind an eight ball that neither affirmative action and multiculturalism nor increasing school budgets will change.

The Thernstroms conclude that equal opportunity can be achieved only when the minority students in the inner cities reach a higher academic achievement.

"The black high school graduation rate has more than doubled since 1960," they write in "No Excuses: Closing the Racial Gap in Learning," a book that fuses analysis and outrage.

"And blacks attend college at a rate that is higher than it was for whites just two decades ago. But the good news ends there. The gap in academic achievement that we see today is actually worse than it was 15 years ago."

10　The problem, the Thernstroms say, is not the lack of a racial mix in public schools. Nor is it the amount of money spent per child or the size of teacher salaries.

What's crucial to enabling children to learn is an educational environment that motivates kids to want to work and study hard.

Such an environment requires teachers who are imaginative and innovative, whose careers are not governed by rigid union rules and whose hiring and firing is community based, where teachers, administrative staffs and parents work together.

The best-kept secret in education is that almost all the achieving inner-city schools are charter schools, operating within the public school system.

They're financed by the public and held to public accountability but are freed from the bureaucratic wrangling that stran-
gled the public system.

Unfortunately, charter schools require a great deal of time and   15
private energy and suffer from many of the shortcomings of voucher
programs. They draw money away from the vested interests.

But they confer extraordinary benefits. Largely independent of
bureaucratic control, they can hire nonunion teachers, choose their
own textbooks and exert discretionary power over their budgets.

When a charter school goes bad, and some have, they're easy
to close. Closing a bad public school is difficult.

Capital City Public Charter School in Washington, which
opened in 2001, exemplifies what a dedicated group of adults can
accomplish for a diverse group of children enrolled in classes
ranging from prekindergarten to the eighth grade.

The school is small, and most of its racially diverse student
body comes from low-income families. Parents choose the school.

The staff operates on a theory that emphasizes project-based   20
instruction to help children meet rigorous academic standards.
They meet them, too.

I observed 7- and 8-year-olds describe a project for planning
a playground. They told me how the models of climbing bars and
see-saws were built to scale, learning how 1 inch on a diagram of
the tiny climbing bars was the equivalent of 1 foot in the real-life
playground.

They did the math without notes, explaining complex ideas
about how the length of the chain of the swing required more
space than was available.

The children were eager to talk about the concepts to any
adult who would listen. Children at this school show gains each
year. No surprise there.

But of course this is a young adventure. What was striking
was the enthusiasm and animation of all the children—black and
white—talking about their work, expressing the joy of learning
with the enthusiasm of kids thinking they're only talking about
fun and games.

This school achieves what elite private schools, which charge   25
tuition of $15,000 a year, achieve.

Charter schools are a compromise between the fat and exhausted public schools and the more controversial vouchers that

enable parents to transfer their children from bad to good public schools.

Schools that don't shape up fail. Charter schools, like vouchers, are innovative and offer fresh opportunities for turning around the racial gap in learning. They're worth trying and watching. They brook no excuses.

Suggestions for Writing and Discussion

1. While Williams and Nieto argue that children of poverty are also victims of unequal education, Abigail and Stephan Thernstrom, authors of the book *No Excuses: Closing the Racial Gap in Learning,* claim that the problem is not segregated schools or lack of funding. Instead, they say that the learning environments have to change in order to motivate students. How might Williams and Nieto respond to this contention?

2. The Thernstroms also claim that dedicated and creative teachers are crucial to the good learning environment. Again, what might Nieto and Williams say to them regarding this point?

3. Analyze the points that Fields makes regarding her observations of a charter school. On what specifics and facts does she base her statements?

EXTENDED CONNECTIONS: CRITICAL THINKING, WRITING, AND RESEARCH

1. Read Chief Seattle's letter (chapter 3) and then research the current conditions of the Pine Ridge Indian Reservation in South Dakota. Write an essay, much along the lines of Chief Seattle's, in which you propose several solutions to the problems that exist for Native Americans on this reservation today.

2. Write a discussion between Richard Rodriguez (chapter 3) and Sonia Nieto regarding multicultural educations in America today. Raise three or four questions that both writers will answer, and come to some conclusions about how to make America a more tolerant culture.

3. Research the current conditions of schools in the Mississippi delta and compare/contrast your findings with those of any two of the readings in this chapter or in chapter 3.
4. Collect several current journal articles written by American educators on the initiative "No Child Left Behind." Compare/contrast these new articles with what you have learned about the ways in which children learn best, according to the readings in this chapter.
5. Read Jonathan Kozol's book on East St. Louis schools, *Savage Inequalities*. How does this book support/refute the pieces in this chapter, including the "Then" essays by Eudora Welty, Malcolm X, and Frederick Douglass?
6. Watch the movie *Dangerous Minds*. Compare/contrast this teacher's experience with situations described in several pieces in this chapter.

CHAPTER 6

Redefining Gender: Men, Women, and Couples

INTRODUCTION

As the lively exchange between Abigail Adams and her husband, John Adams, suggests in this chapter's first reading, gender issues have been a concern for people in the United States since its earliest days. In their correspondence, Abigail raises a question about the role of women in a democratic society. Her husband's response may seem surprising, especially considering that various historical reports identify their marriage as a union of equals. Nonetheless, John's letter indicates how polarizing gender issues can be. In 1851, seventy-five years after the Adamses' now-famous correspondence, Sojourner Truth delivered a fiery speech—the second of this chapter's readings—to a women's rights convention, showing that gender issues still remained problematic. Gayle G. Fischer's essay, the third reading, also looks at the nineteenth century, examining how styles of dress affected the freedom of women.

The Adamses' correspondence, Truth's speech, and Fischer's analysis provide a broad background for thinking about gender-related issues in the United States. The next two sections, "How Do Gender and Society Influence How We Dress?" and "For Better or for Worse: Defining Marriage," focus specifically on controversies related to gender. The first explores women and dress reform. Megan Twohey's interview with Lt. Col. Martha McSally and Tish Durkin's article raise questions about how women in military service should be required to dress.

While there are many controversial gender issues related to today's armed forces, of particular relevance is the way women who serve are impacted by the culture of countries to which they are posted. Should they be forced, when away from their base, to dress as local law requires women to dress? In addition to the argument about dress codes for women in the military, this section provides a thoughtful perspective by Gary Barlow on a fifteen-year-old male student who protested when he was not allowed to wear earrings and high heels in his high school, even though his female counterparts were permitted to do so.

The last section focuses on the changing views of marriage in the centuries since John and Abigail Adams became man and wife. Four articles offer differing perspectives on the rights of gay couples to marry. Gail Mathabane suggests that gay people who wish to marry face many of the same arguments made against interracial marriage as recently as 1967. Ramesh Ponnuru contests that conservatives have not focused in the ways that they should on this issue, while Suneel Khanna recounts his experiences as he and his partner seek the same rights as heterosexual couples. Providing a conservative argument, Dennis O'Brien expresses his reservations regarding gay marriage. Finally, a photo essay explores the issue of same-sex unions.

Thinking about historical views of men and women and about gender roles today in military service and in marriage law offers an opportunity to begin considering the many ways in which our lives are impacted by gender matters.

· THEN ·

SETTING THE CONTEXT: GENDER AND MARRIAGE THEN

Suggestions for Prereading or Journal Writing

1. In what ways might the thoughts and values of women today differ from those of the women who were married to America's founding fathers or women such as Sojourner Truth, who fought for civil rights and women's rights in the nineteenth century?

2. Can you think of any time when you or someone you know
   has experienced discrimination or taunting because of a
   choice of clothes, hairstyle, jewelry, or body art? In what
   ways, if any, was the discrimination or criticism related to
   gender? Explain.

Letters: The Place of Women in the New American Republic

Abigail Adams and John Adams

Abigail Adams was born in 1744 and her husband, John, in 1735. Prior
to their term as president and first lady of the United States, John and
Abigail Adams were passionate supporters of the colonial revolution
against British control. Their letters suggest that theirs was a marriage of
the minds as well as a lifelong romance. The first letter, sent by Abigail
to John while he was in Philadelphia collaborating on the Declaration of
Independence, suggests Abigail's wit as well as her awareness of the need
for increased attention to women's rights in the new republic. John's letters—both to his wife and to his colleague James Sullivan—show that
although he was among the most liberal of the Declaration's framers, he
still considered Abigail's request to "Remember the Ladies" a mere jest
rather than a serious proposal.

LETTER FROM ABIGAIL ADAMS TO JOHN ADAMS, MARCH 31, 1776

I long to hear that you have declared an independency—and by
the way in the new Code of Laws which I suppose it will be necessary for you to make I desire you would Remember the Ladies,
and be more generous and favourable to them than your ancestors. Do not put such unlimited power into the hands of the Husbands. Remember all Men would be tyrants if they could. If
perticuliar care and attention is not paid to the Ladies we are determined to foment a Rebellion, and will not hold ourselves bound
by any Laws in which we have no voice, or Representation.

   That your Sex are Naturally Tyrannical is a Truth so thor-
oughly established as to admit of no dispute, but such of you as

wish to be happy willingly give up the harsh title of Master for the more tender and endearing one of Friend. Why then, not put it out of the power of the vicious and the Lawless to use us with cruelty and indignity with impunity. Men of Sense in all Ages abhor those customs which treat us only as the vassals of your Sex. Regard us then as Beings placed by providence under your protection and in immitation of the Supreem Being make use of that power only for our happiness.

LETTER FROM JOHN ADAMS TO ABIGAIL ADAMS, APRIL 14, 1776

As to Declarations of Independency, be patient. Read our Privateering Laws, and our Commercial Laws. What signifies a Word.

As to your extraordinary Code of Laws, I cannot but laugh. We have been told that our Struggle has loosened the hands of Government every where. That Children and Apprentices were disobedient—that schools and Colledges were grown turbulent—that Indians slighted their Guardians and Negroes grew insolent to their Masters. But your Letter was the first Intimation that another Tribe more numerous and powerfull than all the rest were grown discontented—This is rather too coarse a Compliment but you are so saucy, I wont blot it out.

Depend upon it, We know better than to repeal our Masculine ₅ systems. Altho they are in full Force, you know they are little more than Theory. We dare not exert our Power in its full Latitude. We are obliged to go fair, and softly, and in Practice you know We are the subjects. We have only the Name of Masters, and rather than give up this, which would compleatly subject Us to the Despotism of the Peticoat, I hope General Washington, and all our brave Heroes would fight. I am sure every good Politician would plot, as long as he would against Despotism, Empire, Monarchy, Aristocracy, Oligarchy, or Ochlocracy.—A fine Story indeed. I begin to think the Ministry as deep as they are wicked. After stirring up Tories, Landjobbers, Trimmers, Bigots, Canadians, Indians, Negroes, Hanoverians, Hessians, Russians, Irish Roman Catholicks, Scotch Renegadoes, at last they have stimulated the[m] to demand new Priviledges and threaten to rebell.

LETTER FROM JOHN ADAMS
TO JAMES SULLIVAN,
MAY 26, 1776

. . . The same reasoning which will induce you to admit all men who have no property, to vote, with those who have, for those laws which affect the person, will prove that you ought to admit women and children; for, generally speaking, women and children have as good judgments, and as independent minds, as those men who are wholly destitute of property; these last being to all intents and purposes as much dependent upon others, who will please to feed, clothe, and employ them, as women are upon their husbands, or children on their parents.

As to your idea of proportioning the votes of men, in money matters, to the property they hold, it is utterly impracticable. There is no possible way of ascertaining, at any one time, how much every man in a community is worth; and if there was, so fluctuating is trade and property, that this state of it would change in half an hour. . . .

Depend upon it, Sir, it is dangerous to open so fruitful a source of controversy and altercation as would be opened by attempting to alter the qualifications of voters; there will be no end of it. New claims will arise; women will demand a vote; lads from twelve to twenty-one will think their rights not enough attended to; and every man who has not a farthing, will demand an equal voice with any other, in all acts of state. It tends to confound all distinctions, and prostrate all ranks to one common level.

Suggestions for Writing and Discussion

1. Comment on the tone and purpose of Abigail's letter to her husband and on the tone and purpose of his letter to her. What can you infer about the relationship between the two and about their differing attitudes toward the rights of women?
2. Compare and contrast John's tone and purpose in his letter to his wife with those in his letter to James Sullivan. How do John Adams's public and personal voices differ?

Ain't I a Woman?

Sojourner Truth

Born a slave in 1797 in New York and given the name Isabella, Sojourner Truth took on her new name in 1843. Believing that she had received a message from God to work for the civil rights of all, and particularly for the rights of women, she delivered this speech at a women's rights convention in Akron, Ohio, in 1851.

Well, children, where there is so much racket there must be something out of kilter. I think that 'twixt the negroes of the South and the women at the North, all talking about rights, the white men will be in a fix pretty soon. But what's all this here talking about?

That man over there says that women need to be helped into carriages, and lifted over ditches, and to have the best place everywhere. Nobody ever helps me into carriages, or over mud-puddles, or gives me any best place! And ain't I a woman? Look at me! Look at my arm! I have ploughed and planted, and gathered into barns, and no man could head me! And ain't I a woman? I could work as much and eat as much as a man—when I could get it— and bear the lash as well! And ain't I a woman? I have borne thirteen children, and seen them most all sold off to slavery, and when I cried out with my mother's grief, none but Jesus heard me! And ain't I a woman?

Then they talk about this thing in the head; what's this they call it? [Intellect, someone whispers.] That's it, honey. What's that got to do with women's rights or negro's rights? If my cup won't hold but a pint, and yours holds a quart, wouldn't you be mean not to let me have my little half-measure full?

Then that little man in black there, he says women can't have as much rights as men, 'cause Christ wasn't a woman! Where did your Christ come from? Where did your Christ come from? From God and a woman! Man had nothing to do with Him.

If the first woman God ever made was strong enough to turn 5 the world upside down all alone, these women together ought to be able to turn it back, and get it right side up again! And now they is asking to do it, the men better let them.

Obliged to you for hearing me, and now old Sojourner ain't got nothing more to say.

Suggestions for Writing and Discussion

1. Make a list of the points Truth makes as she argues for women's rights. Then analyze each point and explain how she supports her contentions.
2. Considering the points in Truth's argument, what stereotypical views of women can you infer were part of the American culture in 1851? Do any of those stereotypes persist in any form today? Explain.

"Pantelets" and "Turkish Trowsers": Designing Freedom in the Mid-Nineteenth-Century United States

Gayle V. Fischer

Gayle Fischer, a professor of history, is the author of a book-length study of dress reform and a contributor to an encyclopedia on clothing and social history in the United States. In this excerpt from her article, which first appeared in the spring 1997 issue of *Feminist Studies,* she identifies social and political issues related to the dress reform movement among women in the United States during the mid-nineteenth century and notes an intriguing objection to American women adopting what were regarded as "Eastern" clothing styles.

During the middle of the nineteenth century in the United States, groups of women and individual women who seemed to have little, if anything, in common cast aside their long fashionable gowns and donned trousers worn beneath shortened dresses.[1] [. . .] All these dress reformers, however, were linked by their belief in the superiority of reform dress over contemporary fashionable styles. [. . .]

An understanding of the design origins and the construction techniques of various reform costumes offers clues to how the female reformers may have seen themselves—and how the American public may have interpreted their actions. Although dress reformers meant to send a particular message, observers quite often saw something different from what reformers had intended. Outraged commentators clearly perceived what dress reformers tried to downplay: by wearing pants—of any kind—women appropriated male dress, and, by association, male privilege and power. Understanding that pants had long been considered a male garment and that this association would be difficult to break, most dress reformers sought a version of bifurcated clothing with no masculine associations. Dress reformers faced the challenge of reinterpreting female garments from outside contexts—"Oriental" costume[2] and children's wear—into acceptable female apparel for middle-class American women. [. . .] Surprisingly, when feminists brought orientalized notions of Eastern dress [. . .] instead of male pants, into the service of dress reform they failed to mitigate or mute the blatant act of gender appropriation inherent in the act of wearing trousers. [. . .]

A misconception about reform dress that has persisted into the twentieth century is that dress reformers looked solely to men's clothing as the inspiration for their reform garb—observers considered reform dress "a travesty of male attire."[3] Most of nineteenth-century society, including dress-reforming women, thought male dress superior to female clothing and freely expressed this opinion. Dress reformers, however, wanted to reform female dress for comfortable fit, physical well-being, religious beliefs, women's rights, or work opportunities—not to blur distinctions between the sexes. Whether male clothing actually was more comfortable, convenient, or "natural" does not really matter. Trousers represented physical freedom. And some women imagined being freed from societal restraints as well.

Dress reformers wanted to wear pants, so not surprisingly, their arguments stressed that there was nothing inherently male about trousers and that the garment could be adapted and made feminine. Most dress reformers, as women of their time, could not have conceived of themselves as dressed in "true" male garb of pants, jacket, shirt, collar, tie, and hat and played down references to borrowing clothing from the opposite sex.[4] [. . .]

Mainstream society did not want women to wear men's pants. 5 However, it is difficult to determine if the general public's resistance to female trousers stemmed more from the fear that women would seize male power or from the fear that pants-clad women would be unabashedly "sexy." Most of the diatribes against reform dress printed for mass circulation stressed the opinion that women would somehow become coarsened, more "male," if they wore bifurcated garments. Only a year after the introduction of the "bloomers," cartoons began to appear that depicted one of the biggest fears about reform clothing—that men would become feminine. Numerous articles and essays charged that if women wore the pants then it would logically follow that men would wear dresses and assume the female characteristic of dependence [. . .].

In such a charged atmosphere, at least two groups of dress reformers [. . .] turned away from men's trousers and looked elsewhere for "safer" models. Clothing from Eastern countries was one choice, although the sexual suggestiveness of pantaloons seemed unavoidable. Western travelers to the East showed a great deal of fascination with Eastern clothing and often affected "Oriental" dress while staying in the Middle East. The veil and the ferace (a long, loose robe) captivated Western observers more than any other article of Eastern women's clothing. These articles also suggested eroticism, because they hid the female face and form behind drapery and hinted at the sexual pleasures that could be found beneath the flowing cloth. Fashion historian Valerie Steele has found that images of the harem were considered both exotic and erotic. Decades after the freedom dress debuted, Steele noted that the "notorious jupe-culotte (or harem trouser-skirt) of 1911" caused a scandal, in part, because it indicated the legs.[5] [. . .]

The prevalence of Middle Eastern elements in nineteenth-century fashionable dress supports the theory that foreign dress influenced some later reform garments.[6] The incorporation of "exotic motifs" into Western fashion was a way of adding a "thrill" of something foreign or rare to familiar fashions.[7] [. . .]

Harper's New Monthly Magazine, unlike many other contemporary magazines, enthusiastically featured the "Turkish" costume on its fashion pages. The July 1851 Harper's article freely criticized "the trailing skirts" of Western women and complimented the "more elegant dresses of Oriental women." The accompanying illustrations of Near Eastern women looked remarkably like Western dress with the addition of "Eastern" jewelry and accessories. The magazine included the opinion that women could wear "trowsers" if "properly done." Apparently the proper way for women to wear pants was to wear imitations of those worn in the "Orient," the implication being that docile "Eastern" women and their clothing did not pose a danger to the existing sex-gender system in the West.[8] [. . .]

Opponents of dress reform heard women demanding their rights and saw women wearing a garment they believed belonged exclusively to men. Thus, critical observers claimed they saw men or a "third sex" or even "no sex" when they gazed upon women wearing pants.[9] Antagonists of women's rights dress reformers expended an enormous amount of energy to get the women back in long dresses. Caricatures of cigar-smoking, trouser-wearing feminists proved to be one of the more popular forms of attack; the image of the masculine feminist became synonymous with the image of the "ugly feminist."

Art historian Anne Hollander points out that the "most impor-   10
tant aspect of clothing is the way it looks," and to most nineteenth-century observers it "looked" like the dress reformers, regardless of their different political, social, or religious agendas, wore men's pants.[10] They may have adapted drawers, children's pantalettes, or Turkish trousers, and the reformers may have tried to distance their bifurcated garments from men's trousers, but to most women and men in nineteenth-century America it "looked" like the women stole a male garment and wore it. [. . .] Women in any form of bifurcated garments challenged the mid-nineteenth-century sex/gender system which used the language of clothing to visually distinguish the places of women and men in society. [. . .] Trousers, no doubt, counted as one of manhood's "grand prerogatives," no matter how innocuous the design origins of the garment worn by women. Today trousers—tomorrow, the ballot.

NOTES

1. Short dresses and trousers are commonly referred to as "bloomers," however, technically, "bloomers" only refer to the specific garment worn by Amelia Jenks Bloomer and the women associated with the "women's rights movement" around 1851. Furthermore, as Gerda Lerner noted, not only was the word "bloomer" "odious" to Elizabeth Cady Stanton and others, but it was an "epithet designed to ridicule" feminists. Therefore, the word "bloomer" will not be used to refer to reform garments; instead I will use the names the different dress reformers gave their respective costumes. Gerda Lerner, *The Grimke Sisters from South Carolina* (New York: Schocken Books, 1971), 335; and Alice Stone Blackwell, *Lucy Stone: Pioneer Woman Suffragist* (Norwood, Mass.: Plimpton Press, 1930), 104–13.

2. The most basic definition of Orientalism is a Western interpretation of the Orient (or the East) that focuses on the contrasts between the cul-

tures and ends up revealing more about Western culture than Eastern. The interpretations usually imply that the East is inferior to the West. See Edward Said, *Orientalism* (New York: Vintage Books, 1979); Sarah Graham-Brown, *Images of Women: The Portrayal of Women in Photography of the Middle East, 1860–1950* (New York: Columbia University Press, 1988).

3. Harriet N. Austin, "The Reform Dress," *The Water-Cure Journal* 23 (January 1857): 3; "The Demoralization of Dress," *The Health Reformer* 4 (September 1869): 57; Madame Demorest, "Dress and Its Relation to Health," *The Herald of Health and Journal of Physical Culture* 9 (January 1867): 16.

4. It appears that some women borrowed male dress or elements of male apparel as an avenue to gain power denied them elsewhere in their lives. Some dress reformers introduced features found exclusively in men's clothing into their reform garments: other women, some of whom identified themselves as dress reformers, donned male garb from head to toe. But these were exceptions.

5. Valerie Steele, *Fashion and Eroticism* (New York: Oxford University Press, 1985), 232–33.

6. Susannah Worth, "Embroidered China Crepe Shawls, 1816–1863," *Dress* 12 (1986): 43–54; Jean Gordon Lee, *Philadelphians and the China Trade, 1784–1844* (Philadelphia: Philadelphia Museum of Art, 1984).

7. Jennifer Craik discusses the tension between the exotic and the familiar in *Face of Fashion: Cultural Studies in Fashion* (New York: Routledge, 1994), 17–43.

8. "Turkish Costume," *Harper's New Monthly Magazine* 3 (July 1851): 288.

9. "Woman's Rights," *American Whig Review* 8 (October 1848):374–75.

10. Anne Hollander, *Seeing through Clothes: Fashioning Ourselves* (New York: Avon Books, 1980), 311.

Suggestions for Writing and Discussion

1. Art historian Anne Hollander is quoted as saying that the "most important aspect of clothing is the way it looks." Do you agree with her observation? Explain.

2. Argue for or against the following proposition: Being allowed freedom of choice of dress is an essential right for all people in a free society.

3. Research the resistance to women wearing trousers or pants in the United States, and then explain why you agree

or disagree with the idea that the main reason men objected to this change was that it implied women would then challenge the power of men.

Making Connections: Synthesis and Analysis

1. In comparing Sojourner Truth's speech with the observations in the Adamses' letters, how much do the roles of men and women seem to have changed in the United States from the late eighteenth century (the Adams letters) to the mid-nineteenth century (Truth's speech)?

2. Imagine a panel discussion among John Adams, Abigail Adams, and Sojourner Truth, with Gayle V. Fischer as the moderator. They are asked to address the following topic: In what ways do gender stereotypes affect both men and women? What questions might Fischer ask the panel members? How might they answer? What might Fischer's response to their answers be?

· NOW ·

HOW DO GENDER AND SOCIETY INFLUENCE HOW WE DRESS?

Suggestions for Prereading or Journal Writing

1. In what ways do you think Americans are affected by the laws, rules, and customs of other countries? Have you ever traveled or lived in a country where you were expected to observe laws, rules, or customs that surprised you? Explain.

2. Have you, or anyone you know, ever worn clothing or jewelry considered by others to be appropriate only for the opposite gender? Explain the responses encountered and your evaluation of these responses.

EVALUATING AN ARGUMENT:
TWO POINTS OF VIEW

Taking Off the Abaya
Megan Twohey

Journalist Megan Twohey has been a staff writer for the *National Journal* and the *Moscow Times.* Currently, she lives in Washington D.C., and works as a freelance writer for several journals, newspapers, and magazines, including Salon.com, from which this article (May 16, 2002) is taken. In this piece, Twohey interviews Air Force lieutenant colonel Martha McSally, who filed suit against the Department of Defense to challenge their dress code for servicewomen in Saudi Arabia.

Hours after a victory in her fight to free servicewomen in Saudi Arabia from wearing head-to-foot Muslim robes off base, Lt. Col. Martha McSally talks about her battles as a jet pilot and a woman.

Lt. Col. Martha McSally has done well by the military. Through hard work and model comportment, the 5-foot-3 woman has muscled her way up the ranks to become the top female fighter pilot in the Air Force. During the last decade, she's flown combat missions in the no-fly zone over Iraq, instructed pilots deployed to Kosovo and directed search-and-rescue missions inside Afghanistan.

But the vehicle of McSally's success also has been the source of her oppression. In an environment dedicated to equality, she says, principles have been sacrificed for appearances. For seven years, McSally has been fighting military rules that formerly required and now "strongly encourage" women stationed in Saudi Arabia to wear a head-to-foot Muslim robe called an abaya, to ride in the back seats of vehicles and to be accompanied by men when off base.

McSally, who was stationed in the Muslim kingdom in 2000 and 2001, argues that the rules are unconstitutional because they improperly force women to conform to another country's religious and social customs. Last year, after failing to secure change within the system, she filed suit in U.S. District Court to force the Department of Defense to eliminate the policies. The department says it created the regulations to avoid offending conservative Saudi leaders and to protect U.S. troops from terrorist attacks. But

in January, the DOD agreed to alter the rules, changing the requirement to wear the abaya and ride in the back seat of cars to a policy
in which the practices are "strongly advised." The department still
prevents women in Saudi Arabia from driving off base alone.

The changes are sufficient, argues the DOD, to merit dis-   5
missal of McSally's suit. But McSally has not been placated by
the move. Instead, she has pushed forward with her lawsuit, arguing that when a commanding officer "strongly advises" a young
enlisted woman to do something, it is essentially an order.

Recently, with the suit still pending, McSally brought her case
to Washington, crafting with her home state congressman, Jim
Langevin, D-R.I., a bill that would prohibit the military from requiring or strongly encouraging servicewomen in Saudi Arabia to
wear abayas. On Tuesday, the House of Representatives passed
the bill, and McSally was there to watch. She spoke about her victory in an interview following the vote.

Today was a big day for you. How does it feel to win?

It was pretty overwhelming actually to be sitting up in the gallery
of the United States House of Representatives and be listening to
representatives of Congress speak so strongly on this issue and
then to have this legislation pass after seven long years of being
told that I'm the only one who cares about this issue, that I need
to get over it.

It's a very historic moment for this nation, but also for me
personally. I was a legislative fellow, and I also know that many
freestanding bills do not make it into law. So the battle is won, but
not the war. We need to push the Senate and make sure that when
this legislation gets into conference, the DOD doesn't bully any
changes to the bill's language.

**What do you think is the motivation
behind the DOD policy?**

I've done a tremendous amount of research on this over the years.
The policy came about after Desert Storm. I was told initially that
it was a State Department policy and that it was way above my
pay grade. But I discovered that it was created by a local commander in Saudi Arabia. I don't know the reason.

10   The reason I was given at the time was host nation sensitivity. But Saudis aren't officially asking for it. My belief is that in the bureaucratic way, it was handed down from one commander to the next and that it took on a life of its own. I don't think our DOD was going out to oppress women. But the problem is that the people who came up with the policy are not women. And they didn't seem to think it was a big deal.

I've heard all sorts of defenses for the policy recently that are emotionally palatable at the moment. People say the policy provides protection from terrorist attack or safety for our troops. At face value, those things sound very noble. But in reality they're irrational defenses and have only recently been presented.

Although there is no official Saudi policy requiring women to wear abayas, do you think it's likely that those expectations are so ingrained in Saudi culture that American servicewomen will be at risk if they don't wear them off the base?

Well, this nation is an ally of ours. This is not a combat zone. And this ally has said that the abaya is not a requirement. So I think that we could get assurances from our ally government that our people will not be assaulted in their streets, and that if they are, those who commit the assaults will be punished. Secondly, there's been no evidence to say that wearing the abaya is more safe than not wearing it.

I've talked to women who serve in the embassy and don't wear an abaya who have never been harassed because they're clearly Westerners. Whereas, almost every single servicewoman I know who has worn an abaya has been harassed. It's like if you were to put on a military uniform and come on a base. I'm going to correct the way you wear that thing. As soon as you put that thing on, you're inviting correction within the jurisdiction of the religious beliefs.

Are there any cultural circumstances in which you'd embrace an Arab tradition?

I've heard that when you go into a mosque, some of them ask you to wear the abaya. Personally, I'm not Muslim, and I would not choose to do that. The key is whether it's your choice or not. If you want to put on an abaya in order to get a tour of a mosque, God bless you, feel free. But to be forced to wear it to do your duty is not right.

Is what's going on here in Congress likely to affect your lawsuit?

Well, if this law passes, some of the issues raised in the lawsuit 15 will no longer need to be approached. I met with some of my attorneys today. And we're definitely excited about the legislation. It's got to run its course. And we need to continue to fight the policy in parallel. We made attempts to settle the lawsuit, but they were met with tremendous arrogance. Last Friday, we actually filed an amended complaint because of some of the statements they made in oral argument. We had, for instance, talked about the retaliation that has happened to me. I had tried to play that down. But in the oral arguments, when the other side started to question whether this really happened or whether we're bluffing, we had no choice but to file an amended complaint claiming that the retaliation was real and support the statement with details.

Is there anything you can tell me about the retaliation you have experienced?

The real obvious one was my supervisor refusing to recommend me for squadron command, which is a clear flag for a lieutenant colonel promoted four years early that I failed in some way. Prior to that, the other subtle retaliation was that I was continuously undermined and berated for my disloyalty and poor leadership. You name it, I've heard it all. In America, if things are rough at work, you can go home and escape. In Saudi Arabia, there was no escape.

Do you think your recent transfer from Saudi Arabia to Arizona to work as a flight commander for an air operation center was part of a retaliation?

Actually, it was my choice to go to that job. But it was based on the environment I had going on at the time. I was a national finalist for the White House fellowship. I made the final round of 30 people. They pick 11 to 19. In June, in the middle of all this, I was about to fly to my interview. I was told that I would need to make another three-year commitment to the Air Force after the fellowship.

With everything going on around me, I felt like I had no future in the Air Force. So I withdrew from the fellowship finals. I had always dreamed of doing that fellowship. My decision was an indication of what I was experiencing at the time. At that point, I had two years left of my commitment to the Air Force. If I accepted a flying job, I'd be committed for at least three more years. I have a home and close friends in Tucson, Ariz. Instead, I asked to be sent there for a non-flying job. I said, "Please send me to the job in Arizona, so I can at least recover."

You flew as a fighter pilot in the combat zone over Iraq. What was that like as a woman?

I was immediately deployed to Kuwait to fly over Iraq once I finished my fighter pilot training in 1994. The military changed the policy in 1993 to allow women to be fighter pilots. They identified seven of us who had already passed training.

20   I very much remember the first day I looked down outside my canopy and saw the berm that divides Iraq and Kuwait. I was the most inexperienced person in our squadron. I said a little prayer and hoped I had paid attention in class. I then had over 100 hours of flying time over Iraq during the next several years.

What did you do in Saudi Arabia?

I was responsible for combat search and rescues for initially Iraq and then Afghanistan. After Sept. 11, we had to figure out how to survive in a whole new country with land mines and snow-covered mountains. To get out to every air base and every ship to make sure that all the air crew understood how they were going to survive out there—that was our first challenge. And then we actually kicked off our operation. The tally right now is that we've rescued over 250 Americans from Afghanistan. I wasn't personally there for all of those. But I was there for several months.

How would you characterize your experience in the military as a woman, excluding the abaya issue?

We've come a long way, but we still have a ways to go. The military is still male-dominated. So you're going to have to deal with some attitude problems from time to time, like whether women deserve to serve their country or whether they're competent to be fighter pilots. So I've seen it and could write a book on it. Pretty much every time I've gone into a new unit or a new place, I've had to change people's minds one at a time by my competence and professionalism.

Are you planning on writing a book?

I've thought about it. So many friends have said, "You're keeping a journal of this aren't you?" I haven't had the time. I've actually been asked for the movie rights on this whole issue. So there's supposedly a script being written right now. And I've had some informal offers on book things, but right now, it's just not a priority for me.

If not a book, what do you plan to do when your duty is up a year and a half from now?

Well, I wouldn't expect a book to be my livelihood. It would just be to educate people. I think that if I get out of military service, I will stay in public service for sure. I've always been fascinated with public policy. So maybe some sort of public policy job. Or ministry. I've always wanted to be involved in ministry. You don't have to be a pastor to be involved in ministry. There are many kinds of ministry—you can go feed the people in Afghanistan. I don't know what my own ministry would look like. And I'm kind of open.

If You're a Woman in Saudi Arabia, Just Cover Up. (For Now)
Tish Durkin

Tish Durkin is a political reporter who has written extensively on the Clintons, including a contribution to "Bill Clinton and His Conse-quences," published in the *Atlantic Monthly*. In addition, she covered Hillary Clinton's senatorial campaign for the *New York Observer*. In this article, Durkin argues that American women, including servicewomen, in Saudi Arabia should follow the customs of the country. Describing herself as an admirer of Lt. Col. Martha McSally, who brought suit against the Department of Defense's policy that forced servicewomen to wear abayas when off base, Durkin nevertheless believes that there are important reasons for that policy to remain in place. This article first ap-peared in the *National Journal*, January 19, 2002.

Don't get me wrong. I abhor the idea of a government forcing a woman to cloak herself from head to toe, regardless of her own thoughts on the matter. I marvel at the straight faces with which certain theocracies impose cultural restrictions on visiting Americans, when they would choke upon complying with any such restrictions from Americans. ("Welcome to the United States, sir; the prayer beads must remain in the terminal.") I cringe at the scenario, drawn in *The Washington Post* on January 7, of Martha McSally, an Air Force lieutenant colonel of high caliber and rugged experience, being obliged, as an American military woman serving in Saudi Arabia, to swathe herself in an ankle-length abaya and head scarf and ride in the back seat of a Chevy Suburban, while her blue-jeaned male subordinates sat up front. I applaud McSally's guts in bringing a lawsuit against the Defense Secretary, on the grounds that the abaya rule violates women soldiers' "religious freedom by forcing them to adopt the garb of another faith."

In light of all this, I cannot tell you how much I take issue with myself for taking issue with McSally. But I do take issue with her. (I am delighted, however, to take issue with Sen. Bob Smith, R-N.H., who told the *Post:* "What makes this particularly bizarre is that we are waging war in Afghanistan to remove those abayas, and the very soldiers who are conducting that war have to cover up." No, Senator, we are waging war in Afghanistan to destroy the home base of terrorists who attack Americans. If we were going to wage war over the burqa, we would have started waging it years ago.)

First, let's dispense with the dispensable. I have not read the legal papers, but in a recent address to about 200 girls at the National Cathedral School in Washington, McSally pointed out that the policy she opposes forbids men to adopt traditional Saudi dress but requires women to do so. To my mind, this bolsters the position of the military, for whom the operative issue seems to be to avoid offending the Saudis. Presumably, the Saudis are offended by the idea of men wearing Saudi garb, and offended by the idea of women not wearing Saudi garb. Hence a policy that requires personnel, male and female, to dress so as not to offend. As for the fact that it is the U.S. military, and not the host country, that is actually issuing the requirement, that hardly seems to be the point: If tomorrow the Saudis were to put forth such a request, it is hard to believe that McSally would drop her objection. Clearly, the heart of the issue is that the Saudi Arabian government forces a policy of extremely conservative Muslim dress upon its women, and that the U.S. military, far from setting any counter-example, is imposing that extreme dress upon its own women.

"When [local] customs and values conflict with ones that our Constitution is based on," McSally told the schoolgirls, ". . . that is where you draw the line." Hear, hear, but let's face facts: In many realms of American troop deployment, to draw the line at the Bill of Rights is to draw a very red line that runs way past the question of costume. It isn't just the freedom to dress as the Western Christian she is that McSally may not exercise when she is in Saudi Arabia. She also may not exercise her right to free speech, or to freedom of religion, or to many other freedoms enshrined in our Constitution. If the military is ordered to honor the wishes of a woman who is understandably offended that she must wear an abaya in public, what does it say to the Christian who is understandably offended that he cannot wear a cross?

Of course, one can argue that that is just the point. One can   5
argue that to forfeit one's constitutional rights based on one's geographical location is to betray those rights, and to quell all hope of their propagation to the very parts of the world where they are needed most. But one would have to square that argument with the pitch that the United States is making—and making ever more insistently in the here-there-and-everywhere context of the war on terrorism: We are not going into various countries to make social or political waves, but simply to carry out specific missions toward specific ends. And it is a waste of breath to protest that the abaya rule is nothing on the order of making local waves, but merely an American policy affecting only American soldiers. When those American soldiers are moving among non-American populations, there is no such hermetically sealed thing.

What, then, of our moral standards, or double standards? "If it were in our national security to deploy to South Africa under apartheid," McSally mused in her National Cathedral School remarks, "would we have found it acceptable . . . to segregate African-American soldiers . . . and say, 'It's just a cultural thing'? I don't think so." Really? Let's imagine the following: Those four planes are hijacked, and those 3,000 innocents are killed, not on September 11, 2001, but on September 11, 1981. The worst foreign attack in American history is not the brainchild of a terrorist network based in Afghanistan, but of such a network based in . . . Zimbabwe. The United States concludes that destroying that terrorist network will be greatly facilitated by the cooperation of Pretoria, and greatly hindered by the lack of such cooperation. The odious but well-situated regime agrees to let the United States use its facilities and airspace and all the rest, on the following condition: The U.S. military can make its own rules for its own soldiers on its own bases—but off base, South African rules go. There can be no interracial socializing; a white soldier having a beer with a black soldier will be subject to arrest; the whole, abominable nine yards. Would we find it acceptable for the United States to be not only tempted, but also legally required, to say, "Sorry, we've got a nonracist-anti-terrorism-host-country policy?" I hope not.

I don't say that easily. It would bother me a great deal for our military to cooperate very publicly with, and perhaps enhance the prestige of, a horribly racist regime. And it bothers me a great deal that our military is doing just that right now with horribly sexist regimes. But as an often-bothered inhabitant of the real world, I have to ask: What is the alternative? And as a feminist inhabitant of the real world, I have to ask: What, if anything, would that alternative mean for women?

I'll be honest. The women on whose behalf the abaya requirement concerns me most are not the women of the U.S. military. Not to belittle their concerns, but they signed up, they get paid, they can leave. McSally's lawsuit does not address the rights of Saudi women, nor could it. But it is their abysmal legal status that the abaya rule actually symbolizes. The bitterness of this debate lies in the irony that our presence in Saudi Arabia might appear to lower the status of American women, rather than raise that of Saudi women. And the heart of the apprehension, at least for me, is the possibility that by mimicking the Saudi policy, the United States endorses it—and thus, yet again, relegates the status of women to some vague future realm of endless, toothless conferences that chatter away, utterly apart from the real business of this military engagement or that economic initiative. I have no doubt that this policy makes the United States part of the problem. But I have no faith that repealing it would be any part of the solution. Granted, pussyfooting around blatant misogyny is a lousy way to fight it. But an even worse way is granting privileges to a few foreigners—which is exactly what McSally's victory would amount to. Yes, it would send a message that adult American women can dress themselves and the earth won't quake. But it would mix that message with the message that Americans show up and do whatever they please, no matter where they are—a message that will

be gleefully received, scrambled, and redistributed by conservative Muslim activists, not all of whom, by the way, are men. The
question is: On balance, at this moment, are the rewards of sending the former message worth the risks of sending the latter?

The answer is no. Don't get me wrong. I find the enduring
trend toward ultra-conservatism in the Muslim world to be twisted
and distressing and sad. Far from being resigned to it, I believe
that it can and must be fought. But American women have got to
realize that the more we make the fight about us, the more we lose
it for them. I want to root for McSally, but how can I? Her victory
would be a pain for the military. It would be a gift to those who
want to portray the United States as an arrogant interloper. And
most important, it would be nothing at all for the women for
whom the abaya really is the rule.

Suggestions for Writing and Discussion

1. Twohey quotes McSally as saying that the problem with
   the dress and behavior codes urged on servicewomen in
   Saudi Arabia "is that the people who came up with the policy are not women. And they didn't seem to think it was a
   big deal." Yet, McSally also says, "I don't think our DOD
   [Department of Defense] was going out to oppress women."
   Do you see any contradiction in these statements? Explain
   why or why not.

2. Identify two arguments McSally proposes against servicewomen wearing the abaya when they go off base. Do you
   find these arguments convincing? Explain why or why not.

3. McSally holds high rank in the Air Force and this article
   details many aspects of her military career. Do these points
   make her argument more convincing to you than the same
   points would if they were made by (a) a lower ranking servicewoman, (b) a high-ranking civilian female employee
   of DOD, or (c) a male senator? Give reasons to explain and
   justify your response.

4. Do you agree with Durkin's point that encouraging servicewomen to dress like Saudi Arabian women while
   forbidding servicemen to adopt Saudi male garb "bolsters
   the position of the military"? Explain.

5. Durkin introduces the issue of First Amendment rights.
   How does her explanation of these rights relate to her ar-

gument against McSally's position? How convincing do you find this rebuttal? Explain.

Principal Gives High Heels on Boys the Boot

Gary Barlow

In this article from the *Chicago Free Press* (July 31, 2002), staff writer Gary Barlow reports on a controversy concerning male high school students who choose to wear clothing and jewelry that administrators believe to be appropriate only for female students.

A 15-year-old gay student at the Chicago High School for Agricultural Sciences expressed disbelief last week after the school's assistant principal allegedly told him he had to "dress as a boy" if he wanted to remain at the school.

"I had on some high heels for about 10 minutes," the student said. "She told me as long as I was at the school, I would dress as a boy, that I would not wear anything feminine."

The student also said CHSAS assistant principal Martha Hamilton told him his long hair was "offensive" when she reprimanded him in a hallway July 24.

Hamilton denied making the comment about the student's hair but acknowledged that she told him he couldn't wear high heels.

5   "We don't allow boys to wear high heels and earrings," Hamilton said. "Girls can wear earrings."

Asked whether girls at the school, part of the Chicago Public Schools system, are allowed to wear high heels, Hamilton said, "Girls are allowed to wear whatever shoes are appropriate for girls. How many boys do you know who wear high heel shoes?"

Hamilton said distinguishing what male and female students can wear is not discriminatory.

"It has nothing to do with his sexual orientation," she said. "Before (students) come here, we explain what our policies are. He's one of the ones who signs a contract to abide by them. If there's a problem with this, he can go somewhere else."

But the student said he feels the atmosphere at the school is not good for GLBT students, adding he's the only openly gay student he knows at CHSAS, 3857 W. 111th St.

"Everybody at that school, they look way down on it," he said. 10
He added that he's spoken about the atmosphere at the school with at least one teacher he knows is gay, but said the teacher told him if he spoke out about it, "he would only be causing trouble."

"It's not right for them to tell you how to dress," the student said. "There's other guys, straight guys, who wear their hair long and in braids, and they haven't said anything to them."

The student said Hamilton's actions "were very traumatizing" and expressed additional concerns after Hamilton, following an interview with CFP, called his mother.

CPS chief legal counsel Marilyn Johnson said the school system has a strict policy barring discrimination based on sexual orientation.

"I can tell you this is an issue that arises from time to time," 15 Johnson said. "We deal with these on a case-by-case basis. We do take these seriously."

Johnson said she would discuss the issue with Hamilton and CHSAS officials and take appropriate action.

Rick Garcia, political director of Equality Illinois, expressed outrage at Hamilton's actions.

"It certainly should not be the business of the school to tell this kid what to wear," Garcia said. "If there's no dress code and the child wants to wear heels, then it's not appropriate for them to say he can't."

Each CPS school sets its own dress code. At CHSAS, that code is being revised, according to Hamilton. But Garcia and Johnson agreed that the code cannot be used to discriminate against GLBT students.

"It's entirely possible and necessary to accommodate (issues 20 of) blanket discrimination," Johnson said.

The student, who returns to the school this fall as a sophomore, said he intends to continue dressing in a way that he feels is appropriate.

"I identify as whatever I put on in the morning," he said.

Suggestions for Writing and Discussion

1. From reading this article, what rules can you infer are part of the dress code at the Chicago High School for Agricultural Sciences? What is your response to these rules and to the justifications for them given by the school administra-

tors? Do you find their arguments for these rules convincing? Explain.

2. In addition to the male-female issue, the student who was interviewed for the article claims there is a bias against gay, lesbian, bisexual, and transgendered (GLBT) students at this high school. What evidence does he provide? If his contention is true, do you find his argument convincing? Explain.

Making Connections: Synthesis and Analysis

1. Compare the objections Gayle Fischer describes as aimed against women who worked for dress reform in the nineteenth century to the objections Martha McSally encounters when she challenges the Department of Defense's dress code for military women in Saudi Arabia. What significance do you see in the similarities and differences you observe?

2. Consider two points Martha McSally makes about following Saudi Arabian customs and the ways in which Tish Durkin refutes those points. Whose argument do you find more convincing? Explain.

3. Both McSally and Durkin provide information about their background and expertise. Compare the details each provides and explain whose biographical information creates a more convincing picture for the reader. Do any of the personal details either woman provides raise doubts about her credibility? Explain.

4. Durkin concludes her argument with several paragraphs relating to the treatment of Saudi women by their government, while McSally does not mention this issue. Do you find this point a strength for Durkin's argument? Do you find its omission a weakness for McSally's argument? Explain.

FOR BETTER OR FOR WORSE: DEFINING *MARRIAGE*

Suggestions for Prereading or Journal Writing

1. How would you define an ideal marriage? What qualities would you hope to see in the ideal married couple?

2. Who should have control over the civil rights of those who wish to marry? The federal government? The state government? The federal or state court system? Direct vote of the citizens of a town, state, or country? Explain the reasons for your choice.

EVALUATING AN ARGUMENT: MULTIPLE PERSPECTIVES

Gays Face Same Battle Interracial Couples Fought

Gail Mathabane

Gail Mathabane is a journalist who writes frequently on issues related to interracial marriage. With her husband, Mark Mathabane, she is the coauthor of *Love in Black and White: The Triumph of Love over Prejudice and Taboo.* In this article, which first appeared in *USA Today* on January 26, 2004, she argues that gay couples today face some of the same barriers to marriage that were faced by interracial couples in the United States as recently as 1967.

In his State of the Union address on Tuesday, President Bush hinted that a constitutional ban on gay marriage might be needed if "activist judges" continue to threaten the sanctity of marriage by "redefining marriage by court order."

Although I'm not gay, for 16 years I've been in a marriage that a group of nine "activist judges," led by Chief Justice Earl Warren, legalized in 1967. They did so by striking down the laws of 16 states, mostly in the South, that had considered marriages such as ours illegal, immoral and ungodly.

In other words, I'm white and my husband is black.

Before the U.S. Supreme Court delivered the landmark Loving decision, interracial couples were in the same boat that same-sex couples are in today. They were vilified, persecuted and forbidden to marry. Interracial marriage was considered a felony punishable by five years in a state penitentiary.

Critics of gay marriage point to polls that seem to support 5 their position. In a USA TODAY/CNN/Gallup Poll last month,

65% said they oppose same-sex marriage. But mass opinion should not dictate judicial decisions. In 1948, when California became the first state to strike down a ban on interracial marriage, nine out of 10 Americans opposed such unions.

'LOVING VS. VIRGINIA'

In the Loving case, a Virginia judge had called for the imprisonment of Mildred Jeter, an African-American woman, and Richard Loving, a white man, after they were legally married in the District of Columbia and moved to Virginia, where their marriage was considered a felony.

The judge's ruling had religious overtones similar to those heard in the arguments of today's critics of same-sex marriage: God created the races and placed them on separate continents. The fact that he separated the races shows that he did not intend for them to mix.

On Wednesday, the Ohio Senate approved one of the nation's most sweeping measures against gay marriage. The bill, which passed 18–15, bars unmarried state employees—whether heterosexual or homosexual—from receiving benefits for domestic partners.

Ohio legislators passed the bill on the heels of a landmark ruling last November by Massachusetts' highest court granting gay couples the right to marry under the state's constitution. The court gave the Massachusetts Legislature 180 days to change state laws to make same-sex marriages possible.

10   Like interracial marriages, same-sex marriages are bound to become legal sooner or later, especially since the U.S. Supreme Court struck down state same-sex sodomy laws last June and California recently adopted a domestic partnership law that will give same-sex couples a status similar to marriage when it takes effect next year.

DIFFICULT CHALLENGE AHEAD

In some ways, however, advocates of same-sex marriage face a tougher challenge than did advocates of interracial marriage. The 1996 Defense of Marriage Act and similar state-specific laws defining marriage strictly as a union between a man and a woman are on the books in 37 states; laws against interracial marriages were on the books primarily in the South.

Laws usually change long before public attitudes do. After I got married, a well-meaning North Carolina woman told me that "somewhere in the Bible" it says blacks and whites are not supposed to love each other "because they're different species." I responded that as a minister's daughter, I was quite familiar with the Bible and believed that God loves us all—regardless of race, creed or sexual orientation—and wants us to have happy marriages with faithful spouses of our own choosing.

Some conservatives argue that the government should keep its nose out of people's private lives. I agree. The government should have no role in dictating whether two individuals can marry. Gay marriage, like interracial marriage, is not a threat to the sanctity of marriage and will not upend America's social structure.

The Supreme Court's Loving decision stated that marriage is one of the "vital personal rights" protected under the 14th Amendment. It is time these rights were extended to same-sex couples so they can enjoy the many emotional, financial and social benefits offered by legalized marriage.

Suggestions for Writing and Discussion

1. List the similarities Gail Mathabane notes between objections in 2004 to gay marriage and objections in the past to interracial marriage.
2. What differences do you see between the issues of interracial marriage and those of gay marriage?

Coming Out Ahead: Why Gay Marriage Is on the Way

Ramesh Ponnuru

Writing for the *National Review,* where he is a senior editor, Ramesh Ponnuru traces the growing acceptance of the civil rights of gay men and lesbians. He explains the conservative positions against gay marriage but points out ways in which these arguments often undermine themselves. He concludes by noting that "social conservatives have not yet lost this battle, and their defeat is not quite inevitable." This article appeared on July 28, 2003.

For social conservatives, it seems that the battle over gay rights is nearing an end before it has even fairly begun. It is true that a small majority of the American public continues to believe, as the poll question puts it, that "sexual relations between two adults of the same sex" are "always wrong." It is true, as well, that a slightly larger majority believes that persons of the same sex should not be allowed to marry.

But public opinion has been moving with stunning rapidity. In the 1970s and '80s, the percentage of Americans who believed gay sex was "always wrong" barely budged. The National Opinion Research Center found that 73 percent held that belief in 1973, and 76 percent did in 1990. By 2000, that number had fallen by 16 points. It fell another 6 in the next two years. In 1996, Gallup found that 26 percent of the public supported same-sex marriage. In late June of this year, 39 percent did. Young people support it more than their elders. The trend lines favor gay marriage.

So do legal developments, as Gerard V. Bradley explains. Elite, including legal-elite, opinion favors gay rights more than public opinion does. Still, public opinion influences the courts. If courts had imposed gay marriage in 1990, there would have been a substantial public backlash. Now the idea looks less radical. If the courts move this year, or two years from now, there may yet be a backlash—but perhaps not one large enough to be effective. Three decades after Roe, almost three years after Bush v. Gore, no one is shocked when the courts make the weightiest political decisions.

Another shift in public sentiment is less easily captured in poll numbers: the rise of what one might call an "anti-anti-gay" bloc. People in this group may have qualms about homosexuality and may not support gay marriage. But they are at least as uncomfortable with anything that strikes them as hostile to gay people, with rhetoric that singles them out for criticism, with political figures who seem to spend too much time worrying about them. It is this group—more than gays themselves or even unequivocal supporters of gay rights—that has caused the Bush White House to take a moderate line on gay issues.

5   President Bush opposes gay marriage, "hate crimes" legislation, and even the Employment Non-Discrimination Act. But he has also appointed openly gay officials, refrained from picking fights with the gay lobby, and generally frustrated social-conservative groups. In March, Marc Racicot, then-leader of the Republican

National Committee, met with a liberal gay organization and assured them that bigotry in his party was fading. In April, when Sen. Rick Santorum was being pilloried, Bush expressed support for him—but too tepidly for social conservatives. Some of them warned that traditionalist voters would stay home in 2004. But Bush is responding to political circumstances that run far deeper than today's tactical jockeying and that social conservatives, thus far, have been powerless to change.

The change in public attitudes toward homosexuality has several causes, but three in particular bear mentioning: the effects of the sexual revolution, the changed focus of gay activism in the 1990s, and the ineffectiveness of social-conservative organizations.

Because of the sexual revolution among heterosexuals, social conservatives may have lost on gay marriage as soon as they started debating it. In the 1990s, as liberal journalist E. J. Graff has written in the *Boston Globe,* "the religious right barnstormed the nation warning against 'gay marriage'—with an odd result. For both straight and gay folks, the phrase was transformed from an oxymoron into a real possibility."

Again, most people continue to agree with social conservatives that marriage should be reserved for heterosexual couples. But they do not agree with the premises that underlie that conclusion. The traditional moral argument against homosexual sex has been part of a larger critique of non-marital sex—and, classically, of sex that is not oriented toward procreation within marriage. Social conservatives need no instruction on how the links among sex, procreation, and marriage have been weakened among heterosexuals. They know that many people have adopted what might be called a privatized view of marriage, as an institution whose contours are plastic, whose purpose is to provide emotional satisfaction to the persons concerned, and whose terms are negotiable (and revocable). But they have been slow to see some of the political effects of these social changes.

The logic of the argument against homosexuality now implicates the behavior of a lot of heterosexuals. If the argument is made openly, and cast as a case for traditional sexual morals in general, a large part of the public will flinch. If the argument is made so as to single out gays, the logic vanishes. Social conservatives begin to look as though they are motivated not by principle but by the desire to persecute a minority. If no effective public argument can be made, the prohibition on gay marriage must survive based on tradition and unarticulated reasons. These are weak defenses in a rationalistic and sexually liberated era.

10   By the mid 1990s, social conservatives increasingly relied on the dialectical argument against gay marriage: the claim that acceptance of it logically requires acceptance of polygamy as well. That argument, as far as I can tell, is sound, and it may be effective in the short run. (In the long run it is as likely to increase support for polygamy as it is to decrease support for gay marriage.) But whatever its effectiveness, resorting to the dialectical argument was a sign of political weakness. It meant that gay marriage was not self-evidently objectionable, but had to be condemned because it would lead to other, more objectionable things. It meant that the argument from definition no longer worked.

At the same time that social conservatives were reaching this dead end, the agenda of gay-rights organizations was changing, too. What, after all, have been gays' great demands in recent years? They have asked for the opportunity to serve in the armed forces, to lead Boy Scout troops, to marry and adopt. Social-conservative rhetoric on homosexuality remained stuck in the 1970s, presenting gays as sexual radicals. Social conservatives were really the last squares. Homosexual groups also embraced the quintessential conservative idea of a fixed human nature. Indeed, they pushed an exaggerated form of that idea: genetic determinism. Many people who would otherwise be disposed to object to homosexuality came to believe that gays and lesbians were "born that way." Gay activists had to be ambivalent about this development, given the subtext: Who would choose to be that way? A mildly "homophobic" sentiment was recruited to the side of gay rights.

It has been a powerful ally. Genetic determinism has erased the distinction between being and doing—between, that is, identity and behavior. No space has been left in which to love the sinner and hate the sin; objection is discrimination. Justice Scalia's recent attempt to maintain the distinction, to say that a ban on gays' sexual behavior does not discriminate against people on the basis of their (putatively innate) desires, was widely regarded as both hair-splitting and demeaning.

The most effective gay strategy was not a political strategy at all. It was the choice of individuals to identify themselves openly as homosexuals. Scores of millions of Americans now have friends and relatives whom they know are gay. Perhaps as a strict matter of logic, that should not have affected their views on sexual morality. But logic and eros have never been easy bedfellows, have they?

It was perhaps impossible for social conservatives to resist a tide so strong. But their failure was partly of their own making. They were simultaneously too loving and too hateful. The second point is familiar enough to everyone. For the reasons outlined above, persuasive social-conservative rhetoric on gay rights is difficult to devise. But the rhetoric the social Right actually adopted had the additional burden of lending itself to easy caricature as spiteful, harsh, and obsessive—in part because it was not infrequently all of those things. The Religious Right's love for gays, meanwhile, was not the sort that homosexuals could recognize. It took the form of wanting to save their souls. What religious conservatives wanted was for gays to become ex-gays. The unspoken wish of many other conservatives was for gays to re-closet themselves. Neither had any chance of happening in large numbers.

The proposed marriage amendment to the Constitution nicely 15 illustrates the folly and weakness of organized social conservatism. The amendment will probably fail—most proposed constitutional amendments do. But it may very well be the only way to prevent the incremental judicial imposition of gay marriage. One would think that social-conservative groups would be working as hard as they could to enact it. Yet the Catholic bishops' conference is divided about the amendment. The Family Research Council came out against it, and then declared itself neutral. The council objects to the amendment because, among other things, it would not bar a state legislature from creating same-sex civil unions. The failure of judgment here should be an object lesson for students of politics for ages to come.

When the Massachusetts supreme court brings full-fledged gay marriage to an American state for the first time, the issue will heat up. Anyone who expects President Bush's storied quest for the Catholic vote to strengthen the hand of social conservatives has not been looking at the survey data. *Catholic World Report* recently commissioned a survey that suggested that students at Catholic colleges became more liberal during their time on campus. The freshmen were pro-life, and the seniors pro-choice. What was even more interesting was that a majority of Catholic-college freshmen already favored gay marriage when they got to campus. I suspect that even conservative Catholics who oppose gay marriage are especially sensitive to rhetoric that seems intolerant toward gays as persons.

After Massachusetts, will Republicans find a way to object forcefully to gay marriage and to push for the marriage amendment, without looking intolerant? That would be a tall order even for people who thought deeply about these matters. Social conservatives have not yet lost this battle, and their defeat is not quite inevitable. But that is the way to bet.

Suggestions for Writing and Discussion

1. What details does Ponnuru provide to support the contention that gay marriage receives more support today than it would have in the past?
2. What are the three main reasons the author cites as causing the move toward more approval of gay marriage? Do you agree that these causes have affected public opinion? Explain.

Gay and Ready to Marry

Suneel Khanna

Suneel Khanna, the public relations manager for *Maclean's Magazine,* describes in the May 5, 2003, edition of that publication his search with his partner for acceptance by his family. He also argues that the right to marry should be a basic right for all adults—whether heterosexual or gay. Civil unions, he believes, create a division that condemns gay couples to second-class citizenship.

In this largely personal essay, I put forward an intellectual argument for the legal sanction of same-sex marriage. I'd like to credit author/journalist Andrew Sullivan who previously, in the New Republic, *very strongly articulated the case for this fundamental right.*

"See what an Indian wedding looks like?" My mom is pointing at a photo of herself and my dad taken on July 17, 1963. I'm sitting at the kitchen table with her, my sister, and my boyfriend, Fadi. My dad has retired to the family room, in keeping with his post-dinner ritual. From time to time we can hear a muffled snore escape him. He's obviously fallen asleep watching CNN again. It makes us giggle.

Now that Fadi and I are well into our relationship, I have the courage to bring out our oldest photo album so that I can give him a peep into my family's past. As we enjoy our chai tea, I get a kick out of watching Mummy—yes, that's what I still call her—flip through the pages of images shot in New Delhi 40 years ago. As Fadi examines each photo, Mummy leans in toward him to explain the elaborate Hindu rituals taking place the day she and my dad started life together. Each shot glitters with the fabric of saris and the twinkle of gold jewellery.

My parents have a uniquely naive yet regal look in these photos that is, to me, striking. They seem almost surprised at their fate—yet it's clear they were both proud to be the focal point of two families coming together. I wonder how Fadi and I—two gay men raised in, respectively, Hindu and Islamic families—will continue this sacred tradition if and when our day comes.

Regardless of what we choose, whether our marriage-to-come will be recognized under Canadian law depends on what the courts and government decide in the next few years. Across the country, gay men and women are seeking recognition of their right to marry. Recent rulings in the three most populous provinces, Ontario, Quebec, and British Columbia, have found that the exclusion of same-sex couples from marriage violates the equality rights section of the Charter of Rights and Freedoms, although the B.C. judge held that the discrimination was justified.

Last week, federal lawyers asked the Ontario Court of Appeal [5] to overturn the decision in that province. But Ottawa was also exploring other approaches. Federal Justice Minister Martin Cauchon has presented his cabinet colleagues with a range of options to deal with the issue. Three ministers—Allan Rock, Bill Graham and Sheila Copps—have publicly supported same-sex marriage legislation. But in the absence of cabinet consensus, the matter has gone to a Parliamentary committee for study—an age-old delay tactic to move issues off the front-burner. The committee began its public sessions in Ottawa on Jan. 28, hearing deputations from groups in favour of and opposed to same-sex marriage legislation. Then came town-hall style hearings across the country—Vancouver, Halifax, Iqaluit, Toronto, etc.—with the committee expected to present its findings late this year.

Leaving aside the bizarre notion that consensus is required for formalizing equality in our laws, there is something admirable about a travelling same-sex road show. While Fadi and I would be happy to win our right to marriage equality in court, if necessary, there's also a glimmer of hope that the federal government could pass legislation giving us that right even before being forced to by law. In symbolic and emotional terms, that would be great news for us and for other gay couples: recognition of our right to marry would come from our country's elected officials, rather than our appointed nine rulers in the Supreme Court. We'd see that outcome as bottom-up validation from our families and peers, rather than a top-down decree.

In a way, that hope reminds me of the way I saw Mummy, on that visit home, gently patting Fadi's back as she eagerly turned a page to another set of images. I had a lump the size of a golf ball in my throat. The last time I brought a guy home for her to meet, she had to excuse herself continually as she tried to hide the water pooling up in her eyes. Drama queen. But there she sat this time, showing her potential son-in-law her cherished photos, easily throwing around the term "beta"—or son—when talking to him.

While Fadi may have won Mummy's approval, we don't hold our breath waiting for the federal government's. Asked his opinion on the matter in a recent media scrum, Jean Chretien wouldn't say. "We want to have a committee to consult Canadians and experts on the matter," he said. "If I want to listen, it's not for me to tell you what I think before I listen."

But are you really listening, Mr. Chretien? Not that equality rights should be subject to a popularity contest, but even if they were, it's clear that public support for same-sex marriage legislation is growing. In last year's *Maclean's* year-end poll, 49 per cent of respondents said yes when asked if gay marriages should be legally recognized, while 46 per cent were opposed. Sure, that's a close call—but when you consider that the number of supporters was highest among people under the age of 40 (60 per cent in favour), you can see that a wave of support is building.

10 Marriage is a basic right in any civil society; a fundamental mark of citizenship. Without turning to complex legal arguments, there is an intuitive method of grasping this point. What would be more objectionable to people who believe in the institution of marriage—to be denied a vote in the next federal election or to no longer have legal attachment to their wife or husband? Not a close call.

When such a basic right is involved, the burden of proof should lie with those who want to deny it to a small minority of citizens, not with those who seek to extend it. So far, the opposite has been the case—both in our courts and in Parliamentary hearings. I was horrified to read the minutes of the Feb. 11 appearance of Rita Curley, "Christian Family Life chair" at St. Ignatius Martyr Catholic Church in Ottawa. "To redefine marriage to be more inclusive of homosexuals," said Curley, "is to create a new morality in which homosexuality is not merely tolerated but is normalized and would branch out into sexual activity with babies, children of both sexes, and with animals." Prove, the opponents say, that marriage will not collapse, that this reform will not lead to polygamy and incest and bestiality, that the world will not end and that we won't see the fall of Rome.

There's a very simple argument for same-sex marriage: it's good for gays and lesbians. It provides role models for young gay people who, after the trauma of coming out, can easily lapse into short-term relationships and insecurity without a tangible goal in sight. I would guess that those of us who would choose to embrace such a goal—with all the responsibilities it entails—would do so with more commitment than straight people. That's because we recognize that we are pioneers, and as such are the standard bearers for a new idea. Legal same-sex marriage could also help bridge the gulf between gays and their parents: it could bring the essence of gay life—a gay couple—into the heart of the traditional straight family in a way the family can most understand.

The only way gays and lesbians will achieve equal status in Canada is if we're given the right to marry. It's the only one of four options tabled by the justice ministry that is fair and just. The others are: maintaining the status quo by legislating the "opposite-sex" definition of marriage; retaining that definition while introducing registered partnerships or civil unions for same-sex couples; or leaving marriage to religions, effectively abolishing it as a legally recognized civil institution.

Creating a second class of marriage only perpetuates our second-class-citizen status. Leaving marriage up to individual religions would infuriate far too many Canadians. And most provinces and territories have already begun the process of legislating same-sex partnership benefits and civil unions. So undoing the process of moving toward fairness will simply not be accepted by most Canadians, straight or gay. It's already clear how the future of same-sex marriage in Canada will unfold. What remains to be seen is what side of history the government will find itself on.

15   In the meantime, back at my house, my sister gets up from the table and puts her hand on my shoulder. "More chai?" she asks. "For sure." Fadi and I will need our energy for the road ahead.

Suggestions for Writing and Discussion

1. What are the cultural issues suggested by the narrative Khanna provides, describing his relationship with his parents and his mother's response to his desire to marry his gay partner?
2. Khanna argues that gay men and lesbians will have full civil rights only when they are afforded the right to marry. List arguments you think might be made by proponents and opponents of this proposition.

A More Perfect Union: Reservations about Gay Marriage
Dennis O'Brien

Dennis O'Brien is the author of *The Idea of a Catholic University*. This article was published in the *Christian Century* in January 2004.

We have a bumper sticker on our car: "Keep Vermont Civil." The sticker is a bit tattered, since it goes back to the controversy about "civil unions"—the Vermont law passed in 2000 establishing various legal equivalencies to marital rights for gay and lesbian couples. The legislature had been forced to take action following the 1999 ruling of the Vermont Supreme Court holding that denial of marital rights to such unions violated the Vermont constitution's "common benefits" clause.

In a neat bit of Solomonic judgment, the court both rejected the gay and lesbian plaintiffs' claim that they were entitled to marriage licenses and declared that they were entitled to the benefits "incident on the marital relation." The court ruled that those benefits could be established by granting a marriage license, but that there might be other legislative means to assure proper benefits. The matter of specific statute was handed over to the legislature. The result was "civil unions."

A ruling in November 2003 by the Supreme Judicial Court of Massachusetts similarly affirmed "marital" rights for gay and lesbian couples and handed the matter on to the legislature of the Commonwealth. The tone of the 4–3 decision of the Massachusetts Court appears, however, to push toward an unequivocal affirmation of "gay marriage." That would seem to be the hope and expectation of gay activists. Perhaps "gay marriage" will finally emerge as the statutory provision as it has in Canada and in various European jurisdictions. The heavens will not fall, the republic will not totter if that is the direction of public policy, but I am not enthusiastic about such a result. I prefer the "civil unions" approach.

Anyone who writes on this topic must do so with something akin to despair. Rationality is not on broad display in our discussion about sexuality, from homosexuality to abortion rights and back again. Advocates on all sides misstate their opponents' views and overstate their own to the point where careful discourse disappears. Nevertheless, I think it is worth trying to explicate some of the central claims and key issues that swirl around the discussion of gay marriage. I choose four topics: nature, education, culture and law as relevant to framing moral concerns and public policy.

First, nature: One of the dominant views both within and 5 without the gay community is that sexual orientation is a given, a natural determinant—perhaps the expression of a "gay gene." In his judicious exposition of the arguments for gay marriage, Bruce Bawer states the point succinctly:

> One can approve or disapprove of somebody's actions or opinions, beliefs; but it is meaningless to speak of approving or disapproving of another's innate characteristics. To say that someone approves or disapproves of somebody's homosexuality is like saying that one approves or disapproves of somebody's baldness or tallness.

I think that the gay community puts all too much weight on the notion of natural sexual orientation. In the first place, it just may not be true. If one were to assess sexual orientation by behavior rather than biology, one would be more inclined to Freud's view that our sexuality is polymorphous: heterosexual and homosexual and what all, through a fascinating range of fact and fantasy. Unipolar sexuality may be a strange outlier, not the rule.

The second problem with the idea of a "gay gene" is that it simply bypasses the value of homosexuality. How do we decide that the gay gene is not a defective gene like the gene for sickle cell anemia? Given access to abortion or gene therapy, the decision could be made to eliminate this fault of nature. Indian villagers have traditionally sought abortions for female fetuses; perhaps parents and societies will seek to abort fetuses with a gay gene. Gene therapy may lead to "designer children" who are handsomely tall, definitely not bald—and certainly not gay! If one believes, as I certainly do, that it is immoral to abort gay and female fetuses, that must be because there is some value in the expression of such a sexuality or such a gender. It would be much better for the gay community to argue that homosexuality enriches the range of human values in a way that being bald does not.

The third problem with resting the case on natural sexual orientation is that it needs a middle term to justify sexual behavior. This is as true of heterosexual behavior as of homosexual. The human gene pool is full of behavioral urges that may or may not be worthy of expression. Priests who choose celibacy or couples who choose an active sexual life claim that certain values are being expressed in their abstention from or participation in sexuality.

The standard Catholic position on homosexuality does not condemn homosexual orientation; it does condemn homosexual behavior. Thomas Aquinas is correct, I think, when he says that all human acts are moral acts. Sexual acts and behavior are distinctly human acts in that we can choose to engage in them or not. Not engaging in them may be difficult, but so is checking my anger and all too many other urges. We do not act sexually by automation as animals do when biologically triggered. The gay community has been so exercised to deny that homosexual orientation is chosen that it runs the danger of draining homosexual behavior of its human dimension as a chosen act or life.

10   The real issues about sexuality are choice, life style, and cultural value. On the basis of genes or Freudian polymorphous sex, sexuality in many forms is a fact. The question is, How should society assess and shape various sexual expressions? Is America now more morally sensitive, more well structured in its laws and practices insofar as it accepts publicly avowed homosexual behavior; constructs laws that protect homosexuals from the criminal penalties formally attached to homosexual acts; and allows for civil unions or even gay marriages? On the whole, I am inclined to say that getting gay sex out of the closet and legally protected is a moral and political advance. But that is not because homosexuality is natural but because something of value emerges from it.

Education: If one holds that sexual orientation may be poly-morphous, one should then face the problem of the sexual educa-tion of children and young adults. Admittedly, educating for sexual direction is somewhere between unclear and utter mystery, but to whatever extent parents and educators can give advice and cues for sexual orientation and behavior, one must ask: Are some kinds of sexual lives to be preferred?

Having worked with late adolescents most of my career, I am inclined to think that sexual confusion is as much a fact of life as sexual determination. One of the reasons to be concerned with the notion of natural, genetically determined sexual orientation is that it assumes that inclination is destiny. If a young person flirts with homosexuality, sexual-orientation-by-nature confirms gay identity. Maybe not.

What then should a parent, educator or society in general say to a young person caught in a mixed stew of sexual inclinations? Would it be proper to advise a confused teenager that heterosexu-ality is a preferred sexual life? And if so, what are the grounds for such advice? Difficult and complex as assessing various sexual lives may be, I want to resist the notion that it is a matter of indif-ference. "I don't care. Any sexual life—heterosexual, homosexual, bisexual—is OK. It's all the same. You choose whatever you want."

I am not denying that there can be deep determinations to-ward differing sexual lives. Though I am skeptical that sexual ori-entation is genetic, it certainly can emerge as "second nature": a pattern of desire, circumstance and culture that is virtually inerad-icable. And so I am equally skeptical about the possibility (or morality) of persuading or treating mature homosexuals in order to change their sexual direction.

The issue is not with the mature, stable homosexual (or het-   15
erosexual); it is with the immature, whose sexual orientation may well be relatively open. Is it legitimate morally, politically or spir-itually to commend one or the other sexual orientation? I don't necessarily want to prejudice the question toward heterosexuality; I can imagine a sensitive male homosexual commending the un-usually close bonding and intense sexuality of that relationship as the preferred life choice. The educational problem I want to raise is whether any conversation commending this or that sexual life pattern is legitimate.

Culture: One of the confusions in the sexual polemics of the day is the blurring of the line between natural orientation and chosen behavior. If you have the orientation, then of course behavior should follow and is fully morally legitimate. Sexual libertarians argue that the repression of sexual urges of whatever sort is psychologically disastrous and culturally stultifying. I like this argument because it shifts to issues of moral choice and social values. Repression is bad for you and your society!

Just how far should the value of nonrepression be taken? One of the byproducts of the sexual revolution has been the emergence of bisexuality—presumably a natural given. Advocates of marriage, heterosexual or gay, would both have to agree that bisexual orientation must be repressed in the interests of marital fidelity: One cannot be faithful to a sexual partner if one is having sex with someone of a different sex. Gay marriage advocates are, as they often say, conservatives on the issue of sexual fidelity.

Returning to my sexually confused adolescent: If I am in favor of the spiritual and moral value of sexual fidelity, then I am going to commend traditional marriage. A bisexual life or an "open" marriage is judged as an unacceptable choice, natural inclination to the contrary notwithstanding.

Of course, one can then go on and question the value of sexual fidelity both for partners and the social good. The least negative comment I would make here about "open" sexuality is that while it may be compatible with a large range of other social goods like justice and friendship, it is not clearly conducive to those broader social values. (I credit the distinction to the late Victor Preller.)

20   Can one go any farther in advising the young about sexual life choices? If there is genuine sexual polyvalence and confusion, I would be inclined to commend heterosexuality. Why? Given the drift of this essay, it would have to be because the moral and spiritual values that can be realized in heterosexual life are either impossible or difficult to realize or sustain in homosexual life. At this point, any gay friend will ask how I know about the values of gay life since I haven't lived it!

To be sure. I grant the argument and reinforce it. I suspect that there are deep values that can emerge in certain homosexual lives which are unique to that life and which cannot be replicated in content or depth in heterosexual life. A commitment to heterosexuality obviously attenuates male-male relations from the wilder, deeper passions and revelations of mutual sexuality. That is the price one pays for heterosexual life choice.

Any argument for heterosexuality as a preferred sexual choice does not rest on how this or that heterosexual life works out. Heterosexual marriage can be a human disaster—the divorce statistics attest to that! Homosexual bonding may be deeply valuable and, as noted, reach ranges of the human heart that heterosexuality cannot. Any argument for heterosexuality must deal with broad cultural and spiritual realities.

Having said that, it is obvious that constructing the case for heterosexuality must be as complex and nuanced as the cultural and spiritual trajectories of the human spirit. To short-circuit that long argument, I would say that it comes down to the ancient belief that men and women are different. Luce Irigary puts it well in *An Ethics of Sexual Difference:* "man and woman, woman and man are always meeting as though for the first time because they cannot be substituted for one another."

Why heterosexuality? Because the human spirit can expand as it moves toward the different. It can; it may not. Certainly some homosexual (or celibate) life choices arise from a fear of the different in women (or men). On the other hand, in a society that devalues heterosexuality and marriage through a mix of sentimentality and sexual titillation, the choice of homosexuality may be the choice of the different which is revelatory. So be it. But the final fact is that the bodily, biological difference between men and women is the urtext of the heterosexual narrative. Writing that sexual script is inherently difficult—that is the reason that sentimentality and fantasy are so popular: they conceal the pain of difference and the lessons of loving across that pain.

Law: One might well conclude that commending heterosexuality as a preferred sexual life is educationally legitimate, and then ask: But what about the law? Just because one may commend one life choice over another—being a social worker over being a stock broker—does not mean the preference needs to be legally enforced (there is no law against being a stock broker). Perhaps the issue of gay or heterosexual direction should be left to the subtleties of parental or church guidance. Whether that is the final conclusion or not will depend on how one views the role of law.

For classical philosophers law had an educational function; it was set up to structure individual and communal life in order to produce certain human virtues. In Aristotle's work, [individual and communal life values] are mutually supporting. One needs certain virtues like courage, temperance and justice in order to realize human good, but those virtues are also necessary to be a good citizen. The state, in turn, is bound through the enactment and enforcement of proper laws to educate for virtue both for its own sake and for human prospering.

The educational role of law is at best recessive in the American understanding of law. We tend to view law not as aimed at creating individual or common good but as a means of mediating dispute and keeping civil peace. In so far as that is the dominant view of law in America, "gay marriage" says nothing about the morality of homosexuality one way or the other, it simply guarantees that all "domestic partnerships" (an alternative term considered for "civil unions") are treated equally. All well and good. But I am not certain that one can ever completely erase the educational effect of law.

The law may not deliberately create culture, but it certainly becomes a sign within the culture. Giving legal status to gay marriage does appear to suggest that the difference between gay and heterosexual partnerships is a matter of irrelevance. It will surely make it more difficult for parents or the churches to argue a preference for heterosexual marriage (which I hope they will wish to do). Thus I remain in favor of "civil union" as a concept more in keeping with our restrained sense of law and less tilted toward the equating of gay and heterosexual unions.

Suggestions for Writing and Discussion

1. Summarize O'Brien's views on the four topics he addresses in his discussion of gay marriage.
2. Why does O'Brien favor civil unions for gay and lesbian couples rather than marriage? What differences between the two possibilities do you see?

Making Connections: Synthesis and Analysis

1. Ramesh Ponnuru suggests that the behavior of heterosexual men and women is more of a threat to the institution of marriage than is the possibility of gay marriage. Considering his observations, as well as the observations of the other

writers in this section, what examples support this point of view? How convincing do you find this argument? Explain.

2. After reading all four articles, list the reasons conservative thinkers oppose gay marriage. How do they back up their claims? How convincing do you find these claims? Explain.

3. Suneel Khanna and Dennis O'Brien discuss civil unions as an alternative to the right to marry. Khanna argues against the idea that civil unions confer full civil rights, while O'Brien argues the opposite point of view. After doing research on the distinctions between the legal rights conveyed by marriage laws and the legal rights conveyed by civil unions, explain why you do or do not agree with Khanna.

John Fewings, Same Sex Marriage. Copyright © by John Fewings.

Topics for Writing and Discussion

1. Compare the cartoon "Marriage Controversies" (page 242) with the article by Mathabane. What details in the cartoon suggest the artist's attitude toward the opinions expressed by the figures depicted? In what ways do the points made by Mathabane compare or contrast with the opinions suggested by the cartoon?

2. Compare the message of the text and image in "Help America Save Marriage!" (page 240) with the text and image in the cartoon "Same Sex Marriage" (page 238) and the photograph "Gay Rights Activists" (page 241). In what ways are the couples depicted similar? In what ways are they different?

3. Compare and contrast Dennis O'Brien's (page 231) view of heterosexual marriage with the view implied by the cartoon "Same Sex Marriage."

4. Both "Help America Save Marriage!" and "Two Women Celebrate Their Legal Marriage" (page 242) show newly married couples. How do these images and the text surrounding these images compare and contrast?

EXTENDED CONNECTIONS: FOR CRITICAL THINKING, WRITING, AND RESEARCH

1. Is the issue of equal dress codes for males and females important or trivial? Using details and examples from selections in this chapter as well as from research in various sources (books, online databases, interviews), make one of these two arguments:

   a. An equal dress code for males and females is an important issue that carries real significance related to gender fairness.

   b. An equal dress code for males and females is a trivial issue that only interferes with the attention that should be paid to more significant gender-related topics.

2. Using details and examples from selections in this chapter as well as from research in various sources (books, online databases, interviews), make one of these two arguments:

Help America Save Marriage!

| Home | Purpose of Petition | Inform Family and Friends |

The Massachusetts Supreme Judicial Court has issued a ruling to make homosexual marriage legal. Because of the "full faith and credit" clause in the U. S. Constitution, every other state may be forced to accept the legalization of homosexual marriage by recognizing the Massachusetts decision.

To protect traditional marriage as being a union between one man and one woman, we must unite and amend our Constitution.

To add your name to the petition to defend traditional marriage, fill out the information below.

Inform
Friends & Family

Success of the marriage amendment will require support of millions. Click here to send this petition to others.

Distribute the Petition

Print the petition and distribute it in your church, neighborhood, or civic organizations.

Talking Points on Same Sex Marriage

Print this document to help you discuss why same sex marriage is not a good thing..

Save Traditional Marriage

A Petition to the United States Congress

Traditional marriage is one of the key foundations of a civil American society. This foundation is under attack and needs your support. Congressional Rep. Marilyn Musgrave has introduced before congress the Federal marriage Amendment (H.J. 56) which simply states:

> **"Marriage in the United States shall consist only of the union between a man and a woman. Neither this constitution or the constitution of any state, nor state or federal law, shall be construed to require that marital status or the legal incidents thereof be conferred upon unmarried couples or groups."**

I urge you to use your position in the congress to defend the sanctity of traditional marriage in America by giving this amendment your full and complete support.

Signed,

Title: Mr.
First Name:
Last Name:
Address:

City:
State: Alabama
ZIP:
Email:
Phone Number:

[Submit]

*Web page (www.defeatgaymarriage.com), "Help America Save Marriage!",
urging visitors to petition Congress for the passage of a Federal marriage
amendment "to defend the sanctity of traditional marriage." Used by permission of the National Center for Freedom and Renewal.*

Gay rights activists rally for same-sex mariage in West Hollywood, California, May 19, 2004

    a. The United States has made significant moves toward gender equality since the eighteenth century, and very few further changes are needed.

    b. Although there have been some significant changes in gender equality since the eighteenth century, this country needs to make still more progress.

Two women celebrate their legal marriage during the 34th annual Boston Gay Pride Parade in Boston, Massachusetts, June 12, 2004

Darrin Bell, "Marriage Controversies: 1960 and 2000," March 6, 2000. Copyright © 2000 by Darrin Bell.

3. Several selections in this chapter relate to the rights of gay men and women. Choosing an issue other than gay marriage or dress codes for gay students, investigate a topic related to gay men and lesbians in the United States (for instance, their right to custody of children or to adopt children). Using details and examples from research in various sources (books, online databases, interviews), argue that the right you are investigating should or should not be granted to gay men and lesbians.

CHAPTER 7

Exploring Pop Culture: Media Messages

INTRODUCTION

Americans have a complicated and often contradictory relationship with the icons and industries related to pop culture. For example, long after many people have forgotten that the New England Patriots won the 2004 Super Bowl with a breathtaking last-minute field goal, everyone will remember the moment of Janet Jackson's "wardrobe malfunction" and the way fans' applause gave way to outrage. While some saw the moment as trivial, others, including U.S. Congress members, felt called upon to demand strong censorship standards of the television networks.

The first two pieces in this chapter suggest the long history of censorship. Robert Atkins notes that the desire to control and even ban the work of popular writers, artists, and philosophers dates back at least to the time of the Old Testament. Phillip Taylor provides a look at the music industry in the United States. Beginning with an example from 1957, he demonstrates how often recording artists and their studios have been the target of censorship initiatives.

The first topical question of the next section asks, "Whose Music Is It, Anyway?" Bill Holland provides background information on copyright law, leading to three articles addressing the current music industry controversy related to music sharing through Web sites. Amy Harmon explores arguments for and against the active cooperation of colleges and universities in tracking down students who share music files. Michael Rogers contends that file sharing is wrong and that it will have devastating effects that go beyond the music industry. Cornell student Ben

Kupstas argues for a third possibility—an inexpensive distribution system, noting that "even the musicians and members of the file-sharing community" often support such an alternative.

How could Harry Potter be evil? In the next section, Robert Seltzer provides a look at the reasons for a Texas bonfire at which hundreds of individuals burned copies of the Harry Potter books, while Will Manley discusses reasons for book burning and the power carried by the image of a burning book. Steve Eighinger also offers a view of the arguments for and against the Potter series as books that are appropriate for young people.

Throughout this chapter, issues of First Amendment rights are raised. Who has the right to "own" words or music? Who has the right to forbid words, music, or images to be read, heard, or viewed? The answers to these questions relate to rights and responsibilities with which we are all struggling during the challenging times in which we live.

· *THEN* ·

SETTING THE CONTEXT:
POP CULTURE THEN

Suggestions for Prereading or Journal Writing

1. How would you define the word *censorship*? Does this word hold mainly negative or mainly positive associations for you?
2. Think of an example in which you or someone you know experienced censorship of a book, film, music video, or other item. What was the reason for the censorship? Who was the censor (store owner, public official, school official, parent)? What was your response to this example of censorship?

A Brief and Idiosyncratic History of Censorship

Robert Atkins

Robert Atkins, a fellow at Carnegie Mellon University's STUDIO for Creative Inquiry, offers an intriguing and often frightening look at censorship of various works of art, literature, philosophy, and music. Although in recent years many of these works have been recognized as masterpieces, the critics of their own times (and in some cases later times) found them shocking enough to ban. This article appears on "The File Room," an online artists' project produced jointly by the Randolph Street Art Gallery, the Chicago Department of Cultural Affairs, and the School of Art and Design at the University of Illinois, Chicago.

Should homo sapiens be renamed homo censoris? We're certainly the only species capable of censorship. Where does this troublesome urge come from? Perhaps it's merely an extension of that age-old, apparently hormonal instinct to dominate and control. Whatever its origins, censorship—the prohibition of speech or expression divorced from action—transcends cultural boundaries and predates recorded history. The Old Testament informs us that the Hebrews burned the prophecy of Jeremiah because it was too downbeat. Confucius's writings were incinerated around 250 BC after a change of dynasty made them politically incorrect. The Roman historian Tacitus mistakenly believed that Augustus was the first emperor to destroy books and punish speech, but the Romans had actually taken their cues from the Greeks. To be fair, the Romans should be credited with refining the practice of censorship, as well as with coining the term itself. Beginning in the fifth century BC, they commissioned "censors" whose primary purpose was to conduct the "census," in order to rationalize the collection of taxes. As night follows day, the imposition of moral standards followed the imposition of standards for citizenship. Around the time of Christ, Augustus codified these moral standards into law. But as Tacitus wisely noted about "immoral" books: "So long as the possession of these writings was attended by danger, they were eagerly sought and read: when there was no longer any difficulty in securing them, they fell into oblivion."

So what else is new? That's the thing about censorship—it seems to spring from misguided, but ever-so-human nature. What follows is a sometimes tragic, sometimes inadvertently amusing chronicle of mostly Western milestones in censorship since the fall of the Roman Empire. Rest assured that each of these objects—or agents—of censorship stands for hundreds like it.

VENUS DE MILO. The armless classical statue was tried, convicted and condemned for nudity in Mannheim, Germany, in 1853. Reproductions of that day chastely renamed Venus the Goddess of Liberty. In 1911—in what critics ridiculed as an "elephantiasis of modesty"—Buffalo alderman John Sullivan and local Catholic clergy sought to cover up several reproductions of classical statues including Venus. Circa 1930 reproductions of the statue in Palmolive ads got censor's dots over Venus's breasts, and in Hungary, police burned her photo in a shop window. In 1955, in Winona Lake, IN, a full-scale reproduction was covered in poison ivy by a puritanical housewife hoping to disguise the statue's nudity.

MEDIEVAL FRENCH DRESS. Philipe le Bel of France ruled in 1294 that bourgeois persons might not wear squirrel or gray fur, ermine, precious stones, gold or crowns. To enforce and delineate class distinctions, dukes, counts, and barons with income of 6000 livres a year might annually purchase four robes (suits). Knights with incomes of 3000 livres were allowed just three robes, one of which had to be for summer.

5   MICHELANGELO. On its unveiling in Florence in 1501, onlookers stoned Michelangelo's "David," breaking off an arm. At Forest Lawn Memorial Park in California, the penis on a reproduction of "David" was masked with a fig leaf from 1939–69; its removal caused complaints. In 1969, a poster of "David" in a book shop in Australia was seized by the Sydney vice squad. Michelangelo's "Last Judgment" fresco in the Sistine Chapel proved controversial even before its unveiling in 1541. Blaylo de Cesena, the papal master of ceremonies, warned Pope Paul III, that its nudes were "better suited to a bathroom or roadside wine shop than to a chapel of the Pope." In 1558, veils, draperies and skirts were added. The work was the basis of the publication "Dialogue on the Error of Painters" (1564) by Andrea Gilio da Fabriano, which denigrated nudity in painting. In 1933, a New York court declared a set of pictures of the fresco obscene.

CALVINISM. Under John Calvin's rule, do's and don'ts in mid-16th century Geneva were enforced by annual visits to the populace from a minister and an elder. They checked for violations of the Old and New Testament monitoring, for instance, children's respect for their parents (some children are known to have been beheaded for striking their parents). Other areas of concern that seem far more foreign to us include: 1) the number of dishes that might be served at a meal (even wedding banquets were limited to three courses); 2) the wearing of jewelry, lace, frilly hats, or hair arranged to an "immoral height;" 3) the prohibition of theater and many books (authors of books critical of Calvin had to throw them into fires with their own hands) and 4) staying up past 9 p.m. at inns.

BOWDLER FAMILY. The term "bowdlerize" means to expurgate literature; it comes from the English family that pioneered the commercial cutting—really rewriting—of literature. The most famous Bowdler family members were Thomas and his sister Henrietta Maria. Harriet—who could not bear the indelicacy of dancers at the opera—anonymously published "Sermons on the Doctrines and Duties of Christianity," which ran into 50 printings. Thomas published the "Family Shakespeare," ironically deleting notice of Harriet's participation in the project. It became the best-selling Shakespeare of the 19th century. In 1826, he published "The Family Gibbon," a sanitized, debauchery-free gloss on Edward Gibbon's "The Decline and Fall of the Roman Empire."

WILLIAM SHAKESPEARE. The works of Shakespeare (1564–1616) have been expurgated more often than those of any other English language author except Chaucer. The bard was first bowdlerized by Queen Elizabeth I who cut the passage in "Richard II" in which the king is deposed. In 1660, Sir William Avenant trimmed seven plays with the intention "that they may be reformed of profanities and ribaldry." In the 18th century, by contrast, greater ribaldry was desired. Dryden's version of "The Tempest," for instance, gave Miranda a new—and sexy—twin sister.

SHIKANO BUZAEMON. Shikano Buzaemon, a professional storyteller in theaters, published a collection of stories in 1686. Seven years later, a rumor spread that a talking horse had predicted an epidemic that could be prevented by eating pickled plums. Authorities investigating the run on the plum market and a twenty-fold increase in plum prices traced the rumor to a shopkeeper who got the idea from one of Shikano's stories. Shikano was sentenced to banishment, but died before being deported.

CHARLES SEDLEY. Sir Charles Sedley (1639–1701), was a **10** dramatist, a poet, and an insider at the court of King Charles II.

He was equally well known for his drunken exploits. In June, 1663, he and some friends appeared "inflam'd with strong liquors" on the balcony of the Cock public house in London. They lowered their breeches and "excrementiz'd" on the crowd below, followed by a shower of urine-filled bottles and blasphemous speeches. They were sent to court and found guilty under a novel use of England's obscene-libel laws, which were based on the right to punish or prohibit any act contrary to the public interest. Subsequent obscenity laws in Anglo-Saxon cultures are based on this precedent.

ANTHONY COMSTOCK & GEORGE BERNARD SHAW. Anthony Comstock (1844–1915) was the pioneer of modern American censorship. Starting with a police-assisted raid on a New York bookstore in 1868, the twin goals of Comstock's crusade were the elimination of obscenity and criminalization of abortion and contraception. The Comstock-inspired federal anti obscenity law of 1873 banned items "for the prevention of conception" and this phrase was echoed in similar laws passed by 22 states. (Many remain on the books.) As a special "postal inspector," Comstock abused his considerable powers by raiding the Arts Student League in New York in 1906 for its use of nude models and cautioned that "obscene, lewd and indecent" photos are "commonly, but mistakenly called art." In 1905, Comstock denounced George Bernard Shaw as an "Irish smut dealer" and his New York-bound play, "Mrs. Warren's Profession," as "reekings." The author of this play about prostitution was charged with obscenity in the Court of Special Sessions, but was cleared. Shaw irritated Comstock with his invention of the term "Comstockery," which he characterized as "the world's standing joke at the expense of the US. Europe likes to hear of such things. It confirms the deep-seated conviction of the Old World that America is a provincial place, a second-rate, country-town civilization after all." H.L. Mencken tartly observed of Comstock that "more than any other man he liberated American letters from the blight of Puritanism."

[. . .]

SCOPES TRIAL (1927). Tennessee's Anti-Evolution Act of 1925 outlawed the teaching of Darwinian theory. John Scopes, a young biology teacher, volunteered to be a test case to challenge the law; Clarence Darrow took the case for no fee. He attacked what he regarded as excessive religiosity in the courtroom; objecting to Judge John Raulston's pretrial prayers and having a

"Read Your Bible" sign removed from the courtroom. The obstreperous Darrow went on to demolish William Jennings Bryan's fundamentalist arguments, but still lost the case because he never denied that Scopes had taught Darwinian theory. The Supreme Court later reversed Scopes's conviction on a technicality.

DIEGO RIVERA. Mexican painter Diego Rivera (1886–1957) was among the great muralists of the 20th century. In 1933, capitalist extraordinaire Nelson Rockefeller commissioned a $21,000 mural on the theme of "human intelligence in control of nature," from the socialist artist for the new RCA Building in Rockefeller Center. While working on the 63 x 17' mural in May, 1933, Rivera was dismissed from the project and paid off. Rockefeller objected to Rivera's inclusion of a portrait of Lenin. (His original sketch had simply called for "a great leader.") Rockefeller suggested that Lenin be replaced by an anonymous figure; Rivera volunteered to add Lincoln. No accord was reached and the fresco was destroyed. Rockefeller charged Rivera with propagandizing and Rivera countered that "All art is propaganda."

LENNY BRUCE. Labeled "America's #1 Vomic" by columnist Walter Winchell, Lenny Bruce was the hottest American comedian of the early sixties. His free form fantasies and rambling stories assaulted people accustomed to aw-shucks style humor. He regarded restrictions on free speech as ludicrous and observed that: "A knowledge of syphilis is not an instruction to contract it." He was tried for obscenity in Philadelphia, Beverly Hills, and Chicago during the early sixties, and deported from the United Kingdom in 1964. His Chicago obscenity trial in 1963 was typical for its focus on his mockery of religion. Increasingly embittered and consumed by his legal problems, he died of a drug overdose in 1966.

JOHN LENNON. John Lennon enraged Americans with his 1966 remark that the Beatles were more popular than Jesus. Christian groups burned Beatles records and tried to get the group's music pulled from radio play. Similar protests greeted the cover of his 1968 album "Two Virgins" portraying him and Yoko Ono in the nude. During the early seventies, President Nixon, Senator Strom Thurmond and the FBI tried to have him deported because of his politically incendiary lyrics.

Other censored musicians of the twentieth century include: Kurt Weill and Bertold Brecht (by the Nazis); Dmitri Shostakovich (USSR); the Weavers (by US radio stations during the McCarthy era); the Sex Pistols (UK); the Rolling Stones (UK & US); Jethro Tull (UK); and Elvis Presley, Jim Morrison, Van Morrison, Bob Dylan and the Kingsmen (of "Louie, Louie" fame) almost everywhere. More recently, 2 Live Crew was unsuccessfully tried for obscenity in Federal court in Florida, and Pepsi canceled a contract with Madonna under pressure from Donald Wildmon's American Family Association, which objected to the "blasphemous" music video "Like a Virgin."

CENSORED BOOKS (AND BOOK BURNINGS) IN THE US SINCE 1965. A compilation of six surveys conducted by librarians and libertarian organizations show that the ten, most frequently attacked books in the US since 1965 are: "The Adventures of Huckleberry Finn," "Diary of a Young Girl" (Anne Frank), "Black Like Me," "Brave New World," "The Catcher in the Rye," "Deliverance," "The Electric Kool-Aid Acid Test," "A Farewell to Arms," "Go Ask Alice," "The Good Earth," and "The Grapes of Wrath."

Books recently burned in the US include: "Slaughterhouse Five" at Drake, ND, in 1974; "Of Mice and Men," at Oil City, PA in 1977; "Values Clarification" at Warsaw, IN, in 1977; "The Living Bible" at Glastonia, NC, in 1981; and copies of the "National Geographic," Disney comic books, and "Fifty True Tales of Terror" in Omaha in 1981.

As Tacitus's ancient observation about the allure of banned books reminds us, when it comes to restricting speech and thought, there is precious little new under the sun.

Suggestions for Writing and Discussion

1. In the first paragraph of this article, Robert Atkins speculates on the motives for censorship. Briefly summarize his thoughts on this subject and then explain, with examples you have observed, why you do or do not agree with him.
2. Choose one work that Atkins mentions with which you are familiar. Then write two paragraphs. In the first paragraph, give reasons that this work should be censored. In the second paragraph, explain why the work should not be censored.

First Amendment Rocks Memphis
Phillip Taylor

Phillip Taylor, a writer based in Newport News, Virginia, describes examples of music censorship and the responses of the American recording industry to such censorship, beginning in 1957 with a distributor's doubts about the lyrics of a Jerry Lee Lewis song. This selection first appeared on October 15, 1999, on www.freedomforum.org, an organization concerned with First Amendment rights.

Memphis, Tenn.—Sam Phillips remembers being waist-deep in promotions for Jerry Lee Lewis in 1957 when a Detroit-based record distributor called to express worries about the title of the piano rocker's song, "Whole Lotta Shakin' Goin' On."

Phillips, founder of the legendary Sun Records here, said the distributor was worried about what people might think was "shakin'." He said he refused to delete the word "it" from the "shake it, baby" refrain, believing that the song would get radio airplay without modification. The uncensored record became the third-best-selling song in the country in September 1957.

Phillips said nothing was raised as objectionable about another classic, "Great Balls of Fire."

"But you see how you're wont to make connotations out of something when you want to get rid of it in the first place?" he said.

The man credited with unleashing Elvis Presley upon an unsuspecting world got used to vestiges of censorship but never liked it.   5

"Censorship is the most dangerous thing that God has ever let live or exist on this world," Phillips told an audience of more than 300 journalists gathered yesterday for the 1999 Associated Press Managing Editors National Convention in Memphis' Peabody Hotel. "Because when you start messing with the creative energies of people, you don't have much left in this world."

For a conference program, "Elvis, Music Censorship and the First Amendment," The Freedom Forum's First Amendment Center gathered Phillips, Sir Mack Rice of the Falcons and writer of "Mustang Sally," John Kay of the seminal rock band Steppenwolf and singer-songwriter Jill Sobule.

Charles Overby, chairman and CEO of The Freedom Forum, said a program on music censorship—including a raucous Steppenwolf performance—was just the thing to get the editors thinking about what keeps them free to publish.

"The freedom of the press is not highly regarded somewhat because it is viewed as a special-interest piece of legislation," Overby said. "One of the reasons that's the case is that people in the newspaper business tend to care about freedom of the press and either don't care or don't know or don't understand the other four freedoms."

10   In a recent survey on music censorship, the First Amendment Center found that 54% of Americans polled agreed that musicians should be allowed to sing songs with words that others might find offensive. The poll revealed that 62% agreed that radio stations should be allowed to play songs of a political nature.

But the approval numbers drop significantly when stations play music with themes of violence, drugs or sex. The survey found that 75% of those polled disagreed that stations should be allowed to play songs with violent lyrics, while 81% disagreed about songs about drugs and 68% disagreed about sexually suggestive songs.

The questions were part of a larger survey on the State of the First Amendment that the center released in July.

For yesterday's program, the First Amendment Center took advantage of Memphis' blues and rock-'n'-roll history and used one of the city's favorite sons—Elvis Presley—as a vantage point from which to discuss music censorship.

"When he emerged out of this city, he frightened a lot of people and when he went to places like Jacksonville (Fla.)—they said you can sing but you can't move," said Ken Paulson, executive director of the First Amendment Center and moderator of the program. "And that was a classic example of prior restraint of government."

15   Paulson noted that it was an Elvis appearance on "The Ed Sullivan Show"—one where producers refused to allow cameras to film the rocker below his waist—that gave many young Americans of the time their first taste of censorship.

Sir Mack Rice remembered such concerns while the Falcons were touring in the 1950s with Hank Ballard and the Midnighters, performers of the oft-censored tune "Work With Me, Annie."

"We were in Alabama and the authorities said, 'We're going to let you Midnighters sing, but we don't want no dancing,'" said Rice, who said the bands didn't object then because they wanted first and foremost to sing.

For Jill Sobule, censorship came as her very first single, the 1995 hit "I Kissed a Girl," struggled to find airplay in some markets because of its lesbian theme.

"The positive thing was, if there hadn't been that controversy, the censorship, I wouldn't have sold as many records as I did," said Sobule, noted for songs of social commentary.

For the program, Sobule played and sang a song she had   20 penned only hours earlier with Nashville musician Bill Lloyd about New York City Mayor Rudolph Giuliani and his opposition to the hotly debated "Sensations" exhibit at the Brooklyn Museum of Art. It's called "Call Rudy."

"Call Rudy if your art's a little queer, call Rudy, election year is near," Sobule sang. "Don't call the Whitney, don't call the Met, don't call MOMA, lest you forget. You can be a sensation on every news station, lines around the block to see your degradation. It's your duty, call Rudy."

Steppenwolf's John Kay also drew applause after he related a story where authorities in Winston-Salem, N.C., stifled the band's efforts to play "The Pusher," an anti-drug song banned for the line "God damn the pusher man." Although the band promised not to sing the line, at Kay's urging thousands of fans at the concert shouted out the chorus themselves.

As a refugee from post-war Germany, Kay said he learned at a young age the effects of censorship.

"My growing up in East Germany after World War II made me keenly aware of how wrong things can go when oppression sets in and no one speaks up," said Kay, who then played a solo version of "The Pusher" and later joined his bandmates for "Born to Be Wild" and "Magic Carpet Ride."

For Phillips, the program held in the Peabody Hotel's Skyway   25 marked a sort of return to roots. Before Elvis ever walked through the doors of Sun Studios, Phillips said he spent a half dozen years in the late 1940s and early 1950s engineering broadcasts of big bands for the hotel's rooftop venue.

But something stirred the soul, he said, tempting him to find a sound that represented his poor upbringing in Alabama.

"My only aim was to stay in the business until I could prove, right or wrong, that we needed to be blazing some new trails," Phillips said. "I didn't do it to change the world. I just wanted the world to know some of the things that I was seeing, feeling and hearing even though there wasn't any noise going on."

Looking back on more than five decades of music, Phillips smiled as a man who knows he's right.

"Music has done more to break down areas of censorship, racism, international understanding," he said. "More than all of the damn ambassadors put together, and I mean around the world!"

Suggestions for Writing and Discussion

1. In this article, Phillip Taylor quotes Ken Paulson, executive director of the First Amendment Center, as saying about Elvis Presley, "When he emerged out of this city [Memphis], he frightened a lot of people." From the details Taylor provides, why do you think people were frightened by Presley? To what extent do you think their fears were justified? Explain.

2. Jill Sobule is quoted as saying that she would not have sold as many copies of her 1995 hit "I Kissed a Girl" if there had not been a move to censor the song because of its lesbian theme. To what extent do you think moves to censor simply give extra publicity and visibility to the work in question? Explain with examples.

Making Connections: Synthesis and Analysis

1. Compare Robert Atkins's approach to censorship with Phillip Taylor's. In what ways do their views differ? In what ways are they the same?

2. How do you think the technological changes in mass media (radio, television, film) have affected the issue of censorship? In your response, use examples from both Atkins's and Taylor's articles.

· *NOW* ·

WHOSE MUSIC IS IT, ANYWAY?

Suggestions for Prereading or Journal Writing

1. Should holding a copyright protect an individual's or corporation's right to sell, distribute, and profit from a product? Explain your response with examples.
2. Should institutions such as universities or businesses police their students and employees to make sure they are not violating copyright law? Explain.

EVALUATING AN ARGUMENT: MULTIPLE PERSPECTIVES

Piracy Suits: Shock and Awe
Bill Holland

Bill Holland is an investigative reporter who in January 2001 was awarded several writing prizes for his series of *Billboard* magazine articles addressing the United States Copyright Act. In this article, he provides background information on the file-sharing controversy. The title given is from the editor of this anthology.

The nation's top copyright cop has strongly endorsed the record industry's right to file subpoenas and sue those who illegally download songs over the Internet. During testimony Sept. 8 before the Senate Judiciary Committee, U.S. Register of Copyrights Marybeth Peters provided the clearest federal statement yet in support of industry efforts to combat piracy.

In addition to endorsing those efforts, spearheaded by the Recording Industry Assn. of America (RIAA), she said that if pending court cases go against the industry, Congress would have to remedy the situation. "Mr. Chairman, make no mistake. The law is unambiguous," she said. "Using peer-to-peer networks to copy or distribute copyrighted works without permission is infringement, and copyright owners have every right to invoke the power of the courts to combat such activity."

As head of the U.S. Copyright Office, Peters is the official interpreter of U.S. intellectual property law. She told lawmakers that a review would be necessary even if it means revisiting the underlying legal principle regarding copyrighted material put forth in the landmark 1985 Supreme Court case Sony v. Betamax. That decision gave the makers of video recording machines limited liability for any illegal copying on their devices.

Her testimony comes as the U.S. Court of Appeals is about to take up two important court challenges. In a case being heard in Washington, D.C., Verizon argues that the record industry's use of the information subpoena process authorized in the Digital Millennium Copyright Act (DMCA) is illegal. The other case before a federal court in Central California involves the RIAA's appeal of a lower court's ruling absolving Grokster, Kazaa and other file services from liability for content traded over their networks.

5   Peters made clear that in her view, the RIAA, representing copyright owners, is on solid legal ground in both cases. "The Digital Millennium Copyright Act represents a carefully crafted and balanced bargain, which utilizes the incentives created by pre-existing doctrines to encourage all stakeholders to work cooperatively to realize the potential of the Internet while respecting legal rights," she testified. "Taken together, the positions of Kazaa and Grokster, along with the arguments now made by Verizon, if they prevail, will leave copyright owners with little or no remedy against the most widespread phenomena of [copyright] infringement in the history of this country," she continued. "Thus," she said, "it is incumbent upon this committee and this Congress to see that if the judiciary fails to enforce the DMCA and therefore fails to provide the protection to which copyrighted works are entitled, the legislature does."

Peters told Judiciary Committee chairman Sen. Orrin Hatch, R-Utah, that every court that has addressed the issue has agreed that such activity is infringement. "It can also be a crime, and the perpetrators of such a crime are subject to fines and jail time," she said. She added that efforts to "rationalize or justify" illegal behavior with allegations of inflated profits or unfair dealings with recording artists are "diversionary tactics" that do not alter the fundamental fact that they are trying to defend illegal activity.

"There are some," she said, "who argue that copyright infringement on peer-to-peer systems is not truly harmful to copyright owners and may even help them generate new interest in their products. The law leaves that judgment to the copyright owner, and it ought not to be usurped by self-interested third parties who desire to use the copyright owner's work," she said.

Peters characterized Grokster and Kazaa, which the Central District of California ruled are not liable as secondary copyright infringers, as businesses that are "dependent upon massive copyright infringement." "Any application of the law that allows them to escape liability for lack of knowledge of those same infringements is inherently flawed," she said. Peters added that hanging over all these cases is the Supreme Court's decision on Sony. "It is perhaps a commentary on that opinion that almost 20 years later, we still have such uncertainty that three courts seem to interpret and apply it in three different ways," she said. "If the case law evolves as to compel the opposite result [of findings of liability for the owners of Kazaa and Grokster], I believe Sony should be revisited either by the Supreme Court or by Congress."

Suggestions for Writing and Discussion

1. Identify three points that Marybeth Peters makes against the practice of file sharing. How convincing do you find her arguments?

2. What is meant by "peer-to-peer" transfer of copyrighted data? What arguments can you think of for making such transfers legal? What arguments might be made against such transfers?

Recording Industry Goes after Students over Music Sharing

Amy Harmon

Investigative reporter Amy Harmon provides an in-depth look at students who claim that the recording industry's lawsuits against those who run file-sharing Web sites are alienating the very customers essential to the industry's survival.

College Park, Md.—Jason, a senior at the University of Maryland, ran one of the most popular Web sites on campus out of his shoebox dorm room here. The site let his 8,500 fellow dorm residents search for music files, among other things, stored on one another's computers and copy them in seconds.

Then came the news that the record industry had filed lawsuits against four students running similar sites at other universities, accusing them of enabling large-scale copyright infringement and asking for billions of dollars in damages. Within an hour, Jason, who insisted on anonymity for fear of being sued himself, had dismantled his site.

"I don't think I was doing anything wrong," said Jason, a computer science major. "But who wants to face a $98 billion debt for the rest of their lives? I was scared."

The lawsuits, filed on April 3, are the most aggressive legal action the record industry has ever directed against college students, who in recent years have exercised an enduring predisposition to consume large quantities of music by copying it over the Internet without ever paying for it. College campuses, the record industry says, have become far and away the prime locus for online piracy.

5   Wary of alienating young customers who continue to generate a large chunk of their revenue, record companies until recently focused on prodding university administrators to discipline their students. But freshman orientation sessions on respect for intellectual property have had little effect. With CD sales in a tailspin that record executives attribute at least partly to the downloading frenzy in academia's hallowed halls, they said they needed to try another approach.

Record executives say the lawsuits—singling out four students at three colleges—mark a turning point in the battle they have been waging since Napster popularized Internet music trading three years ago. (A federal judge in 2001 ruled that Napster had abetted copyright infringement, and it has been off line since.) The unauthorized copying of digital music that has become as routine a part of college life as cramming and keg parties may have finally lost some of its charm.

"We have decided to bring to the attention of universities just how much music piracy is going on on college campuses and universities," said Cary Sherman, president of the Recording Industry

Association of America, which brought the suits, "and we think that message has been received."

College students are not the only ones copying music off the Internet. But students, who often justify their behavior by arguing that CD's are too expensive and that artists do not get the money anyway, may be more hostile toward the music industry than most. Many say record labels should accept that the Internet has irrevocably changed their business and instead offer new services, like chat sessions with artists or early ticket sales for concerts, which they would be willing to pay for. Others say they buy as many or more CD's as they ever did because they are able to sample music free and discover artists they like.

"This is just more crazy litigation that shows everyone over 40 not understanding the future of music," said Thomas Geoghegan, 21, a history major at Maryland and a frequent user of Jason's site before it was so abruptly removed.

College administrators say they are mindful of their responsibility to teach students that what they are doing is wrong. They are also aware of the expense they are incurring as the constant flow of large media files strains campus networks.

At the same time, they want to protect students' privacy and rights to free speech and stay out of the role of monitoring what is sent over their networks. As a result, most colleges have simply sent warnings to students whom industry groups have reported as downloading copyrighted material. Some have required students to write papers on copyright law or have temporarily deprived them of Internet access. But such measures have had little impact.

"It's been very difficult because students have grown up viewing the Internet as a place where you go to get lots of free access to things," said Graham Spanier, president of Pennsylvania State University. "As we have tried to educate our students, half of them understand it's like going into a store and putting a CD in your pocket and the other half just can't see it that way."

The threat of legal retribution may be improving their vision. Since the record industry filed its lawsuits, officials say they have seen over a dozen internal campus Web sites devoted to music-sharing go dark.

The complaints charge Daniel Peng, a student at Princeton University; Joseph Nievelt, a student at Michigan Technological University; and Aaron Sherman and Jesse Jordan, both students at Rensselaer Polytechnic Institute, with directly infringing copyrights by providing dozens of songs from popular artists to other students to copy.

15   They also charge the students with contributing to much broader infringement by running programs that indexed tens of thousands of songs stored on other computers connected to the campus network by students who chose to make them available to copy. Accusing the four of having "taken a network created for higher learning and academic pursuits and converted it into an emporium of music piracy," the lawsuits ask for $150,000 for each of the recordings listed on the students' Web sites, but recording industry officials acknowledge that having made their point, they expect to settle out of court.

    The proliferation of campus file-trading networks appears to have started two years ago, when many universities capped the amount of bandwidth allotted to each student.

    In response, students began using programs that would let them share files over the superfast networks that connect computers on campus, without relying on the Internet.

    Because those files may be notes from Psych 101, family pictures or music by bands that choose to distribute it freely, some academic community members argue that the students running the programs should not be held accountable for how others may have used them. By singling out the technology, they say, the record industry has also raised First Amendment issues in what otherwise could have been a straightforward copyright infringement case.

    "If this becomes more about a challenge to the technology than about downloading music for recreational purposes, that is a serious concern for us," said Peter McDonough, general counsel for Princeton. "Because we emphatically believe the technologies themselves are not illegal."

20   That is also the conclusion of Brendan Dolan-Gavitt, 19, a freshman at Wesleyan University who has continued to run his own site, which indexes the shared files of every computer on the Wesleyan network.

    Mr. Dolan-Gavitt took his site down the day after the suits were filed but put it back up the next day after poring over copyright statutes. He said that if a copyright holder notified him of an infringing file in his index, he would remove it, just as the law says. His mother is nervous, but "I just figured if there was something I was going to take a stand on it might as well be this," he said.

Even before the lawsuits, university administrators felt the heat of the music industry's stepped-up anti-piracy campaign. In recent months, entertainment companies have barraged administrators with complaints documenting alleged copyright infringement over their networks. Several colleges, in turn, issued more stringent policies regarding student behavior.

Harvard University warned undergraduates this month that they would lose their Internet access for a year if they illegally shared copyrighted material more than once. The United States Naval Academy punished 85 students who were found to have downloaded copyrighted movies and songs through the academy's Internet connection. Penn State warned students that file-sharing could lead to huge fines and jail time, and deprived 220 students of high-speed Internet connections in their dorms after finding that they were sharing copyrighted material. A committee of university presidents and entertainment industry executives are in the process of formulating strategies to address the illegal activity on campus. One idea under consideration: negotiating campuswide licenses for legal online music services, which colleges could provide as part of a standard student activities fee along with recreation facilities and newspaper subscriptions.

Colleges have a financial interest in working with the entertainment industry to solve the downloading problem: the free bandwidth they provide to students is getting more and more expensive, and they must constantly investigate all of the entertainment industry's complaints to avoid being held liable for the infringement themselves.

The peremptory lawsuits have also angered some college   25 administrators.

"They have apparently changed their minds about wanting to work cooperatively with universities," said Curtis Tompkins, president of Michigan Tech, who vented his frustration in an open letter to the recording industry association. "To pick four individuals out of thousands and line them up against the wall and say, 'Here's the firing squad,' is not the way you deal in higher education."

Just how successful the industry's tougher tactics will be is unclear. On a recent afternoon at Maryland, a student who once used Jason's site showed a reporter how to log on to another local network instead.

"We can't live without it," said Eric Lightman, a junior majoring in computer science. "If one goes down, another comes up."

On the other hand, an advertisement for a new administrator for Jason's site willing to "take on whatever legal risks may come about" has so far received no replies.

Suggestions for Writing and Discussion

1. Do you agree or disagree with the argument that file sharing should be legal because CDs are too expensive? Explain.
2. What role do you believe college administrators and information technology offices should play in enforcing the laws against file sharing? Explain.

Why the Record Companies Have to Play Hardball

Michael Rogers

Michael Rogers, who began his reporting career for *Rolling Stone* and now serves as editor and general manager of Newsweek.com, provides a thoughtful, balanced view of why record companies must sue those individuals—even junior high school students—who violate copyright law by downloading music.

Sept. 23—I *know* about free music: I started my working life at *Rolling Stone* and for a decade never once paid for music. Then I moved to *Newsweek* to write about technology and discovered that the labels would no longer send me all their new releases for free. I went into such shock that it was over a year before I could actually bring myself to *pay* for a recording. "Free" is a price tag that sticks in your mind.

And that's why the record companies—with their desperate strong-arm tactics of suing junior high school students—have no choice. They are an industry caught in a technology-driven shift in public attitude that threatens the livelihood of every creative profession whose product can be rendered as bits. It has happened before and it will likely happen again—and when it does there is really no recourse for the threatened but to stake out territory and go to war.

The music industry has actually gone through this before. Back in the early days of radio, broadcasters happily filled their programs not only with recorded music, but also readings from plays, magazine articles and books. Finally, in 1923, ASCAP (the American Society of Composers, Artists and Performers)—after trying to resolve the matter peacefully with licensing offers—began to sue radio stations to enforce their copyrights.

At that time, many radio stations were still fairly tiny enterprises, often run by hobbyists, without a clearly viable business model. There was great hue and cry over the lawsuits—big, bad ASCAP was beating up on tiny, defenseless broadcasters. One pioneer radio station, WOR in Newark, New Jersey, was big enough to fight back in court, arguing that they were not broadcasting for profit, but rather to provide a free cultural service. But the court ruled that WOR needed to compensate music owners for the use of their property and not long thereafter, "ether advertising" appeared—the birth of the commercial.

In the current lawsuit offensive, the record industry is again 5 going after broadcasters: only this time, they are the individuals who make copyrighted music files available to the Web audience of millions—and who, like WOR, argue that they're just innocent participants in popular culture. But this time there's an even bigger threat: because file-sharing has widely come to be seen as a harmless and victimless activity.

Earlier this summer, the Pew Internet & American Life Project (entirely unaffiliated with the record industry) found that fully two-thirds of all Internet users who download music or share files do so without regard to or concern over copyright. And that percentage had actually increased since a similar study in 2001. More recently, the Business Software Alliance (a group funded by software manufacturers) issued a study showing that "digital piracy" was not confined to music: on campuses, 26 percent of students have downloaded movies, with only 4 percent paying for it most of the time and that another 23 percent have downloaded application software (like Excel or Photoshop) with only a third paying.

In short, this is more than a minor squabble about whether the record industry charges too much for CDs, or whether musicians already make enough money from T-shirts and concerts. Rather, it's a sea change in public perception of what constitutes theft of intellectual property. And virtually all media will ultimately face this issue. Movies would be in the same crisis as music were it not for bandwidth constraints and the lack of quality playback options. Television shows are increasingly pirated, now that technologies like BitTorrent make the download process easier. And while it may take a decade, even the book business will someday rely on digital distribution (e-books will already be a $10 million business this year).

Critics, of course, say that you can't ever defeat technology—that file sharers will always come up with new ways to hide their activities, through elaborate encryption schemes and the password-protected "dark Internet." Actually, that would probably be fine with the music industry: if you make file-sharing sufficiently difficult and underground, then most people will opt for legal ways to buy music. And the remaining bunch of illegal file-sharers will begin to look much more like a criminal conspiracy—similar to the gangs that currently counterfeit CDs—and will be that much easier to prosecute.

The argument is often made that the music industry, seeing the Internet challenge, should have simply built an easy-to-use online music system, and therefore their customers wouldn't have been "forced" to break the law. But this isn't how business works. Radically remaking a distribution system that has evolved over decades isn't as simple as having the board of directors say, "Make it so." The current way CDs are manufactured and distributed may be inefficient, corrupt and wasteful, but it's also an ecology of many interdependent businesses, all of whom are making an acceptable living. So there's internal resistance to making sudden changes—and there's no way the record industry is going to alienate their current distribution channels before they fully figure out how to make money online.

10   Even so, the music industry is moving online and it's already clear that the efforts are bearing fruit—especially the success of Apple's Music Store, which sold its ten millionth song earlier this month. But that can't be taken as evidence that all customers will be willing to pay money for music (as opposed to getting it for free) simply because the process is made easy. If file-sharing continues to be seen as a socially acceptable free alternative to paying for an artist's work, it wouldn't make any difference how ardently Sheryl Crow promotes the service. Free is everyone's favorite price, until it becomes abundantly clear that the offer is no longer available.

Suggestions for Writing and Discussion

    1. What is the tone of this article? Cite specific phrases and sentences that suggest the attitude of the author toward the

record companies, radio stations, and those who practice
file sharing.

2. Rogers suggests that in the near future both movies and
books will become part of the pool of resources that can
be shared through the Web. If this should happen, how do
you think the film and publishing industries might be affected? How might movie fans and readers be affected?

File Sharing Wars: Version 2:0

Ben Kupstas

Cornell student Ben Kupstas, himself a musician, makes a plea for a
compromise among the recording industry, music fans, and musicians.
He argues that there are reasonable alternatives to the extremes of both
the free file sharing of fans and the aggressive lawsuits filed by some
record companies. This article first appeared in the September 11, 2003,
edition of the *Cornell Daily Sun.*

If, by analogy, we see the RIAA as a one-eyed (maybe blind) giant
like Goliath and we see underdogs like Shawn Fanning (the now
deified Napster founder) and Jesse Jordan (one of the college students sued by the RIAA this past April) as modern-day Davids,
then Apple may just be this fable's closest thing to Gandhi. Their
message has always seemed to be, "Can't we all just get along"—
the musicians, the record companies, the fans, and the technology.

Since its inception, Apple has fought the battle against the PC
at least partly by catering to artistically minded computer users,
specifically musicians. With the recent plethora of laptop-toting
composers, producers, and performers, the PowerBook by Apple
has emerged as the musician's computer of choice (everyone from
Jim O'Rourke to Cex to Kid 606 uses a Mac). Many of the modern editing software and digital synthesizers are tailored to Macs,
and as the computer is fast becoming a studio and stage touchstone
as integral as the guitar, the PowerBook is the veritable Stratocaster
of this revolution. So, Apple is no stranger to the realm of music.

In the post-Napster world of music distribution, the war is
still against the PC, but the acronym now refers to political correctness (at least as dictated by the RIAA). While many in the
music industry are scrambling to either exploit modern distribution technologies (file-sharing stalwarts like Kazaa and Limewire)

or stomp it out completely (the Philistine RIAA), few are seriously and realistically proposing ways of helping this mess evolve into a mutually beneficial arrangement. Apple's iTunes is thus far the most feasible and appealing alternative to the current state of anarchic trading and absurd lawsuits, a climate that ultimately alienates the fans, the artists, and the distributors.

In April, while the RIAA was busy prosecuting undergraduates for hundreds of millions of dollars, Apple head honcho Steve Jobs launched the iTunes Music Store, which basically sells songs for $.99 each (adding up to roughly the price of individual songs on full-length CDs). What makes Apple the apparent "good guys" in this story are the relationships they've been fostering with independent record labels and individual artists. Apple has expressed a commitment to helping independent labels, and representatives from labels such as Matador and Sub Pop have already met with Apple to discuss possible partnerships. Bands like Dashboard Confessional are now top-sellers for iTunes. While mainstream artists are still a major part of Apple's initiative, their attempts to befriend the indie crowd have been largely successful. In a *Rolling Stone* interview, Sub Pop boss Jonathan Poneman said he is "psyched" about their participation with iTunes, which pays the label about $.65 per song.

5   Even the musicians and members of the file-sharing community are supporting iTunes. In an interview with Magnet, Radiohead frontman Thom Yorke expressed his endorsement of iTunes. In the words of one Soulseek user, "Apple has done the unthinkable by convincing labels and artists that making it easy for people to do the right thing is infinitely more constructive and lucrative than throwing money into a fight against the consumer that smacks a little too much of the drug war" (from the Soulseek message board).

So, Apple has stepped up to the plate preaching peace through iPods. Concerns about the looming death of the album aside, iTunes is looking like the people's choice for the future of legal musical distribution.

Suggestions for Writing and Discussion

    1. Explain the analogy Kupstas uses in the first paragraph. Why might the RIAA be compared to Goliath and college students who are sued for copyright infringement be seen as modern-day Davids? And how does Apple figure into the picture as the "closest thing to Gandhi"?

2. To what extent do services such as iTunes, which provide very inexpensive copies of individual songs, undermine the argument that file sharing should be legal because CDs are too expensive?

Sharing or Pirating?
Doonesbury Cartoon Sequence

Gary Trudeau

With a dialogue between Mike and his daughter Alex, cartoonist Gary Trudeau suggests that there may be a generation gap in the interpretation of the ethics of file sharing.

Topics for Writing and Discussion

1. Explain the ethical issue that faces Mike Doonesbury and his daughter Alex.
2. Choose one argument Mike makes and one argument Alex makes and explain why you agree or disagree with each of them.

Making Connections: Synthesis and Analysis

1. Create a list for each of the articles and the Doonesbury cartoon in this section. On each list, note the claims for and against file sharing. When the lists are complete, go back and evaluate the evidence used to support the claims.

Which do you find convincing? Which do you find unconvincing? Explain.

2. Ben Kupstas argues that there should be a way for musicians, record companies, fans, and technology to all work together. He suggests a possible solution. How effective do you find his argument? Explain.

3. The Doonesbury cartoon suggests that there is a generation gap in the question of "cyber-ethics." Do you agree that, in general, people in their teens, twenties, and thirties are more apt to approve of such practices as file sharing than are those in older generations? Explain why you do or do not agree.

IS HARRY EVIL?

Suggestions for Prereading or Journal Writing

1. What comes to mind when you hear the phrase "book burning"? Explain your response.

2. Why might some people believe that the Harry Potter books should be kept away from children? What is your response to these beliefs?

Harry and History[1]

Elizabeth D. Schafer

Elizabeth D. Schafer, an independent historian from Auburn, Alabama, writes for the *History News Service,* describing the background of censorship that has preceded and led up to the controversy surrounding the Harry Potter series. This article first appeared on November 13, 1999.

Teenage wizard Harry Potter, the hero of a popular children's book series, routinely outwits fantastical creatures in his quests to vanquish evil forces. But some parents think Harry is the evil being who should be subdued.

---

1. Editor's title.

Mimicking the paranoid Chicken Little, a fictional character who assumes the sky is falling when an acorn hits him, the anti-Potter parents are forming illogical conclusions similar to those of generations of book censors before them. These protesters demand the banning of Harry Potter books from public schools. They say the books are too scary and border on the occult. Some have even accused the books' author, Joanne K. Rowling, of being a witch seeking converts.

Book banning is a familiar foe of American education and peaks during cycles of political and cultural conservatism. "Censorship reflects a society's lack of confidence in itself," United States Supreme Court Justice Potter Stewart remarked. "It is a hallmark of an authoritarian regime."

The Potter protesters emulate previous censors. Since colonial times, adults have regulated what children read. Early American children's books instructed with moral examples. The literary ancestors of Harry Potter, adventure and fantasy stories, became popular after 1850. Around that time, attitudes toward children changed. Children were encouraged to indulge in imaginative play. However, concerned parents criticized books that addressed what they considered taboo subjects such as magic.

5   Book-banning strategies throughout American history reflect the country's changing culture. Like Harry Potter, Mark Twain's novels, featuring boyish rascals, have occasionally been accused of absurd transgressions. In 1885, literary elites thought "The Adventures of Huckleberry Finn" was too crude for refined readers. Twenty years later, critics complained that the characters were poor role models. By the 1950s, civil rights advocates censured Twain's characters for using racist language.

With National Children's Book Week just around the corner, even more attention has been drawn to the fact that this year the Harry Potter stories join earlier children's novels that have been challenged. In the 1950s, J.D. Salinger's "The Catcher in the Rye" inflamed censorious adults who were afraid their children might use slang to imitate the protagonist, Holden Caulfield. Censors of the 1990s are concerned about the magical spells Harry Potter casts.

In a different decade, Harry Potter might not have suffered from such a ludicrous backlash. Censorship was mostly dormant until the election of Ronald Reagan in 1980. Book banning gained new momentum as groups and individuals publicly imposed their punitive opinions against literature, especially fantasies such as the Potter novels. Children's books were burned, pulled from shelves and removed from required reading lists. Selected passages and illustrations were cut out or inked over.

Recycling predecessors' rhetoric, censors of the 1990s, many of whom came of age in the 1980s, have focused on perceived evil in children's books. Book banners, primarily members of the Moral Majority and religious right, assume their beliefs should be embraced by all Americans. Instead of prohibiting what their children can read, these censors try to limit all children's access to literature they deem inappropriate.

They label targeted books dangerous because they claim the stories provide bad examples for impressionable children. Protesting parents say books like Harry [P]otter are subversive and do not promote family values.

Many school administrators quickly appease censors to avoid   10 awkward publicity. They condemn the Harry Potter books as potentially threatening. Opponents argue that censorship is detrimental to students' intellectual development.

Like the boorish non-wizard Muggles in the Harry Potter novels, most censors lack imagination. Unable to separate reality from fantasy, they are oblivious to the books' theme of love conquering evil. Harry's true magic is that he is empowered by his compassion and tolerance of others.

Potter's antagonists misinterpret out-of-context sentences because they refuse to read the books. This undisciplined scrutiny is a typical book-banning pattern. Even ministers have preached against heroic Harry Potter's battle with his archenemy Lord Voldemort. They say the books' popularity is evidence of Satanic influence.

Mark Twain enjoyed the publicity and profits he gained from censorship. He wrote his publisher that the censors "have given us a rattling tip-top puff which will go into every paper in the country." He predicted the notoriety gained would sell at least an additional 25,000 copies. And Harry Potter's author is surely benefiting from the censors' misguided attempts as curious readers flock to bookstores and buy her books.

If efforts to restrict children's books like Harry Potter are successful, they can cause more harm than eradicating valuable literature. "You don't have to burn books to destroy a culture," Ray Bradbury, author of "Fahrenheit 451," warned. "Just get people to stop reading them."

15   As long as conservatism prevails, Harry Potter may rival Huck Finn and Holden Caulfield to become one of America's most banned boys.

Suggestions for Writing and Discussion

1. Elizabeth Schafer quotes United States Supreme Court justice Potter Stewart, who said, "Censorship reflects a society's lack of confidence in itself. It is a hallmark of an authoritarian regime." What do you think he meant by this comment? In your response, include a definition of the phrase "authoritarian regime."

2. Schafer cites three different reasons that Mark Twain's classic American novel *The Adventures of Huckleberry Finn* has been banned or challenged in the United States. List the three reasons and then discuss whether you think any of the three would justify removing the book from a middle-school library.

" 'Potter' Book Burning Was Misguided"
Robert Seltzer

Writing for the *El Paso Times,* Robert Seltzer explores some of the issues related to a book burning led by a pastor in Alamogordo, Texas. Seltzer examines the reasons the congregation chose to burn the Harry Potter books and, while defending their First Amendment rights, makes an argument against their actions. This article first appeared on January 4, 2002.

It was a waste of time, energy and lighter fluid.

If Harry Potter could survive evil rivals, fiendish relatives and mountain trolls, what chance did a "holy bonfire" have?

Oh, hundreds of individuals tossed the "Harry Potter" books into the fire, turning the hero and his exploits into ashes.

But for every book consumed by the flames of intolerance, millions more remain intact—most of them beyond the reach of the match-wielding zealots in Alamogordo, where Christ Community Church orchestrated the bonfire earlier this week.

5   To destroy all of them, the congregation would have to turn the world into a furnace.

And, then, Harry Potter would not be a literary character; he would be a martyr.

Does the church really want that?

Does it want to fuel an even greater passion for a series of books it already deems evil?

FREE SPEECH

The bonfire might have been disgusting, even contemptible—a waste of matches that could have been used to light a yule log. But the church members acted in, well, good faith. They saw an evil, the propagation of what they interpreted as witchcraft and devil worship, and they responded—a response protected by the First Amendment.

While the church members might have exercised a right, how- 10 ever, that does not mean they were right to exercise it. They did not kill Harry Potter; Harry Potter will live as long as children read—and adults should rejoice in that.

More than 40 million illiterate adults live in the United States, according to the National Institute for Literacy. Do we want their children to follow in their tragic footsteps—a fate worse than anything a witch or warlock could conjure?

Harry Potter has encouraged millions of children to abandon their video games, if only a few hundred pages at a time. If that is witchcraft, we should glory in the magic. Give a child a compelling book, and you have the best baby-sitter money can buy, as any parent can attest.

And the wizard?

If Harry Potter is evil, we should hurl "The Wizard of Oz" into the same bonfire. And "Macbeth." And "Le Morte D'Arthur." And . . . .

When people set fire to books, they practice the worst kind of 15 tyranny. They try to stifle the one thing we should prize above all else—our imaginations. They will never succeed. "The Grapes of Wrath," "The Adventures of Huckleberry Finn," "I Know Why the Caged Bird Sings"—all have been banned and burned, and all have survived.

The Harry Potter books may dramatize the art of witchcraft, but they also explore courage, loyalty and love—qualities that we should encourage, not condemn. The children who read the books are wiser than the adults who burn them. If only we could eradicate intolerance as easily as we do works of art.

Suggestions for Writing and Discussion

1. Robert Seltzer implies that burning books will "fuel an even greater passion" for the readings that have been destroyed. Do you agree with this observation? What examples from other media, such as television or film, might support or challenge this point?

2. Although Seltzer opposes the book burning, he believes that it is a right guaranteed by the First Amendment to the Constitution. Do you agree? If not, do you think another amendment should be passed to deny book burners legal rights?

In Defense of Book Burning
Will Manley

Will Manley, a columnist for the *American Libraries Journal,* has been writing on issues related to censorship and libraries for more than twenty years. In this article, he first argues that book burning is an effective way to make a strong statement but then questions why anyone would want to burn the Potter books, which he claims have "turned kids away from television, videos, and computer games and back into books." This article first appeared in March 2002.

If you want to make a strong statement about something, it's hard to find a stronger image to use than fire. When God revealed himself to Moses, he did so as a burning bush. When Jesus attempted to describe the pain of hell, he conjured up a terrifying portrait of eternal flames. When the white-hooded thugs of the Ku Klux Klan rode menacingly through the rural South to stir up the hatred of racism, they burned crosses on people's front yards. When antiwar dissidents protested U.S. involvement in the Vietnam War, they burned the American flag. When Buddhist monks protested the corrupt Diem regime in South Vietnam, they burned themselves. When the Nazis wanted to rid Germany of dangerous and undesirable ideas, they burned piles and piles of books.

Unfortunately, book burning is back in business, but not in Germany. It's happening right here in the U.S., and, oddly, it has nothing to do with our worldwide war on terrorism. In fact, there's probably been a book burning at a church or school near you. The target is Harry Potter, hero of millions of children. Harry is a fictional young boy who can perform extraordinary feats of magic. The fact that he has captured the hearts and imaginations of children has driven some clerics and parents into fits of frustration and rage. It's the kind of rage that bursts into fire.

The whole book-burning phenomenon is actually quite difficult to understand. You would think that Harry would be a cause for celebration by anyone sincerely interested in young people. With a wave of a wizard's wand he has done the utterly impossible. He has turned kids away from television, videos, and computer games and back into books. I never thought I'd see the day when kids would line up outside of a bookstore just to buy a book! Miraculously, that is what happens whenever a new Potter title is released, and that is precisely why Harry is driving his enemies crazy.

He's so popular that they think that he might mesmerize young children, turning them away from God and toward the black arts. Never mind the fact that Harry is a force of goodness and courage in a world that is creeping with evildoers. It's actually hard to think of a character in all of children's literature that is more a Goody Two-shoes than young, innocent Harry. In fact from a literary perspective, the only thing that I don't like about Harry is that he seems too good to be true. His sidekicks, Ron and Hermione, are much more appealing because they do have some minor character flaws.

So, how do you deal with a wizard who is mesmerizing your 5 children? If you're really clueless about the magical arts, you will do something stupid like trying to burn him in hopes that he will instantly vanish. Anyone who knows anything about wizards or sorcerers, however, recognizes that this approach is probably the worst thing that you can do. Wizards have a way of miraculously reappearing stronger than ever, and in Harry's case that is exactly what is happening. It's actually quite magical—the more you burn Harry, the more he multiplies. As a result, his creator, J. K. Rowling, is laughing all the way to the bank. I wonder how the book burners feel about helping finance her new castle in Scotland.

Book burnings bring big publicity. Nothing provokes public interest more than a fire, and nothing helps to sell books more than public interest. Book burners, therefore, are playing right into Harry's wily hands. He's not a wizard for nothing.

Not only are they clueless about wizards, the book burners are equally clueless about kids. What's the old expression—"don't tell kids not to put beans up their nose because that's exactly what they will do as soon as you turn your back." The same thing holds true here. If you burn a book because you don't want your child to read it, don't you think the kid will make it his first order of business to seek the book out on his own? He might even go to the public library to read it.

Oh, I get it—these book burnings are really a ruse to get kids back into libraries.

Suggestions for Writing and Discussion

1. What is the tone of this essay? To formulate your response, compare and contrast the title of the article with the points the author makes within the article.
2. In the first paragraph of this article, Manley notes, "If you want to make a strong statement about something, it's hard to find a stronger image to use than fire." After considering the examples he provides, think about other examples that might support or challenge Manley's point.

The Harry Potter Controversy: Dark Fantasy or Gateway to the Occult?

Steve Eighinger

Steve Eighinger, a staff writer for the *Herald-Whig* in Quincy, Illinois, interviews Potter proponents and opponents, suggesting arguments for and against the censoring of the popular series. This article first appeared in July 2003, following the release of the fifth installment of the Potter books, *Harry Potter and the Order of the Phoenix.*

That Harry Potter kid is causing trouble—again.

English author J.K. Rowling's fifth installment of the mega-popular Harry Potter series has refueled the controversy over whether or not the books promote interest in the occult, especially among younger readers.

Potter critics and supporters are passionate about their positions concerning Harry, who is now a teenager in the fifth of what eventually will be a seven-book succession. Rowling's fifth book, "Harry Potter and the Order of the Phoenix," was released in late June.

The series' initial offering showcased Harry as an 11-year-old wizard raised by abusive relatives who enrolls at Hogwarts School of Witchcraft and Wizardry. As the series has progressed, the storylines have become gradually darker, as Rowling said they would.

"The Harry Potter thing comes up quite often," said Drew   5
Massey, a youth pastor at the Tabernacle of Praise Church in Hannibal, Mo.

Massey said the Harry Potter books tend to glamorize witchcraft and sorcery, and can pique an interest in such subjects among readers. Massey said he advocates not reading the Potter books or seeing the movies, but feels such a decision needs to be made on a personal basis.

"It's kind of tricky, but if you're not sure about whether something is good or bad (for you spiritually) . . . just avoid it," Massey said. "For every black and white, there's a bit of a gray area."

Massey said I Thessalonians 5:22 reminds, "Avoid every kind of evil."

"I can't tell you what is junk and what is not—that is up to each person's discretion," Massey said. "Each person needs to talk to God about it. I don't try and push my convictions on another person. Why would I call your parents to ask what my curfew is?"

In an interview with CNN, Rowling said, "I have met thou-   10
sands of children now, and not one time has a child come up to me and said, 'Ms. Rowling, I'm glad I've read these books because now I want to be a witch.' They see it for what it is. It is a fantasy world and they understand that completely. I don't believe in magic, either."

Donna Cogdan, manager at Waldenbooks in the Quincy Mall, said she has received scattered complaints about the Harry Potter books.

"I've had some people come in and complain that we are selling them, but there hasn't really been that many," she said. "We have had maybe three or four since the series started."

Cogdan defends the Harry Potter books.

"It is not witchcraft," she said. "It is no different than Star Trek, Star Wars or 'Lord of the Rings.' To me, it gets kids reading who might normally not."

15   Cogdan also said a larger number of adults buy the Harry Potter books.

"I once had a mother and daughter come in and buy two, because they both wanted to read it at the same time," Cogdan said.

The Rev. Rod Bakker of First Presbyterian Church in Quincy is strongly against the Harry Potter books and the movies. Bakker said he did not make up his mind on the subject until the initial controversy erupted and he read the first Harry Potter book.

"There are people in society who practice witchcraft and we do not need to encourage it," Bakker said. "The difference between Star Trek and Harry Potter is that Star Trek is 100 percent pure fantasy. I'm not sure Harry Potter is."

Bakker said if Harry Potter proponents would take the time to check, the spells talked about in the books are actual witchcraft writings "with a couple of the words changed."

20   "There is a dark side, there are satanists and there are people involved in witchcraft," Bakker said. "The Harry Potter books skate a little too close to those. I would not say I had forbid my own children from reading (the Harry Potter books) . . . but I suggested they didn't. And they didn't."

John Andrew Murray is headmaster at St. Timothy's-Hale, an Episcopal school in Raleigh, N.C., and a writer who believes Harry Potter can be a harmful read.

"By disassociating magic and supernatural evil, it becomes possible to portray occult practices as 'good' and 'healthy,' contrary to the scriptural declaration that such practices are 'detestable to the Lord.' This, in turn, opens the door for less discerning individuals—including, but not limited to, children—to become confused about supernatural matters," Murray said on the www .family.org Web site.

"With the growing popularity of youth-oriented TV shows on witchcraft—'Sabrina, the Teenage Witch,' 'Charmed,' 'Buffy the Vampire Slayer'—a generation of children is becoming desensitized to the occult. But with Hollywood's help, Harry Potter will likely surpass all these influences, potentially reaping some grave spiritual consequences," Murray said on the www.worthynews .com Web site.

The Rev. Bob Jallas of All Saints Catholic Church in Quincy says he sees nothing wrong with the Harry Potter books or movies.

25   "I have not read any of the books, but I have seen a Harry Potter movie and enjoyed it," Jallas said.

Jallas said he does not think any children will be driven to "devil worship" as a result of the series. "I think (the controversy) is overblown."

Jallas said he has no plans to read the current Harry Potter book, but said he will probably see the movie when it comes out.

Charles Colson, a columnist for christianitytoday.com, also defends the Harry Potter phenomenon. He says the magic and sorcery in the books is "purely mechanical, as opposed to occultic."

"Harry and his friends cast spells, read crystal balls and turn themselves into animals—but they don't make contact with a supernatural world," he writes. "(It's not) the kind of real-life witchcraft the Bible condemns."

Love him or hate him, Harry Potter appears to be with us 30 through at least two more installments.

Suggestions for Writing and Discussion

1. Drew Massey, a pastor, is quoted as saying that "if you're not sure about whether something is good or bad (for you spiritually)" you should "just avoid it." Do you agree? Explain.

2. Two of the people interviewed for this article disagree about whether *Harry Potter* is more dangerous than *Star Trek* or *Lord of the Rings*. What differences and similarities do you see among these works? What arguments, pro and con, could you make to the proposition that *Harry Potter* is no more dangerous than either *Star Trek* or *Lord of the Rings*?

Making Connections: Synthesis and Analysis

1. Consider the tone of each of these articles. Which do you see as objective, reporting each side of the controversy in a neutral way? Which do you see as proposing an argument for one side or the other? What specific phrases or word choices indicate to you the writer's beliefs on the topic?

2. From each article, find at least two reasons that have been given for banning the Potter books and at least two reasons that have been given for opposing such a ban. Which reasons do you find more convincing? How would you add to the arguments either for or against the censorship?

3. From reading the articles by Robert Seltzer and Will Manley, develop arguments for and against the following proposition: "Burning books is never an appropriate means of protest, no matter what their content."

EXTENDED CONNECTIONS: FOR CRITICAL THINKING, WRITING, AND RESEARCH

1. Several of the articles in this chapter deal with the history of censorship. Choose one aspect of this history—perhaps the censoring of one specific work of art, literature, or music—and do research in various sources (books, online databases, interviews). Then write an argument explaining why you do or do not think the censorship was warranted by the circumstances you have discovered.

2. Research the history of book burning. In addition, consider issues of First Amendment rights (as mentioned, for instance, by Robert Seltzer). As you pursue your research, consult various sources (books, online databases, interviews). Then write an argument for or against the following proposition: "Public book burnings should be banned in the United States."

3. Choose a controversial issue related to ethics and the Internet. As you pursue your research, consult various sources (books, online databases, interviews). Then write an argument proposing that your view of this controversy is worthy of consideration.

CHAPTER 8

Coping with Change: Technology and Work

INTRODUCTION

By our very nature, we humans are curious beings. As Alexander Pope wrote in *The Essay on Man,* we are the "glory, jest, and riddle of the world." Captured in this phrase is the reality that within each of us, and thus within all of our societies and cultures, we possess both the capacity for greatness and the capacity for ridiculousness. The fact that we possess both and so often choose the ridiculous may be one of the riddles to which Pope refers.

In this chapter, we will explore how technology has both presented Americans with opportunities for a better quality of life and at the same time created greater problems and conundrums. Such is the essence of Henry George's opening chapter, "The Great Enigma of Our Times," from his nineteenth-century book on economics, *Progress and Poverty.* His observations lead to a question that is still current: How is it great wealth and severe poverty live side by side in America? Addressing the issue of technology and communications, Tom Standage looks to history to see how the wheel simply keeps getting reinvented. In his piece, he examines how the telegraph was another one of those riddles, a "mixed blessing" that became the ancestor of the Internet.

Finally, leaping forward to the 1950s, Benjamin Darling captures vintage tips for teens, which reveal how much the world has changed in the past fifty years. Darling's advice for teens includes how to answer the telephone and how to call a member of the opposite sex.

Past concerns, connections, and ideals serve as material ripe for discussion and with which we can compare our modern world.

282

Fittingly, since the technology that most affects learning is the advent of the personal computer and the Internet, the first four pieces in the "Now" section deal with how the use of computers both enriches and endangers students today. In "The Cyber Children Have Arrived," Dan Johnson highlights the benefits and drawbacks of students having access to computers at home and in the classroom. Peter Coffee and Reid Goldsborough discuss computers in the workplace and how this technology might contribute to a dearth of manners as well as a strong web of online community relationships.

However, as Goldsborough also states, some people, primarily men, end up isolated and lonely in their dependence on a computer as their primary link to human relationships. And chat rooms—the new, modern way to communicate—how safe are they? In "Deadly Chatter," Susan Horsburgh and Johnny Dodd describe how one high school dropout overdosed on drugs and died as a result of the advice he received from his "friends" in a chat room for drug devotees.

Just as the computer age has given us the choice between meaningful learning and destructive practices, so, too, have advances in the fields of science and medicine. People should not fear or ban recent advances made in cloning human beings, claims Michael Shermer in the next reading, "I, Clone." This position, however, violates the beliefs and values of many of the world's moral and ethical leaders, including in the Roman Catholic Church and the Muslim community. Conflicts have arisen, too, with other advancements in medicine. Human beings can now be kept alive on life support even though they are unable to connect or respond on any meaningful human level. In "Embracing Life, Accepting Limits," Peter Setness, a doctor himself, writes about the agony of keeping his elderly father alive.

In a similar manner, these same complexities concerning the moral complications that euthanasia presents are seen quite clearly in Vickie Chachere's piece on the recent case involving Terri Schiavo. In the case of this 39-year-old woman who has been in a vegetative state for thirteen years, the battle has yet to be won over who has the right to make decisions concerning her future: her husband, who wants to discontinue the life support of medical technology, or her parents, who insist that she stay alive in this comatose state. This case in Florida, which is currently in the court's hands, may set precedence for America's moral, ethical, and legal options in the near future—options that may confirm the "glory, jest, and riddle" of our own humanity.

· *THEN* ·

SETTING THE CONTEXT:
TECHNOLOGY THEN

Suggestions for Prereading or Journal Writing

1. Reflect on the modern technologies on which you depend on a daily basis, such as cell phones, television, computers, automobiles. Now imagine that you live one hundred years ago, when these technologies have not yet been invented. Write about your life back then. How does it compare to your life today? In what ways do you feel more

LET US MAKE YOU FAT
50c Box Free
We Want to Prove at Our Own Expense That It Is No Longer Necessary to Be Thin, Scrawny, and Undeveloped

"Gee! Look at that pair of skinny scarecrows! Why don't they try Sargol?"

Let Us Make You Fat, advertisement, October 1915

connected to yourself and others? In what ways might you be more isolated?

2. Explore this question: In the days before the Internet, were human relationships more real or less real than they are today?

3. Discuss the ways in which technology has the capacity to create both poverty and wealth within the same society.

Topics for Writing and Discussion

1. What is your immediate response to this ad? What does it reflect about the concerns and values of society in 1915?

2. The fine print that accompanied this ad stated that "skinny men fail to gain social or business recognition on account of their starved appearance," and skinny women need to "fill out hollows in their cheeks, neck, and bust, to get rid of that 'peaked' look." Why might people back then have been so embarrassed to be thin? How does that compare to today's concerns?

The Great Enigma of Our Times
Henry George (1839–1897)

In the nineteenth century, Henry George was the third most famous American, following Mark Twain and Thomas Edison. However, this man who was admired for his deep curiosity, great wit, and intelligence, had no more than an sixth-grade education. Though he had to stop his formal schooling in order to work, he continued his self-education by reading, among others, economist Adam Smith and the philosopher John Stuart Mill. Because George was an unknown, he could not find anyone to print his book, *Progress and Poverty,* which he wrote after his long days as a printer. However, undeterred, he and his friends set the type themselves and published the book. Within a few months, George's book, which was by all accounts a brilliant, radical theory on the relationship between culture and industry, was known not only in America but around the world. While many did not agree with George's answers to the disturbing questions he raised about wealth and poverty ("How could there be greed when all had enough?"), more than 100,000 people attended his funeral procession in Brooklyn when he died. Today, his theories on economics are still regarded as brilliant insights into the interconnectedness and complexities of an advancing world order.

The utilization of steam and electricity, the introduction of improved processes and laboursaving machinery, the greater subdivision and grander scale of production, the wonderful facility of exchanges, have multiplied enormously the effectiveness of labour.

It was natural to expect, and it was expected, that laboursaving inventions would lighten the toil and improve the condition of the labourer; that the enormous increase in the power of producing wealth would make real poverty a thing of the past.

Could a Franklin or a Priestley have seen, in a vision of the future, the steamship taking the place of the sailing vessel, the railway train of the waggon, the reaping machine of the scythe, the threshing machine of the flail; could he have heard the throb of the engines that in obedience to human will, and for the satisfaction of human desire, exert a power greater than that of all the men and all the beasts of burden of the earth combined; could he have seen the forest tree transformed into finished lumber—into doors, sashes, blinds, boxes or barrels, with hardly the touch of a human hand; the great workshops where boots and shoes are turned out from improved facilities of exchange and communication—sheep killed in Australia eaten fresh in England, and the order given by the London banker in the afternoon executed in San Francisco in the morning of the same day; could he have conceived of the hundred thousand improvements which these only suggest, what would he have inferred as to the social condition of mankind?

It would not have seemed like an inference. Further than the vision went it would have seemed as though he saw, and his heart would have leaped and his nerves would have thrilled, as one who from a height beholds just ahead of the thirst-stricken caravan the living gleam of rustling woods and the glint of laughing waters. Plainly, in the sight of the imagination, he would have beheld those new forces elevating society from its very foundations, lifting the very poorest above the possibility of want, exempting the very lowest from anxiety for the material needs of life. He would have seen those slaves of the lamp of knowledge taking on themselves the traditional curse, those muscles of iron and sinews of steel making the poorest labourer's life a holiday, in which every high quality and noble impulse could have scope to grow.

And out of those bounteous material conditions he would have 5 seen arising, as necessary sequences, moral conditions realizing the golden age of which mankind has always dreamed. Youth no longer stunted and starved; age no longer harried by avarice; the man with the muck-rake drinking in the glory of the stars! Foul things fled; discord turned to harmony! For how could there be greed when all had enough? How could there be the vice, the crime, the ignorance, the brutality, that spring from poverty and the fear of poverty, exist where poverty had vanished? Who should crouch where all were freemen? Who oppress where all were peers?

More or less, vague or clear, these have been the hopes, these the dreams born of the improvements which give this wonderful era its pre-eminence. They have sunk so deeply into the popular mind as radically to change the currents of thought, to recast creeds and displace the most fundamental conceptions.

It is true that disappointment has followed disappointment. Discovery upon discovery and invention after invention have neither lessened the toil of those who most need respite nor brought plenty to the poor. But there have been so many things to which it seemed this failure could be attributed that up to our time the new faith has hardly weakened. We have better appreciated the difficulties to be overcome, but not the less trusted that the tendency of the times was to overcome them.

Now, however, we are coming into collision with facts which there can be no mistaking. From all parts of the civilized world come complaints of industrial depression; of labour condemned to involuntary idleness; of capital massed and wasting; of pecuniary distress among business men; of want and suffering and anxiety among the working classes. There is distress where large standing armies are maintained, but there is also distress where the standing armies are nominal; there is distress where protective tariffs are applied, but there is also distress where trade is nearly free; there is distress where autocratic government yet prevails, but there is also distress where political power is wholly in the hands of the people; in countries where paper is money, and in countries where gold and silver are the only currency. Evidently, beneath all such things as these, from local circumstances but are in some way or another engendered by progress itself.

This association of poverty with progress is the great enigma of our times. It is the central fact from which spring industrial, social, and political difficulties that perplex the world, and with which statesmanship and philanthropy and education grapple in vain. From it come the clouds that overhang the future of the most progressive and self-reliant nations. It is the riddle that the Sphinx of Fate puts to our civilization, which not to answer is to be destroyed. So long as all the increased wealth which modern progress brings goes but to build up great fortunes, to increase luxury and make sharper the contrast between the House of Have and the House of Want, progress is not real and cannot be permanent.

All-important as this question is, pressing itself from every 10 quarter painfully upon attention, it has not yet received a solution which accounts for all the facts and points to any clear and simple remedy. This is shown by the widely varying attempts to account for the industrial depressions. They exhibit not merely a divergence between vulgar notions and scientific theories, but also show that the concurrence which should exist between those who avow the same general theories breaks up upon practical questions into an anarchy of opinion.

The ideas that there is a necessary conflict between capital and labour, that machinery is an evil, that competition must be restrained and interest abolished, that wealth may be created by the issue of money, that it is the duty of the government to furnish capital or to furnish work, are rapidly making way among the great body of the people who keenly feel a hurt and are sharply conscious of a wrong. Such ideas, which bring great masses of men, the repositories of ultimate political power, under the leadership of charlatans and demagogues, are fraught with danger; but they cannot be successfully combated until political economy shall give some answer to the great question which shall be consistent with all her teachings and shall commend itself to the perceptions of the great masses of men.

It must be within the province of Political Economy to give such an answer. For Political Economy is not a set of dogmas. It is the explanation of a certain set of facts. It is the science that seeks, in the sequence of certain phenomena, to trace mutual relations and to identify cause and effect, just as the physical sciences seek to do in other sets of phenomena. It lays its foundations upon firm ground. The premises from which it makes its deductions are truths that have the highest sanction; they are axioms that we all recognize; upon them we safely base the reasoning and actions of everyday life and they may be reduced to the metaphysical expression of the physical law that motion seeks the line of least resistance— namely, that men seek to gratify their desires with the least exertion. Proceeding from a basis thus assured, its processes, which consist simply in identification and separation, have the same certainty. In this sense it is as exact a science as geometry, which, from similar truths relative to space, obtains its conclusions by similar means, and its conclusions when valid should be as self-apparent. And although in the domain of Political Economy we cannot test our theories by artificially produced combinations or conditions, as may be done in some of the other sciences, yet we can apply tests no less conclusive, by comparing societies in which different conditions exist, or in imagination by separating, combining, adding or eliminating forces or factors of known direction.

That Political Economy, as at present taught, does not explain the persistence of poverty amid advancing wealth in a manner that accords with the deep-seated perceptions of man; that the unquestionable truths that it does teach are unrelated and disjointed; that it has failed to make progress in popular thought—must be due, it seems to me, not to any inability in the science when properly pursued, but to some false step in its premises, or overlooked factor in its estimates. And as such mistakes are generally concealed by the respect paid to authority, I propose in this inquiry to take nothing for granted. I propose to beg no question, to shrink from no conclusion, but to follow truth wherever it may lead. If the conclusions that we reach run counter to our prejudices, let us not flinch; if they challenge institutions that have long been deemed wise and natural, let us not turn back.

Suggestions for Writing and Discussion

1. In your own words, what really is the "great enigma" as George sees it between poverty and wealth?

2. George writes that with all of the advancements humans have made to improve their lives, we should be living in a dream world, a golden age, where all social problems should be virtually eliminated. Why, then, aren't Americans living in a utopian state?

3. Industrialization, it seems, has put the world on a collision course. As George writes, "From all parts of the civilized world come complaints of industrial depression. . . ." Why might he have so carefully chosen the phrase "the civilized world"?

4. George contends that as long as "all the increased wealth . . . goes but to build up great fortunes," there can be no future

progress at all. Does this theory ring true in light of today's American society? What do you think?

5. Combining the laws of physics, philosophy, science, and economics, George concludes that the reason societies will not rise up despite their mounds of wealth is that "men seek to gratify their desires with the least exertion." What is your understanding of this thought, and based on your own experience and observations do you find it to be true?

The Nineteenth-Century Internet

Tom Standage

As a former engineering and computer student at Dulwich College and Oxford University, Tom Standage now serves as the technology correspondent for *The Economist.* In addition to countless articles he has penned regarding the impact of technology on society, Standage is also the author of two recent books, *The Neptune File* and *The Turk.* He lives with his wife and daughter in Greenwich, England, and can be reached at www.tomstandage.com.

A jaded editor once said, "There are no new stories, just new reporters."

His point even extends to the Internet. Although the Internet has truly been revolutionary, if you go back 150 years, to the height of the Victorian age, you find that the electric telegraph caused remarkably similar effects.

Yet today the telegraph is forgotten. What happened to it? And what does its fate say about what lies ahead for the Internet?

If you find it hard to believe that the Internet is merely a modern twist on a 19th-century system, consider the many striking parallels. For a start, the telegraph, like the Internet, changed communication completely. While the Internet can turn hours into seconds, the telegraph turned weeks into minutes. Before the telegraph, someone sending a dispatch to India from London had to wait months before receiving a reply. With the telegraph, communication took place as fast as operators could tap out Morse code.

Consider, also, the hype around the telegraph. The Internet   5
hysteria of the late 1990s was nothing compared with the excitement greeting the completion of the first trans-Atlantic telegraph

cable in 1858. There were hundred-gun salutes in Boston and New York. There were fireworks, parades, and special church services. Tiffany & Co. bought the leftover portion of the Atlantic cable, cut it into four-inch pieces, and sold them as souvenirs. The completion of the cable was widely seen as the most momentous event since the discovery of the New World. People speculated that the telegraph would bring about world peace.

Even the concerns about the telegraph sound familiar. It was criticized for encouraging a dangerous overdependence among users. It raised at least as many concerns about security as the Internet has—and with good reason. Criminals and pranksters found many ingenious ways to profit. One favorite scam was to telegraph the result of a sporting event to an accomplice in a distant town where the results were still unknown, so that he could place a bet on the winning team or horse.

Before too long, many telegraph users came to see it as a mixed blessing. Businessmen, who were keen adopters of the technology because it enabled them to keep track of distant markets and overseas events, found that it also led to an acceleration in the pace and stress of life. One harassed New York executive complained in 1868: "The businessman of the present day must be continually on the jump. The slow express train will not answer his purpose, and the poor merchant has no other way in which to work to secure a living for his family. He MUST use the telegraph." Information overload existed even then.

Although chat rooms are treated as a recent phenomenon, telegraph operators had the equivalent. Several operators on the same line could communicate with each other, tell jokes, and exchange gossip. The bored and lonely played chess and draughts over the wires, using a numbering system to identify the squares of the board. Tensions between skilled users in the cities and clueless part-time operators in rural areas led to angry exchanges similar to the "flame" wars that happen online today.

Just as inevitably, romances flourished online. (Telegraphy was regarded as a suitable job for young women, because it wasn't too strenuous.) There were several telegraphic weddings. One took place with the groom and his bride at a remote military base in Arizona and the minister 650 miles away in San Diego. The wedding was "attended" by dozens of operators who listened over the wires.

As long as the Internet has followed the telegraph's trajectory [10] thus far, it's likely that history will serve as a good guide for how the latest communication revolution will unfold.

It was the telegraph's fate ultimately to be overshadowed by several of its offspring. When the telephone was invented, in 1876, it was known as the "speaking telegraph." People assumed it would be used to speed the transmission of telegrams—operators could simply read them out to each other, rather than using Morse code. The telegraph survived for decades after the telephone was invented because there were some things—such as long-distance communication—for which it was better suited, but the telephone was, of course, a far more significant technology in its own right. The telegraph also spawned the stock ticker, which used telegraph technology with special ticker-tape printers to provide a continual stream of market data. Teletype machines employed the technology to send messages quickly and easily from an alphanumeric keyboard, rather than using Morse code.

The Internet can, thus, expect to be eclipsed by offspring devices that use Internet technology but are geared to specific markets and tasks and make the technology available to everyone. Access to the Internet on mobile devices, in the form of hand-held computers or smart phones, seems to be the most promising area.

Tellingly, just as the telephone was mistakenly viewed as simply a "speaking telegraph," the mobile Internet is still mistakenly perceived as a portable version of the Web—an approach that is impractical given the bandwidth constraints and small screens of mobile devices. History suggests that the mobile Internet will be different, and will become far larger, than today's PC-based Internet, which will continue to exist alongside it. Other task-specific devices, such as Internet-capable music players, game consoles, e-mail pagers, and Web pads will emerge. Although most "Internet appliances" have failed so far when attempting to tackle specific tasks, it's important to remember that many of the telegraph's offspring, such as a device that transmitted handwriting, were stillborn, too.

The sign of a truly mature technology is that it becomes invisible. You notice it only when something goes wrong: when the lights don't come on, or when there is no dial tone. By mutating into easier-to-use technologies that were better suited to specific tasks, the telegraph threw off its nerdy origins. In the process, the telegraph became ubiquitous and was transformed into a variety of instant communications devices that have been almost unnoticed, but integral, parts of everyday life. The same will surely happen to the Internet.

Suggestions for Writing and Discussion

1. Standage claims that the completion of the trans-Atlantic cable was "seen as the most momentous event since the discovery of the New World." Discuss the ways in which this invention may have created a whole new world.
2. According to Standage, how are the telegram and the Internet similar? What other similarities might they share, similarities that Standage does not address here?
3. Standage includes an anecdote about how the telegraph also had its own version of chat rooms. However, what do you feel is a basic difference between modern-day chat rooms and the old telegraph online romances that Standage does not address?
4. If the telegraph technology is indeed the "creator" of our modern communications systems, such as telephones and the Internet, has it reached its pinnacle of evolution? In other words, continuing the analogy of the family tree of technology, where might the Internet branch out next, and what will these offspring be like?

Tips for Teens
Benjamin Darling

Benjamin Darling, a collector of vintage ads, pamphlets, and nostalgia, has edited several books, including *Helpful Hints for Housewifes, Let's Be Safe, Helpful Hints for Teens,* and most recently *Vixens of Vinyl,* a collection of album covers from the 1940s and 1950s. He also has written and published a nonfiction book, *Shakespeare on Fairies and Magic.*

LETTER ETIQUETTE

A letter is a piece of private property. It is considered a serious breach of good manners to open a letter addressed to another (even a member of your own family) or to read a letter you find lying about opened. Keep in mind, too, that letters are not intended for general circulation like a newspaper. The boy or girl who, for amusement or curiosity, shows a sentimental or confidential letter he or she has received reveals coarse feelings. Do not write any very personal message on a postcard. This is not considerate. A postcard is hardly more private than a poster.

Do not seal a letter that you give to a friend to deliver. If it is a letter of introduction, you will probably show it to him anyway.

Who writes the first letter when two friends separate? The one who has gone away, regardless of sex.

TELEPHONE TACTICS

Telephoning comes into its own during the teen years. The instrument which was used only casually during childhood is jealously guarded by adolescents as a priceless means of communication. Dates are made and broken over it. What to wear and where to go and what to do are all discussed over it.

How to Place a Telephone Call

There is a know-how of telephoning another that is well to master.   5 Since most teenagers live with their families or in dormitories where they share the use of the phone, certain basic courtesies should be recognized. For example, when you put through a call, ask at once for the person to whom you wish to speak, giving your name, in this way: "Hello, is Jane there please? This is Edith calling." When Jane comes to the phone repeat the salutation: "Hello, Jane. This is Edith." Then give the message you called to deliver. If Jane is not there or cannot come to the phone, you may leave a message for her if you keep it short and simple. Long, involved messages get twisted and are a nuisance to transmit. If you cannot get your message into a few words, leave word that you will call her back later or that you would like her to call you when she gets in. Thank the person to whom you have been talking, and hang up courteously.

Reserve your kidding and teasing for those who appreciate such fooling. Asking Jane's father if he knows who is calling is apt to get you in Dutch with Jane's family and to put Jane on the spot too. Nor is it wise to be too "cute" and full of nonsense with others of the family who may answer the phone. Keep your request and your message short and simple.

How to Answer a Phone

If you are expecting a call, it is well to be close by when it comes through. When the phone rings do not quickly take it for granted that it is your call; give the person on the other end of the line a chance to identify himself before you salute him. Picking up the receiver and saying, "Hi, sweetheart!" just may cause your dad's boss to sputter in consternation!

Your salutation starts best with your identification. You may simply repeat the number of your phone, immediately assuring the other party that the correct number has been connected. Or you can answer the phone by the formula, "Hello, this is the Gaynor residence." Another variation is to say, "Yes? This is John Gaynor speaking."

DATING DOS AND DON'TS

How to Ask a Girl for a Date

When a boy wants to ask a girl for a date, there are several rules to follow and pitfalls to avoid. First of all, he invites her specifically for a particular occasion, giving her the time, the place, and the nature of the affair. He says, for example, "May I take you to the game in Hometown Gym at two next Saturday afternoon?" Knowing all the relevant facts, she has a basis upon which to refuse or to accept. In the second place, he is friendly and acts as though he really wants her to accept his invitation. He looks at her with a smile while he waits for her reply. If she accepts, he seems pleased and arranges definitely for the time at which he will call for her. If she refuses, he says that he is sorry and suggests that perhaps another time she will go with him.

How Not to Ask Her

10   Boys find that girls do not like the indirect approach that starts, "What are you doing next Friday night?" That puts the girl "on a spot." Boys should not act as though they expect to be refused, as Amos does when he says, "I don't suppose you'd like to go on a date with me, would you?" This back-handed kind of invitation is apt to make the girl feel uncomfortable and is a mark of the boy's feeling of insecurity, too.

Girls do not like to be asked for dates at the last minute. It is no compliment to call a girl up the very evening of an affair. Even if she is free, she may be reluctant to accept such an eleventh-hour invitation. If circumstances have made it impossible to ask early for the date, then go right ahead, of course. Be frank about it. It sometimes happens that a girl has had no other invitation to an affair she wants very much to attend. Girls protest, too, that some boys try to date them for months ahead. Beth put her uncertainty about such an invitation this way: "Why sure, Mac, I'll go with you to the Prom next year if we both still think it's a good idea when the time comes."

Since asking a girl for a date is both a compliment and an invitation, a boy needs have no fear of using the simplest, most direct, and friendliest approach he can muster. He might be surprised to know how eager the girl has been to hear the words he is struggling to say!

Suggestions for Writing and Discussion

1. Out of all the advice included in this reading from the 1950s, which "rules" seem the most outdated? How have the values beneath these rules changed, and are these changes in values for the better or not?

2. What advice, albeit outdated, might serve teenagers well in our American society today? Explain.

3. Synthesizing the advice that Darling has collected here, what does the fabric of society look like to you? A patchwork quilt? A tapestry? A checkerboard of black and white? How does that compare to what our society in general looks like now?

4. Take any one of the issues that Darling addresses and rewrite it for teenagers today. Comparing your advice to the advice that is now fifty years old, what specific changes have occurred regarding American values, morals, and ethics?

Making Connections: Synthesis and Analysis

1. Compare and contrast these three pieces in terms of what they reflect about America's beliefs and value systems. Which values are still present in society today, and which ones have fallen by the wayside?

2. What, specifically, were the problems that industrialization and nineteenth-century inventions were addressing? In what ways did technology solve those problems? In what ways did technology create a further set of unforeseen problems?
3. People have a tendency to look to their own pasts as "the good ol' days." Using these three pieces as your sole support, write an essay in which you argue that yes, the nineteenth and twentieth centuries were better than the times we live in now, or that no, the quality of our lives now is better than "back then."

· *NOW* ·

HOW HAS THE INTERNET CHANGED HOW WE RELATE TO ONE ANOTHER?

Suggestions for Prereading or Journal Writing

1. Reflect on how much time your actually spend using the Internet. What do you primarily use it for—to do research, to write to friends, to meet new people, to share new interests? Imagine now your life without this resource. How does it change?
2. Based on your own experience, what do you think is more "true": the words a person uses or the actions and unspoken messages that can be observed, such as body language and facial expressions? Write about someone you know well, and analyze how you came to this conclusion.
3. What are, in your opinion, the advantages of writing to someone instead of meeting or seeing them in person? What are the drawbacks?

Topics for Writing and Discussion

1. To whom, specifically, would this site appeal? Explain.
2. How effective is this website ad for bringing in new clients? Explain.

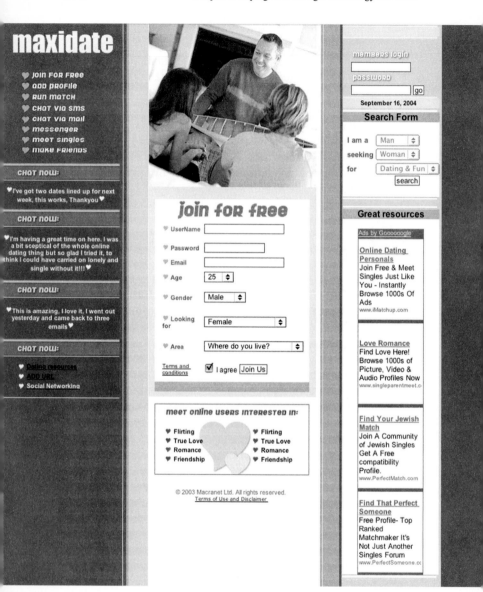

"Maxidate: It's Fun and Free!" Copyright © Macranet Limited. Used by special permission of Leon Chaddock. All rights reserved.

The Cyber Children Have Arrived
Dan Johnson

Dan Johnson is a contributor to *Futurist*. The following article first appeared in September 2001.

The majority of U.S. children are following a digital path to the future: Most of them are working on computers at school, and two-thirds of them have computers in their homes.

"Children's growing use of computers brings with it both the promise of enriched learning and the risk of possible harm," writes Richard E. Behrman, editor of *Children and Computer Technology,* a collection of articles analyzing the impacts of computers on children.

Computer technology is enhancing instruction in the classroom by engaging students and giving teachers new teaching tools. Computers are especially effective in enabling children to better understand core concepts in science and mathematics. Computer-based applications that use modeling and simulations have become important tools in teaching scientific concepts.

The simulation program ThinkerTools, for example, helps students visualize the concepts of acceleration and velocity. One controlled study found that middle-school students who used ThinkerTools were able to outperform high-school physics students in a test that required them to apply basic Newtonian principles to real-world problems. Researchers think that the computer program makes science more interesting. Computers are also helping a broader student population learn mathematics by reducing paper-based revision; this makes it easier for students to see the effects of changing one notation in an equation and gives them rapid feedback on incorrect answers.

5   The interactivity of some computer learning programs appears to boost student comprehension. In one study, sixth-graders who created a multimedia computer presentation for a social studies project tested higher than students who studied the same material in a textbook. In a separate study, first-graders who used an interactive computer storybook significantly outperformed those who simply read the story.

Outside of the classroom, millions of U.S. children are routinely participating in a diverse media culture. Approximately

8.6 million children and 8.4 million teenagers were online in 1998; by 2002, the total number is expected to reach 38.5 million, according to Jupiter Communications. Children are using the Internet to maintain contact with friends and family and to form online communities with like-minded peers.

The downside of all this connectivity is that kids are also exploring a world designed for them by adults, such as Web sites created by marketers who want to sell them the latest toys.

"For the most part, the heavily promoted commercial sites, sponsored mainly by media conglomerates and toy companies, are overshadowing the educational sites," warns Kathryn C. Montgomery, president of the Center for Media Education.

To guard children against commercial exploitation and unscrupulous adults online, Montgomery argues that "safe zones" should be created in cyberspace: Web sites that would be shielded from both marketers and predators. The sites should also be "designed to enhance children's learning and development, not merely keep them free from harm," she writes.

A central concern of *Children and Computer Technology* is   10
the need to monitor children's computer use: "The amount of time and the types of activities that children engage in while using computers are key factors influencing whether computer technology has positive or negative effects on their development." The report stresses the role of parental supervision in containing the harmful side effects of excessive computer activity:

- Obesity in children is linked to sedentary time spent watching television—or sitting in front of a computer screen.
- Repetitive-strain injuries can result when children work at computer stations designed for adults, and too much screen time can affect a child's vision.
- Teenagers may experience loneliness, depression, and a decline in "real world" social activity as a result of overexposure to chat rooms and excessive Web surfing.
- Playing violent computer games is correlated with increased aggression in children.

Despite such perils, parents and teachers recognize that children must prepare for life and work in the future by becoming computer literate, and troubling disparities exist between rich and poor children. "Only about 22% of children in families with annual incomes of less than $20,000 had access to a home computer in 1998, compared to 91% of those families with annual incomes of more than $75,000," writes education professor Henry Jay Becker.

In order to bridge the "digital divide," *Children and Computer Technology* recommends significant initiatives from government and the private sector to boost low-income families' access to computers and the Internet—at home, at school, and in libraries and community centers. Efforts to develop more useful online content, train teachers and parents to encourage children's computer use, and publicize models of success could help equalize access to computer opportunities for all children.

Suggestions for Writing and Discussion

1. In this piece, Johnson reports that the use of computers has been both beneficial and potentially dangerous for children today. Based on the information Johnson provides, would you say he leans toward one position or the other? Explain.

2. How credible do you find Johnson's claims of four harmful side effects—obesity, eye injuries, depression, and violence—as being a direct result of excessive computer use by children today? What other factors might contribute more than computers to these four problems? Explain.

3. What are the advantages to a computer-enhanced education versus one that does not rely on computers? What are the drawbacks?

4. What specific problems with learning and education do computers address? Reflect on other ways in which these problems could be addressed.

5. Who or what is most responsible for a child's ultimate success in school: parents, teachers, schools, technology, environment, the students themselves? If you had to eliminate one of these factors, which one would you deem as least important? Explain.

There's a Bad Example on Every Desk
Peter Coffee

Peter Coffee is a contributing writer to *eWeek*. This article first appeared on April 15, 2002. Coffee welcomes feedback to his comments in this piece, or, as he says, a "courteous letter," which can be sent to peter_coffee@ziffdavis.com.

There's been lots of comment about this month's report on our bad manners—formally titled "Aggravating Circumstances: A Status Report on Rudeness in America," produced by Public Agenda for the Pew Charitable Trusts. So far as I know, though, I'm the first to point out that report's most glaring oversight. This report ignores a terrible influence on our courtesy and consideration: a bad example to which we're exposed, in many cases, for 3 to 7 hours of the day. I'm not talking about television or even e-mail or chat rooms; I'm talking about computer applications.

Software doesn't apologize, at least not in any meaningful way, when it can't do what we want. An application fails to complete an operation and leaves it to us to figure out that we need to do it over. You'd fire a retail clerk who pretended not to notice a customer, then charged the customer twice for the same purchase, but Web sites do this all the time.

Using computers deconditions our habits and practices of courtesy. Before we had PCs on almost every desk, we got things done by talking to people. White-collar workers handwrote documents for someone else to type: You could, in principle, make dozens of revisions, but you knew that you would eventually build up a level of ill will in the typing pool. You tried to get it right the first time or to tolerate less than the perfect turn of phrase. Live and let live—but now, we just want what we want when we want it.

We conduct our daily lives by interacting with software: It doesn't care whether or not we smile, and it's totally insensitive to whether we gently tap the Enter key or brusquely smack it down. We become accustomed to demanding, rather than requesting, and we unlearn the skill of making someone feel good about doing what we need.

We may think that we're getting used to working with these 5 machines that treat us so badly, but we may not realize the toll that it takes. Research at MIT, measuring people's reactions while playing video games, found that muscle tension and other physical signs of anger were more pronounced when software malfunctioned than when their character "died" in the course of the game. It looks as if we'd rather do our best, or die trying, than be treated with a lack of respect.

I'm not suggesting a return to a labor-intensive workplace. I am suggesting that systems can be designed with good manners in mind and that it's about time we did so.

Suggestions for Writing and Discussion

1. What is the author's point about software applications and common courtesy?
2. Coffee claims that computers "decondition" our habits of respect and courtesies toward one another. Based on this claim, how do you think he maintains an awareness of courtesy himself?
3. What point is Coffee making in the research found at MIT about video games and our values? To what extent do you agree with this conclusion?

For Love of the PC
Reid Goldsborough

Reid Goldsborough is a syndicated columnist and author of the book *Straight Talk about the Information Highway.* He can be reached at reidgold@netaxs.com.

Joe, a computer programmer, was talking with his psychotherapist.

"You've got to help me," he says. "I've fallen in love with my computer, but I know I can never marry her."

"Well, it's good you haven't totally lost touch with reality," says the therapist.

"Oh, it could never work," says Joe. "She wants a career."

5   Making fun of computer geeks, as this joke from "The Official Computer Freaks Joke Book" does, can be fun.

In defense of the geeks, however, computers can captivate.

They allow you to communicate with droves of people at the same time. They help you write more efficiently than a typewriter

or pen and paper. They keep information neat and tidy, eliminating reams of paper lists and files. They let you budget, forecast
and plan more effectively than with a calculator or table. And they
put a different spin on education than traditional books.

Computers empower people, a critical element in today's
world where the lone worker bee often feels irrelevant among the
buzzing corporate hives.

Computers also introduce new things into a culture fascinated
by the latest and greatest. From snazzy monitors to sleek central
processing units, the computer market redefines itself with each
new piece of equipment, stirring hype and excitement.

The morphing market does reflect the great strides made by   10
the computer industry. A run-of-the-mill personal computer today
is 10 times faster than it was five years ago. Despite this increase
in power, the cost of computer hardware—and most software—
has not gone up, but down.

And when it's not crashing or freezing, a computer is always
there when you need it. If you know what you're doing, it does
what you want, unconditionally—unlike other human beings. In
some ways, a computer mimics the human mind and becomes an
extension of you.

It's no wonder people love these machines.

But anything taken to excess, including computers, can be
harmful, according to Dr. Richard Johnson, a psychologist from
Fort Washington, Pa., who works with computer addicts.

Computers can isolate people, Johnson says. If you replace
important social, occupational, educational or recreational activities by sitting in front of your computer, you've gone too far.

Although men most often fall prey to computers, Johnson   15
says, women can get wrapped up, too.

People who are overly involved with their computers may be
trying to fill a void or to block out perceived shortcomings in their
lives. People can use a computer in a dysfunctional way to deal
with guilt or shame, or to avoid tackling difficult decisions or facing responsibilities. Because their lives aren't perfect, some
people obsess about their computers, trying to make them perfect.

But though computers can isolate, they can also connect.
Many people have developed online friendships and romances
that have blossomed off line. People use the Internet to find old
friends and classmates. E-mail and instant messaging are easy,
low-cost ways for faraway family and friends to stay in touch.

As with everything else, computers are about moderation. As long as you keep things in perspective, there's nothing wrong with being a nerd, a word coined by Dr. Seuss in his 1950 book, "If I Ran the Zoo." Or, for that matter, a geek, dweeb, wonk or freak.

Deadly Chatter
Susan Horsburgh and Johnny Dodd

Susan Horsburgh and Johnny Dodd are contributing writers for *People Magazine.* This piece first appeared on February 24, 2003.

Brandon Vedas was sitting by himself at his bedroom computer in the early hours of Jan. 12, but he was hardly alone.

"Take one capsule."

"Takea thousant [sic]!"

"I wanna see if you survive or if you just black out."

5 As other members of a chat room devoted to drug users cheered him on, Vedas, 21, downed one prescription pill after another while smoking pot.

"Do it," wrote one of his pals.

"Cram it."

But as dawn approached—and with a half dozen other chatters watching via a Webcam—the dangerous game was taking its toll on Vedas. "I told u I was hardcore," he boasted to his buddies in a final burst of coherence.

Minutes later he lost consciousness for good.

10 Vedas's lethal overdose might have been remembered like any other case of a young man gone before his time. As it happens, however, it was something of a first: a deadly round of truth or dare viewed live over the Internet. According to a transcript of the chat room found on the Web by Vedas's brother a week later, several of his online pals did send warnings during the two-hour binge—"man don't die," "who's calling the cops when he passes out?"—but none actually called police or alerted Vedas's mother, who, for part of the time at least, was asleep in the next room.

"What has the world come to when people are watching someone die on a Webcam?" asks Vedas's mother, Nancy Russell, 52, who discovered Brandon's body when she tried to rouse him to work at the University of Phoenix computer technology department.

Emergency workers found bottles of Klonopin, methadone, Restoril and Inderal stashed around his room. "If only someone had encouraged him to get help, then maybe he would have just overdosed. Brandon would be in counseling now, instead of dead."

Brandon's brother Rich, 28, a Huntington Beach, Calif., sales rep, says he has spoken with three of the people who were in the chat room. One, according to Rich, claimed that he dialed 911, but the dispatcher said he couldn't help. Meanwhile police have rejected Russell's request to file charges against the people who encouraged her son to take drugs that morning. "There was no coercion or duress. He could have stopped taking pills anytime he wanted to," says Phoenix Police Dept. Sgt. Randy Force. "This is a guy who had a history of drugs, and it caught up with him." (Tests to determine Vedas's exact cause of death are still pending.) As for the reaction of those who witnessed the death online, says Internet scholar John Perry Barlow, "young people by nature like to play around with the edge of death. What makes this different is that the edge was blunted by being virtual. It must have been like a video game."

Still, for Brandon's family, the feeling remains that his friends abandoned him when he needed them most. "We're in complete shock," says Rich, the second of Russell's five children with computer technician Richard Vedas, whom she divorced in the late '80s. The youngest of the kids, Brandon was a high-tech whiz who dropped out of high school at 16 but earned a G.E.D. and managed to land impressive jobs writing software and building networks. "He was a classic computer dork in a lot of ways," says Rich.

But Brandon could also be immature, his brothers say. About 3½ years ago, when his mother remarried, he moved out of the family home and discovered Phoenix's rave scene. According to his brother Brett, 23, a Phoenix bartender, Brandon began using a wide range of drugs, including Ecstasy, LSD and speed. Then, just as abruptly as he had stumbled, Vedas seemed to pick himself back up. "One day he just realized, 'This is probably going to kill me,'" says Brett. About a year ago Brandon began seeking help from a doctor, who prescribed medicine for depression. He also moved back in with his mother. "He assured me he was turning his life around," says Russell, who adds that Brandon had just landed his job and started dating a new girl. "He seemed so positive," she says.

Russell is adamant that her son would never have intentionally 15 killed himself. But after his final Internet session, she says, the family did discover Brandon was well-known in chat rooms for drug devotees, where he went by the name Ripper and had been using the drugs prescribed by his doctor to get high. "I was so oblivious to what he was doing," says Russell. "We're hoping his death will make people more aware of what's going on around them."

Suggestions for Writing and Discussion

1. Reid Goldsborough contends that a computer, in some ways, "mimics the human mind and becomes an extension" of the person using it. Given this belief, who is responsible, then, for Brandon Vedas's death ("Deadly Chatter")?
2. Which one of these pieces do you find most effective and why? Which one provides the most "proof" for its claims?
3. Both authors address the issue of how computers can simultaneously isolate people and yet keep them connected at the same time. How do you reconcile these two seemingly opposing forces?
4. What are the underlying causes within our modern society that might make the use of computers such an attractive alternative to real, personal relationships?

Making Connections: Synthesis and Analysis

1. Based on the four articles in this section, would you say that computers have enriched our personal lives or not? Write an essay in which you argue and support your position.
2. Construct a discussion among the authors of these four pieces based on three questions that you raise about the use of computers today. After their discussion, present your conclusions on their areas of agreement and disagreement.

MEDICAL TECHNOLOGY: HOW MUCH IS TOO MUCH?

Suggestions for Prereading or Journal Writing

1. What are the reasons that Americans, in general, are so reluctant to talk about or plan for death? Write about your own feelings concerning death. What are your greatest fears? What are your deepest hopes?

2. When it comes to end-of-life decisions and the person who is dying does not have a living will, who do you think should be responsible for making medical decisions: someone in the person's family, the doctor in charge, or the courts?

3. If the technology were available so that you could clone yourself, would you or wouldn't you? Explain.

"CC" (Cloned cat, child of "Rainbow")

Topics for Writing and Discussion

1. What is your first reaction upon seeing little "CC"?

2. What reasons might the photographer have had for putting "CC" in a laboratory beaker?

I, Clone

Michael Shermer

This article first appeared in *Scientific Magazine* in April 2003. In addition to being a freelance writer, Michael Shermer is publisher of *Skeptic Magazine* and the general editor of the *Skeptic Encyclopedia of Pseudoscience*.

THE THREE LAWS OF CLONING WILL PROTECT CLONES AND ADVANCE SCIENCE

In his 1950 science-fiction novel *I, Robot,* Isaac Asimov presented the Three Laws of Robotics: "1. A robot may not injure a human being, or, through inaction, allow a human being to come to harm. 2. A robot must obey the orders given it by human beings except where such orders would conflict with the First Law. 3. A robot must protect its own existence as long as such protection does not conflict with the First or Second Law."

The irrational fears people express today about cloning parallel those surrounding robotics half a century ago. So I would like to propose Three Laws of Cloning that also clarify three misunderstandings: 1. A human clone is a human being no less unique in his or her personhood than an identical twin. 2. A human clone has all the rights and privileges that accompany this legal and moral status. 3. A human clone is to be accorded the dignity and respect due any member of our species.

Although such simplifications risk erasing the rich nuances found in ethical debates over pioneering research, they do aid in attenuating risible fears often associated with such advances. It appears that the Raelians have not succeeded in Xeroxing themselves, but it is clear that someone, somewhere, sometime soon is going to generate a human clone. And once one team has succeeded, it will be Katy bar the door for others to bring on the clones.

If cloning produces genetic monstrosities that render it impractical as another form of fertility enhancement, then it will not be necessary to ban it, because no one will use it. If cloning does work, however, there is no reason to forbid it, because the three common reasons given for implementing restrictions are myths. I call them the Identical Personhood Myth, the Playing God Myth, and the Human Rights and Dignity Myth.

The Identical Personhood Myth is well represented by activist 5 Jeremy Rifkin: "It's a horrendous crime to make a Xerox of someone. You're putting a human into a genetic straitjacket." Baloney. He and fellow cloning critics have the argument bass ackward. As environmental determinists, they should be arguing: "Clone all you like—you'll never produce another you, because environment matters as much as heredity." The best scientific evidence to date indicates that roughly half the variance among us is accounted for by genetics and the rest by environment. It is impossible to duplicate the near-infinite number of permutations that come into play during the development of each individual, so cloning is no threat to unique personhood.

The Playing God Myth has numerous promoters, among the latest was Stanley M. Hauer, a professor of theological ethics at Duke University: "The very attempt to clone a human being is evil. The assumption that we must do what we can do is fueled by the Promethean desire to be our own creators." In support of this myth, he is not alone. A 1997 Time/CNN poll revealed that 74 percent of 1,005 Americans answered "yes" to the question "Is it against God's will to clone human beings?" Balderdash. Cloning may seem to be "playing God" only because it is unfamiliar. Consider earlier examples of once "God-like" fertility technologies that are now cheerfully embraced because we have become accustomed to them, such as in vitro fertilization and embryo transfer.

The Human Rights and Dignity Myth is embodied in the Roman Catholic Church's official statement against cloning, based on the belief that it denies "the dignity of human procreation and of the conjugal union," as well as in a Sunni Muslim cleric's demand that "science must be regulated by firm laws to preserve humanity and its dignity." Bunkum. Clones will be no more alike than twins raised in separate environments, and no one is suggesting that twins do not have rights or dignity or that they should be banned.

Instead of restricting or preventing the technology, I propose that we adopt the Three Laws of Cloning, the principles of which are already incorporated in the laws and language of the U.S. Constitution, and allow science to run its course. The soul of science is found in courageous thought and creative experiment, not in restrictive fear and prohibitions. For science to progress, it must be given the opportunity to succeed or fail. Let's run the cloning experiment and see what happens.

Suggestions for Writing and Discussion

1. Shermer bases his main point—that cloning should not be forbidden—on what three laws? How complete do you find his thinking here, and can you think of any other laws that might apply to this issue?
2. How would you characterize Shermer's tone in this piece? Point to several examples that support your answer.
3. Out of the three myths that Shermer presents, which one do you think he supports most effectively? Which one is the weakest?
4. What effects of cloning is Shermer not addressing in this piece? Imagine, for example, that you are a clone. How might this affect your identity as well as your sense of self?

Embracing Life, Accepting Limits
Peter A. Setness

This article by Peter Setness, who is a physician, first appeared in *Postgraduate Medicine* in August 2003.

A PHYSICIAN'S POSITION IS UNIQUE WHEN A LOVED ONE FACES DEATH

The poet Dylan Thomas wrestled with the death of his father through his writings, specifically the poem "Do not go gentle into that good night."(n1) I am not a gifted poet, but I, too, have wrestled with the same issue as of late. My own father slowly died over the past 3 months. Although he was 86 years old and had lived a rich and fruitful life, watching this man I loved and respected pass away was indescribably painful at times.

In a matter of months, the tumor in his brain transformed him from an alert and active octogenarian to a weak, fragile shell who no longer recognized our family. We had to face deciding, with the aid of his physician, when prolonging his life through the use of science ended and prolonging his death began. We used terms such as supportive care and comfort measures and discussed what each meant in my father's case. And unlike Dylan Thomas, I found myself wishing to see my father pass peacefully and comfortably, rather than having to "rage, rage against the dying of the light."

This experience has caused me to reflect on the role we physicians play when our patients become terminally ill. We practice in a time when a wide range of options are available for those nearing the end of life. Modern medicine offers medication and technology capable of keeping the terminally ill alive for much longer than ever thought possible. Concurrently, debates rage in our society over whether the hopelessly ill have a right to passive or active euthanasia.

LIFE-SUSTAINING MEASURES

Medical science now offers us the ability to sustain life under remarkably adverse conditions. Patients whose prognosis would have been deemed hopeless just a decade or two ago now routinely receive lifesaving and life-prolonging care. There is no doubt that these advances in technology offer a much-appreciated second chance to those who are critically injured or suffering from debilitating diseases. Even patients with terminal conditions can experience longer lives, thanks to our ability to support the body in the face of overwhelming odds. Advances in transplant therapy, chemotherapy, medication management, surgical intervention, and mechanical support all offer patients a chance at extended survival.

However, potential drawbacks to these medical miracles exist. 5 Seizing every opportunity to stave off death may result in prolonged suffering for the patient. Families may cling to unrealistic hopes that medical science can offer a last-minute cure or reprieve. Conscientious physicians may be reluctant to abandon the fight without exhausting every weapon in their arsenal.

THE "DEATH WITH DIGNITY" MOVEMENT

On the other end of the spectrum, the Hemlock Society advocates that "every hopelessly ill, mentally competent American should have access to the full range of end-of-life choices, including the option of hastening one's death . . ."(n2) The society and other groups like it support and actively lobby for enforceable laws that protect doctors who wish to aid patients in ending their life. Thus far, only Oregon has passed such legislation, but initiatives have been brought before the legislatures in four other states. (The US Department of Justice has challenged the Oregon law as a violation of the federal Controlled Substances Act, and the federal courts have yet to decide the matter.(n3))

The Netherlands became the first country to legalize mercy killing when a controversial euthanasia law took effect in 2002.(n4) The law allows patients who have extreme suffering to request euthanasia and lets doctors carry out mercy killing in these cases without fear of prosecution. Specifics of the law require that the patients be of sound mind when making the request and face a future of "unbearable, interminable suffering," although their condition need not be terminal or life-threatening. The request to die must be voluntary and originate with the patient.

Countries such as France, Belgium, and Australia are exploring similar measures. In the Netherlands, there already is talk of widening the scope of the law. However, public opinion around the world remains largely opposed to legalized euthanasia. The United Nations Human Rights Committee has gone on record saying it is not convinced that the Dutch system can prevent abuses such as pressure to request euthanasia being exerted on the patient [.]

"AND YOU, MY FATHER, THERE ON THE SAD HEIGHT . . ."(n1)

In an address last year to a scientific congress of physicians, Pope John Paul II urged them to pursue scientific research but reminded them, "There are limits which cannot be humanly overcome."(n5) He further noted that resorting to extreme measures to keep the terminally ill alive does not respect the patient. He stated, "Certainly one cannot forget that man is a limited and mortal being."

10   Throughout my career I have leaned toward providing supportive care in the terminal phases of life. When a patient nears death because of a terminal condition, I believe there comes a time when it is appropriate to set aside heroic measures so that the dying process may proceed. Watching my father slip away only served to strengthen my belief that this middle ground is the best course.

As much as I loved and respected my father, I was prepared to let him go when the time came. Birth and death are part of the cycle of our earthly existence, and both have their appointed time.

As a matter of fact, within days of my father's passing, my daughter delivered our first grandchild—a healthy baby boy named Samuel. Life and death . . . the cycle continues.

REFERENCES

(n1.) Thomas D. *The selected poems of Dylan Thomas 1934–1952.* Rev. ed. New York: New Directions, 2003:122.
(n2.) Hemlock Society USA. *What Hemlock believes.* Available at: http://www.hemlock.org/about/beliefs.asp. Accessed May 29, 2003.
(n3.) Carson T. *Oregon, US battle in court over assisted suicide.* Available at: http://www.dwd.org/fss/news/reut.05.07.03.asp. Accessed May 29, 2003.
(n4.) *Dutch legalise euthanasia.* Available at: http://news.bbc.co.uk/1/hi/world/europe/1904789.stm. Accessed May 29, 2003.
(n5.) Pope: excess treatment disrespects terminally ill. *Star Tribune* Mar 24, 2002.

Suggestions for Writing and Discussion

1. According to Setness, what are the three main choices that patients may have when they are suffering from a hopeless, terminal condition?
2. In this piece, Setness does not use medical terminology even though the publication for which he is writing is geared toward medical professionals. Instead, he refers to poetry and quotes John Paul II. What effect might these references have on his readers? What do they reflect about Setness himself?
3. What reasons might Setness offer for not embracing what the Hemlock Society advocates for the terminally ill? In what instances might a person experience "unbearable, interminable suffering" but not be terminally ill?
4. What decisions might Setness have had to make in regard to his father's death? Would these decisions be easier to make in a physician's role or from the son's perspective? Explain.

Court: Removal of Brain-Damaged Woman's Feeding Tube Can Proceed

Vickie Chachere

Vickie Chachere's article on the controversy surrounding the Terri Shiavo case first appeared in the *Naples Daily News* on October 15, 2003.

Pinellas Park—An appeals court refused to block Tuesday the removal of a severely brain-damaged woman's feeding tube, one of the last hopes her parents had for keeping her alive.

The 2nd District Court of Appeal in Lakeland rejected two motions filed by an attorney for the parents of Terri Schiavo, who is scheduled to have the feeding tube removed Wednesday at her husband's request.

"Our legal remedies are exhausted," Bob and Mary Schindler's attorneys said in a statement Tuesday afternoon.

Schiavo, 39, is expected to die within two weeks after the tube is removed. She has been in a vegetative state since suffering a heart attack in 1990.

5   The Schindlers have waged a long legal battle against her husband, Michael Schiavo, saying their daughter could be rehabilitated but has never been given the chance.

Michael Schiavo says he is carrying out his wife's wishes that she not be kept alive artificially. Pinellas Circuit Court Judge George Greer has ordered the tube be removed at 2 p.m. Wednesday.

The Schindlers' attorney, Pat Anderson, had asked the appeals court to remove Greer—who has repeatedly ruled in favor of Michael Schiavo—and filed an emergency motion seeking a stay and therapy for Terri to determine if she can eat on her own.

"It certainly appears the legal options for the Schindlers are diminishing very quickly," said George Felos, the attorney representing husband Michael Schiavo. "So many unexpected things have happened in this case, we are just going to take it one day at a time."

Meanwhile, anti-abortion activists who have joined the Schindlers in their fight stepped up protests outside the hospice where Terri Schiavo now lives.

10   Bob Schindler, along with national anti-abortion activist Randall Terry, released a secretly recorded videotape of Terri Schiavo made in defiance of Greer's order to not photograph or tape her.

The tape prompted a letter from Michael Schiavo's attorneys threatening to block the Schindlers' unsupervised visits with their daughter, a threat that Mary Schindler said Tuesday night was already being carried out.

She said guards blocked her from seeing her daughter at 5 p.m. Tuesday, telling her that she could only visit in the future with Michael Schiavo present.

"He's the guardian. He doesn't need the court to tell him he can do that," Mary Schindler said. "He can just do it."

Bob Schindler Jr., Terri's brother, said family attorneys were attempting to find ways to allow the family to visit her without her husband being present.

"Essentially, this means we've been barred from seeing Terri," 15 Schindler Jr. said.

The tape was made in August 2001 and shows Mary Schindler attempting to communicate with her daughter. Bob Schindler made the videotape by smuggling a small camera into her room under his shirt, and said the family also had a Nevada therapist secretly trying to treat his daughter over the telephone earlier this year.

Doctors have testified that the noises and facial expressions Terri Schiavo makes are reflexes and do not indicate that she has enough mental capabilities to communicate with others.

Bob Schindler said he is releasing the videotape in hopes it will spur Gov. Jeb Bush to intervene. Bush has sided with the parents in court filings, but has not taken any other action.

The Schindlers want the Department of Children & Families to investigate whether Michael Schiavo exploited his wife by using money awarded to her in a malpractice lawsuit to pay attorneys fees rather than for therapy.

The governor's office has said there is nothing Bush can do to 20 stop the removal of the tube.

Still, the governor said Tuesday the case is "very troubling."

"This is not an easy situation for anyone," Bush said. "But at the end of the day, if it's possible for this woman to be able to continue to live without life support, then she should be able to do that . . . I don't know if that's the case or not, we'll never know if it stands where it is right now."

Bob Schindler said he has made no formal request of the governor to attempt to stop the tube removal, nor has the family ever made a formal complaint to DCF on their allegations of exploitation.

Schindler said he may still file a complaint in the coming days.

"The game isn't over," he said. "There is still time on the clock." 25

Suggestions for Writing and Discussion

1. Who are the key players in the decision to either sustain Terri Schiavo's life or to remove the feeding tube that has been keeping her alive for more than a decade? Regardless

of how you feel about this case, who do you think should have the authority to make these decisions and why?

2. What more might you need to know about this case in order to understand Michael Schiavo's actions? What more might you need to know about Terri's parents, the Schindlers, in order to understand their point of view?

3. If Terri Schiavo had made a living will, then her wishes about what she would want, should she ever be in a vegetative state, would have to be followed. What reasons can you offer as to why Terri Schiavo did not have a living will?

4. Since this article came out, Governor Bush did indeed overturn the court order to remove the feeding tube. What evidence in this piece questions his authority to make such a decision?

Making Connections: Synthesis and Analysis

1. What are the moral dilemmas within each piece presented here? What are the ethical dilemmas? Which ones revolve primarily around one's ethical beliefs, and which ones affect the morals of American society as a whole?

2. Research the current status of Terry Schiavo or the current state of cloning in America. What changes can you see happening based on your new information?

3. Imagine you are running for a prominent public office. How would you respond to the following questions from reporters: What are your feelings about cloning? What are your feelings about medical advances and the prolonged suffering of terminally ill patients? What are your feelings about children and the Internet? Write a platform, using specific scenarios that will both explain and support your views.

EXTENDED CONNECTIONS: FOR CRITICAL THINKING, WRITING, AND RESEARCH

1. Write a research paper on one specific concern that directly affects college students and the Internet. Issues that are found within this text include file sharing, human relationships, and chat rooms. Other topics of interest might include

buying research papers from Internet sources, the advent of instant messaging, and using personal Web sites as "authorities." Consider using outside written sources, personal interviews, and surveys for your research.

2. How effectively are computers being used in America's classrooms today? Blending issues from chapter 5 with those raised in this chapter, focus on one aspect of educational reform and argue whether or not computers will make a difference.

3. Write a feature essay in which you trace the roots of the Terri Schiavo case from its very beginnings to where it is today. Within this research, find other cases that compare to this case, and make a prediction for what the outcome will finally be.

4. What are the most effective ways of helping those who live in poverty? Using several essays from several different chapters, come to some conclusions about what key factors allow people to succeed in America today.

5. Focus on the differences in gender in America, and come to some conclusions as to how modern relationships compare/contrast with relationships in the past and how technology has been a major factor in these changes.

6. Trace the history of cloning: Where did it begin, where is it now, and what is the American government's stance on the issue? Based on other changes that have taken place between "then" and "now," what predictions can you make about the possibility of widespread human cloning in the future?

CHAPTER 9

Going to College: Race and Privilege in College Admissions

INTRODUCTION

According to the American dream, anyone who tries hard enough can go to college. Succeeding at higher education, achieving academic honors, and earning degrees have long been viewed as opportunities equally available in the democratic society of the United States.

However, even a casual look at the history of education shows a very different picture. During the early years, for example, African Americans were held in slavery and were denied the right to literacy. Once they were emancipated and could legally learn to read, their educational institutions were segregated and were often "separate but not equal."

Until the early years of the twentieth century, many medical authorities regarded women as delicate creatures, whose reproductive systems would be damaged by higher education. Even as late as the 1960s, women were denied admission at some of the country's most prestigious colleges and universities.

With the increasing population of Jewish immigrants arriving from Russia and eastern Europe in the late nineteenth and early twentieth centuries, many colleges and universities set quotas so that Jewish students, who were often perceived as extremely gifted intellectually, would not occupy too many places in any given class year. These quotas persisted in some institutions until the late 1950s.

In addition to gender, race, and ethnic discrimination, however, there are other, sometimes more subtle, ways in which the possibilities for realizing college dreams in America are rendered unequal. This chapter explores issues related to race and privilege in the college admissions process.

Describing a small town in Arkansas in the 1940s, Maya Angelou provides a historical perspective for the inequities in access to college preparation. Her memoir addresses the way black Americans were routinely discouraged from aspiring to higher education. Moving ahead to the 1950s and 1960s, Mike Rose, the son of Italian immigrants, describes the barriers of economic and social class he encountered during his elementary and high school years. And Borgna Brunner provides a useful history and timeline on affirmative action.

Looking at recent college admissions policies and focusing on race-based affirmative action, Brent Staples reflects on the ways both he and President Bush's advisor Condoleezza Rice have benefited from affirmative action, and two related articles suggest the complexities of affirmative action admission at the University of Michigan.

While race-based affirmative action makes college admission available to some students, many other students who come from privileged socioeconomic backgrounds are given preference because of their families' connections or because they are related to alumni of a particular institution. Articles by John R. MacArthur and Todd Gitlin explore the many aspects of class-based affirmative action.

Finally, two readings look at additional factors that affect college admission. An article from the *Christian Century* notes the preferential treatment given to athletes, and Michael Arnone examines the increasing use of writing coaches to assist students who have the economic means with their college and scholarship application essays.

While most people in the United States view educational opportunities as a basic right, the perspectives on college admission in this chapter suggest that gaining admission to college in America may be much more complicated than many aspiring students believe.

· *THEN* ·

SETTING THE CONTEXT: COLLEGE THEN

Suggestions for Prereading or Journal Writing

   1. Are there any ways you have observed in which the college classroom experience is different for women than it is for men? Explain.

   2. In your opinion, how seriously do most American students take their education today? Using your own experience as well as your observations, consider this question: Is education in this country considered a right or a privilege? Explain.

   3. If you could go back and change anything about your past educational experiences, what would you change? Explain.

Graduation in Stamps
Maya Angelou

Originally named Marguerite Johnson, Maya Angelou was born in St. Louis in 1928. During her early years, Angelou and her brother grew up in Stamps, Arkansas, under the watchful, loving eye of their grandmother, whom they called "Momma." Unfortunately, her grandmother's boundless energy and affection could not protect Angelou from the pain of poverty, segregated schools, and violence at the hands of both whites and blacks. During a brief stay with her mother, she was raped by her mother's lover and shortly after that returned to her grandmother's home in her beloved Stamps. Best known for her highly praised autobiography *I Know Why the Caged Bird Sings* (1968), from which this selection is taken, Angelou is also a Pulitzer Prize–winning poet and has served as poet laureate of the United States.

The children in Stamps trembled visibly with anticipation. Some adults were excited too, but to be certain the whole young population had come down with graduation epidemic. Large classes were graduating from both the grammar school and the high school. Even those who were years removed from their own day of glorious release were anxious to help with preparations as a kind of dry run. The junior students who were moving into the vacating classes' chairs were tradition-bound to show their talents for leadership and management. They strutted through the school and around the campus exerting pressure on the lower grades. Their authority was so new that occasionally if they pressed a little too hard it had to be overlooked. After all, next term was coming, and it never hurt a sixth grader to have a play sister in the eighth grade, or a tenth-year student to be able to call a twelfth grader Bubba. So all was endured in a spirit of shared understanding. But the graduating classes themselves were the nobility. Like travelers with exotic destinations on their minds, the graduates were remarkably forgetful. They came to school without their books, or tablets or even pencils. Volunteers fell over themselves to secure replacements for the missing equipment. When accepted, the willing workers might or might not be thanked, and it was of no importance to the pre-graduation rites. Even teachers were respectful of the now quiet and aging seniors, and tended to speak to them, if not as equals, as beings only slightly lower than themselves. After tests were returned and grades given, the student body, which acted like an extended family, knew who did well, who excelled, and what piteous ones had failed.

Unlike the white high school, Lafayette County Training School distinguished itself by having neither lawn, nor hedges, nor tennis court, nor climbing ivy. Its two buildings (main classrooms, the grade school and home economics) were set on a dirt hill with no fence to limit either its boundaries or those of bordering farms. There was a large expanse to the left of the school which was used alternately as a baseball diamond or a basketball court. Rusty hoops on the swaying poles represented the permanent recreational equipment, although bats and balls could be borrowed from the P.E. teacher if the borrower was qualified and if the diamond wasn't occupied.

Over this rocky area relieved by a few shady tall persimmon trees the graduating class walked. The girls often held hands and no longer bothered to speak to the lower students. There was a sadness about them, as if this old world was not their home and they were bound for higher ground. The boys, on the other hand, had become more friendly, more outgoing. A decided change from the closed attitude they projected while studying for finals. Now they seemed not ready to give up the old school, the familiar paths and classrooms. Only a small percentage would be continuing on to college—one of the South's A & M (agricultural and mechanical) schools, which trained Negro youths to be carpenters, farmers, handymen, masons, maids, cooks and baby nurses. Their future rode heavily on their shoulders, and blinded them to the collective joy that had pervaded the lives of the boys and girls in the grammar school graduating class.

Parents who could afford it had ordered new shoes and ready-made clothes for themselves from Sears and Roebuck or Montgomery Ward. They also engaged the best seamstresses to make the floating graduating dresses and to cut down secondhand pants which would be pressed to a military slickness for the important event.

5   Oh, it was important, all right. Whitefolks would attend the ceremony, and two or three would speak of God and home, and the Southern way of life, and Mrs. Parsons, the principal's wife, would play the graduation march while the lower-grade graduates paraded down the aisles and took their seats below the platform. The high school seniors would wait in empty classrooms to make their dramatic entrance.

In the Store I was the person of the moment. The birthday girl. The center. Bailey had graduated the year before, although to do so he had had to forfeit all pleasures to make up for his time lost in Baton Rouge.

My class was wearing butter-yellow piqué dresses, and Momma launched out on mine. She smocked the yoke into tiny crisscrossing puckers, then shirred the rest of the bodice. Her dark fingers ducked in and out of the lemony cloth as she embroidered raised daisies around the hem. Before she considered herself finished she had added a crocheted cuff on the puff sleeves, and a pointy crocheted collar.

I was going to be lovely. A walking model of all the various styles of fine hand sewing and it didn't worry me that I was only twelve years old and merely graduating from the eighth grade. Besides, many teachers in Arkansas Negro schools had only that diploma and were licensed to impart wisdom.

The days had become longer and more noticeable. The faded beige of former times had been replaced with strong and sure colors. I began to see my classmates' clothes, their skin tones, and the dust that waved off pussy willows. Clouds that lazed across the sky were objects of great concern to me. Their shiftier shapes might have held a message that in my new happiness and with a little bit of time I'd soon decipher. During that period I looked at the arch of heaven so religiously my neck kept a steady ache. I had taken to smiling more often, and my jaws hurt from the unaccustomed activity. Between the two physical sore spots, I suppose I could have been uncomfortable, but that was not the case. As a member of the winning team (the graduating class of 1940) I had outdistanced unpleasant sensations by miles. I was headed for the freedom of open fields.

Youth and social approval allied themselves with me and we 10 trammeled memories of slights and insults. The wind of our swift passage remodeled my features. Lost tears were pounded to mud and then to dust. Years of withdrawal were brushed aside and left behind, as hanging ropes of parasitic moss.

My work alone had awarded me a top place and I was going to be one of the first called in the graduating ceremonies. On the classroom blackboard, as well as on the bulletin board in the auditorium, there were blue stars and white stars and red stars. No absences, no tardiness, and my academic work was among the best of the year. I could say the preamble to the Constitution even faster than Bailey. We timed ourselves often: "Wethepeopleofthe-UnitedStatesinordertoformamoreperfectunion . . ." I had memorized the Presidents of the United States from Washington to Roosevelt in chronological as well as alphabetical order.

My hair pleased me too. Gradually the black mass had lengthened and thickened, so that it kept at last to its braided pattern, and I didn't have to yank my scalp off when I tried to comb it.

Louise and I had rehearsed the exercises until we tired out ourselves. Henry Reed was class valedictorian. He was a small, very black boy with hooded eyes, a long, broad nose and an oddly shaped head. I had admired him for years because each term he and I vied for the best grades in our class. Most often he bested me, but instead of being disappointed, I was pleased that we shared top places between us. Like many Southern black children, he lived with his grandmother, who was as strict as Momma and as kind as she knew how to be. He was courteous, respectful and soft-spoken to elders, but on the playground he chose to play the roughest games. I admired him. Anyone, I reckoned, sufficiently afraid or sufficiently dull could be polite. But to be able to operate at a top level with both adults and children was admirable.

His valedictory speech was entitled: "To Be or Not to Be." The rigid tenth-grade teacher had helped him write it. He'd been working on the dramatic stresses for months.

15 The weeks until graduation were filled with heady activities. A group of small children were to be presented in a play about buttercups and daisies and bunny rabbits. They could be heard throughout the building practicing their hops and their little songs that sounded like silver bells. The older girls (non-graduates, of course) were assigned the task of making refreshments for the night's festivities. A tangy scent of ginger, cinnamon, nutmeg and chocolate wafted around the home economics building as the budding cooks made samples for themselves and their teachers.

In every corner of the workshop, axes and saws split fresh timber as the woodshop boys made sets and stage scenery. Only the graduates were left out of the general bustle. We were free to sit in the library at the back of the building or look in quite detachedly, naturally, on the measures being taken for our event.

Even the minister preached on graduation the Sunday before. His subject was, "Let your light so shine that men will see your good works and praise your Father, Who is in Heaven." Although the sermon was purported to be addressed to us, he used the occasion to speak to backsliders, gamblers and general ne'er-do-wells. But since he had called our names at the beginning of the service we were mollified.

Among Negros the tradition was to give presents to children going only from one grade to another. How much more important this was when the person was graduating at the top of the class. Uncle Willie and Momma had sent away for a Mickey Mouse watch like Bailey's. Louise gave me four embroidered handkerchiefs. (I gave her three crocheted doilies.) Mrs. Sneed, the minister's wife, made me an underskirt to wear for graduation, and nearly every customer gave me a nickel or maybe even a dime with the instruction "Keep on moving to higher ground," or some such encouragement.

Amazingly the great day finally dawned and I was out of bed before I knew it. I threw open the back door to see it more clearly, but Momma said, "Sister, come away from that door and put your robe on."

20 I hoped the memory of that morning would never leave me. Sunlight was itself still young, and the day had none of the insistence maturity would bring it in a few hours. In my robe and

barefoot in the backyard, under cover of going to see about my new beans, I gave myself up to the gentle warmth and thanked God that no matter what evil I had done in my life He had allowed me to live to see this day. Somewhere in my fatalism I had expected to die, accidentally, and never have the chance to walk up the stairs in the auditorium and gracefully receive my hard-earned diploma. Out of God's merciful bosom I had won reprieve.

Bailey came out in his robe and gave me a box wrapped in Christmas paper. He said he had saved his money for months to pay for it. It felt like a box of chocolates, but I knew Bailey wouldn't save money to buy candy when we had all we could want under our noses.

He was as proud of the gift as I. It was a soft-leather-bound copy of a collection of poems by Edgar Allan Poe,[1] or, as Bailey and I called him, "Eap." I turned to "Annabel Lee" and we walked up and down the garden rows, the cool dirt between our toes, reciting the beautifully sad lines.

Momma made a Sunday breakfast although it was only Friday. After we finished the blessing, I opened my eyes to find the watch on my plate. It was a dream of a day. Everything went smoothly and to my credit. I didn't have to be reminded or scolded for anything. Near evening I was too jittery to attend to chores, so Bailey volunteered to do all before his bath.

Days before, we had made a sign for the Store, and as we turned out the lights Momma hung the cardboard over the door-knob. It read clearly: CLOSED: GRADUATION.

My dress fitted perfectly and everyone said that I looked like a   25
sunbeam in it. On the hill, going toward the school, Bailey walked behind with Uncle Willie, who muttered, "Go on, Ju." He wanted him to walk ahead with us because it embarrassed him to have to walk so slowly. Bailey said he'd let the ladies walk together, and the men would bring up the rear. We all laughed, nicely.

Little children dashed by out of the dark like fireflies. Their crepe paper dresses and butterfly wings were not made for running and we heard more than one rip, dryly, and the regretful "uh uh" that followed.

---

1. *Edgar Allan Poe:* (1809–1849) American editor, critic, poet, and short-story writer. A brilliant, haunted man, Poe created poems and stories that combined the beautiful with the grotesque, the real with the fantastic.

The school blazed without gaiety. The windows seemed cold and unfriendly from the lower hill. A sense of ill-fated timing crept over me, and if Momma hadn't reached for my hand I would have drifted back to Bailey and Uncle Willie, and possibly beyond. She made a few slow jokes about my feet getting cold, and tugged me along to the now-strange building.

Around the front steps, assurance came back. There were my fellow "greats," the graduating class. Hair brushed back, legs oiled, new dresses and pressed pleats, fresh pocket handkerchiefs and little handbags, all home-sewn. Oh, we were up to snuff, all right. I joined my comrades and didn't even see my family go in to find seats in the crowded auditorium.

The school band struck up a march and all classes filed in as had been rehearsed. We stood in front of our seats, as assigned, and on a signal from the choir director, we sat. No sooner had this been accomplished than the band started to play the national anthem. We rose again and sang the song, after which we recited the pledge of allegiance. We remained standing for a brief minute before the choir director and the principal signaled to us, rather desperately I thought, to take our seats. The command was so unusual that our carefully rehearsed and smooth-running machine was thrown off. For a full minute we fumbled for our chairs and bumped into each other awkwardly. Habits change or solidify under pressure, so in our state of nervous tension we had been ready to follow our usual assembly pattern: the American national anthem, then the pledge of allegiance, then the song every Black person I knew called the Negro National Anthem. All done in the same key, with the same passion and most often standing on the same foot.

30   Finding my seat at last, I was overcome with a presentiment of worse things to come. Something unrehearsed, unplanned, was going to happen, and we were going to be made to look bad. I distinctly remember being explicit in the choice of pronoun. It was "we," the graduating class, the unit, that concerned me then.

The principal welcomed "parents and friends" and asked the Baptist minister to lead us in prayer. His invocation was brief and punchy, and for a second I thought we were getting back on the high road to right action. When the principal came back to the dais, however, his voice had changed. Sounds always affected me profoundly and the principal's voice was one of my favorites. During assembly it melted and lowed weakly into the audience. It had not been in my plan to listen to him, but my curiosity was piqued and I straightened up to give him my attention.

He was talking about Booker T. Washington,[2] our "late great leader," who said we can be as close as the fingers on the hand, etc. . . . Then he said a few vague things about friendship and the friendship of kindly people to those less fortunate than themselves. With that his voice nearly faded, thin, away. Like a river diminishing to a stream and then to a trickle. But he cleared his throat and said, "Our speaker tonight, who is also our friend, came from Texarkana to deliver the commencement address, but due to the irregularity of the train schedule, he's going to, as they say, 'speak and run.'" He said that we understood and wanted the man to know that we were most grateful for the time he was able to give us and then something about how we were willing always to adjust to another's program; and without more ado—"I give you Mr. Edward Donleavy."

Not one but two white men came through the door offstage. The shorter one walked to the speaker's platform, and the tall one moved over to the center seat and sat down. But that was our principal's seat, and already occupied. The dislodged gentleman bounced around for a long breath or two before the Baptist minister gave him his chair, then with more dignity than the situation deserved, the minister walked off the stage.

Donleavy looked at the audience once (on reflection, I'm sure that he wanted only to reassure himself that we were really there), adjusted his glasses and began to read from a sheaf of papers.

He was glad "to be here and to see the work going on just as 35 it was in the other schools."

At the first "Amen" from the audience I willed the offender to immediate death by choking on the word. But Amens and Yes, sir's began to fall around the room like rain through a ragged umbrella.

He told us of the wonderful changes we children in Stamps had in store. The Central School (naturally, the white school was Central) had already been granted improvements that would be in

---

2. *Booker T. Washington:* (1856–1915) African American educator who founded Tuskegee Institute, a post–high school institution of learning for black students who were not, at that time, admitted to most colleges and universities. He was criticized by many African American leaders because he argued that social equality could not be attained—and should not be a goal for African Americans—until they had, on their own, attained economic independence.

use in the fall. A well-known artist was coming from Little Rock to teach art to them. They were going to have the newest microscopes and chemistry equipment for their laboratory. Mr. Donleavy didn't leave us long in the dark over who made these improvements available to Central High. Nor were we to be ignored in the general betterment scheme he had in mind.

He said that he had pointed out to people at a very high level that one of the first-line football tacklers at Arkansas Agricultural and Mechanical College had graduated from good old Lafayette County Training School. Here fewer Amen's were heard. Those few that did break through lay dully in the air with the heaviness of habit.

He went on to praise us. He went on to say how he had bragged that "one of the best basketball players at Fisk sank his first ball right here at Lafayette County Training School."

40　　The white kids were going to have a chance to become Galileos[3] and Madame Curies[4] and Edisons[5] and Gauguins[6], and our boys (the girls weren't even in on it) would try to be Jesse Owenses[7] and Joe Louises.[8]

Owens and the Brown Bomber were great heroes in our world, but what school official in the white-goddom of Little Rock had the right to decide that those two men must be our only heroes? Who decided that for Henry Reed to become a scientist he had to work like George Washington Carver,[9] as a bootblack, to buy a lousy microscope? Bailey was obviously always going to be too small to be

---

3. *Galileo:* (1564–1642) Italian astronomer and physicist. He discovered many physical laws, constructed the first telescope, and confirmed the theory that the earth moves around the sun. 　4. *Madame Curie:* (1867–1934) Polish-born French physicist. She won the Nobel Prize in 1911 for the discovery of metallic radium. 　5. *Thomas Alva Edison:* (1847–1931) One of the most productive American inventors. Among his significant inventions were the record player, the motion picture, the incandescent lamp, and a system for the distribution of electricity. 　6. *Paul Gauguin:* (1848–1903) French painter, associated with the impressionists, noted especially for rejecting traditional naturalism and, instead, using nature as an inspiration for abstract symbols and figures. 　7. *Jesse Owens:* (1913–1981) African American track star who won four gold medals at the 1936 Olympics, which were held in Berlin. Owens made a mockery of Hitler's contention that "Aryan" athletes were superior to all others. 　8. *Joe Louis:* African American boxer. Holder of the heavyweight title, Louis was known as the Brown Bomber. 　9. *George Washington Carver:* (1864–1943) African American agricultural chemist. Born a slave, he later taught at Tuskegee Institute, where he carried out research that led to crop diversification in the South. He is particularly credited with discovering new uses for crops such as peanuts and soybeans.

an athlete, so which concrete angel glued to what county seat had decided that if my brother wanted to become a lawyer he had to first pay penance for his skin by picking cotton and hoeing corn and studying correspondence books at night for twenty years?

The man's dead words fell like bricks around the auditorium and too many settled in my belly. Constrained by hard-learned manners I couldn't look behind me, but to my left and right the proud graduating class of 1940 had dropped their heads. Every girl in my row had found something new to do with her handkerchief. Some folded the tiny squares into love knots, some into triangles, but most were wadding them, then pressing them flat on their yellow laps.

On the dais, the ancient tragedy was being replayed. Professor Parsons sat, a sculptor's reject, rigid. His large, heavy body seemed devoid of will or willingness, and his eyes said he was no longer with us. The other teachers examined the flag (which was draped stage right) or their notes, or the windows which opened on our now-famous playing diamond.

Graduation, the hush-hush magic time of frills and gifts and congratulations and diplomas, was finished for me before my name was called. The accomplishment was nothing. The meticulous maps, drawn in three colors of ink, learning and spelling decasyllabic words, memorizing the whole of *The Rape of Lucrece*[10]—it was for nothing. Donleavy had exposed us.

We were maids and farmers, handymen and washerwomen, and   45 anything higher that we aspired to was farcical and presumptuous.

Then I wished that Gabriel Prosser and Nat Turner[11] had killed all whitefolks in their beds and that Abraham Lincoln had been assassinated before the signing of the Emancipation Proclamation, and that Harriet Tubman[12] had been killed by that blow on her head and Christopher Columbus had drowned in the *Santa Maria*.

---

10. *The Rape of Lucrece:* A narrative poem, 1855 lines long, written by William Shakespeare.   11. *Gabriel Prosser, Nat Turner:* Leaders of slave rebellions. In 1800, Prosser recruited several hundred slaves to attack Richmond. Before they could attack, they were betrayed, and the leaders of the rebellion were captured and executed. In 1831, Turner led a group of slaves who eventually killed 57 white men, women, and children as a protest against slavery.   12. *Harriet Tubman:* (1820–1913) An African American abolitionist who escaped from slavery in 1849 and worked with the underground railroad, leading more than 300 slaves north to freedom.

It was awful to be Negro and have no control over my life. It was brutal to be young and already trained to sit quietly and listen to charges brought against my color with no chance of defense. We should all be dead. I thought I should like to see us all dead, one on top of the other. A pyramid of flesh with the whitefolks on the bottom, as the broad base, then the Indians with their silly tomahawks and tepees and wigwams and treaties, the Negroes with their mops and recipes and cotton sacks and spirituals sticking out of their mouths. The Dutch children should all stumble in their wooden shoes and break their necks. The French should choke to death on the Louisiana Purchase (1803) while silkworms ate all the Chinese with their stupid pigtails. As a species, we were an abomination. All of us.

Donleavy was running for election, and assured our parents that if he won we could count on having the only colored paved playing field in that part of Arkansas. Also—he never looked up to acknowledge the grunts of acceptance—also, we were bound to get some new equipment for the home economics building and the workshop.

He finished, and since there was no need to give any more than the most perfunctory thank-you's, he nodded to the men on the stage, and the tall white man who was never introduced joined him at the door. They left with the attitude that now they were off to something really important. (The graduation ceremonies at Lafayette County Training School had been a mere preliminary.)

50   The ugliness they left was palpable. An uninvited guest who wouldn't leave. The choir was summoned and sang a modern arrangement of "Onward, Christian Soldiers," with new words pertaining to graduates seeking their place in the world. But it didn't work. Elouise, the daughter of the Baptist minister, recited "Invictus," and I could have cried at the impertinence of "I am the master of my fate, I am the captain of my soul."

My name had lost its ring of familiarity and I had to be nudged to go and receive my diploma. All my preparations had fled. I neither marched up to the stage like a conquering Amazon, nor did I look in the audience for Bailey's nod of approval. Marguerite Johnson, I heard the name again, my honors were read, there were noises in the audience of appreciation, and I took my place on the stage as rehearsed.

I thought about colors I hated: ecru, puce, lavender, beige and black.

There was shuffling and rustling around me, then Henry Reed was giving his valedictory address, "To Be or Not to Be." Hadn't he heard the whitefolks? We couldn't *be,* so the question was a waste of time. Henry's voice came clear and strong. I feared to look at him. Hadn't he got the message? There was no "nobler in the mind" for Negroes because the world didn't think we had minds, and they let us know it. "Outrageous fortune"? Now, that was a joke. When the ceremony was over I had to tell Henry Reed some things. That is, if I still cared. Not "rub," Henry, "erase." "Ah, there's the erase." Us.

Henry had been a good student in elocution. His voice rose on tides of promise and fell on waves of warnings. The English teacher had helped him to create a sermon winging through Hamlet's soliloquy. To be a man, a doer, a builder, a leader, or to be a tool, an unfunny joke, a crusher of funky toadstools. I marveled that Henry could go through the speech as if we had a choice.

I had been listening and silently rebutting each sentence with   55 my eyes closed; then there was a hush, which in an audience warns that something unplanned is happening. I looked up and saw Henry Reed, the conservative, the proper, the A student, turn his back to the audience and turn to us (the proud graduating class of 1940) and sing, nearly speaking.

> Lift ev'ry voice and sing
> Till earth and heaven ring
> Ring with the harmonies of Liberty . . .[13]

It was the poem written by James Weldon Johnson. It was the music composed by J. Rosamond Johnson. It was the Negro national anthem. Out of habit we were singing it.

Our mothers and fathers stood in the dark hall and joined the hymn of encouragement. A kindergarten teacher led the small children onto the stage and the buttercups and daisies and bunny rabbits marked time and tried to follow:

> Stony the road we trod
> Bitter the chastening rod
> Felt in the days when hope, unborn, had died.
> Yet with a steady beat

---

13. "Lift Ev'ry Voice and Sing"—words by James Weldon Johnson and music by J. Rosamond Johnson. Copyright by Edward B. Marks Music Corporation. Used by permission.

Have not our weary feet
Come to the place for which our fathers sighed?

Every child I knew had learned that song with his ABC's and along with "Jesus Loves Me This I Know." But I personally had never heard it before. Never heard the words, despite the thousands of times I had sung them. Never thought they had anything to do with me.

On the other hand, the words of Patrick Henry[14] had made such an impression on me that I had been able to stretch myself tall and trembling and say, "I know not what course others may take, but as for me, give me liberty or give me death."

60 And now I heard, really for the first time:

We have come over a way that with tears has been watered,
We have come, treading our path through the blood of the
    slaughtered.

While echoes of the song shivered in the air, Henry Reed bowed his head, said "Thank you," and returned to his place in the line. The tears that slipped down many faces were not wiped away in shame.

Suggestions for Writing and Discussion

1. Identify details that suggest the curriculum in various subjects at Marguerite Johnson's (Maya Angelou's) school. How does this curriculum compare with the expectations for the students of this school as expressed by the graduation speaker, Mr. Donleavy?

2. How did members of the Stamps community regard education? Choose details from the preparations for the graduation, as well as from Angelou's description of the ceremony, to support your response.

Topics for Writing and Discussion

1. The individuals in this photograph are protesting the federally ordered integration of Arkansas schools. Their signs

---

14. *Patrick Henry:* (1726–1799) A leader of the American Revolution who was admired for his skills as a public speaker. The rallying cry "Give me liberty or give me death" is attributed to him.

"Race Mixing Is Communism," Arkansas, 1954

state "Race Mixing Is Communism." What do you think these signs mean? In your response, include a definition of communism.

2. List all the visual elements you see in this photograph and then speculate on the way these protesters would interpret the symbolism of the flags they are holding.

"I Just Wanna Be Average"
Mike Rose

Born to immigrant Italian parents in 1944, Mike Rose is an outstanding scholar and teacher, known especially for his autobiographical book on the school experiences of America's underclass, *Lives on the Boundary* (1989). "I Just Wanna Be Average," a chapter from that book, shows the terrifying ways students can slip through the cracks in the educational system.

It took two buses to get to Our Lady of Mercy. The first started deep in South Los Angeles and caught me at midpoint. The second drifted through neighborhoods with trees, parks, big lawns, and lots of flowers. The rides were long but were livened up by a group of South L.A. veterans whose parents also thought that Hope had set up shop in the west end of the country. There was Christy Biggars, who, at sixteen, was dealing and was, according to rumor, a pimp as well. There were Bill Cobb and Johnny Gonzales, grease-pencil artists extraordinaire, who left Nembutal-enhanced swirls of "Cobb" and "Johnny" on the corrugated walls of the bus. And then there was Tyrrell Wilson. Tyrrell was the coolest kid I knew. He ran the dozens like a metric halfback, laid down a rap that outrhymed and outpointed Cobb, whose rap was good but not great—the curse of a moderately soulful kid trapped in white skin. But it was Cobb who would sneak a radio onto the bus, and thus underwrote his patter with Little Richard, Fats Domino, Chuck Berry, the Coasters, and Ernie K. Doe's mother-in-law, an awful woman who was "sent from down below." And so it was that Christy and Cobb and Johnny G. and Tyrrell and I and assorted others picked up along the way passed our days in the back of the bus, a funny mix brought together by geography and parental desire.

Entrance to school brings with it forms and releases and assessments. Mercy relied on a series of tests, mostly the Stanford-Binet, for placement, and somehow the results of my tests got confused with those of another student named Rose. The other Rose apparently didn't do very well, for I was placed in the vocational track, a euphemism for the bottom level. Neither I nor my parents realized what this meant. We had no sense that Business Math, Typing, and English-Level D were dead ends. The current spate of reports on the schools criticizes parents for not involving themselves in the education of their children. But how would someone like Tommy Rose, with his two years of Italian schooling, know what to ask? And what sort of pressure could an exhausted waitress apply? The error went undetected, and I remained in the vocational track for two years. What a place.

My homeroom was supervised by Brother Dill, a troubled and unstable man who also taught freshman English. When his class drifted away from him, which was often, his voice would rise in paranoid accusations, and occasionally he would lose control and shake or smack us. I hadn't been there two months when one of his brisk, face-turning slaps had my glasses sliding down the aisle. Physical education was also pretty harsh. Our teacher was a stubby ex-lineman who had played old-time pro ball in the Midwest. He routinely had us grabbing our ankles to receive his stinging paddle across our butts. He did that, he said, to make men of us. "Rose," he bellowed on our first encounter; me standing geeky in line in my baggy shorts. "'Rose'? What the hell kind of name is that?"

"Italian, sir," I squeaked.

"Italian! Ho. Rose, do you know the sound a bag of shit 5 makes when it hits the wall?"

"No, sir."

"Wop!"

Sophomore English was taught by Mr. Mitropetros. He was a large, bejeweled man who managed the parking lot at the Shrine Auditorium. He would crow and preen and list for us the stars he'd brushed against. We'd ask questions and glance knowingly and snicker, and all that fueled the poor guy to brag some more. Parking cars was his night job. He had little training in English, so his lesson plan for his day work had us reading the district's required text, *Julius Caesar,* aloud for the semester. We'd finish the play way before the twenty weeks was up, so he'd have us switch parts again and again and start again: Dave Snyder, the fastest guy at Mercy, muscling through Caesar to the breathless squeals of Calpurnia, as interpreted by Steve Fusco, a surfer who owned the school's most envied paneled wagon. Week ten and Dave and Steve would take on new roles, as would we all, and render a water-logged Cassius and a Brutus that are beyond my powers of description.

[. . .]

Students will float to the mark you set. I and the others in the vocational classes were bobbing in pretty shallow water. Vocational education has aimed at increasing the economic opportunities of students who do not do well in our schools. Some serious programs succeed in doing that, and through exceptional teachers—like Mr. Gross in *Horace's Compromise*—students learn to develop hypotheses and troubleshoot, reason through a problem, and communicate effectively—the true job skills. The vocational track, however, is most often a place for those who are just not making it, a dumping ground for the disaffected. There were a few teachers who worked hard at education; young Brother Slattery, for example, combined a stern voice with weekly quizzes to try to pass along to us a skeletal outline of world history. But mostly the teachers had no idea of how to engage the imaginations of us kids who were scuttling along at the bottom of the pond.

And the teachers would have needed some inventiveness, for 10 none of us was groomed for the classroom. It wasn't just that I didn't know things—didn't know how to simplify algebraic fractions, couldn't identify different kinds of clauses, bungled Spanish translations—but that I had developed various faulty and inadequate ways of doing algebra and making sense of Spanish. Worse yet, the years of defensive tuning out in elementary school had given me a way to escape quickly while seeming at least half alert. During my time in Voc. Ed., I developed further into a mediocre student and a somnambulant problem solver, and that affected the subjects I did have the wherewithal to handle: I detested Shakespeare; I got bored with history. My attention flitted here and there. I fooled around in class and read my books indifferently—the intellectual equivalent of playing with your food. I did what I had to do to get by, and I did it with half a mind.

But I did learn things about people and eventually came into my own socially. I liked the guys in Voc. Ed. Growing up where I did, I understood and admired physical prowess, and there was an abundance of muscle here. There was Dave Snyder, a sprinter and halfback of true quality. Dave's ability and his quick wit gave him a natural appeal, and he was welcome in any clique, though he always kept a little independent. He enjoyed acting the fool and could care less about studies, but he possessed a certain maturity and never caused the faculty much trouble. It was a testament to his independence that he included me among his friends—I eventually went out for track, but I was no jock. Owing to the Latin alphabet and a dearth of *R*s and *S*s, Snyder sat behind Rose, and we started exchanging one-liners and became friends.

There was Ted Richard, a much-touted Little League pitcher. He was chunky and had a baby face and came to Our Lady of Mercy as a seasoned street fighter. Ted was quick to laugh and he had a loud, jolly laugh, but when he got angry he'd smile a little smile, the kind that simply raises the corner of the mouth a quarter of an inch. For those who knew, it was an eerie signal. Those who didn't found themselves in big trouble, for Ted was very quick. He loved to carry on what we would come to call philosophical discussions: What is courage? Does God exist? He also loved words, enjoyed picking up big ones like *salubrious* and *equivocal* and using them in our conversations—laughing at himself as the word hit a chuckhole rolling off his tongue. Ted didn't do all that well in school—baseball and parties and testing the courage he'd speculated about took up his time. His textbooks were *Argosy* and *Field and Stream,* whatever newspapers he'd find

on the bus stop—from the *Daily Worker* to pornography—conversations with uncles or hobos or businessmen he'd meet in a coffee
shop, *The Old Man and the Sea.* With hindsight, I can see that Ted
was developing into one of those rough-hewn intellectuals whose
sources are a mix of the learned and the apocryphal, whose discussions are both assured and sad.

And then there was Ken Harvey. Ken was good-looking in a
puffy way and had a full and oily ducktail and was a car enthusi-
ast . . . a hodad. One day in religion class, he said the sentence
that turned out to be one of the most memorable of the hundreds
of thousands I heard in those Voc. Ed. years. We were talking
about the parable of the talents, about achievement, working hard,
doing the best you can do, blah-blah-blah, when the teacher called
on the restive Ken Harvey for an opinion. Ken thought about it,
but just for a second, and said (with studied, minimal affect), "I
just wanna be average." That woke me up. Average? Who wants
to be average? Then the athletes chimed in with the clichés that
make you want to laryngectomize them, and the exchange became
a platitudinous melee. At the time, I thought Ken's assertion was
stupid, and I wrote him off. But his sentence has stayed with me
all these years, and I think I am finally coming to understand it.

Ken Harvey was gasping for air. School can be a tremen-
dously disorienting place. No matter how bad the school, you're
going to encounter notions that don't fit with the assumptions and
beliefs that you grew up with—maybe you'll hear these dissonant
notions from teachers, maybe from the other students, and maybe
you'll read them. You'll also be thrown in with all kinds of kids
from all kinds of backgrounds, and that can be unsettling—this is
especially true in places of rich ethnic and linguistic mix, like the
L.A. basin. You'll see a handful of students far excel you in
courses that sound exotic and that are only in the curriculum of
the elite: French, physics, trigonometry. And all this is happening
while you're trying to shape an identity, your body is changing,
and your emotions are running wild. If you're a working-class kid
in the vocational track, the options you'll have to deal with this
will be constrained in certain ways: you're defined by your school
as "slow"; you're placed in a curriculum that isn't designed to lib-
erate you but to occupy you, or, if you're lucky, train you, though
the training is for work the society does not esteem; other students
are picking up the cues from your school and your curriculum and
interacting with you in particular ways. If you're a kid like Ted

Richard, you turn your back on all this and let your mind roam where it may. But youngsters like Ted are rare. What Ken and so many others do is protect themselves from such suffocating madness by taking on with a vengeance the identity implied in the vocational track. Reject the confusion and frustration by openly defining yourself as the Common Joe. Champion the average. Rely on your own good sense. Fuck this bullshit. Bullshit, of course, is everything you—and the others—fear is beyond you: books, essays, tests, academic scrambling, complexity, scientific reasoning, philosophical inquiry.

15   The tragedy is that you have to twist the knife in your own gray matter to make this defense work. You'll have to shut down, have to reject intellectual stimuli or diffuse them with sarcasm, have to cultivate stupidity, have to convert boredom from a malady into a way of confronting the world. Keep your vocabulary simple, act stoned when you're not or act more stoned than you are, flaunt ignorance, materialize your dreams. It is a powerful and effective defense—it neutralizes the insult and the frustration of being a vocational kid and, when perfected, it drives teachers up the wall, a delightful secondary effect. But like all strong magic, it exacts a price.

My own deliverance from the Voc. Ed. world began with sophomore biology. Every student, college prep to vocational, had to take biology, and unlike the other courses, the same person taught all sections. When teaching the vocational group, Brother Clint probably slowed down a bit or omitted a little of the fundamental biochemistry, but he used the same book and more or less the same syllabus across the board. If one class got tough, he could get tougher. He was young and powerful and very handsome, and looks and physical strength were high currency. No one gave him any trouble.

I was pretty bad at the dissecting table, but the lectures and the textbook were interesting: plastic overlays that, with each turned page, peeled away skin, then veins and muscle, then organs, down to the very bones that Brother Clint, pointer in hand, would tap out on our hanging skeleton. Dave Snyder was in big trouble, for the study of life—versus the living of it—was sticking in his craw. We worked out a code for our multiple-choice exams. He'd poke me in the back: once for the answer under *A,* twice for *B,* and so on; and when he'd hit the right one, I'd look up to the ceiling as though I were lost in thought. Poke: cytoplasm.

Poke, poke: methane. Poke, poke, poke: William Harvey. Poke, poke, poke, poke: islets of Langerhans. This didn't work out perfectly, but Dave passed the course, and I mastered the dreamy look of a guy on a record jacket. And something else happened. Brother Clint puzzled over this Voc. Ed. kid who was racking up 98s and 99s on his tests. He checked the school's records and discovered the error. He recommended that I begin my junior year in the College Prep program. According to all I've read since, such a shift, as one report put it, is virtually impossible. Kids at that level rarely cross tracks. The telling thing is how chancy both my placement into and exit from Voc. Ed. was; neither I nor my parents had anything to do with it. I lived in one world during spring semester, and when I came back to school in the fall, I was living in another.

Switching to College Prep was a mixed blessing. I was an erratic student. I was undisciplined. And I hadn't caught onto the rules of the game: why work hard in a class that didn't grab my fancy? I was also hopelessly behind in math. Chemistry was hard; toying with my chemistry set years before hadn't prepared me for the chemist's equations. Fortunately, the priest who taught both chemistry and second-year algebra was also the school's athletic director. Membership on the track team covered me; I knew I wouldn't get lower than a C. U.S. history was taught pretty well, and I did okay. But civics was taken over by a football coach who had trouble reading the textbook aloud—and reading aloud was the centerpiece of his pedagogy. College Prep at Mercy was certainly an improvement over the vocational program—at least it carried some status—but the social science curriculum was weak, and the mathematics and physical sciences were simply beyond me. I had a miserable quantitative background and ended up copying some assignments and finessing the rest as best I could. Let me try to explain how it feels to see again and again material you should once have learned but didn't.

You are given a problem. It requires you to simplify algebraic fractions or to multiply expressions containing square roots. You know this is pretty basic material because you've seen it for years. Once a teacher took some time with you, and you learned how to carry out these operations. Simple versions, anyway. But that was a year or two or more in the past, and these are more complex versions, and now you're not sure. And this, you keep telling yourself, is ninth- or even eighth-grade stuff.

20   Next it's a word problem. This is also old hat. The basic elements are as familiar as story characters: trains speeding so many miles per hour or shadows of buildings angling so many degrees. Maybe you know enough, have sat through enough explanations, to be able to begin setting up the problem: "If one train is going this fast . . ." or "This shadow is really one line of a triangle . . ." Then: "Let's see . . ." "How did Jones do this?" "Hmmmm." "No." "No, that won't work." Your attention wavers. You wonder about other things: a football game, a dance, that cute new checker at the market. You try to focus on the problem again. You scribble on paper for a while, but the tension wins out and your attention flits elsewhere. You crumple the paper and begin daydreaming to ease the frustration.

The particulars will vary, but in essence this is what a number of students go through, especially those in so-called remedial classes. They open their textbooks and see once again the familiar and impenetrable formulas and diagrams and terms that have stumped them for years. There is no excitement here. *No* excitement. Regardless of what the teacher says, this is not a new challenge. There is, rather, embarrassment and frustration and, not surprisingly, some anger in being reminded once again of long-standing inadequacies. No wonder so many students finally attribute their difficulties to something inborn, organic: "That part of my brain just doesn't work." Given the troubling histories many of these students have, it's miraculous that any of them can lift the shroud of hopelessness sufficiently to make deliverance from these classes possible.

[. . .]

Jack MacFarland couldn't have come into my life at a better time. My father was dead, and I had logged up too many years of scholastic indifference. Mr. MacFarland had a master's degree from Columbia and decided, at twenty-six, to find a little school and teach his heart out. He never took any credentialing courses, couldn't bear to, he said, so he had to find employment in a private system. He ended up at Our Lady of Mercy teaching five sections of senior English. He was a beatnik who was born too late. His teeth were stained, he tucked his sorry tie in between the third and fourth buttons of his shirt, and his pants were chronically wrinkled. At first, we couldn't believe this guy, thought he slept in his car. But within no time, he had us so startled with work that we didn't much worry about where he slept or if he slept at all. We wrote three or four essays a month. We read a book every two to three weeks, starting with the *Iliad* and ending up with Hemingway. He gave us a quiz on the reading every other day. He brought a prep school curriculum to Mercy High.

[. . .]

Even MacFarland's barbs were literary. If Jim Fitzsimmons, hung over and irritable, tried to smart-ass him, he'd rejoin with a flourish that would spark the indomitable Skip Madison—who'd lost his front teeth in a hapless tackle—to flick his tongue through the gap and opine, "good chop," drawing out the single "o" in stinging indictment. Jack MacFarland, this tobacco-stained intellectual, brandished linguistic weapons of a kind I hadn't encountered before. Here was this *egghead,* for God's sake, keeping some pretty difficult people in line. And from what I heard, Mike Dweetz and Steve Fusco and all the notorious Voc. Ed. crowd settled down as well when MacFarland took the podium. Though a lot of guys groused in the schoolyard, it just seemed that giving trouble to this particular teacher was a silly thing to do. Tomfoolery, not to mention assault, had no place in the world he was trying to create for us, and instinctively everyone knew that. If nothing else, we all recognized MacFarland's considerable intelligence and respected the hours he put into his work. It came to this: the troublemaker would look foolish rather than daring. Even Jim Fitzsimmons was reading *On the Road* and turning his incipient alcoholism to literary ends.

There were some lives that were already beyond Jack MacFarland's ministrations, but mine was not. I started reading again as I hadn't since elementary school. I would go into our gloomy little bedroom or sit at the dinner table while, on the television, Danny McShane was paralyzing Mr. Moto with the atomic drop, and work slowly back through *Heart of Darkness,* trying to catch the words in Conrad's sentences. I certainly was not MacFarland's best student; most of the other guys in College Prep, even my fellow slackers, had better backgrounds than I did. But I worked very hard, for MacFarland had hooked me. He tapped my old interest in reading and creating stories. He gave me a way to feel special by using my mind. And he provided a role model that wasn't shaped on physical prowess alone, and something inside me that I wasn't quite aware of responded to that. Jack MacFarland established a literacy club, to borrow a phrase of Frank Smith's, and invited me—invited all of us—to join.

25   There's been a good deal of research and speculation suggesting that the acknowledgement of school performance with extrinsic rewards—smiling faces, stars, numbers, grades—diminishes the intrinsic satisfaction children experience by engaging in reading or writing or problem solving. While it's certainly true that we've created an educational system that encourages our best and brightest to become cynical grade collectors and, in general, have developed an obsession with evaluation and assessment, I must tell you that venal though it may have been, I loved getting good grades from MacFarland. I now know how subjective grades can be, but then they came tucked in the back of essays like bits of scientific data, some sort of spectroscopic readout that said, objectively and publicly, that I had made something of value. I suppose I'd been mediocre for too long and enjoyed a public redefinition. And I suppose the workings of my mind, such as they were, had been private for too long. My linguistic play moved into the world; . . . these papers with their circled, red B-pluses and A-minuses linked my mind to something outside it. I carried them around like a club emblem.

One day in the December of my senior year, Mr. MacFarland asked me where I was going to go to college. I hadn't thought much about it. Many of the students I teach today spent their last year in high school with a physics text in one hand and the Stanford catalog in the other, but I wasn't even aware of what "entrance requirements" were. My folks would say that they wanted me to go to college and be a doctor, but I don't know how seriously I ever took that; it seemed a sweet thing to say, a bit of supportive family chatter, like telling a gangly daughter she's graceful. The reality of higher education wasn't in my scheme of things: no one in the family had gone to college; only two of my uncles had completed high school. I figured I'd get a night job and go to the local junior college because I knew that Snyder and Company were going there to play ball. But I hadn't even prepared for that. When I finally said, "I don't know," MacFarland looked down at me—I was seated in his office—and said, "Listen, you can write."

My grades stank. I had A's in biology and a handful of B's in a few English and social science classes. All the rest were C's—or worse. MacFarland said I would do well in his class and laid down the law about doing well in the others. Still, the record for my first three years wouldn't have been acceptable to any four-year school. To nobody's surprise, I was turned down flat by USC and UCLA. But Jack MacFarland was on the case. He had received his bachelor's degree from Loyola University, so he made calls to old professors and talked to somebody in admissions and wrote me a strong letter. Loyola finally accepted me as a probationary student. I would be on trial for the first year, and if I did okay, I would be granted regular status. MacFarland also intervened to get me a loan, for I could never have afforded a private college without it. Four more years of religion classes and four more years of boys at one school, girls at another. But at least I was going to college. Amazing.

Suggestions for Writing and Discussion

1. In what way does Rose's title, "I Just Wanna Be Average," reflect the central idea of this excerpt from his book? What is ironic about the title?
2. Rose's experience was based on what is known in education as tracking or homogeneous grouping. Did the schools you attended use this system of grouping? How did grouping (or nongrouping) work out for you? From your own experiences, what do you see as the advantages and disadvantages of tracking?

Bakke and Beyond: A History and Timeline of Affirmative Action

Borgna Brunner

Borgna Brunner has written extensively on controversial issues related to civil rights. As a senior editor of *Information Please Almanac,* he compiled the following history and timeline of race-based affirmative action, tracing the major arguments on both sides of this important topic.

In its tumultuous, nearly 40-year history, affirmative action has been both praised and pilloried as an answer to racial inequality. The policy was introduced in 1965 by President Johnson as a method of redressing discrimination that had persisted in spite of civil rights laws and constitutional guarantees. "This is the next and more profound stage of the battle for civil rights," Johnson asserted. "We seek . . . not just equality as a right and a theory, but equality as a fact and as a result."

A TEMPORARY MEASURE TO LEVEL THE PLAYING FIELD

Focusing in particular on education and jobs, affirmative action policies required that active measures be taken to ensure that blacks and other minorities enjoyed the same opportunities for promotions, salary increases, career advancement, school admissions, scholarships, and financial aid that had been the nearly exclusive province of whites. From the outset, affirmative action was envisioned as a temporary remedy that would end once there was a "level playing field" for all Americans.

BAKKE AND REVERSE DISCRIMINATION

By the late '70s, however, flaws in the policy began to show up amid its good intentions. Reverse discrimination became an issue, epitomized by the famous Bakke case in 1978. Allan Bakke, a white male, had been rejected two years in a row by a medical school that had accepted less qualified minority applicants—the school had a separate admissions policy for minorities and reserved 16 out of 100 places for minority students. The Supreme Court outlawed inflexible quota systems in affirmative action programs, which in this case had unfairly discriminated against a white applicant. In the same ruling, however, the Court upheld the legality of affirmative action per se.

A ZERO-SUM GAME FOR CONSERVATIVES

Fueled by "angry white men," a backlash against affirmative action began to mount. To conservatives, the system was a zero-sum game that opened the door for jobs, promotions, or education to minorities while it shut the door on whites. In a country that prized the values of self-reliance and pulling oneself up by one's bootstraps, conservatives resented the idea that some unqualified minorities were getting a free ride on the American system. "Preferential treatment" and "quotas" became expressions of contempt. Even more contentious was the accusation that some minorities enjoyed playing the role of professional victim. Why could some minorities who had also experienced terrible adversity and racism—Jews and Asians, in particular—manage to make the American way work for them without government handouts?

"JUSTICE AND FREEDOM FOR ALL" STILL IN ITS INFANCY

Liberals countered that "the land of opportunity" was a very different place for the European immigrants who landed on its shores than it was for those who arrived in the chains of slavery. As historian Roger Wilkins pointed out, "blacks have a 375-year history on this continent: 245 involving slavery, 100 involving legalized discrimination, and only 30 involving anything else."

Considering that Jim Crow laws and lynching existed well into the '60s, and that myriad subtler forms of racism in housing, employment, and education persisted well beyond the civil rights movement, conservatives impatient for blacks to "get over" the legacy of slavery needed to realize that slavery was just the beginning of racism in America. Liberals also pointed out that another popular conservative argument—that because of affirmative action, minorities were threatening the jobs of whites—belied the reality that white men were still the undisputed rulers of the roost when it came to salaries, positions, and prestige.

BLACK-AND-WHITE POLEMICS TURN GRAY

The debate about affirmative action has also grown more murky and difficult as the public has come to appreciate its complexity. Many liberals, for example, can understand the injustice of affirmative action in a case like *Wygant* (1986): black employees kept their jobs while white employees with seniority were laid off. And many conservatives would be hard pressed to come up with a better alternative to the imposition of a strict quota system in *Paradise* (1987), in which the defiantly racist Alabama Department of Public Safety refused to promote any black above entry level even after a full 12 years of court orders demanded they did.

THE SUPREME COURT: WARY OF "ABSTRACTIONS GOING WRONG"

The Supreme Court justices have been divided in their opinions in affirmative action cases, partially because of opposing political ideologies but also because the issue is simply so complex. The Court has approached most of the cases in a piecemeal fashion, focusing on narrow aspects of policy rather than grappling with the whole.

Even in *Bakke*—the closest thing to a landmark affirmative action case—the Court was split 5–4, and the judges' various opinions were far more nuanced than most glosses of the case indicate. Sandra Day O'Connor, often characterized as the pivotal judge in such cases because she straddles conservative and liberal views about affirmative action, has been described by University of Chicago law professor Cass Sunstein as "nervous about rules and abstractions going wrong. She's very alert to the need for the Court to depend on the details of each case."

LANDMARK RULING BUTTRESSES AFFIRMATIVE ACTION

10 But in a landmark 2003 case involving the University of Michigan's affirmative action policies—one of the most important rulings on the issue in twenty-five years—the Supreme Court decisively upheld the right of affirmative action in higher education. Two cases, first tried in federal courts in 2000 and 2001, were involved: the University of Michigan's undergraduate program (*Gratz v. Bollinger*) and its law school (*Grutter v. Bollinger*). The Supreme Court (5–4) upheld the University of Michigan Law School's policy, ruling that race can be one of many factors considered by colleges when selecting their students because it furthers "a compelling interest in obtaining the educational benefits that flow from a diverse student body." The Supreme Court, however, ruled (6–3) that the more formulaic approach of the University of Michigan's undergraduate admissions program, which uses a point system that rates students and awards additional points to

minorities, had to be modified. The undergraduate program, unlike the law school's, did not provide the "individualized consideration" of applicants deemed necessary in previous Supreme Court decisions on affirmative action.

In the Michigan cases, the Supreme Court ruled that although affirmative action was no longer justified as a way of redressing past oppression and injustice, it promoted a "compelling state interest" in diversity at all levels of society. A record number of "friend-of-court" briefs were filed in support of Michigan's affirmative action case by hundreds of organizations representing academia, business, labor unions, and the military, arguing the benefits of broad racial representation. As Sandra Day O'Connor wrote for the majority, "In order to cultivate a set of leaders with legitimacy in the eyes of the citizenry, it is necessary that the path to leadership be visibly open to talented and qualified individuals of every race and ethnicity."

Suggestions for Writing and Discussion

1. According to Borgna Brunner, what was the original reason that the policy of affirmative action for jobs and education was instituted? In your response, refer to and define the phrase "level the playing field."
2. What was the *Bakke* case and why was it significant in the history of affirmative action in the United States?

Making Connections: Synthesis and Analysis

1. Angelou and Rose both write about expectations for particular groups of individuals. Angelou describes the way her own expectations and the expectations of her community were in conflict with those of the authorities who ran her school system. Rose describes the expectations of his teachers, his fellow students, and himself, based on the way he and his classmates were tracked. Using examples from these essays and from your own experiences, make an argument for or against the following proposition: The expectations of others are extremely important in determining the academic success or failure of a student.
2. After reading the three selections in this section, speculate on the possible motivations (positive and negative) of the

following individuals or groups as they explained and acted on their expectations for particular groups of students: Mr. Edward Donleavy, proponents of the Stanford-Binet test given to Mike Rose when he entered Our Lady of Mercy High School, Rose's English teacher, Mr. MacFarland, President Lyndon Johnson, and Allan Bakke.

· *NOW* ·

WHAT ARE THE BENEFITS AND CHALLENGES OF RACE-BASED AFFIRMATIVE ACTION?

Suggestions for Prereading or Journal Writing

1. What do you consider the skills, abilities, and educational background necessary for academic success? Do you believe there are some groups of people in America who are less likely to have these qualifications? Explain.
2. How would you define "classroom diversity"? What are the benefits and challenges you might expect in a diverse educational culture?

EVALUATING AN ARGUMENT: MULTIPLE PERSPECTIVES

Pondering Condoleezza Rice's Affirmative Action Problem—and Mine

Brent Staples

Educated at Widner University and the University of Chicago, where he earned a doctorate in psychology in 1982, Brent Staples is a journalist who writes regularly for the *New York Times,* where this article first appeared on February 1, 2003. Staples offers a nuanced discussion of the advantages and disadvantages that many well-known African Americans see in race-based affirmative action programs.

With African-Americans spread throughout the government, President Bush has assembled what may be the blackest administration in American history. But black voters have been waiting warily to see what impact, if any, this will have on policy. The pessimists predicted that nothing of substance would change, except that Republicans would try to legitimize anti-black positions by lining up the black faces for photo opportunities at the White House.

Secretary of State Colin Powell's refusal to be used has made him the only Republican on the national stage who is revered and respected in the black community. His public support for affirmative action at the University of Michigan—and his candid disagreement with the White House's decision to attack it—have underscored his reputation for independence.

Condoleezza Rice, the national security adviser, has had a more difficult time, partly because some in The White House have tried to use her as political cover for the administration's attack on affirmative action. The ink on the Michigan brief was scarcely dry when an article appeared in the *Washington Post* based on a news leak asserting that Ms. Rice had played a central role in persuading the president to attack race-sensitive admissions policies at the University of Michigan.

People close to her say Ms. Rice was enraged by the article. She subsequently disputed it, both in a statement from the White House and in a television interview, where she parted company with the president by saying that race should be used as one factor among many in the college admissions process. Unlike Mr. Powell—who simply said that reasonable people could disagree—Ms. Rice straddled the issue, saying that she supported both race-sensitive admissions and a Bush administration amicus brief that could lead to those policies' being declared illegal.

Some who know Ms. Rice have dismissed this as an attempt ₅ to display loyalty to the president while disagreeing with his policy. But a closer look at the facts of Ms. Rice's life suggests a clear ambivalence about notions of collective identity and the significance of race-based remedies for discrimination. This is hardly unique. Those of us who were born black in the 1950's remember it well.

Ms. Rice spent her early years at the epicenter of the civil rights movement, in Birmingham, Ala. Children of my generation and hers were barred from the local amusement park, confined to segregated schools and subjected to what a cousin of Ms. Rice's described to Nicholas Lemann of *The New Yorker* as a "presumption of inferiority" that ground many of them down, day by day.

Ms. Rice's father, John Wesley Rice Jr., was a high school counselor who kept aloof from the civil rights movement and the demonstrations featuring fire hoses and police dogs that provoked outrage around the world. The Rices shielded their daughter from blunt-force racism and did not embrace the collective sense of racial identity that animated the early movement.

Like many social conservatives of his time, Mr. Rice preached a gospel of individual uplift, stressing that personal merit and hard work were more important than collective action in overcoming even virulent racism. A friend of mine who knew him as a student was arrested in the Birmingham demonstrations and says that Mr. Rice disapproved of his action, believing that "A" students did not need to demonstrate and get arrested.

At a time when black Americans were denied basic fairness across the board, the theory that hard work could trump racism was both noble and patently false. My parents nevertheless used it to spawn an overachieving son who took a Ph.D. at the University of Chicago. The hard-work axiom allowed many successful black people to believe that their accomplishments would have been possible even without the civil rights movement—at least until racism slapped them in the face. I was out on my own and in my 20's before I grasped the omnipresence of racism and understood that many people thought me less capable because my skin was black. Mr. Powell was no doubt raised on the merit gospel too, but encountered reality when he saw black Army officers with stellar records passed over for promotion for reasons of race.

10   Ms. Rice's insulation was more dramatic than mine or Mr. Powell's. As Mr. Lemann wrote, she grew up believing that her upward progress was a natural consequence of the preparation drummed into her by her parents, and was "almost insulted by the idea that collective action and government intervention were essential to her own life." This is consistent with Republican dogma, but does not reflect the way the world has actually worked either in general or for the meteoric Ms. Rice.

There were several points at which her blackness (and her gender) doubtless helped to open doors that might well have remained closed to brilliance alone. To put it another way, her blackness and her gender added to her appeal, especially in the context of the white, mainly male foreign-policy boys' club.

Like Ms. Rice, I have spent my professional life in jobs where I was the only black person in the room. Nestled snugly among the powerful, many of us are tempted to assert that the best always rise to the top—and that those who do not reach the apex themselves are held back by lack of merit alone.

Some critics suspect Ms. Rice of working behind the scenes to kill off affirmative action while pretending to support it in public. It seems more likely to me that she is still struggling toward an understanding of the roles that race—and racism—have played in the life of Condoleezza Rice and the life of the nation.

Suggestions for Writing and Discussion

1. Summarize what Brent Staples calls the "difficult time" Condoleezza Rice has faced in her position as national security advisor. What does Staples mean when he says that "some in The White House have tried to use her as political cover for the administration's attack on affirmative action"?

2. What does Staples suggest are some of the fundamental differences between the way he views affirmative action and the way he believes Rice views affirmative action?

AT THE UNIVERSITY OF MICHIGAN: TWO VIEWS FROM THE *WASHINGTON POST*

The two articles that follow appeared in the *Washington Post* in 2003. They provide two very different views of the effect race-based affirmative action has had on students who aspire to attend the University of Michigan.

At U-Michigan, Minority Students Find Access—and Sense of Isolation

AFFIRMATIVE ACTION DEBATE INTENSIFIES EMOTIONS ON CAMPUS

Ann Arbor, Mich.—Erin Hendrix was headed up the walkway to her home in Detroit's cozy Rosedale Park community when her mother charged out the front door, frantically waving a letter from the University of Michigan.

"Oh, baby, I'm so proud of you!" Elaine Lewis-Hendrix said. "You were accepted with a full scholarship!"

But Hendrix, then 17, wasn't joyful that spring day in 2000. Black students at the university had warned her that its image of racial diversity was an illusion, so she hoped that her 3.78 grade-point average at an elite suburban high school, along with her 1260 SAT score, would bring a full scholarship offer from a school outside the state.

"I was thinking, 'Oh, great, this pretty much seals my fate,'" Hendrix said.

5   Her ambivalence toward the university is shared by many black and Latino students in Michigan. While they are eager to attend one of the most prestigious state universities in the nation—considered the Harvard of the Midwest—they are also wary of the social environment that awaits them there. In the months leading up to today's arguments at the Supreme Court over whether Michigan can consider race in its undergraduate and law school admissions, students said, the tensions have risen.

Michigan's racial demographics are not remarkably different from those of other major state universities, but the schoolyard debate over how minority applicants are admitted has magnified every perceived white insult, and the hurt and anger that result.

Within the past year, in an episode unrelated to the controversy over affirmative action, the white-run independent student newspaper poked fun at minority student organizations by using expletives to lampoon their names. As attention focused on the Supreme Court cases, someone scrawled a racial epithet across a sidewalk on the campus yard, and a white student organization held a bake sale offering discounted treats for black and Latino students.

"This kind of stuff affects me personally," said Marisa Darden, a 19-year-old sophomore who is black. "I am personally offended. One of the reasons I chose to come to UM is their boastful reputation on diversity. But I have to make a choice between socializing with black people or socializing with white people, because this campus is extremely segregated."

Seventy-five percent of the university's students are white, and they control campus life from the student government to the pep squad. Hendrix, who shares a class with Darden, quickly discovered how little-understood blacks are.

After making the 45-minute drive from Detroit to the Ann **10** Arbor campus, Hendrix moved into a dorm where roughly 70 percent of the students are white. One day, she recalled, a white student asked her if there were any good neighborhoods in Detroit. Her father had told her never to drive there, especially after 5 p.m. on a Friday.

"There was this overwhelming feeling that I didn't belong," Hendrix said. "I feel so isolated. I call my friend at Spelman College and say I want to transfer." But she hasn't sought out the historically black college in Atlanta because a Michigan degree is too valuable a credential, and her father would forbid it.

Monique Perry, a 20-year-old junior, said white students asked her to make them copies of rap CDs. "I've never owned a rap CD in my life," said Perry, who was raised in Detroit and was a top student at the city's elite Cass Technical High School.

Darden said that at her dorm, a white student asked, "How do you wash your hair?"

Despite those complaints, Michigan is quite diverse compared with the nation's elite public universities. At the University of California at Berkeley, underrepresented minorities make up only 15 percent of undergraduates; at Michigan, the proportion is 25 percent. Still, school officials in Ann Arbor say they are seeking a more diverse campus.

"One of the reasons why we're defending our affirmative action **15** policy so strongly is that we're not there yet," said Julie Peterson, a University of Michigan spokeswoman. The school has programs designed to bring students together, Peterson said, "because it's not enough to just have people here. You have to do the work."

Godfrey Dillard, an attorney for the Detroit branch of the NAACP Legal Defense and Educational Fund, said the nuanced suffering of minorities at Michigan has not been argued in the legal challenge to Michigan's undergraduate admissions process, which pits a white complainant against the university. Although the Supreme Court has ruled that the legal system cannot remedy historical discrimination, some observers of the case feel that Michigan's history sits like an elephant in the courtroom.

The university was founded in 1817 but did not admit a black student until more than 50 years later. As recently as 1960, the university's campus housing and fraternities were segregated. The percentage of Latino and Native American students barely registered above zero.

In 1954, there were 200 black students at Michigan, according to school records. Twelve years later, there were 400, barely more than 1 percent of the total student population of 32,000. At that time, 55 percent of Detroit's 300,000 students were black.

At the start of the 1970s, frustrated African American students at Michigan organized the Black Action Movement, requesting more minority enrollment. The request was first rejected by the university, then accepted after the students held a strike, and later abandoned it.

20   A university investigation in 1980 found that 85 percent of black students surveyed said they experienced severe racial isolation and discrimination by their peers. Eight years later, Provost James Duderstadt started the "Michigan Mandate" to increase the number of students and faculty of color.

The mandate acknowledged "prejudice, bigotry, discrimination and even racism" on campus and later instituted an admissions system that awarded applicants points for several attributes, such as grades, test scores, home town and alumni in the family.

When Jennifer Gratz, a white student, applied to the university's College of Literature, Science and Arts in 1995, she was not among approximately 4,000 students who made the cut. She sued, claiming that the school's policy of awarding 20 points on a 150-point scale to minority applicants for their race unfairly helped them pass her in the line for a place at the school.

Since then, university lawyers and affirmative action advocates have noted that the system awards six points to applicants from the state's rural areas, which are overwhelmingly white, and up to 10 points to those from high schools that offer honors courses, which many inner-city high schools don't offer. Children of alumni, who are more likely to be white, also receive points.

Peterson said that at least 42 white and Asian students with grade-point averages and test scores lower than Gratz's were admitted the year she applied.

25   The point system has become an issue not only in the Supreme Court, but also on campus.

Everette Wong, a Chinese American, sided with Gratz. "You shouldn't get 20 points just because you're a minority," said the 20-year-old sophomore. "If I am getting triple-bypass surgery, do I want a doctor who got C's and not A's?"

Ben Wanger, 20, a white sophomore, said, "I think the best people deserve to get the best. Racism isn't as rampant as it used to be."

That is true, other students said, but they are still mindful of Michigan's past.

"I benefited from affirmative action," said Paul Spurgeon, 20, a white sophomore. "My grandfather went to UM, and I benefited from that. If you look at the television, and if you listen to students in my class, you don't see them attacking me. They attack blackness and race."

Helen Basterra, a 23-year-old junior from England, said, "I find it astonishing the amount of people who are against affirmative action. America is a colorblind society, but there's such division on campus. It goes to show you how much race is a factor in this society."

The issue also resonates beyond the campus, in neighborhoods where black Michigan high school students are thinking about where they want to go to college.

"As a minority, it really concerns me," said Danyel Currie, who at 17 is on her way to becoming the first in her family of four to graduate from high school. "I'll be one of the first people affected. It's important, because if affirmative action is struck down by the court, resegregation and inequality will be a fact of life."

She carries a 3.8 grade-point average while taking advanced courses and finished in the 98th percentile of students who took the PSAT. Recruitment letters are cluttering her mailbox. Without affirmative action, Currie said, the letters would almost certainly dwindle, and so would offers of financial aid. Her mother is raising three children on a waitress's wages, so she needs a scholarship.

She's watching the Supreme Court case closely. The University of Michigan hasn't contacted her—which is okay with her. "I'm not sure I want to go there," she said, "because of the social climate and because I want to go to a small, liberal arts college that's more intimate."

If Currie turned down an offer from Michigan, Ashley Maltbia said, she would happily take her place. Maltbia, 14, is a freshman at Renaissance High, the daughter of a teacher, and full of ambition.

"I would love to go," she said. "I feel like it would be a great experience. It's so diverse. All my life I've been going to one-race schools."

Janeé Moore, a 16-year-old junior, said Maltbia would likely be trading one race for another at Michigan. Like Hendrix, she has heard people talk about Michigan's lack of diversity.

"I have a friend who's going there, and she says there are just two black men. I would never date," she joked.

"I want to go because UM has more prestige, bottom line. It's the number one Michigan school. I'll just have to deal with it."

A Dream Denied Leads Woman to Center of Suit

GRATZ'S REJECTION BY U-MICH. LED HER TO FIGHT AGAINST RACE-CONSCIOUS ADMISSIONS

Oceanside, Calif.—Jennifer Gratz has heard it all. That she's a pawn of the right. That she's hijacked the language of the civil rights era. That her lawsuit against the University of Michigan's affirmative action policy cloaks a deeper agenda about race.

"Totally crazy," says the 25-year-old, shaking her head.

The facts. In 1995, Gratz was a high school student with a 3.8 GPA, the golden face of her yearbook when she applied to the University of Michigan and was rejected. Two years later, she helped lead a class action lawsuit against the university, alleging that the school's admissions policies gave an unfair edge to minority applicants.

With her case now at the Supreme Court, Gratz has become the central figure in a sprawling ideological debate over affirmative action. It is her story that will challenge the fairness of race-conscious admissions programs: Gratz represents the white working-class striver passed over in the name of diversity.

5   "I can't tell you exactly how my life would be different, because I wasn't given the opportunity," says Gratz, who left Michigan two years ago and now lives in the rugged hills north of San Diego. She is not the forensic scientist she thought she'd become; she is a software trainer for a vending machine company called SupplyPro.

Newly married, Gratz is sitting in the kitchen of her light-filled stucco house in a planned community. It's the morning after Valentine's Day, when her husband surprised her with homemade ravioli and a chocolate soufflé. A pair of Betty Crocker cookbooks rest on the kitchen counter. Relaxed and polished, Gratz is a bene-factor of innate intelligence and careful coaching by those whose cause she is championing. After six years as a plaintiff, she is still handled with care: Her lawyers in Washington allow a sit-down interview with a reporter, but the conversation is monitored via speaker phone, with occasional interjections.

To some degree, Gratz was snapped into machinery that was churning before she received her rejection letter. The battle began in 1978 when the Supreme Court ruled in Regents of the University of California v. Bakke that race could be used as a factor in admitting students but that quotas were forbidden. In 1996, a fed-eral appeals court in Texas barred the consideration of race in ad-missions and financial aid.

In 1995, events were taking hold in Michigan. A cache of documents forced into public view revealed Michigan's admis-sions process. The group of lawyers who won the Texas case was looking for another. From this confluence emerged Gratz.

Gratz wasn't an activist or grass-roots warrior. She was a teenager whose rejection by her dream school shook her confi-dence and sense of fairness. She had spent years polishing her credentials for the University of Michigan, working hard, volun-teering, studying, even chairing blood drives. Then the dream was snatched away. A minority student with the same GPA and test scores as Gratz would have likely been accepted under Michigan's policy.

Michigan acknowledges that it weighs race when considering 10 applicants. To process the more than 25,000 undergraduate appli-cations that flood in each year for the 5,000 coveted spots, the school uses a point system to score each prospective student. Black, Latino and Native American applicants are awarded extra points because they belong to groups the university says are un-derrepresented on campus. In the 2002 class, blacks made up al-most 9 percent of Michigan's freshman class, Latinos 6 percent and Native Americans almost 2 percent.

"We want to have a class that thinks about issues from different backgrounds," says Mary Sue Coleman, the university's president.

The notion galls Gratz. Atmospheres can't be "engineered," she says. Points for being a minority?

"That would be like me deciding, 'Hey, I want to feed the hungry but I don't have any means to do that, so I'm going to go rob a grocery store,' " she says. "It's still illegal, even though my intentions are good."

The University of Michigan is one of the most idyllic campuses in America. On fall Saturdays, when 107,000 fans jam into Michigan Stadium and shatter NCAA attendance records, a sonic halo lifts over Ann Arbor. The splendor is secondary to academics: Michigan is one of two public institutions consistently ranked among the nation's top 10 universities.

15   Gratz grew up 45 minutes away in Southgate, a working-class suburb of Detroit where many in her neighborhood pulled shift work at the auto assembly plants. Her dad was a police sergeant who worked $10-an-hour moonlighting jobs as a security guard; her mom was a secretary. Neither parent finished college. On Saturday afternoons in the Gratz house, Michigan football ruled the TV. Gratz attended St. Pius Catholic School through the eighth grade and then set her sights on studying forensic medicine at Michigan.

At Southgate Anderson High, she did it all: student government, National Honor Society, science club, spirit club, cheerleader. In Michigan, cheerleading is a sanctioned sport involving stunts and occasional calls for an ambulance. Gratz was so competitive that she used visualization techniques to enhance her performance. "I definitely loved the physical aspects of cheering, of knowing that I could hold a girl above my head," she says.

Race was almost a nonissue at Southgate, because 94 percent of its students were white. The prom was held at the Grecian Center next to the Greek Orthodox church. Gratz would arrive home after a 12-hour day packed with school and extracurricular activities, her dinner waiting on a plate in the kitchen.

Southgate didn't offer Advanced Placement courses, but as a senior Gratz took precalculus and three honors courses. Her GPA was 3.8, and she scored a 25 out of 36 on her ACT college entrance exam.

"Jennifer did everything we asked her to do, and more," says a former assistant principal, Ron Dittmer. "I wouldn't ask any more of my own daughter."

20   Gratz was so confident that she'd make the cut at Michigan that she applied to no other colleges. The wait-list letter was the first bad sign. Then in April of her senior year, after weeks of running home from school to check the mail, came the thin letter of

rejection. Through her tears, Gratz uttered her now-famous rejoinder: "Dad, can we sue?"

It was an odd reaction for a 17-year-old. But Gratz said she suspected something amiss, if not precisely that she'd been passed over because she was white. "Everyone knew bits and pieces," she says, about the premium Michigan placed on diversity. Gratz was in a state of shock. She was so embarrassed by the rejection that she told no one, not even her boyfriend of three years. She hurriedly applied to the University of Notre Dame but didn't get in. She was accepted into the honors program at the University of Michigan's campus in Dearborn.

Dearborn: "You've got four or five buildings where you take your classes," Gratz says, with none of the luminosity she reserves to describe Ann Arbor. "No dorms, the U-Mall with 40 or 50 tables where you could sit around waiting for your next class to start. It wasn't college."

Ann Arbor: "They bring in recruiters from across the country and from around the world."

Dearborn: "They bring in recruiters from metro Detroit."

She began her freshman year, commuting the 15-minute drive 25 from her parents' home.

Around the same time, a University of Michigan philosophy professor named Carl Cohen read in the *Journal of Blacks in Higher Education* that acceptance rates for blacks at top-tier universities were higher than for whites. Suspicious of his own university's admissions system, Cohen filed a Freedom of Information Act request.

The documents showed that Michigan used a grid to evaluate applicants, in part based on race. The grid launched everything: Cohen's testimony before the Michigan legislature sparked four Republican lawmakers to take up the cause.

One of the politicians was then-state Rep. Deborah Whyman, who called the Center for Individual Rights, a conservative Washington law firm that was hot off its 1996 victory in the Texas affirmative action case.

"We laid out a game plan," says Whyman. "When it came down to finding plaintiffs, I did it." She did talk radio shows and gave news interviews about a possible lawsuit against Michigan.

Gratz's parents saw a newspaper article and clipped it for their 30 daughter, who was working at a summer cheerleading camp but still living at home. Immediately, Gratz knew she wanted to be part of some effort against Michigan. She pictured herself stuffing envelopes. She called Whyman's office and gave her vital statistics: her high school GPA, test scores and extracurricular activities.

Whyman says she forwarded 200 names to CIR; the law firm's Curt Levey says that only "six or seven" were ever seriously considered. One was Gratz, who met with CIR attorneys at a Courtyard Marriott near the Detroit airport. A plaintiff was born.

The lawsuit was filed in October 1997 on behalf of Gratz and Patrick Hamacher, another student wait-listed from Michigan's undergraduate program. A separate lawsuit was filed against the University of Michigan Law School. Oral arguments in both cases are scheduled for April 1 before the Supreme Court.

Gratz absorbed most of the heat. Walking out of the courthouse after her case had been sent to the U.S. Court of Appeals for the 6th Circuit, a protester screamed at Gratz, "racist bitch!"

"I'm exactly the opposite," she would later say. "I'm standing up and saying people should not be treated differently because of their skin color."

35   After Cohen's documents were made public, Michigan changed its admissions process, replacing the grid with the point system that is being challenged. On this "Selection Index Worksheet," a perfect GPA is worth 80 points. Having a parent who attended Michigan is worth up to four points. Scholarship athletes are awarded 20 points. A perfect SAT score brings 12 points and an excellent essay gets one point. Being an underrepresented minority brings 20 points.

"To assume a minority can't go to the University of Michigan without that 20 points is crazy," says Gratz. "There are plenty of kids who could stand on their own."

Gratz has been confronted with every angle of the argument. Aren't legacy points also a form of preference? "Four points," she says, not 20. Besides, minorities can also be legacies.

In a classroom setting, could a black student's viewpoints enrich a discussion about racial profiling? "Everyone in the country views racial profiling as wrong," Gratz says. "That's exactly what the University of Michigan is doing: racial profiling. There are race-neutral ways to run an admissions process."

What about affirmative action acting as a remedy for society's past discriminatory practices? Her lawyer won't allow her to answer. "That's a policy question," says Levey.

40   As for her own life, Gratz says she decided not to transfer to Ann Arbor after her sophomore year at Dearborn; too many of her

core courses wouldn't have carried over. She received her math degree in 1999. She took a job with a credit union in Michigan, continuing to live at home. She then switched to a Los Angeles–based company, which brought her to California.

When Gratz first contemplated joining the lawsuit, friends cautioned her that prospective employers might not look favorably on her stance against affirmative action. But as time passed, she says, "I found just the opposite."

Gratz says she was sidetracked by a system that works against whites, but she has made the best of her life. "I'm not an angry or bitter person," she says, gently picking up one of her cats, Bandit. Gratz and her husband, Rob Whyte, a 31-year-old software developer, recently honeymooned in Jamaica and are decorating their new house.

"I'm proud of her," Whyte says, taking a break from installing a satellite dish on their roof on a Saturday morning. "She's standing up for something that a lot of us believe is the right thing."

Far from living in racial exile, Gratz says she is surrounded by diversity. "I have co-workers from all over the place, from England, from Japan," she says of her job at her San Diego com-pany. "We have a friend from South Africa. The head coach at Wayne State University where my dad coaches baseball is African American."

Hanging in Gratz's closet is a University of Michigan sweat 45 shirt. It is a rich and painful irony, this love for the school that spurned her. Gratz was in an airport recently when she noticed that standing nearby was University of Michigan football coach Lloyd Carr. A major celebrity sighting.

"I want you to know my wife is very excited to be standing next to the Michigan football coach," Gratz's husband told Carr. Introductions were made, and Gratz explained how she was such a die-hard fan that she watched last season's games on her computer.

Asked if it's hard to think about minority students who walk the grounds of the Ann Arbor campus, Gratz says with the slightest bit of edge, "They've been given an opportunity to go to an excellent school. Good for them."

Suggestions for Writing and Discussion

1. Describe some of the responses minority students have encountered at University of Michigan from students who

oppose affirmative action. If you were a college ombuds-man, what processes might you suggest to help students from both groups understand the perspectives of those whose views are different from their own?

2. If it were possible for you to write a new admissions pol-icy that would address the concerns of Jennifer Gratz, how would you word it?

Making Connections: Synthesis and Analysis

1. Many proponents of affirmative action believe that a di-verse classroom provides advantages to all students and professors. List possible reasons to support this claim. Then write an essay proposing the responses you believe any of the writers whose articles appear in this chapter might give to support or refute this claim.

2. Borgna Brunner, Brent Staples, and the *Washington Post* article "At U-Michigan, Minority Students Find Access" all suggest reasons why some minority students see prob-lems with race-based affirmative action. Identify the rea-sons in each of these articles, examine the evidence given to support the claims, and then explain your evaluation of these viewpoints.

HOW DO CLASS AND OTHER FACTORS INFLUENCE ADMISSIONS?

Suggestions for Prereading or Journal Writing

1. How is class defined in America? For instance, what crite-ria would you use in deciding whether a particular individ-ual or family was "lower class," "middle class," or "upper class"? Explain.

2. What role do you think socioeconomic status plays in deter-mining opportunities available to individuals in today's American society? Do you think class is more or less im-portant in this country today than it was in the past? Explain.

3. Do you think students with particular talents in such areas as music, acting, and athletics should be given preferential

treatment in college admissions? Should they be given preferential treatment in being awarded scholarships? Explain.

EVALUATING AN ARGUMENT: MULTIPLE PERSPECTIVES

The Great Unmentionable in American Society: Class

John R. MacArthur

John R. MacArthur, publisher of *Harper's Magazine,* wrote this article, which first appeared in the February 7, 2003, edition of the *Providence Journal* (Providence, Rhode Island). In the article, he points out that while many are willing to discuss race-based affirmative action, they are often uncomfortable looking at the barriers that class distinctions create for students seeking admission to college.

As an American in good standing, I know that I'm supposed to be obsessed with race. But when the Bush administration intervened last month in favor of a lawsuit challenging the University of Michigan's "affirmative-action" rules, my thoughts turned not to bigotry and skin color, but to the great unmentionable secret in our society: class.

I know that class is an unpopular subject from direct experience; nothing stops conversation at a New York cocktail party more abruptly than the evocation of economic inequality in our great land. In London or Paris, such musings might provoke a lively discussion, invective or a yawn, but nobody would take exception to the topic itself.

Stateside, the mere suggestion of class divisions sets off silent alarm bells, frequently leaving you alone with your white wine and canape.

Class makes people so uncomfortable that they'd even prefer to discuss racism. And it doesn't matter much if you're talking to someone in the upper or lower class. The well-off don't want to hear it, because it offends their sense of entitlement; the less well-off still hope that the slogans about social mobility are true: America, the land of equal opportunity, where poor immigrants become billionaires—the radical social experiment that gives the lie to Marxist theories of stratification and alienation.

5   More than a conceit, this is scripture in the Republican Book of Common Prayer, written with fireplace charcoal in the log-cabin-to-White House vernacular of Abraham Lincoln.

The truth about class in America is somewhat different from the happy images of classless consumers on TV commercials. In the book "Dynamics of Child Poverty in Industrialized Countries" (2001), economists Peter Gottschalk and Sheldon H. Danziger reported on the fate of a racially diverse group of children whom they studied over 22 years, from 1970 to 1992.

Dividing the kids by family income into five segments, they found that of the children constituting the poorest 20 percent of the sample, 6 in 10 stayed in the bottom income bracket after 10 years, and 9 in 10 stayed in the bottom two income brackets in the same period.

The 1980s boom helped not at all: Children on the bottom two economic rungs stayed put over the succeeding decade. Born poor, stay poor.

In the top 20 percent followed in the study, only 2.4 percent fell to the bottom step.

10   Race does play a disproportionate role in poverty, of course. The U.S. Census reports that the current poverty rate among black children is 30 percent, compared with 9.5 percent for non-Hispanic white children.

But there are also many millions of disadvantaged white children—among the downwardly-mobile members of Barbara Ehrenreich's "Nickel and Dimed" lower middle class—who don't attract sociologists but who never make it into the country-club set. These are the class victims of industrial decline, youngsters whose parents lost their decent-paying factory jobs because of NAFTA and "Permanent Normal Trade Relations" with China.

America's class cover-up goes beyond rags-to-riches mythology. When rich-kid candidate George W. Bush hurled the absurd accusation at well-to-do-kid Al Gore of engaging in "class warfare" (merely because Gore had noted America's accelerating income gap), I thought back to my own childhood, in monied Winnetka, Ill. It was a time when upper-class distinction was very much out of fashion.

By the late 1960s and early '70s, guilt about growing up rich had reached epidemic proportions. Every teenage boy I knew understood that kids from our world could beat the Vietnam draft by exploiting inherited privileges unavailable to our working-class compatriots. We also knew that wealth was of immeasurable advantage in getting into good colleges, including out-of-state public universities.

In those days, a son of Winnetka could afford to stay in school as long [as] it took to stay out of the Army. Then, in 1971, when the draft lottery finally replaced the student deferment, the young man—like my older brother—could afford a draft lawyer to fight a 1-A classification. If he was the son of a public figure with appearances to keep up, such as George W. Bush and Dan Quayle, he could arrange easy duty in the National Guard or, as in Al Gore's case, a short, soft tour in Vietnam as an army "reporter."

The Selective Service System's class bias in favor of my 15 crowd was deliberate. "At the heart of this conscious effort at social engineering was the concept of 'channeling,'" writes Christian P. Appy, author of "Working Class War."

"The basic idea was to use the threat of the draft and lure of educational and professional deferments to channel men into non-military occupations that the Selective Service believed vital to the 'national health, safety and interest.'"

It's no surprise that about 80 percent of enlisted men in Vietnam came from poor or working-class families.

Selective Service was just one of many affirmative-action programs for the rich and the upper middle class. The ability to pay tuition when applying for admission to college has been a huge advantage (no matter what the schools assert); so is having an alumnus or alumna parent, especially one who contributes lots of money.

In allegedly egalitarian public grammar and high schools, affirmative action for the rich presents itself through the levy of the class-ridden property tax, which funds the greater share of public-school budgets nationwide. With a few exceptions, the wealthier districts get the best public schools simply because wealthier people live in them.

But of all the affirmative-action programs—formal and infor- 20 mal—that benefit the rich, none can beat the tax code. Absent compensatory social programs to redress the head starts granted to some Americans at birth, a low (38.6 percent) maximum income-tax rate guarantees a society in which inherited privilege holds the upper hand. Now the son of Greenwich, Conn., and Houston oil money, President Bush, proposes to eliminate the dividend and inheritance taxes altogether. The rich, it seems, are never rich enough.

With our inequalities in plain sight, how is it that so many people are so easily conned by the myth of classless America?

For one thing, certain rich people wear elaborate disguises. In Winnetka, we donned blue workshirts and blue jeans and listened to blues music to conceal our true status; the Bushes, father and son, hide their Wall Street roots behind a preposterous Texas facade of regular-guy entrepreneurial roughness—as if the practice of raw capitalism somehow placed the well-paid boss on the same social and moral level as his underpaid employee.

And the fable of "stakeholder" democracy has been remarkably effective among laboring folks and upscale types alike. Encouraged by unscrupulous politicians such as the Bushes and—especially—Ronald Reagan and Bill Clinton, a great many Americans were lately fooled into buying stock at the top of a market bubble. Now they're paying the price in extended working hours and delayed retirement.

We live in a huckster society, and vast numbers of citizens sustain themselves psychically with the adman's dream of getting rich quick.

25   Among intellectuals who ought to know better about economic reality, we can partly blame the French aristocrat Alexis de Tocqueville, who told us what we wanted to hear about ourselves. "Nothing struck me more forcibly than the general equality of condition among the people," he famously and blindly wrote at the beginning of *Democracy in America,* published in 1835. "There are no paupers . . . everyone has property of his own."

A Tocqueville critic, the historian Edward Pessen, has pointed out that in 1831–32, "most Americans of white as well as black skin had no property, paupers abounded, less than one white Southern family in four owned slaves, most working people and small-farmers . . . fared poorly, and striking inequality of fortunes was the rule during the period of his visit."

Apart from the slaves, doesn't this sound very familiar?

Suggestions for Writing and Discussion

1. Why does John MacArthur call class "the great unmentionable secret in our society"? Do you agree with him? Explain.

2. According to MacArthur, how did class bias affect the Selective Service System during the Vietnam War era?

"Legacies" Are Affirmative Action
Todd Gitlin

Todd Gitlin, professor of journalism and sociology at Columbia University, makes the argument that the preferential admission of "legacies," students who are related to graduates of a particular college or university, is actually a kind of affirmative action for an already-privileged group of individuals. This article first appeared in *Newsday,* February 2003.

When I heard President Bush was opposing the University of Michigan's affirmative action programs, I thought back to the time when I took New York's citywide test for admission to the Bronx High School of Science, then considered by many the best public high school in the country. It was 1956. I'd never seen a test I hadn't aced. I had a stellar record in junior high school and was about to win its medal for general excellence.

Imagine my astonishment a few weeks later when I was lugubriously informed that I hadn't made the cut. Was I hearing this straight? Finished at age 13! Most of my friends were heading to Bronx Science, but I was ruined! Meritocracy had inspected me and shoved me aside. I was more than distraught; I was utterly baffled.

In the days that followed a cavalry was summoned to ride to my rescue. My parents were high school teachers. They were friendly with the head of Bronx Science's English Department, who had taught my mother in college, whose wife had been my first-grade teacher and whose children were friends of mine. Soon thereafter I was called in for a meeting with Bronx Science's guidance counselor. I sat in the man's office and took a test that included a lot of tricky spatial-relations exercises. Not my strongest suit, but the results must have assured him that my citywide admissions exam had been an anomaly.

The next thing I knew, I was admitted to Science. Relieved, reprieved and redeemed. And more than a touch embarrassed at my unorthodox route in. But I also had no doubt that I was receiving my just deserts. Nothing was wrong with me; something must have been wrong with the test. Call it human error or unacknowledged jitters. I could only assume—I still assume—that I had skipped a line on the answer sheet and proceeded to record a long list of answers on the wrong lines.

5 Over the next three years, the mystery of just how I'd flunked the exam morphed into my private comedy. I graduated from Bronx Science as valedictorian, with awards in mathematics and English. I was a finalist in the Westinghouse Science Talent Search. I got into Harvard, with scholarships. The world told me that something had been wrong with a test, not with me.

The point is what, in the college admissions business, they call "legacies." What they mean, in plain English, is connections. In my slight way (teachers' families not being tycoons, exactly), I benefited from a kind of legacy—my parents' profession and contacts. The more usual legacy, of course, is a leg up in admissions when your parents preceded you at the college in question, especially when they are called something like George H.W. Bush and have an impressive donation record. Obviously, the most flagrant example in recent years is the incumbent president, admitted to Yale on the strength—if that is the right word—of Andover grades that are, to this day, locked in a safe in the registrar's office at that exclusive private school.

We don't normally think of "legacies" as affirmative action, but that is exactly what they are: second and third chances, extra points, special interventions. Athletes benefit from special attention of a distinct kind. So do musicians and others deemed to be specially talented. So do residents of thinly populated states, which Harvard, for one, cultivated in the name of diversity. You can make a case for some of these private byways to meritocratic success—but the point is that there was no golden day when objective measurements were permitted to pass for pure meritocracy. Holy test scores and high school grades are recently built shrines. Those who proclaim that the admissions issue boils down to a flat choice of "merit" vs. "affirmative action" forget how many (if you will) unmerited doors there are to admissions. We don't get righteously indignant about low test scores unless they belong to certain skin-tagged minorities.

By filing a brief with the Supreme Court to oppose the University of Michigan's affirmative action programs, the nation's legacy-in-chief blithely ignores generations of affirmative action from which he and many another fortunate son and daughter have profited. Such is the dishonesty of our present debate.

Suggestions for Writing and Discussion

1. Summarize the opening narrative example in Todd Gitlin's article and explain how this example supports his contention that "legacies" are affirmative action.
2. What arguments can you think of to oppose Gitlin's point of view? Are there good reasons why children of alumni should be given preference in college admissions? Explain.

It Pays to Play

Editorial, *The Christian Century*

This brief article, which appeared on March 7, 2001, in *Christian Century* magazine, raises important questions about the preferential treatment given to the applications of student athletes at selective liberal arts colleges.

How do you get admitted to one of those small, highly selective liberal arts colleges? Of course, you need excellent grades in high school and an impressive SAT score. But lots of kids bring those credentials. How can you make sure you stand out among the crowd?

Be a jock. Yes, it's athletes that Harvard, Bowdoin and Williams are craving. That's the unexpected news from a study on sports and college life by James L. Shulman and William G. Bowen.

The authors of *The Game of Life* point out that the percentage of students playing intercollegiate athletics at selective liberal arts schools is much higher than at the large universities most of us associate with big-time college athletics. That's because the small liberal arts schools field teams in just as many sports—from football to squash to soccer—as the large universities do, but with a much smaller student body to draw from. Athletes make up 32 percent of the male student body at schools like Harvard and Williams, as opposed to only 5 percent at a school like the University of Michigan.

This would be a wonderful sign of the participatory possibilities at small schools, except for the fact that selective colleges aren't content just to see which brainy kid shows up and wants to play quarterback. Intent on fielding competitive teams in every sport, the selective colleges make sure that each entering class includes talented athletes who can fill slots on their many teams. That means they have to search for quarterbacks, soccer goalies and third basemen.

5   It also means that athletes get preferential treatment at admissions time. Being an athlete is even more of an advantage than having a family connection to the school or being a member of a racial minority. In the case of one of the schools studied, athletes had a 48 percent better chance of being admitted than those with similar SAT scores. A child of an alumnus had a 25 percent better chance, and a black student had an 18 percent better chance.

Athletes not only get admitted despite relatively low test scores and grades. They also regularly finish their college careers in the bottom of the class. In light of this result, Shulman and Bowen question whether the nation's most highly rated colleges should be devoting so much of their educational resources to students who are not the best equipped to take advantage of them— all for the sake of having strong sports teams. Even if one regards intercollegiate sports as a significant part of college life, one has to wonder why sports play this large a role in the institution.

At a time when many voices are clamoring for colleges to stop using race as a factor in admissions, the biggest affirmative-action program is not for racial minorities but for athletes. The critics of affirmative action might want to turn their attention to the value, fairness and social costs of that policy.

Suggestions for Writing and Discussion

1. Why do you think this article claims that the news that universities and colleges like Harvard, Bowdoin, and Williams aggressively recruit athletes is "unexpected." Were you surprised by this information?
2. Do you agree that giving preference to athletes is a form of affirmative action? Explain.

Online Editors Scrutinize Admissions Essays of the Skittish—for a Fee
Michael Arnone

Michael Arnone, writing for the *Chronicle of Higher Education*, raises questions of ethics related to students who use coaches or online editing services to help with their applications for college admission and scholarships. This article first appeared on February 6, 2002.

To the consternation of admissions officials, many college and graduate-school applicants are now hiring online editors to go over their application essays. The editing companies cater to applicants skittish about their writing ability, ambitious to get into the institution of their choice, or just looking for a second opinion.

Companies large and small are hawking their virtual red pencils to applicants seeking entry or a return to academe. Not surprisingly, these companies—with names such as IvyEssays, EssayEdge, and Accepted.com—emphasize that the personal essay is a crucial part of the application. Many of them advertise that they can improve an applicant's chances of getting into a particular college by helping craft the essay.

Some sites edit all kinds of applications, while others focus on a few or even just one type of degree. For example, Clear Admit works exclusively to get applicants accepted into master-of-business-administration programs. Some of the companies help on the essays only, while others guide customers through the entire application process, so that they end up with an integrated package.

Prices vary widely among companies—EssayEdge's most popular essay-editing service costs $60, while Sanford Kreisberg, founder of the Cambridge Essay Service, offers a complete application package for a flat $1,800 rate. The philosophy of "You get what you pay for"—and the income of the applicant—determines which company applicants pick.

College admissions officials and experts, though, are worrying more and more that people who use these services seek an unfair advantage in the application process to get a benefit that may not exist. Colleges expect applicants to submit their own work without undue outside assistance, says Mark Cannon, deputy executive director of the National Association for College Admission Counseling. Assistance with grammar, for instance, is acceptable, he says, but applicants shouldn't let anyone else develop ideas or write any portion of their essays for them. 5

How much help applicants should—and do—receive has been a growing question for admissions officials for years, Mr. Cannon says. The buzz among those making admissions decisions is that the increasing use of computers and the Internet has fueled the controversy, he says.

"The name of the game in the admissions process is fairness," says Barmak Nassirian, associate executive director of the American Association of Collegiate Registrars and Admissions Officers. Online-editing companies, he says, further widen the gap between the haves and the have-nots. "They allow less-accomplished but well-off students to improve their applications," Mr. Nassirian says.

Admissions professionals are also concerned that the companies warp applicants' expectations of what they must do to get into and pay for college. Robin G. Mamlet, director of admissions and financial aid at Stanford University, says: "I am concerned about the message that students must surely absorb: that who they are is not enough, that they must be packaged and presented in order to pass muster. Nothing could be further from the case."

It's not even clear whether such packaging and presentation of admissions essays really works. Students consistently overestimate the importance of the admissions essay, says Sarah Meyers McGinty, a university supervisor at the Harvard Graduate School of Education who has studied the undergraduate application process. The courses a student takes in high school, the grades received, and scores on standardized tests are more important criteria at all but a few colleges, she says.

10   "An essay would be a very unstable credential to base an admissions decision on," says Marlyn McGrath Lewis, director of admissions at Harvard University's Harvard College. An essay can help admissions officers understand a student's undergraduate record, she says, but the record itself is a much more important criterion for admission.

"The college essay is rarely critical," says Mr. Kreisberg, of the Cambridge Essay Service. Applicants to graduate schools, though, are older and must explain what they've been doing since they graduated, he says. Getting assistance on essays makes a big difference if the finished essays help the students stand out in admission officers' minds.

Whether or not the essay is the linchpin, the companies argue that they deliver what they promise. Customer testimonials litter their Web sites. EssayEdge states that 94 percent of its customers are admitted to at least one of their favorite colleges and 66 percent get admitted to their first choice.

[. . .]

"You can use all the help you can get when you're unsure about your application," says Mark S. Bartholomew, a second-year law student at Lewis & Clark College. He credits Deone M. Terrio, president and editor-in-chief of EssayAdvice, with getting him into his first-choice law school even though his grades weren't the best. "Grades and tests are set in stone, but you can always improve your writing," Mr. Bartholomew says.

Many customers want to hedge their bets on getting into the most prestigious and selective colleges by going with companies that claim to have close links with Harvard, Stanford, and similar institutions. For example, on many of its Web pages EssayEdge says, "Put Harvard-Educated Editors to Work for You!"

While editing ability is important, an editor's knowledge 15 of the applicant is also crucial, says Mary Carroll Scott, vice president of the College Board and of member relations for Collegeboard.com, which does not offer editing services. "Someone who knows you is usually the best person to help you do your writing," she says.

Applicants might be better off seeking free advice from their parents and friends, Ms. McGinty says, adding that hiring a company to help write an essay would be no better or worse than having anyone else edit from scratch. If an applicant does hire a company, he or she should choose one that takes the time to get to know its customers.

Some small companies do spend a good deal of time working with applicants and get a chance to know them. Mr. Kreisberg says he works intensively with his customers for several weeks, doing four or five drafts each of up to seven essays. Ms. Terrio, of EssayAdvice, says she spends hours on the phone and on e-mail learning about her customers.

Other companies offer less personalized service. EssayEdge, one of the larger companies, has 175 to 200 editors and promises turnaround times of 24 or 48 hours, depending on the package bought. Customers get a one- to two-page critique of their essay plus an edited copy.

Most companies make a point of saying on their Web sites that they help their customers write the essays, rather than writing the essays for them. But some offer to sell customers purportedly successful essays as references, and some of those, such as

IvyEssays, warn that they will help prosecute people who plagiarize that material.

20 Plagiarism is hard to spot, but admissions officials usually can recognize it as something that doesn't ring true with the rest of the application, or as something they've read before, says Ms. Lewis, of Harvard. She and her peers say that they encounter a handful of plagiarized essays each year and deal with each case individually. The expectation, though, is that applicants will do their own work. "We do operate on trust," she says.

Suggestions for Writing and Discussion

1. Do you think it is ethical for students to hire experts to edit their college essays? Explain.
2. In what way would the use of application coaches and college-essay editors constitute a form of affirmative action?

Making Connections: Synthesis and Analysis

1. After reading the articles in this section, develop an argument for or against the following proposition:

   Academic achievement, demonstrated by SATs and high school grades, should be the only factor considered for college admission.

2. After reading the articles in this section, make a list of the reasons you think that children in this country who come from families with a high income might have advantages over others in understanding the college admissions process, scoring well on college entrance exams, or developing special abilities such as dance, music, and sports. Then identify evidence you might cite to support or argue against these reasons.

Topics for Writing and Discussion

1. List the many possible definitions of "affirmative action" or "special privilege" in the college admissions process that these political cartoons represent.

Copyright © 2003 by Signe Wilkinson. Used by permission of The Cartoonist Group.

Copyright © 2003 by Signe Wilkinson. Used by permission of The Cartoonist Group. Editorial cartoons by Signe Wilkinson.

2. Relate any one (or more) of these cartoons to any of the essays in this chapter. What comparisons and contrasts do you see? What significance do you see in these similarities and differences?

3. Identify the point of view of the artist in any one of these political cartoons. What arguments could you make to support that point of view? How might you argue against that point of view?

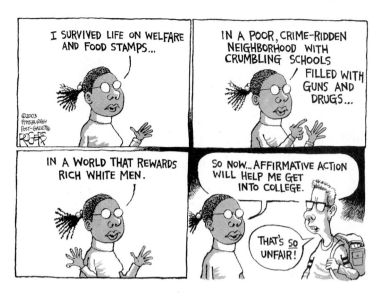

Editorial cartoon by Rob Rogers, 2003. Rob Rogers reprinted by permission of United Feature Syndicate, Inc.

Editorial cartoon by Mike Peters, 2000. Copyright © 2000. Reprinted by special permission of King Features Syndicate.

Segregation   Affirmative Action   The American Way

Editorial cartoon by Chase Exon, June 2003. Copyright © 2003 by Chase Exon. Used with permission of the author.

EXTENDED CONNECTIONS: FOR CRITICAL THINKING, WRITING, AND RESEARCH

1. Research the use of quotas both in the past and more recently, for instance quotas that limited the numbers of Jewish or Asian students that could be accepted into a university or college. Use various sources (books, online databases, interviews). Then write a paper explaining how such quotas are or are not like race-based affirmative action programs.

2. Research preferential admissions programs for athletes, musicians, dancers, or other groups of specially talented students. Use various sources (books, online databases, interviews). Then write an argument, proposing that such programs be eliminated, retained, or altered in some way.

3. Research the arguments for and against open admissions policies (policies that accept all students, no matter what their intellectual abilities, cultural background, race, economic status, or talents, on a first-come, first-accepted basis). Use various sources (books, online databases, interviews). Make an argument that such policies would or would not create more fairness in the college admissions process.

PART THREE

Research and Documentation

THE RESEARCH QUESTION

Most research papers begin with the writer identifying a question. For instance, in a history course the research question might be "Was President Lincoln a racist?" or in a business class the question might be "How has Internet crime impacted small business?" These questions lead to an investigation of sources, both primary and secondary. For a psychology paper beginning with a research question on memory, the *primary source* might be the writer's own observation of second-grade students as they worked on a task requiring memorization. *Secondary sources* might include books and scholarly articles written about the way young children develop memorization strategies. The process of investigating the initial question may lead to a research paper that has mainly an *informative aim* or a *persuasive aim.*

The Informative Research Paper

An example of an informative paper would be one that started with a question such as "How does memory work?" After some preliminary investigation, that question might be narrowed to something like "What are the main strategies that young children use when faced with a memorization task?" The writer would consult several sources, checking especially for places where one author's view of memory strategies was contradicted by another's, noting those discrepancies, and then trying to find sources that would confirm one view or another. The aim of the paper itself would be to inform the reader about memorization strategies that young children use, perhaps to acquaint an audience of future grade school teachers with this information. While even an informative paper must be persuasive in the sense that it must convince the reader of its accuracy, it is quite different from the research paper that has persuasion as its primary aim. However, the research process for writing both types of papers is similar.

The Persuasive Research Paper

The aim of a persuasive research paper is to convince readers that a particular point of view is worthy of consideration. Often the research question that begins the process addresses a controversy. For example, Kimberly Waibel, in her paper on interracial adoption (pages 399–410) began with the question "Is interracial adoption beneficial or harmful to the adopted child?" The question itself implies that some readers would argue that interracial adoption is harmful, while others would argue that it is beneficial. Starting with a question, rather than an assumption (such as "Interracial adoption is beneficial for the child") helps the writer keep an open mind. It also helps the writer gather and evaluate information before refining a question and then restating it as a thesis. To explore both sides of a controversial issue, it is especially important to understand how to locate and evaluate sources.

LOCATING SOURCES

To locate sources to explore the research question, to help define the thesis for the research paper, and to gather evidence to support claims related to the thesis, the following steps are essential:

1. *Become familiar with the library at your college or university.* Most academic libraries have in-person orientation sessions and online tutorials on their Web site to help students learn about available resources. Take advantage of these opportunities. Even if you are very familiar with your local library, academic libraries have different resources and, often, different ways of organizing these resources.

2. *Get to know the librarians and library assistants.* These highly trained professionals and paraprofessionals are there to make your work easier. While they will not do research for you, they can often suggest processes that will make your work much more efficient and effective.

3. *Use electronic searches.* Electronic searches include
   a. Using the library's *online catalog* to find *books* that may be checked out of your library or borrowed through *interlibrary loan.*
   b. Using the library's online catalog to locate *special encyclopedias, reference works, handbooks,* and *general histories.* These valuable resources can provide background information for almost any research project. These books are usually kept in the library's reference room and often cannot be checked out; however, most libraries provide photocopiers, which students can use for a small fee.
   c. Searching *online databases* to which your library subscribes to find newspaper articles, scholarly articles, and other online resources. In some cases, you will be able to access the articles directly. In other cases, you may have to find them in the library or order them through interlibrary loan. These databases are paid for by the library and include many resources that are not available on standard Internet search engines.
   d. Searching the *Internet.* While most people have used the Internet to find information, using search engines such as Teoma.com, Google, AltaVista, and Yahoo, there are many ways to make these searches more effective. In addition, Internet resources must be evaluated carefully. (See page 382).
4. *Develop effective strategies for searching electronic resources.* Using online catalogs, databases, or Internet search engines can be much more effective when you take the time to explore and understand the distinctive features of each electronic resource. In addition, learning how to use search terms effectively can save you time and lead you more quickly to useful information. As you develop strategies for searching electronic resources, consider the following guidelines.

Guidelines for Using Electronic Resources

1. Understand the *distinctive features* of an electronic resource. Read the descriptions of the resource to discover answers to the following questions:

- Can you search by author's name? If so, do you need to reverse the author's first and last names? (Walker, Alice instead of Alice Walker)
- Can you search by title?
- Can you search for a phrase, or must you use a key word?
- Can you organize the hits by date so that you can find the most recent materials quickly?
- Does the database arrange hits in order, with those most likely to be relevant appearing first?

2. Understand how to use *search terms*. (The use of search terms can vary according to the electronic resource you are using, but most use at least some of the following strategies.)
- Enclose phrases in quotation marks: "Vietnam War"
- Enclose proper names with more than one word in quotation marks: "Flannery O'Connor"
- Use the word AND or the plus sign (+) to make your search more specific:
    violence AND women
    violence AND women AND "New York"
    violence+women
- Use parentheses and the word OR to find common synonyms for your key terms:
    violence AND (women OR females)
- Use the words AND NOT or the minus sign (−) with no space after it to avoid getting information that will not address your topic:
    vegans AND NOT vegetarians
    vegans−vegetarians
- Use the asterisk (*) to *truncate* (shorten) terms in order to find variations of the words:
    mechan* (will find mechanical, mechanic, mechanism)

EVALUATING INTERNET RESOURCES

Perhaps the most important thing to keep in mind when you are using Internet resources is that one of the system's greatest strengths—the amazing amount of information it provides—can also challenge writers with a potentially great pitfall. For example, when you use resources from a library, you can be certain that nearly all of the information you obtain has gone through a process of evaluation for reliability and accuracy. The information in most books, for instance, is assessed not only by the author but also by a series of editors and reviewers. Also, in a library trained librarians are available to help you make evaluations of articles in magazines and journals, if you have questions about their currency or about the philosophy of their publishers and authors. On the other hand, anyone with access to an online computer can publish anything he or she wants on the Internet. If you are using the Internet in your dorm room or at home, there are no librarians handy to help you evaluate sources. The following guidelines suggest considerations for making such evaluations.

Guidelines for Evaluating Internet Resources

With each new resource you consider, think about the following issues:

- **Authority:** What are the credentials of the individual or organization who has posted the information? For example, information posted by a professor at a university is likely to be more accurate than a research paper written by a seventh-grade student on the same topic.
- **Source:** Where does the information come from? Is it from an academic institution, a business, a government organization, or an individual? You can tell the source (also called the *domain*) by looking at the last part of the Web address. Typical domain indicators are .com (businesses); .gov (government agencies); .org (nonprofit organizations); .mil (military). A tilde (~) in a Web address means that the page belongs to an individual. This person may have expertise in the area you are researching, or he or she may simply be expressing undocumented opinions. You need to be careful about using such sites to gather data for research papers because it is difficult to be sure of their accuracy.
- **Intent:** What is the intention of the Web site? Does it aim to simply give a brief overview of the topic you are covering? If so, it might not provide the depth you need for a

really useful resource. Does it aim to sell a product? If so, the information about that product may be slanted.

- **Currency:** How recently has the site been posted or updated? Is it up-to-date? Many research topics require the writer to have absolutely current information in order to make accurate judgments. To check the currency of a site, look for a posting or revision date at the beginning or end. Another way to evaluate currency is to test *links* that are provided by the Web site. Links are words or phrases that are usually underlined or in bold print. You should be able to click on these words or phrases and get to other sites containing information relevant to the topic of the site you are currently visiting. If the links have become outdated and are nonfunctional, the site you've found may not be current.

TAKING NOTES

Some sources are so useful that you'll want to take many notes; others may be worth only a sentence or two of general summary; still others may turn out not to be useful at all. Before you start taking notes, skim the table of contents or the subheads. This quick look may tell you that the source isn't one you can use. If, however, it does seem to contain relevant information, read through it. Then take notes, which can be your responses to the source as well as a report of what the source says. Just be sure to indicate somehow which notes are your own evaluations.

There are a number of ways to take notes. You can write your notes on index cards; you can type your notes—or keep just the bibliographical information—on a computer; or you can annotate photocopies and highlight key passages. Or you can use some combination of techniques. Many writers like to photocopy articles so that they can refer to them throughout the drafting process, as they sharpen the focus of the paper and build their argument. Although every writer has a different system for taking research notes, there are two basic guidelines to follow as you develop a system for yourself.

- Be organized.
- Summarize and paraphrase instead of copying long quotations.

Be Organized

Use a new page or a new index card for each new note or piece of information so that you can easily rearrange your notes as you draft your paper. (Make sure you identify the source on each note.) Arranging the information in different ways can give you a feel for the different ways your paper could be organized. For example, what you may at first regard as a piece of evidence for your "supporting details," you may later decide to treat as a separate "claim."

Keep all your notes together. As you conduct your research, you may find an argument that sounds similar or flatly contradictory to one you previously encountered. Having all your notes in one place will make it easy to cross-reference arguments and facts.

Record the complete bibliographical information for each source you consult. It is much easier to delete information about sources you don't end up using than to try to retrace your steps and find missing information about sources you do use. Some writers keep bibliographical notes on 3 × 5 cards and content notes on 4 × 6 cards so that the two kinds can be easily differentiated. Those who keep their notes on computer make a separate file for their source notes, which they can alphabetize with a simple command (if the entries begin with the author's last name). If you choose to keep the source information on note cards (one source per card) or to photocopy it directly from the sources, you can arrange the cards or photocopies in alphabetical order when it's time to type the page of references or works cited for your paper.

Summaries, Paraphrases, and Quotations

Before you begin making notes about a source, read through it. Then make a note that summarizes the article or chapter. Next, consider whether there are any particularly important or useful ideas expressed in the work; if there are, paraphrase them. Writing a paraphrase requires using your own words to express an idea in a source. Make a note of a quotation only if the idea needs to be expressed in the exact words of the source. Figures 1, 2, and 3 are examples of a summary note, a paraphrase note, and a quotation note based on the following paragraphs. (Notice that the source, including the page number, is indicated at the top of each note.)

> Human actions bring about scarcities of renewable resources in three principal ways. First, people can reduce the quantity or

Figure 1. Summary note card.

> *"Environmental Change," Homer-Dixon,*
> *Boutwell, and Rathjens, p. 40*
>
> *The major human causes of shortages of renewable resources are*
> *(1) overconsumption, (2) overpopulation, and (3) unequal*
> *distribution.*

Figure 2. Paraphrase note card.

> *"Environmental Change," Homer-Dixon,*
> *Boutwell, and Rathjens, p. 40*
>
> *There are three major human causes of shortages of renewable*
> *resources. (1) People consume the resources or dilute their quality*
> *faster than the resources can regenerate. (In this regard, a*
> *sustainable economy is one that uses resources only as fast as they*
> *can be renewed.) (2) Population increases put excessive demand on*
> *the supply of resources. (3) A few people take control of the*
> *resources and restrict distribution of them.*

Figure 3. Quotation note card.

> *"Environmental Change," Homer-Dixon,*
> *Boutwell, and Rathjens, p. 40*
>
> *Homer-Dixon, Boutwell, and Rathjens use financial terms to*
> *describe resource consumption. Depleting resources faster than they*
> *can be renewed is "the consumption of the resource's 'capital.'"*
> *Accordingly, a sustainable economy is one that "leaves the capital*
> *intact and undamaged so that future generations can enjoy*
> *undiminished income."*

degrade the quality of these resources faster than they are renewed. This phenomenon is often referred to as the consumption of the resource's "capital": the capital generates "income" that can be tapped for human consumption. A sustainable economy can therefore be defined as one that leaves the capital intact and undamaged so that future generations can enjoy undiminished income. Thus, if topsoil creation in a region of farmland is 0.25 millimeter per year, then average soil loss should not exceed that amount.

The second source of scarcity is population growth. Over time, for instance, a given flow of water might have to be divided among a greater number of people. The final cause is change in the distribution of a resource within a society. Such a shift can concentrate supply in the hands of a few, subjecting the rest to extreme scarcity.

> Thomas Homer-Dixon, Jeffrey Boutwell, and George Rathjens, "Environmental Change and Violent Conflict," *Scientific American,* February 1993, pp. 38–45.

INTEGRATING QUOTATIONS

Your paper should not be a "quotation dump" in which you string together a large number of quotations without any of your own interpretations or remarks. Instead, it should express your own ideas and opinions, which you have developed and refined in the course of your research. The appropriate use of quotations is as *evidence that supports the claim or warrant at hand.* If you are relying on a claim with the backing of expert testimony or statistics, quoting that material will strengthen your argument's credibility by showing your reader that your opinion is an informed one.

Always integrate quotations gracefully into your text; don't just drop them in. Quoted material should flow into your prose. Compare these two treatments of a quotation:

Incorrect: Samuel Johnson also praised London. "When a man is tired of London, he is tired of life."

Correct: As Samuel Johnson once remarked, "When a man is tired of London, he is tired of life" (Boswell 231).

Notice how the quotation in the second example is part of the sentence. A common way to incorporate quotations is to use phrases such as "once remarked," "as one expert has said," "as one critic has observed," and "as one study has found."

Notice also that the second example leaves no doubt about who said the quoted words and, moreover, indicates where they can be found. The parenthetical reference between the end quotation marks and the period identifies the author and the page number of the work where the quotation can be found. The full bibliographical information for the source is at the end of the paper under the author's name in the list of works cited.

Plagiarism

Plagiarism means taking someone else's words or ideas and passing them off as your own. However minor or innocent such an act might seem to you, any attempt to deceive one's audience violates the spirit of the objective pursuit of truth. Institutions of higher learning always expect you to act as part of this great tradition, and the penalties for plagiarism are stiff, ranging from an F to expulsion.

The most obvious kind of plagiarism is to use someone's exact words as if they were your own—for example, to repeat Samuel Johnson's aphorism "When a man is tired of London, he is tired of life" without acknowledging that the words are Johnson's. But there are other forms of plagiarism, such as writing, "When a man is tired of Manhattan, he is tired of life." To avoid plagiarism, you would need to add a phrase like "to borrow from Samuel Johnson."

Another kind of plagiarism occurs when a paraphrase does not acknowledge the source. Here is an example:

Original passage:	"Anyone who knows the frantic temper of the present schools will understand the transvaluation of values that would be effected by [the abolition of grades]. For most of the students, the competitive grade has become the essence. The naïve teacher points to the beauty and the ingenuity of the research; the shrewd student asks if he is responsible for that on the final exam."—Paul Goodman, p. 34
Example of plagiarism:	If grades were abolished, our entire set of educational values would be upset. Many students see their grades as the essence of academic success; while their teachers may concern themselves only with their subject matter, the students want to know what they will need to know to pass an exam.

Although only a few exact words from the original appear in the example (*values, essence*), the exact idea is repeated without any credit to Paul Goodman. An example of quoting without plagiarizing would be

> Correctly quoted: Paul Goodman has argued that abolishing grades would result in a "transvaluation of values" concerning education as a whole. Many students view their grades as the "essence" of education and are more concerned with what they need to know for exams than with the "beauty and ingenuity" of their subject matters (Goodman 34).

In general, when in doubt, provide a citation. This will save you the embarrassment of being accused of academic dishonesty.

DOCUMENTING SOURCES

The most obvious purpose of parenthetical references is to provide the source of information or of a quotation. Parenthetical references are used primarily to provide a list at the end of the paper. There are several systems for citing references. This text explains the MLA (Modern Language Association) system.

The MLA System

The Modern Language Association (MLA) format for identifying sources is used primarily by scholars in English, foreign languages, and other humanities disciplines. The parenthetical references in the text, which identify the author and usually the pages, refer to a list of works cited, which are arranged alphabetically by author.

Parenthetical References Parenthetical references include the author's last name and the page number of the source, for example, "(Goodman 34)," as shown above at the end of the correctly quoted version of the passage by Paul Goodman.

> If the author's name is mentioned in the sentence, only the page number is needed in the parenthetical reference.
>
> If you are discussing an entire work, you do not need to include page numbers in the parenthetical reference.

If you consulted more than one work by the same author, include a shortened version of the title in your citation (underline titles of books; enclose titles of essays and articles in quotation marks): (Goodman, Growing Up 34).

If the work has two or three authors, use all their names: (Goodman and Strong 143-44).

If the work has more than three authors, use the first name and *et al.:* (Goodman et al. 134).

If the work, such as a brief newspaper article, is not signed, identify it with a short version of the title: ("Education" 44).

If a statement has two or more sources, separate them with a semicolon: (Goodman 34; Strong 98-99).

If you consulted sources by authors with the same last name, differentiate them by including their first initials or first names in the parenthetical references: (Paul Goodman 34; Percival Goodman 178-79).

List of Works Cited   The complete information about the works identified in the parenthetical references comes on a separate page, titled "Works Cited," at the end of the paper. The entries are double-spaced, and the second and subsequent lines of each entry are indented half an inch (or five spaces if you are using a typewriter).

The formats for common and not-so-common sources can be found in the sixth edition of the *MLA Handbook for Writers of Research Papers* (New York: Modern Language Association of America, 2003). (Also see the MLA Web site at http://www.mla .org/style.) Every writer of research papers should consult this handbook when preparing his or her final draft. However, here are examples of formats for most of the kinds of sources you are likely to use.

BOOKS

Book by a Single Author

Willeford, Charles. New Hope for the Dead. New York:

Ballantine, 1985.

Book by Two or Three Authors

Killian, James, and Robert Cole. <u>Medical Ethics in</u>
<u>America</u>. Boston: Globe, 1991.

Book by More Than Three Authors

Barker, Francis, et al. <u>1642: Literature and Power in</u>
<u>the Seventeenth Century</u>. Essex, Eng.: U of Essex,
1981.

Two or More Books by the Same Author

Sullivan, Michael. <u>The Arts of China</u>. Berkeley: U of
California P, 1967.

---. <u>The Birth of Landscape Painting in China</u>.
Berkeley: U of California P, 1961.

---. <u>The Meeting of Eastern and Western Art</u>. Berkeley:
U of California P, 1989.

Book by a Corporate Author

Editors, Inc. <u>How to Write Effective Prose</u>. New York:
Editors, 1990.

Edited Book

Peil, Manfred, ed. <u>Modern Views on Classic Films</u>. Los
Angeles: Smithdon, 1992.

Book with an Author and an Editor

Donne, John. <u>Poetical Works</u>. Ed. H. J. C. Grierson. 2
vols. Oxford: Oxford UP, 1912.

Book without an Author or an Editor

Merriam-Webster Dictionary of English Usage.

Springfield, MA: Merriam-Webster, 1989.

Translated Book

Trebelli, Salvatore. My Life on Stage. Trans. Erin

Cairns. New York: Musicland, 1972.

Book Edition Other Than the First

de Man, Paul. Blindness and Insight: Essays in the

Rhetoric of Contemporary Criticism. 2nd ed.

Minneapolis: U of Minnesota P, 1983.

Republished Book

Mitchell, Juliet. Woman's Estate. 1971. New York:

Vintage, 1973.

Multivolume Series

Chambers, E. K. The Elizabethan Stage. 5 vols. Oxford:

Clarendon, 1923.

Volume in a Multivolume Series

Twichett, Denis, and Michael Lowe, eds. The Ch'in

and Han Empires, 221 B.C.-A.D. 220. New York:

Cambridge UP, 1986. Vol. 1 of The Cambridge

History of China. 15 vols. to date. 1978- .

Book in a Series

Bruner, Charlotte H., ed. The Heinemann Book of

African Women's Writing. Heinemann African

Writers Series. London: Heinemann, 1993.

PARTS OF BOOKS

Selection in an Anthology or Compilation

Neary, Adam. "The Impossibility of Utopia." Essays in
Modern Political Theory. Ed. Lenore Kingsmore.
New York: Political, 1982. 176-92.

Signed Article in an Encyclopedia

Ruoff, A. Lavonne Brown. "Native American Prose and
Poetry." Benét's Reader's Encyclopedia of
American Literature. Ed. George Perkins, Barbara
Perkins, and Phillip Leininger. New York: Harper,
1991.

Unsigned Article in an Encyclopedia

"Coffee." Encyclopaedia Britannica. 1992 ed.

Introduction, Preface, Foreword, or Afterword

Sirr, Lauren. Preface. School Certification and Its
Critics. Chicago: Copper, 1982. v-xii.

PERIODICALS

Newspaper Article

Donner, Matthew. "The Plight of the Intern." New
York Times 1 Apr. 1990, sec. 2: 1+.

Article in a Monthly Magazine

Pinho, Genero. "Revitalizing Traditional Opera." Opera
Monthly Feb. 1991: 77-89.

Article in a Journal Paginated by Year or Volume

Gale, Richard P. "The Environmental Movement and
the Left: Antagonists or Allies?" Sociological
Inquiry 53 (1983): 179-99.

Article in a Journal Paginated by Issue

Stevenson, Warren. "'The Tyger' as Artefact." Blake
Studies 2.1 (1969-70): 9.

Unsigned Article or Editorial

"Finally a Solution." Editorial. Nation 16 Dec. 1988: 12.

Review

Cather, Willa. Rev. of The Awakening, by Kate Chopin.
Pittsburgh Leader 8 July 1899: 6.

ELECTRONIC SOURCES

Online Sources

Sengers, Phoebe. "Breakdown." Surfaces 4.5 (1994): 25
pp. 14 Apr. 1994 <http://
www.harfang.cc.unmontreal.ca.txt>.

CD-ROMs and Portable Databases

The Civil War: A Newspaper Perspective. CD-ROM.
Nashville: Folio, 1990. Accessible Archives, 1994.

Article in a Journal

Jaffrey, Anne. "To Live or to Die." American Health 8.1
(1999): 34-38. 25 Jan. 2004 <http://www.reasu
.edu/amheal/jaffrey8(1).htm>.

Article in a Newspaper

"Gay Marriages on City Hall Steps." New York Times
on the Web 2 Mar. 2004. 3 Mar. 2004 <http://
www.nytimes.com/opinion/htm>.

Article in a Reference Database

"Chopin, Kate." Encyclopedia.com. 1996. Electric
Library. 14 Oct. 2003 <http://www.encyclopedia
.com/articles/05975.html>.

Professional Site

Business Studies Program. Ed. Katherine Moss. July
2001. Krasoe U. 3 Mar. 2004 <http://www.bsp
.krasoe.edu/academic/business-studies/hm.html>.

Online Subscription Service or Database

Manley, William. "In Defense of Book Burning."
American Libraries 33.3 (2002): 96-98. EBSCOhost
Research Databases. EBSCO Publishing. Rivier
Coll. Lib., NH. 29 Feb. 2004 <http://www.epnet
.com/ebsco/>.

OTHER SOURCES

Unpublished Dissertation

Yount, Neala Schleuning. "'America: Song We Sang
without Knowing'--Meridel Le Sueur's America."
Diss. U of Minnesota, 1978.

Government Document

United States. General Accounting Office. Siting of
Hazardous waste Landfills and Their Correlation
with Racial and Economic Status of Surrounding
Communities. Washington: GPO, 1983.

Lecture, Speech, Address

Freudenberg, Nicholas. "The Grass Roots
Environmental Movement: Not in Our Backyards."
Annual meeting of American Assoc. for the
Advancement of Science. New Orleans. 15 Feb.
1990.

Film

12 Monkeys. Dir. Terry Gilliam. Perf. Bruce Willis, Brad
Pitt, and Madeline Stowe. Universal, 1995.

Television or Radio Program

"Satanic Cults and Children." Geraldo. CBS. WCBS,
New York. 19 Nov. 1987.

Recording

Barber, Samuel. "Adagio for Strings," op. 11. Perf.
Smithsonian Chamber Players. Cond. Kenneth
Slowik. Metamorphosis. BMG, 1995.

Live Performance

The Tempest. By William Shakespeare. Dir. Carey
Perloff. Perf. David Strathairn, Graham Beckel,

David Patrick Kelly, and Vera Farmiga. Geary
Theater, San Francisco. 30 Jan. 1996.

Work of Art

Vermeer, Jan. Young Woman with a Water Jug. ca.
1664-65. Metropolitan Museum of Art, New York.

Court Decision

Brown v. Board of Ed. 347 US 483. 1954.

Interview, Unpublished Letter, E-Mail, or Other Personal Communication

Moreno, Gloria. Personal interview. 29 Mar. 1996.

Meredith, Lloyd. E-mail to the author. 14 Jan. 1996.

MLA FORMAT

Running heads:
writer's last name
and page
number.

Waibel   1

Kimberly Waibel

Introductory
heading: double-
spaced at left
margin. Writer's
name, instructor's
name, course,
date.

Professor Moekle

Writing 39C

15 November 1998

Title: Capitalize
first letter of most
words (see style
guide for details).
Do not underline
or italicize.
Center.

Changing Views toward Interracial Adoption

While not all positions for social workers

require dealing directly with issues related

to adoption, many social service agencies

encounter concerns related to today's

Double-space
throughout.

changing family structure. Because adoption

is an important part of that changing

structure, it is essential that future social

workers understand the complexities of

interracial adoption. (The terms "interracial"

and "transracial" adoption, which are

Define important
terms.

interchangeable, refer to adoptions in which

the child belongs to one race and the

prospective parents, or one of the

prospective parents, to another.) Transracial

adoption has historically followed a

Waibel 2

dramatically changing pattern. For example, during the thirty years from 1958 to 1988, the Child Welfare League of America (CWLA) issued four different policy statements reflecting the League's view of interracial adoption (Simon, Alstein, A.R.I.). Considering the four different policy views of the CWLA and examining possible reasons for the changes will provide essential background information on this controversial topic.

Provide a thesis introducing the topic of the research.

The Child Welfare League of America is an agency that lobbies for and develops policy statements related to the well-being of children and adolescents in the United States. One of their concerns is adoption, and they would certainly have been aware of the fact that following World War II, there was a great increase in international adoption, with many of the children having fathers who had been in the American military (Bagley, Young, Scully). The placement of these

Citation: For paraphrase, give author's last name in parentheses. Period goes outside parentheses.

children, some of whom were of mixed race,
led adoption agencies within the United
States to try interracial adoption as a way to
find homes for the minority children they
served. These adoptions, however, often
faced condemnation by the families and
communities of the adopting parents, as well
as challenges from the legal system. In 1955,
a case known as In re Adoption of a Minor
was decided in Washington, D.C. The case
involved a child born to an unmarried white
couple. The birth mother then married a
black man. With the mother's permission, the
black man filed a petition to adopt the child.
The court refused, citing that the child would
lose the social status of a white man because
his "official father" would be black (Simon,
Alstein, A.R.I. 40). Although the court of
appeals reversed the district court's ruling,
the first ruling is an example of the strong
prejudices of this time period.

Waibel   4

In 1958, the CWLA published its guide

Standards for Adoption Service, which

reflects the racist attitudes of the era. This

publication gave guidelines that specifically

promote inracial (same-race) adoption as the

only acceptable form of adoption. Under the

subtitle "Matching," the CWLA held that

"Physical resemblances should not be a

determining factor in the selection of a home,

with the exception of such racial

characteristics as color" (Simon, Alstein,

A.R.I. 4). During the same year that this

policy was issued, 1958, the rate of

interracial adoption, which had risen every

year since 1945, began to drop. Several

experts agree that the position stated by the

CWLA, as well as the public attitudes

leading to that position, influenced many

adoption agencies to stop encouraging or

even permitting interracial adoption (Austin;

Bagley, Young, Scully).

Direct quotation requires page number as well as author's last name. Here, shortened version of title is given because more than one source by same authors has been used.

Parenthetical reference indicates paraphrase information came from two sources.

Waibel   5

As the country moved into the 1960s,
however, changes occurred to bring pressure
on agencies such as the CWLA to change
their views. For example, Martin Luther
King, Jr., was leading the nation's civil rights
movement, which promoted racial harmony
and the full integration of black people into
society. According to Jane Marent, Ph.D.,
professor of sociology, this movement led
some social workers to argue strongly that
transracial adoption should be looked at as
acceptable. In addition, Dr. Marent stated,
some proponents of the civil rights
movement believed that interracial adoption
would further the cause of racial integration.
Furthermore, both the National Association
for the Advancement of Colored People
(NAACP) and the National Urban League
made statements endorsing transracial
adoption as a reasonable alternative to
traditional adoption (McRoy). Subsequently,

Use of expert testimony to support points being made.

Waibel   6

in the late 1960s, the CWLA reversed its

earlier position, now stating that ". . .

Ellipses indicate
omitted words.

families who have the capacity to adopt a

child whose racial background is different

from their own . . . should be encouraged to

consider such a child" (McRoy 149). In

response to the changing times, as reflected

by the reversal of the CWLA policy,

approximately 5,000 to 10,000 transracial

adoptions occurred between 1967 and 1972

(Simon, Alstein, <u>Transracial Adoption</u> 156).

    In 1972, however, a new influence, which

Example of
transitional
sentence to
guide reader into
new paragraph.

was to influence yet another change in

CWLA policy, made its voice heard. At its

annual conference, the National Association

of Black Social Workers (NABSW) developed

an official statement strongly opposed to

interracial adoption. The 5,000 members of

the association passed a resolution stating

that "black children in white homes are cut

off from the healthy development of

themselves as black people" (McRoy 150).

Furthermore, the NABSW went so far as to

call transracial adoption "a form of genocide"

(Simon, Alstein, <u>A.R.I.</u> 15). Support for the

NABSW came from African American

separatists who surfaced in response to the

civil rights movement. These separatists

believed that integration would destroy the

sense of black identity and pride. Several of

these separatist groups reinforced the

NABSW's position by stating that the

adoption of black children by white families

would be detrimental to the African

American community as a whole (Hayes 30).

As a result, the CWLA again reversed their

position, restating the importance of inracial

placements in order to facilitate a child's

integration into its adoptive family (McRoy

150). Following the statements made by the

NABSW and the CWLA, the rate of transracial

adoptions decreased dramatically. In 1975,

Waibel   8

the last year the federal government

collected information on adoption statistics,

the number of transracial adoptions was 831,

as reported by the Department of Health,

Education, and Welfare. This number is

much lower than the record high in 1971

when 2,574 transracial adoptions were

recorded (Simon, Alstein, <u>A.R.I.</u> 5).

The most recent statement from the

CWLA, its 1988 <u>Standards for Adoption</u>

<u>Services</u>, shows yet another change. While

the organization still maintains inracial

adoption to be the best alternative, the new

policy states, "If aggressive, ongoing

recruitment efforts are unsuccessful in

finding families of the same ethnicity or

culture, other families should be considered"

(Simon, Alstein, <u>A.R.I.</u> 32). This statement

indicates that the objections of such

organizations as the NABSW are being taken

seriously, yet interracial adoption is now

Citation must be given for statistics.

Title of book is underlined.

Waibel   9

looked at as a reasonable alternative to

having the children remain in the custody of

the state where, according to social worker

Eric Blogden, they are often simply moved

from one crowded foster home to the next.

The latest change in the CWLA's statement

is supported by the results of a twenty-year

study, carried out from 1971 until 1991 by

sociologists at the University of Illinois. This

study included 133 families who adopted

children interracially. The families and

children were contacted regularly and were

found by researchers to have done very well.

In fact, in publishing some of the results of

the survey, sociology professor Rita Simon

notes the following:

> In conclusion, I want to emphasize
>
> that the findings in our study are
>
> neither unique nor unusual. All of
>
> the studies, even those carried out
>
> by researchers who were initially

Author's name given in lead-in, so it does not appear in parentheses following quote.

Quotation of more than four lines should be indented one inch, double-spaced. No quotation marks. Parenthetical citation comes after period.

Waibel   10

skeptical, reported that transracial

adoptees grow up emotionally and

socially adjusted, and aware of and

comfortable with their racial identity.

(76)

For future social workers, continuing to

watch the policy statements of organizations

such as the CWLA and the NABSW will

provide a way to follow the developing views

on interracial adoption. This topic continues

to be highly controversial, and because it

may well touch the lives of people who seek

help from various social service agencies,

future social workers should make

themselves aware of the complex history and

the continuing changes related to this

important issue.

Conclusion sums up findings and rationale for research.

Waibel   11

Works Cited list
goes on new
page. Title
(Works Cited) is
not underlined.
Only first letters
are capitalized.

Works Cited

Austin, Judy, ed. Adoption: The Inside Story.

Washington, D.C.: American University

Press, 1991.

Bagley, Christopher, Loretta Young, and

Anne Scully. International and

Double-space
throughout.

Transracial Adoptions. Montpelier,

Vermont: Ashgate, 1993.

Blogden, Eric. Personal interview. 10 Nov.

1998.

Entries are
alphabetical
according to first
word (usually
author's last
name).

Hayes, Peter. "Transracial Adoption: Politics

and Ideology." Child Welfare 72 (1993):

301-10.

Marent, Janet, Ph.D. Personal interview. 13

First line starts
at margin.
Subsequent
lines are
indented
one-half inch.

Nov. 1998.

McRoy, Ruth G. "An Organizational

Dilemma: The Case of Transracial

Adoptions." Journal of Applied

Behavioral Science 25.2 (1989): 145-60.

Period at the end
of each entry.

Simon, Rita James. "Transracial Adoptions:

Experiences of a Twenty-Year Study."

Waibel   12

American Sociologist 27.3 (1996):

79-90.

Simon, Rita James, and Howard Alstein.

Adoption, Race, and Identity. New York:

Praeger, 1992.

---. Transracial Adoption. New York: Wiley,

1977.

Credits

Text Credits

Adams, Abigail and John, Excerpts from "Letters: The Place of Women in the New American Republic." Reprinted by permission of the publisher from *The Adams Papers: Adams Family Correspondence, Volume I,* edited by L.H. Butterfield, Cambridge, Mass.: The Belknap Press of Harvard University Press. Copyright © 1963 by the Massachusetts Historical Society.

Angelou, Maya, "Graduation in Stamps" from *I Know Why the Caged Bird Sings* by Maya Angelou. Copyright © 1969 and renewed 1997 by Maya Angelou. Used by permission of Random House, Inc.

Arnone, Michael, "Online Editors Scrutinize Admission Essays of the Skittish—for a Fee," *The Chronicle of Higher Education,* February 6, 2002, Vol. 50, Issue 3. Copyright © 2002 The Chronicle of Higher Education. Reprinted with permission.

Atkins, Robert, "A Brief and Idiosyncratic History of Censorship" from *The File Room* website, created by Antonio Muntadas and currently hosted by The National Coalition Against Censorship. Used by special permission of the author.

Baltimore Sun, "Conservative Backlash," editorial, *Baltimore Sun,* August 22, 2003. Copyright © 2003 The Baltimore Sun. Used by permission.

Bartlett, Donald L. and James B. Steele, "Wheel of Misfortune," *Time,* December 16, 2002, Vol. 160, Issue 25. Copyright © 2002 TIME Inc. Reprinted by permission.

Barlow, Gary, "Principal Gives High Heels the Boot," *Chicago Free Press,* July 31, 2002. Used by permission of Gary Barlow, Chicago Free Press.

Brunner, Borgna, "Bakke and Beyond: A History and Timeline of Affirmative Action." Copyright © 2004 Pearson Education, publishing as *Infoplease.* Used by permission.

Chachere, Vickie, "Court: Removal of Brain-damaged Woman's Feeding Tube Can Proceed." Reprinted with permission of The Associated Press.

Chicago Tribune, "An education in citizenship," editorial. Copyright © 2003 Chicago Tribune Company. Used with permission.

Christian Century, "It Pays to Play," editorial. Copyright © 2001 Christian Century. Reprinted with permission from the March 7, 2001 issue of the *Christian Century.*

Coffee, Peter, "There's A Bad Example on Every Desk." Reprinted from *eWeek,* April 15, 2002, with permission. Copyright © 2002 Ziff Davis Publishing Holdings, Inc. All Rights Reserved.

Conlin, Michelle, "The New Gender Gap" reprinted from *Business Week,* May 26, 2003, Issue 3834 by special permission. Copyright © 2003 by The McGraw-Hill Companies.

Darling, Benjamin, From *Tips for Teens* by Benjamin Darling. Copyright © 1994 by Benjamin Darling. Used with permission of Chronicle Books LLC, San Francisco. Visit ChronicleBooks.com.

de Poyen, Jennifer, "Seeing Stars and Stripes: Amid all the Flag-Waving, a Writer Begins to Paint." Copyright © 2002 National Arts Journalism Program. This essay originally appeared in *Articles,* the journal of the National Arts Journalism Program, No. 8, 2002, "After." Used with permission.

Durkin, Tish, "If You're a Woman in Saudi Arabia, Just Cover Up (for Now)." Copyright © 2002 by National Journal Group Inc. All rights reserved. Reprinted by permission.

Eighinger, Steve, "The Harry Potter Controversy: Dark Fantasy or Gateway to the Occult?" *The Herald-Whig,* July 24, 2003. Steve Eighinger, Staff Writer; *The Herald-Whig,* Quincy, IL. Reprinted with permission.

Fears, Darryl, "At U-Michigan, Minority Students Find Access—and Sense of Isolation," *The Washington Post,* April 1, 2003. Copyright © 2003 The Washington Post. Reprinted with permission.

Fields, Suzanne, "Charter Schools Blaze Trail to Racial Equality," *The Washington Times,* November 20, 2003. Copyright © Suzanne Fields. Used with permission.

Fischer, Gayle, "'Pantalets' and 'Turkish Trowsers': Designing Freedom in the Mid-Nineteenth-Century United States" was originally published in *Feminist Studies,* Volume 23, Number 1 (Spring 1997): 111-140. Used by permission of the publisher, *Feminist Studies,* Inc.

Gitlin, Todd, "Legacies Are Affirmative Action," *Newsday,* February 10, 2003. Copyright © Todd Gitlin. Used by permission.

Goldsborough, Reid, "For Love of the PC," *Community College Week,* June 24, 2002, Vol. 14, Issue 23. Reprinted with permission from *Community College Week,* www.ccweek.com.

Guy, Sandra, "Scientists Raise Concerns About Impact of Patriot Act," *Chicago Sun-Times,* July 30, 2003. Copyright © 2004. Reprinted with special permission from the Chicago Sun-Times, Inc.

Harmon, Amy, "Recording Industry Goes After Students Over Music Sharing," *The New York Times,* April 23, 2003. Copyright © 2003 by The New York Times Co. Reprinted with permission.

Holland. Bill, "Courts: A Powerful Boost." Copyright © 2004 VNU Business Media, Inc. Used with permission.

Horsburgh, Susan & Johnny Dodd, "Deadly Chatter," *People,* February 24, 2003. Copyright © 2003 Time Inc. All rights reserved.

Howe, Irving, "At Ellis Island" from *World of Our Fathers* by Irving Howe. Reprinted by permission of Nicholas Howe, Literary Executor of Irving Howe.

Hull, Ann, "A Dream Denied Leads Woman to Center of Suit," *The Washington Post,* February 23, 2003. Copyright © 2003 The Washington Post. Reprinted with permission.

Illes, Judith, "Tattoos in Ancient Egypt." Used by permission of *Tour Egypt Monthly Magazine.*

Johnson, Dan, "The Cyber Children Have Arrived," originally published in the September-October 2001 issue of the *Futurist.* Used with permission from the World Future Society, 7910 Woodmont Ave., Suite 450, Bethesda, MD 20814

Khanna, Suneel, "Gay and Ready to Marry," *Maclean's,* May 5, 2003. Author's note: In this largely personal essay, I put forward an intellectual argument for the legal sanction of same-sex marriage. I'd like to credit author/journalist Andrew Sullivan who previously, in *The New Republic,* very strongly articulated the case for this fundamental right. Used with permission.

King, Martin Luther, Jr., "I Have a Dream" is reprinted by arrangement with the Estate of Martin Luther Ling, Jr., c/o Writers House as agent for the proprietor New York, NY. Copyright © 1963 Martin Luther King Jr., copyright renewed 1991 Coretta Scott King.

Kingston, Maxine Hong, "Secrets" from *The Woman Warrior* by Maxine Hong Kingston. Copyright © 1975, 1976 by Maxine Hong Kingston. Used by permission of Alfred A. Knopf, a division of Random House, Inc.

Kravets, David, "Terrorist Attacks Prompt Changes in American's Legal Rights." Reprinted with permission of The Associated Press.

Seltzer, Robert, "Potter Book Burning Was Misguided," *El Paso Times,* January 4, 2002. Used by permission of the *El Paso Times.*

Setness, Peter, "Embracing Life, Accepting Limits." Copyright © The McGraw-Hill Companies, Inc. Reprinted with permission from *Postgraduate Medicine,* August 2003.

SF Gate, "Don't Turn on the Flag," editorial, *SF Gate,* February 27, 2003. Copyright © 2003 by San Francisco Chronicle. Reproduced with permission of San Francisco Chronicle via the Copyright Clearance Center.

Shermer, Michael, "I, Clone," *Scientific American,* April, 2003, Vol. 288, Issue 4. Copyright © Michael Shermer. Used by permission.

Standage, Tom, "The 19th Century Internet," *Context,* August-September 2002. Used by permission of the author. Tom Standage is technology editor of *The Economist* and author of *The Victorian Internet.*

Staples, Brent, "Pondering Condoleezza Rice's Affirmative Action—and Mine," *The New York Times,* February 1, 2003. Copyright © 2003 by The New York Times Co. Reprinted with permission.

Taylor, Philip, "First Amendment Rocks Memphis," from the web site *The Freedom Forum,* October 15, 1999. Copyright © 1999 First Amendment Center. Used by permission.

Tripaldi, Tara, "The Fight About the Flag," *Touchstone,* February 27, 2003. Used by permission of the author.

Twohey, Megan, "Taking Off the Abaya" first appeared in Salon.com, at http://www.Salon.com. An online version remains in the *Salon* archives. Reprinted with permission.

Welty, Eudora, "Clamorous to Learn" is reprinted by permission of the publisher from *One Writer's Beginnings* by Eudora Welty, pp. 22-29, Cambridge, Mass.: Harvard University Press. Copyright © 1983, 1984 by Eudora Welty.

Williams, Richard, "No Child, Even Native Americans, Left Behind." Used with permission of Richard B. Williams, President & CEO, American Indian College Fund.

Photo Credits

p. 23 top: © Dion Ogust/The Image Works; p. 23 bottom: © Image 100/Royalty-Free/Corbis; p. 24: © Jean-Marc Giboux/Getty Images; p. 25: © Sonda Dawes/The Image Works; p. 26: © Nicolas Asfouri/AFP/Getty Images; p. 75: © Corbis; p. 76: Courtesy of The Advertising Council, Inc; p. 87: © Joe Raedle/Getty Images; p. 100: © Bill Aron/PhotoEdit Inc; p. 137: Courtesy of GE; p. 142: © David Buffington/Getty Images; p. 163: © Photodisc; p. 181: © Merri Cyr/Nonstock; p. 241: ©Hector Mata/AFP/Getty Images; p. 242: © Darren McCollester/Getty Images; p. 284: Comfort Magazine 1915; p. 308: © 2005 Richard Olsenius/National Geographic Image Collection; p. 334: Library of Congress, Prints & Photographs Division, LC-U9-2908-15

Color Insert

p. 1 top: © Corbis; p. 1 bottom: Library of Congress, Prints & Photographs Division, WWI Posters, LC-USZC4-8307; p. 2 top: © Henry Diltz/Corbis; p. 3 top: © Hisham Ibrahim/Getty Images; p. 2 bottom: NASA Headquarters - Greatest Images of NASA (NASA-HQ-GRIN); p. 3 bottom: Pastel Painting, "United We Stand" © 2004 Tom Sierak, www.tomsierak.com; p. 4: © Corbis; p. 5: US Postal Service; p. 6 top: ©Steve Holland/AP Wide World Photo; p. 7 top: ©Terry Vine/Getty Images; p. 6 bottom: ©David Greedy/Getty Images; p. 7 bottom: © Todd A. Gipstein/Corbis; p. 8: The Seattle Times Via AFP/AFP/Getty Images

Index